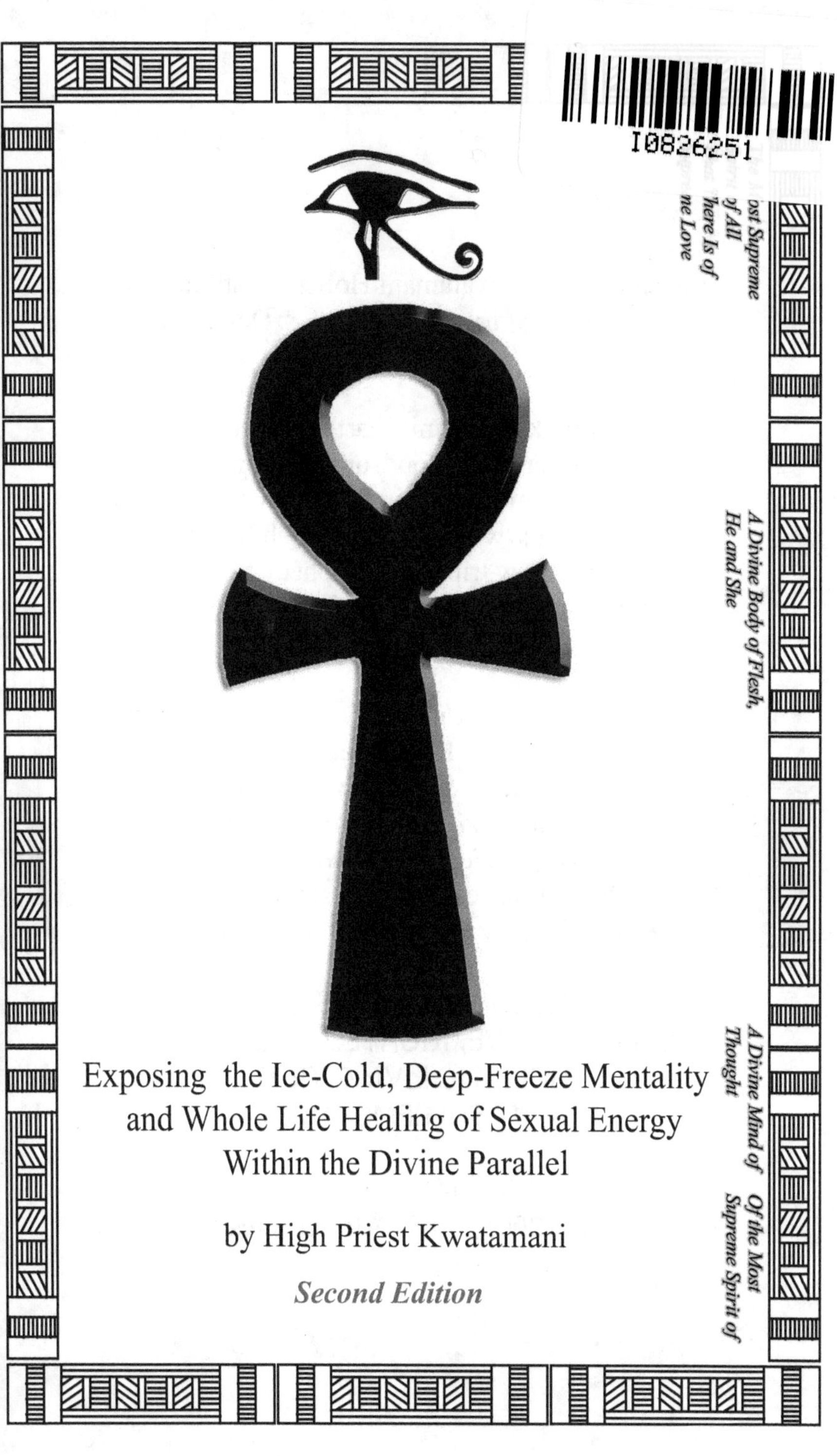


I0826251

# Exposing the Ice-Cold, Deep-Freeze Mentality and Whole Life Healing of Sexual Energy Within the Divine Parallel

by High Priest Kwatamani

***Second Edition***

Published by the Kwatamani Holistic Institute of
Brain Body & Spiritual Research & Dev., Inc.

email: kwatamani@earthlink.net
kwatamani@livefoodsunchild.com
kwatamani@tripleninepropheсy.tv
website: http://www.livefoodsunchild.com
http://www.tripleninepropheсy.tv
http://www.myspace.com/kwatamani

*Editors:*
High Priest Kwatamani and
Royal Priestess Gail Kwatamani
*Feminine Spirit Translator for the
High Priest Kwatamani*:
Royal Priestess Gail Kwatamani
*Technical Editor:* Queen Bea Kwatamani

MANIFESTING THE EXPRESSIONS OF
SUPREME LOVE, RIGHTEOUSNESS &
THE HOLISTIC LIVING TRUTH
ABOUT SUPREME LOVE

Second Edition
Copyright © 2005, 2008. All rights reserved

## Warning:

This text is brought to you within
the Divine Intervention
of the Most High Plan
and is rated **TRIPLE SSS.**
For Seriously Sacred Spirits only.

We advise that you do not go beyond this page
unless you are most sincere about gaining
divine spirit consciousness.

Again we say:
This book is not for casual readers and
is not written for casual readers or those who are
fundamentalists of the religious kind.
All messages are spiritually encoded within to resurrect
the weak and feeble spirit of Man, He and She.

Please take this warning very seriously
and proceed with caution, whole life detoxing at work.

***Please read the fine print***

*This text is written within the vibration of spirit code
to resurrect divine spirit consciousness
within the sacred presence of Man, He and She.
For best results, with the least amount of interpersonal conflict, it is a
prerequisite that one consumes
raw and living fruits, vegetables, seeds and nuts
to achieve divine clarity.
Additionally, this text should be read three times --
One for the brain, one for the body and one for the spirit.*

***Let***
***The***
***Most***
***Supreme***
***Spirit***
***Of***
***Love***
***Be***
***Your***
***Guide***

# Table of Contents

# Attuning in the Key of Life

Despite any appearance to the contrary, the sacred spirit presence of the Divine Children of the Sun is alive and well. The Most High Essence of Life and Supreme Love has never been extinguished, even though the mental and physical presence of Man, He and She, has been severely depleted and devitalized, leading to massive disease and disorder. The spread of the energy that is opposite of Supreme Love that resulted from The Deep-Freeze Invasions against the sacred garden culture severely devastated Man, He and She. The toxic consumption of this energy that is opposite of Supreme Love instigated a planetary cycle of Disorder.

The cycle of Disorder was foreseen and comprehended within divine spirit consciousness. The completion of this depleted and devitalized cycle was also foreseen. The Ancient and Sacred Ancestral Ones left messages that were coded and sealed for protection prior to the time of The Deep-Freeze Invasions. The emergence of the sacred spirit presence out of the rubble and decay of despair is the inevitable renewal process of whole life energy. However, the further decline of the lost and astray mind is the opposite parallel that will also run its course.

The energy that is opposite of Supreme Love was identified as being a foreign and toxic substance within the sacred spirit presence of Man, He and She. The whole life system is equipped with an immune mechanism to neutralize and rid the system of foreign and toxic substances. This immune mechanism or self-healing ability is present to ensure that divine order will eventually be restored within the whole-life system.

The toxic patterns of violating and depleting the life energy of others are encoded within the energy that is opposite of Supreme Love. All that is witnessed and experienced by Man, He and She, in the chaos, conflict and confusion of the death consumption culture is the consequence of toxic consumption. The agonizing symptoms of toxic consumption are afflicting massive populations of Man, He and She, upon the planet Earth.

Because of mutation and degeneration, the Most Sacred and Ancient Ancestral Presence has been blocked from re-cycling into the physical seen. The mass majority of Man, He and She, no longer embody the sacred codes of whole life energy. The mother spirit has been so defiled and degraded that the generations of Man, He and She, have become the reflection of a depleted state of being. Toxic consumption depletes the brain and body temple of Man, He and She. All that can manifest from toxic consumption is a weak and feeble presence, a mutation and degeneration of the sacred presence of Man, He and She.

The Sacred and Ancient Ones foretold of the time when the Most Supreme Unseen Essence of Life and Supreme Love would amass enough intensity to once again establish a presence in the seen. The ancient temples of the sacred garden culture housed mystery schools and served as the learning centers of the divine social economic family community. The priests and priestesses as initiates into the sacred circle of divine wisdom, divine knowledge and divine understanding are charged with the duty, obligation and responsibility to serve as spiritual teachers and spiritual healers.

The priests and priestesses uphold the integrity of divine oneness by serving as the medium for the Most Supreme Unseen Essence of Life and Supreme Love to be fully expressed and enacted in the seen presence. Within this context of divine spirit consciousness, the sacred spirit presence of the High Priest serves as the central figure and focal point of divine guidance and divine protection, as the voice and embodiment of the Sacred and Most Ancient Ancestral Father Spirit of Man, He and She.

The divine consumption of whole life energy within the sacred garden culture is a mystery to the lost and astray mind. The consumption of raw and living fruits, vegetables, seeds and nuts is just the first step to reclaiming the holistic living way of life of the Divine Children of the Sun. The consumption of whole life energy for brain, body and spirit must be comprehended.

The High Priest Kwatamani has emerged from within the Most Supreme Unseen Essence of Life and Supreme Love to bring forward the divine reality that has been veiled from the lost and astray mind until this time. There have been many who declare a knowing and a spiritual sight, yet they continue to consume of toxic vibrations and sensations. One's attitudes and behaviors reveal whether or not one still exists within toxic and depleted energy.

The High Priest Kwatamani establishes the divine example that bears witness to the fact that the Seed of Life when it is planted grows into the sacred garden culture. The High Priest Kwatamani in divine union with the Sacred Mother Spirit calls for the coming forward of all who recognize themselves as the sons and daughters of the sacred garden culture. Connect with your inner spirit sense. Fully appreciate this most precious moment of life that is for the living.

Meditate upon the divine spirit genius of the Most Supreme Seen and Unseen as anointed by the Most Supreme Mother Spirit of Life and delivered through the sacred spirit presence of the High Priest Kwatamani. The I now open the Womb of Life and present the divine message of the High Priest Kwatamani, supreme soothsayer, supreme soul seer and supreme spiritual healer.

*Inner-Spective by Royal Priestess Gail Kwatamani*
*Spokeswoman for the Kwatamani Royal Sisterhood*

# Introduction: Divine Solutions—Plan of Action

# Introduction: Divine Solutions—Plan of Action

Before the last Ice Age, the sacred garden culture flourished in its radiant glory all across the planet Earth. These ancient communities existed long before the appearance of a mutated breed upon the planet and the prehistoric references to the cave-dwelling tribes or the nomadic pastoral tribes. Research indicates that the last major Ice Age ended approximately 10,000 years ago. While northern regions of the planet froze under glaciers and sheets of ice, the Divine Children of the Sun with the golden tan continued to refine and expand the splendor of a holistic living way of life within the sacred garden culture. The ancient civilizations of Kemet, Nubia, Indus Valley and Mesopotamia would be the extension to other majestic Ethiopian communities, such as the Olmeks in the Americas, and the Xia and Shang Li communities of Li Min populations of China. Many other Afrikoid/Nubian communities extended throughout Asia, Malaysia, Australia and "pre-invasion Europe," inclusive of England. These Afrikoid/Nubian populations who adhered to the practices and principles of the sacred garden culture will herein be referred to as the Divine Children of the Sun with the golden tan.

At the conclusion of the last Ice Age, a tragic event began to unfold, and that unfolding has served to destabilize the entire planet. The mass populations of Man, He and She, have fallen into the grips of a mentality that originated from the deprivation of an ice-cold, deep-freeze environmental experience. Thus, the I in I herein use the term "ice-cold, deep-freeze mentality." The consequences of this mishap upon the mass populations and the lingering ill-effects of the deprivation upon those who were bred in this toxic mental state have produced a terrorizing history of devastation. This devastation produced a population that suffered massive degeneration and mutation. This devastation has manifested an opposition culture that stands in contradiction against the divine origin of Man, He and She. The I in I identify this opposition culture by its primary characteristics. The opposition culture is a culture of death consumption where devitalized and depleted energy is the primary focus of every level and degree of consumption. Thus, the I in I herein use the term "death consumption culture."

Those Divine Children of the Sun who suffered the devastation, degeneration and mutation and then inflicted the ice-cold, deep-freeze mentality on other populations will herein be referred to as the lost and astray Children of the Sun who lost their tan, i.e. the mutated breed. The Divine Children of the Sun who suffered the vicious attacks from the cold-blooded invaders of the ice-cold, deep-freeze mentality and who, through generations, eventually lost the connection to their divine presence will herein be referred to as the Children of the Sun with the golden tan, i.e. the suntanned Children.

In examining the traumatic state and condition of Man, He and She, within the death consumption culture, especially the condition of the suntanned Children, it becomes clear that there is a dire need for a plan of action. The dire need for a divine plan of action intensifies when viewing the fact that massive disorder, chaos and degenerative programming have been orchestrated against and assimilated by the suntanned Children. This revelation is extremely critical, especially since the suntanned Children most closely reflect the original DNA blueprint encoded in Man, He and She.

A more focused and wholesome direction must be taken than has been presented in the past by those suffering from the plagues of the ice-cold, deep-freeze mentality. Man, He and She, in general, must begin to understand that concepts of superiority and inferiority were created in a few wretched and decaying minds and spread like a plague as a massive distortion of holistic living reality. The attitudes and behaviors of those who defined themselves as superior reveal that they were simply masterminding the destruction of the original presence of Man, He and She, through overt and covert means. Attitudes of hostile aggression and vicious greed simply breed more of the same. As long as one continues to do the same thing over and over again while expecting different results, one is merely practicing insanity.

The fact is power concedes nothing without a struggle. Therefore, one must not fall into the trap of believing that simple words or expressions, such as peace, love, and godliness will ever overcome the corrupt, corroded, and capitalizing attitudes and behaviors that lurk just beneath the surface of those words. The lost and astray mind is deeply entrenched in the death consumption culture as it wallows in the vibrations and sensations of the energy that is opposite of Supreme Love.

The I in I remind you to keep it in the forefront of every reasoning when consuming this text that what a thing appears to be may not be what it is. What it is said, defined or accepted to be may not be what it is. All things depend on the nature of the energy and on what side of the parallel one is consuming from. Let us be clear from the onset that there is the Most High Essence of Life as the Most Supreme Seen and Unseen. The most sacred and supreme energy of the Most High Essence of Life manifests as the Most Supreme Spirit of Love, Righteousness and the Holistic Living Truth about Supreme Love. The prerequisite for the Supreme Love vibration is divine spirit consciousness. Divine spirit consciousness is fueled by the divine consumption of raw and living fruits, vegetables, seeds and nuts, i.e. the fruits of the trees of life within the sacred garden culture.

Let us be reminded that there is the opposite side of the divine parallel which manifests through the ice-cold, deep-freeze mentality and is fueled by the death consumption culture. This energy is unquestionably the energy that is opposite of Supreme Love. The meaning of words then must be examined in accordance with which side of the parallel one is consuming from. If one refers to hunter, gatherer and herder within the cultural reference of the sacred garden culture, the word "herder" would not have a translation. The closest parallel would refer to one who harvests the crop and stores and preserves seeds, nuts and sun-dried fruits. One may define hunting as foraging or seeking out fruits and vegetables and their seeds and plants to seed for one's environmental garden. One would hunt or seek these fruits, vegetables, seeds and nuts and one would gather them to re-plant in one's garden or to consume. That is as far as the meaning of these words could extend within the sacred garden culture, because the whole life energy defines the meaning and context of every attitude and every behavior and every relationship of every living thing within the Essence of Life.

On the opposite side of the parallel, herder reflects the enslaving vibrations that capture and imprison the life energy of other living beings/creatures to consume of their physical presence. Hunter refers to the killer vibrations that destroy and consume the remains of slaughtered beings/creatures. Gathering refers to the raiding and pillaging vibrations that diminish and steal from the belongings of others in order to increase one's personal gain. The meaning and context of words within the death consumption culture can only reflect the energy that is opposite of Supreme Love.

What is the divine solution? Is this not a dreadful and wretched situation for Man, He and She? Power concedes nothing, absolutely nothing, without a struggle, so one can forget about power conceding in these vibrations of degeneration and mutation. One can forget about the idea of power conceding in the perpetuation of the death consumption culture. One can forget about the idea of power conceding in the perpetuation of the energy that is the opposite of Supreme Love. One can forget about power conceding anything at all without a deep-rooted, deadly, massive and deceptive struggle to maintain the ice-cold, deep-freeze mentality. Even when it appears that power is conceding, in truth and reality, power is only conceding another deception as a statement that power has conceded absolutely nothing…without a struggle. And so this vicious cycle continues within so many of Man, He and She, without a struggle.

The struggle is massive and great, but the struggle is not a political struggle, an economic struggle, a religious struggle or a military struggle. The struggle is against the universe; the struggle is against what is called nature, the struggle is against the most Supreme Seen and Unseen Essence of Life. The struggle is amassed within the lost and astray minds of those who have mutated and degenerated into a state of superior inferiority. The struggle continues within the lost and astray minds of Man, He and She, who worship, idolize and devote themselves to the degeneration and mutation that is looked upon and held in high esteem.

The struggle is within self as the self-destruct mechanism of the mutated and degenerated cells becomes activated. Yes, there is selective breeding within the death consumption culture. There are selective breeding systems that have been in practice for generations and generations. Those within the elite power structure of the social economic order were offspring of those selective breeding ideologies, thoughts, beliefs, and attitudes. A divine parallel is that there is a selective breeding process within the holistic living way of life of the sacred garden culture. There is a selective breeding process within the vibrations of the Most Supreme Spirit of Love. There is a selective breeding of the holistic living truth about Supreme Love. There is a selective breeding of divine spirit consciousness in the mind of thought and reason. There is selective breeding of our sacred physical presence as Man, He and She, in divine order. This is the mission. This is the challenge.

Within the war zone of massive confusion and toxic illusions, delusions, fantasies and dreams about life after death and all the other cop-outs that have been amassed to keep passivity in the lost and astray mind of Man, He and She, there is a struggle. Man, He and She, has a challenge. The I in I have come upon the planet Earth to inspire, amass, and assemble the attitudes and behaviors of the Supreme Love vibration. The challenge is not about conflict, confusion, lust, lies, illusions, death and deadly destruction. The challenge is not about revolutions, rebellions, marches or protests. The challenge is not about perpetuating the energy that is opposite of Supreme Love in any manner or degree.

In fact, the challenge is about creating harmony by every divine means necessary. The challenge is about multiplying the Supreme Love vibration, multiplying divine spirit consciousness, and gathering the divine and sacred few to go forward and multiply divinity in the offspring. The challenge is to secure the holistic living presence of Man, He and She, upon the earth as a continuation into the eternal presence that we are. We are a life force entity. We are divine spirit presence. We have a body of flesh that we reside within. We have a brain that produces divine thought and reasoning when in divine order. We are the glory of the holistic living presence of Man, He and She, when in divine order.

This text deals with the social economic and religious attitudes and behaviors of the ice-cold, deep-freeze mentality. It is but the first step in re-organizing the divine presence of the sacred sons and daughters of Man, He and She. Before we indulge in the modern deceptions of masters and grand masters of deceit, let us get a brief feel for the historical whitewash of the holistic living truth regarding the ancient presence of the Divine Children of the Sun and their travels throughout the planet Earth. In viewing the whitewash and horrifying consequences, it will be necessary to track the movements of the lost and astray Children of the ice-cold, deep-freeze mentality.

Within the ice-cold, deep-freeze mentality, there are two major camps regarding the presence of man upon the earth, i.e.

the origin of Man, He and She. The evolutionists believe that Man, He and She, evolved as "modern man" from the "lower primates," i.e. apes, about 100,000 years ago. The creationists believe that god created the world in 4,000 B.C., i.e. six thousand years ago. These two groups spend a massive amount of time arguing, refuting, destroying and covering up data that would otherwise give all of Man, He and She, a clearer perspective on the historic pathways of the Children of the Sun. There is no possibility of divine clarity when one is reasoning from the toxic infusions that have inundated one's thinking process. There is a reasoning that is beyond these two opposing camps. However, so long as the lost and astray Children of the ice-cold, deep-freeze mentality are in charge, the Holistic Living Truth about Supreme Love will never ever be acknowledged.

Within the divine parallel, the sacred spirit presence reveals the cycles of life upon the planet Earth. As it was, as it is and as it continues to be. Consume this divine energy and set your spirit free.

*The Wholly Messenger*
*High Priest Kwatamani*
*Supreme soothsayer, supreme soul seer*
*and supreme spiritual healer*

# Chapter One:
# Exposing the Thought and Reasoning of the Ice-Cold, Deep-Freeze Mentality

# Chapter One: Exposing the Thought and Reasoning of the Ice-Cold, Deep-Freeze Mentality

Holistic living health is a state of well-being that includes optimum mental functioning, optimum physical functioning and optimum spiritual functioning that maintains a harmonious whole life system. The divine order of brain, body and spirit serves to advance the whole life presence of Man, He and She. Therefore, a basic formula of holistic living health is: whole life energy is needed to maintain a whole life system, or simply, life begets life. The whole life system of every living cell includes elements of brain: the codes and messages, the body: structure and form, and the spirit: life energy. Each holistic living element must be nourished in order to maintain holistic living health. Only the raw and living fruits, vegetables, seeds and nuts provide whole life energy as the optimum fuel for the living cells of Man, He and She.

Disorder is the state and condition in a whole life system when the elements of brain, body and spirit receive deficient fuel, i.e. fuel that is insufficient to maintain a consistent and optimum level of functioning. Disorder occurs in a malnourished brain element as codes and messages are confused, in error or undecipherable. Disorder occurs in a malnourished body element as the structure and form become merely adequate in function, leading to breakdown, chaos and deterioration. Disorder occurs in the malnourished spirit element as the life energy becomes weak, feeble and depleted. Sickness and disease, such as obesity, diabetes, cancer, high blood pressure, manic depression, fibroids, and prostate conditions are symptoms of disorder within the body of Man, He and She. Likewise, crime, war, violence, rape, dysfunctional relationships and suicide are symptoms of disorder within the larger body of Man, He and She.

The nature of disease and disorder within the death consumption culture can be described as the invading and conquering presence of foreign and toxic agents. Foreign or outsider forces are toxic when they disrupt the functioning of healthy cells and therefore undermine the functioning of the whole life system. The process of invasion occurs as a result of toxic consumption. Toxic consumption is when a harmful and damaging substance enters one's body temple either because one has ingested toxins or one has become infected by environmental factors. Difficulties arise when toxic consumption continues and one begins to accumulate the damaging effects in one's mental, physical and spiritual state of being.

The state of disease and disorder is the direct consequence of a way of life that was born and bred in the "killer" vibrations of hunting, scavenging and herding. This state of disease and disorder is the direct consequence of being out of order with the divine laws of the universe of the Most High Essence of Life and Supreme Love. The error messages have been persistent, and yet the mass majority of Man, He and She have continued to plunge deeper and deeper into the vibrations of lust, lies, illusions, confusion, death and deadly destruction. As conditions progressively worsen within the death consumption culture, and the ravages of sickness, disease, disorder and dysfunction begin to take their toll on the individual and on the collective body of Man, He and She, there will be a divine and sacred few who seek whole life healing.

Make no mistake: consumption is the basis of order or disorder within any whole life system. Either one is of a whole life consumption pattern, i.e. divine consumption, that promotes holistic living health, or one is of a toxic consumption pattern, i.e. dead, devitalized and depleted consumption that will lead to deterioration, degeneration and mutation. Therefore, the death consumption culture is a culture that perpetuates and maintains patterns of toxic mental, physical and spiritual consumption. One would expect to find massive symptoms of disorder within such a culture.

The I in I am reminded here by ancient ancestral wisdom that power concedes nothing without a struggle. The power of the culture of disorder concedes absolutely nothing for any reason, not even if it is headed for a crash course collision of fatality. The I in I am also reminded that until one can identify the root and foundation of a problem, it is impossible to find a divine solution. It is clear that every problem has a birthplace, and so, to examine the problem of self-destruction that is facing Man, He and She, what better place to look than within the mental, physical and spiritual consumption patterns of Man, He and She?

The objective of this text is to pinpoint the patterns of the ice-cold, deep-freeze mentality so that we may go forward with a deeper comprehension of the challenges that are facing Man, He and She, especially the historic target population. There are key points of clarity regarding the ice-cold, deep-freeze mentality as it perpetuates hostile aggression against the original descendants of Man, He and She upon the planet Earth, i.e. the Children of the Sun with the golden tan. Let us unravel the complex nature of the superiority and inferiority syndrome within the ice-cold, deep-freeze mentality as it threatens the mental, physical and spiritual health and well-being of every single consumer of this toxic and fatal vibration.

When we say every single consumer, it matters not whether one is conscious or unconscious, knowing or unknowing, willing or unwilling. So long as one is a consumer of the death consumption culture, one is being plagued by the ice-cold, deep-freeze mentality. It matters not whether one considers oneself as a part of the master race or the racist elite; it matters not whether one considers oneself conservative, radical or liberal; it matters not whether one belongs to the upper, middle or lower class; it matters not whether one considers oneself to be in the historic target group or above the historic target group…. In other words, it matters not whether one is blonde or bald or natty, natty dread. So long as one is consuming of the toxic, depleted and devitalized culture of death consumption, one is indulging in the ice-cold, deep-freeze mentality.

Consuming of the ice-cold, deep-freeze mentality causes mental, physical and spiritual warfare. What the I in I mean is that the most vicious warfare is the warfare within. As one begins to review the chronic sickness and disease that afflicts the internal organs, the brain and the central nervous system, one will know beyond a shadow of a doubt that a most vicious and cruel war is going on within the body—an internal war with fatal consequences. Therefore, consuming of dead, devitalized, and depleted food substances is the primary factor of biological warfare and will definitely cause degeneration, mutation, and a fatal attraction to lust, lies, illusions, confusion, death and deadly destruction.

### *Sex and Violence*

Violence has come to be known as hostile aggression and the infliction of pain and suffering. We normally think of violence as an act inflicted by one against another. Violence is usually seen as having a perpetrator and a victim. What is often not realized is that violence can be self-inflicted. In fact, violence can be programmed into one's memory to the point that an individual will spend the majority of his or her life participating in suicidal missions of violence and self-destruction. These kinds of aggressive acts can actually be introduced into the gene pool. The kinds of violent acts that one commits against the wholly presence of Man, He and She, are those acts which cause harm and damage to one's mental, physical and spiritual state of being. One can cause violence within the cell structure, violence that can actually mutate the cell life form, by consuming toxic and depleted substances.

Each life system is designed to absorb different levels and degrees of food, ranging from the scavenger creatures to the carnivorous creatures and then the highest level of consumers, the herbivorous creatures or consumers of the fruits of the Tree of Life.

Levels in the food chain are determined by the relationship of consumer with the consumed. The violence of the carnivore that must kill to eat represents a vibration of existence that affects the entire system, including the behaviors and characteristics of that creature. Additionally, the scavenger who follows behind the kill to consume of the rot and the decomposition of the kill establishes a relationship of living off of the dead. The cells of living matter encode the vibrations and sensations of that creature's life presence. Within the moments of the death of a being/creature, signals are sent throughout the body as chemical messages and electrical impulses. The cells retain the vibrations of fright, fear, pain, suffering, anguish and alarm that register within the being/creature's system at the time of slaughter and death. The toxic vibrations are then consumed along within the dead cells as food substance.

On the other hand, green plants maintain life energy from the sunlight relationship even after they are harvested unless cooking or freezing is applied. The sun's natural heat and the body's natural heat are all that are necessary to activate the life processes that move from photosynthesis in the green plant to digestion and metabolism in the body temple. The fiery pits of the ice-cold, deep-freeze mentality were an inferior substitute for the solarized charge that activates whole life consumption. As a result, cooking food substances causes a breakdown of the plant cell structure: protein codes are denatured, enzymes are disrupted and destroyed, and the life energy of the plant is depleted. Death consumption refers to the acts of violence used to deplete the life energy of one's food source and then the act of consuming the dead remains. Whether one slaughters and kills directly, or whether one goes to the supermarket or restaurant to buy the top cut of a slaughtered cow and cooked vegetables, death consumption represents violence. It is clear that a majority of Man, He and She, has mutated and degenerated into scavenger consumption patterns regardless of how sophisticated and elite one may consider oneself to be.

It is reasonable to assume that Man He in the ice-cold, deep-freeze environment would track behind scavenging animals, pick up the carcass and take it away from the animals. If one has ever witnessed a pack of hungry hyenas tearing into dead flesh, one can comprehend the attitudes and behaviors that would develop in Man He within the scavenger vibration. For example, it is noted that hyenas are well-adapted to the scavenger way of life. It is noted that hyenas consume every scrap of dead flesh often leaving only horns and tail. It is amazing that there are so many of Man, He and She, who consume on a lower scavenger lifestyle than even the hyena. Studies show that hyenas will eat almost anything, even another hyena from the pack if it has been dead long enough. In fact, none of the scavengers have a problem consuming carcass, waste, bowels or stool remains.

During a battle for food with other scavengers, it is easy to conclude that Man He in the ice-cold, deep-freeze environment used a rock or stick to ward off aggressive competitors. Hostile aggression became a way to secure food substances. Intentional killing became a practiced behavior that eventually turned Man He from a scavenger into a predator. It is noted that predatory animals have sharp teeth, large, piercing claws, and the speed to chase down their prey. Man, He and She, does not have these physical traits. Man, He and She, however mutated and degenerated into a predatory mentality where thought and reasoning was confined to vibrations of hunting, ways to entrap and kill one's prey. Within the culture of death consumption, methods and instruments of killing were a priority, and the hunter was glorified in his ability to swiftly kill. Research indicates that the creation of weapons, such as a dart stick now called the atlatl, was what brought man out of a scavenger lifestyle and placed him within the predatory vibrations of hunter scavenger.

When Man, He and She, began to consume like a scavenger and then a predator, it should be very clear that over a period of time, the DNA would mutate and that degeneration of the cells would create character disorders.

### *Breeding in Captivity*

Domestication is defined within the hunting, scavenging and herding culture as a process by which a population of animals becomes adapted to the captor and the captive environment. Studies show that domestication of the dog occurred long before that of any other animal species by the end of the last Ice Age. According to research, the gray wolf became the domesticated wolf which then became the dog. Research indicates that the genes of the gray wolf are almost exactly the same as the genes of the dog. It is noted that the gray wolves that ate the scavenger scraps and leftovers from humans began a process of mutation many thousands of years ago which altered certain physical traits and behavior characteristics. It is noted that over many generations, selection by humans for traits that were of benefit to them resulted in an animal that differed from the gray wolf in behavior and physical appearance. The gray wolf that consumed the scraps started to act and look like a young immature wolf even when it was a full-grown adult; its powerful jaws weakened considerably and it became more submissive.

By controlling the food substances that a captive population consumes and by controlling the breeding process, one can actually control the attitudes, and behaviors of a population. It comes as no surprise that the death consumption culture is a pet-keeping culture. Pets represent a form of enslavement where the captive animal is considered a favorite companion although the relationship is actually one of owner and property. All societies within the death consumption culture were born and bred from the hunter and herder mentality that perpetuates toxic values, norms and moral standards based on the consumption of dead, devitalized and depleted food substances. The process of domestication involves a systematic strategy of modifying the behaviors of an animal in order to produce a tame, docile, obedient pet, show piece or servant. The owner/master then uses toxic thought and reasoning to justify the acts of enslavement with statements about how loyal the slave is and how well the slave is treated. Oh, excuse me, we are talking about the pet here not the slave. Pet dogs are even dressed in fancy rhinestone collars with fancy leashes, sweaters, and hats to the amusement of their owners with the projection that the dog is enjoying being a spectacle. Pet dogs are taught tricks and given snack treats for being obedient. The pet dog has come a long way from its ancestor the gray wolf. The domestication of animals, the herding of livestock and the maintaining of zoos all bear a striking parallel to the vibrations of corralling female slaves as concubines throughout the history of the death consumption culture.

There have been many experiments on animals in captivity. Studies show that captivity and altering natural consumption patterns have an adverse effect on chimpanzees and other animals. The more the consumption patterns differ from the natural and innate foods that would be eaten in the natural habitat of the animal, the more character disorders develop that are in sharp contrast to the animal's innate behaviors. Every aspect of an animal's life is shaped and determined by the environment it lives in, starting with the food that is available or unavailable. How an animal finds food and how it secures a food supply is a function of mental and physical behaviors that are both learned and innate.

There have been many attempts to feed dead flesh, cooked commodities, etc. to creatures who are naturally fruit and vegetable eaters, such as the gorilla. The adverse effects on the creature in captivity have been grave and severe. Research indicates that when gorillas are brought into captivity and fed on low-fiber diets containing meat and eggs, they suffer from many common human disorders: cardiovascular disease, ulcerative colitis, and high cholesterol levels to name a few. In many instances, the zoos and the experimenters lose the creature, because that creature refuses to consume of the toxic, dead and devitalized food substances that a scavenger would gladly devour. The individuals who favor the keeping of zoos and medical experimentation on animals tend to be staunch supporters of the death consumption culture; and they have little innate sensitivity to suffering and enslavement in the first place.

The I in I am sure that someone will be quick to point out that Man, He and She, is different from the animals. Certainly, Man, He and She, has the distinct ability to reason and need not be restricted or limited by environmental conditions. If environmental conditions are not conducive to a holistic living way of life, then Man, He and She, has the ability to respond with corrective actions. A crucial lesson has been learned from the ice-cold, deep-freeze experience. Unfortunately, it is clear that the warning signals to depart the increasingly frigid vibrations were met with lethargy, apathy and complacency. Messages went unheeded; the comfort zone was wide and familiar until the deep freeze set in.

By the time the snow became blinding, the thoughts and reasoning of Man, He and She, had already wandered into a scavenger mentality. The comprehension of divine consumption was dismissed and rejected for the dead remains left behind from the animals. When Man, He and She, adapted their thinking and reasoning to behaviors of the scavengers in the ice-cold, deep-freeze environment, acts of death consumption became reasonable, normal and even acceptable. Toxic changes in the energy of thought send toxic signals to the cells. Toxic changes in the energy of food consumption send toxic signals to the cells. Toxic changes in the brain and body, i.e. malnutrition, result in a depletion of one's life energy presence. As a result, the thought and reasoning of the lost and astray mind no longer expresses the Supreme Love vibrations of Man, He and She's divine presence. The lost and astray mind of Man, He and She, would in fact perpetuate the ice-cold, deep-freeze mentality which is the manifestation of an energy that is opposite of Supreme Love. The lost and astray mind of the ice-cold, deep-freeze mentality would perpetuate the death consumption culture. The death consumption culture would be the forwarding mechanism of degeneration and mutation.

***Scavenger Relationships***

There is no question that a majority of Man, He and She, has become scavengers, i.e. consumers of dead and devitalized food substances. The point here is for Man, He and She, to become well aware that you are a sum total of all that you consume, mentally, physically and spiritually. The results of toxic consumption, i.e. dead and devitalized food substances, have caused a massive character assassination against the divine characteristics of Man, He and She. Man, He and She, has mutated and degenerated completely out of character because of death consumption. Instead of peaceful and harmonious relationships, death consumption breeds the hostile aggression and violence of carnivorous and predatory characteristics. The dominant relationship of this degenerated and mutated breed of man is based on the I-me-my syndrome, regardless of the hurt and harm inflicted upon another life entity.

When one begins to consume of depleted and devitalized energy, mutation and degeneration is bred in a body temple divinely designed to consume of the raw and living fruits, vegetables, seeds and nuts, i.e. the fruits of the trees of life. Glaring circumstances continue to arise regarding the hostile and non-compassionate, predator-like behaviors that have become part of the new characteristics of the mutated and degenerated breed of Man, He and She. The level and degree of mutation and degeneration that occurs as result of death consumption within the body temple of Man, He and She, is massive. This body temple requires the whole life energy of raw and living fruits, vegetables, seeds and nuts in order to function in divine order. Therefore, when one is consuming of depleted and devitalized food substances, one is actually engaged in acts of violence and acts of violation against one's whole life presence. Man, He and She, violates sacred laws of divine order when they introduce the vibrations of depletion and devitalization into their whole life system. The errors of consumption are manifested throughout the body system of Man, He and She, and beyond into every relationship and social structure that they encounter.

At the highest level, the plateau has been assigned to that glorious phenomenon called Man, He and She. Any practice other than the divine consumption assigned to Man, He and She, causes degeneration and mutation within the original DNA blueprint of excellence that initially formulated this glorious creation, this glorious presence known as Man, He and She. Environmental factors are key and important, because the body consumes of the solarized energy. The melanin within the body is an energy collecting mechanism. Melanin absorbs sunlight energy and sends off energy from its solarized relationship. The whole life factors of earth, wind, rain and the heat of life, the sun, is in a divine order that allows the plants to absorb the wholesome vibrations of a supreme life formation to be consumed and assimilated into the body of flesh, the mind of thought and the sacred spirit presence of Man, He and She. Thus, Man, He and She, would be blueprinted, and the key to that blueprint is divine consumption.

### *Spreading the Plague*

The nature of sex and violence practiced within the hunting and herding culture of the ice-cold, deep-freeze mentality has led to a mutation and degeneration in the sexual relationships of Man, He and She. Disorder in the relationship of the male and the female continues to cause the spread of many sexually transmitted diseases that infect millions and millions each year. The introduction of syphilis into the human population is said to be from sheep that were the original carriers of the bacteria. While the debate continues on the exact origin of syphilis and how it passed to Man, He and She, several facts are clear. Research indicates that in the fifteenth century a violent syphilis epidemic spread throughout Europe, killing, blinding and maiming millions of people. It is noted that lack of sanitation, overflowing garbage, lack of sewage control, poor personal hygiene, consumption of tainted and rotting animal flesh, and living in close quarters with domesticated animals reflected the general living environment of Europe during what is called the Middles Ages.

Findings reveal that the conditions of overpopulation in the city areas coupled with a depleted environment of unclean living conditions provided the circumstances for several massive plagues, such as the bubonic plague, to invade and reduce massive populations throughout Europe. It is noted that millions of Europeans were wiped out by the fatal infectious diseases. Those who survived the plagues continued to mutate and degenerate because of genetic codes that further reflected the presence of toxic foreign agents in the body. The offspring of the plague survivors were born and bred with the mutations and degenerations that allowed them a physical tolerance to the plague even as they were carriers of the plague. Physical tolerance of a toxic environment, physical tolerance of toxic consumption and physical tolerance of a toxic way of life simply means that the offspring had degenerated to the point of adapting within the unhealthy conditions of a depleted environment. In fact, the offspring became conditioned or programmed into depleted and toxic consumption patterns, a depleted and toxic environment, and a depleted and toxic way of life, leading to the consequences of a depleted and toxic mental state of being. The depleted and toxic mental state of being is expressed in morals, values and norms that completely contradict the divine and innate presence of Man, He and She. Clearly this was merely a further stage of deterioration of the mutated and degenerated mind of thought born and bred of the ice-cold, deep-freeze mentality.

The presence of massive disease, disorder, dysfunction and depletion is a clear and obvious sign that toxic agents are at work, mentally, physically and spiritually. When the so-called New World was invaded by Europeans during the fifteenth century, those who were identified as "American Indians" were exposed to the massive and deadly infectious diseases that the Europeans carried. The carriers of the plagues of disease and disorder, known in this case as *conquistadores*, were noted to rape the "American Indian" females and spread infection.

It has been reported that when Christopher Columbus encountered the "New World" and its suntanned populations, he reported to his queen:

> So tractable, so peaceable, are these people, that I swear to your Majesties there is not in the world a better nation. They love their neighbors as themselves, and their discourse is ever sweet and gentle, and accompanied with a smile; and though it is true that they are naked, yet their manners are decorous and praiseworthy.[1]

---

[1] Online Source: http://www.americanindiansource.com/columbusday.html

After encountering the "peaceable" and "gentle" population of suntanned Children, Christopher Columbus continued in the tradition of the ice-cold, deep-freeze mentality, establishing the pattern of violent conquest in the "New World."

> In 1493 Columbus returned with an invasion force of seventeen ships, appointed at his own request by the Spanish Crown to install himself as "viceroy and governor of [the Caribbean islands] and the mainland" of America, a position he held until 1500. Setting up shop on the large island he called Espa–ola (today Haiti and the Dominican Republic), he promptly instituted policies of slavery (encomiendo) and systematic extermination against the native Taino population. Columbus's programs reduced Taino numbers from as many as eight million at the outset of his regime to about three million in 1496. Perhaps 100,000 were left by the time of the governor's departure. His policies, however, remained, with the result that by 1514 the Spanish census of the island showed barely 22,000 Indians remaining alive. In 1542, only two hundred were recorded. Thereafter, they were considered extinct, as were Indians throughout the Caribbean Basin, an aggregate population which totaled more than fifteen million at the point of first contact with the Admiral of the Ocean Sea, as Columbus was known.[2]

Formal proclamations of taking land in the name of the king, the empire, and the pope, were a Spanish tradition established by practices and procedures of Christopher

---

[2] *Indians Are Us: Genocide and Culture in Native North America.* Ward Churchill. Common Courage Press, 1994.

Columbus's first voyages to the "New World." It is noted that after 1513, an official document called the Requirement or *Requerimiento* was given to the Spanish invaders under the authority of the Spanish Crown and the pope. History states clearly that throughout the period of Spanish invasions, upon landing and encountering the native populations who would come to greet them, the Spanish invaders would read this *Requerimiento.* It is noted that this document would immediately be read aloud regardless of any language barrier. Findings reveal that the Spanish invaders' procedure was that if the natives succumbed to their dominance, then the natives would be allowed to live, but if the natives resisted at any time then the Spanish invaders were required to commence the acts of genocide under the authority of the church and the state. An excerpt from the *Requerimiento* reveals a common expression of the attitudes and behaviors of the ice-cold, deep-freeze mentality:

> I certify to you that, with the help of God, we shall powerfully enter into your country, and shall make war against you in all ways and manners that we can, and shall subject you to the yoke and obedience of the Church and of their highnesses; we shall take you, and your wives, and your children, and shall make slaves of them, and as such shall sell and dispose of them as their highnesses may command; and we shall take away your goods, and shall do you all the mischief and damage that we can, as to vassals who do not obey, and refuse to receive their lord, and resist and contradict him; and we protest that the deaths and losses which shall accrue from this are your fault,

> and not that of their highnesses, or ours, nor of these cavaliers who *come with us*..."[3]

It is amazing that after the "American Indians" were infected with the plagues of these diseases unleashed by the ice-cold, deep-freeze mentality, analysts who reasoned from the ice-cold, deep-freeze mentality would later declare the "American Indian" as the original carriers of such diseases. It is noted that the infectious diseases of the "white" man virtually wiped out the entire dark-skinned "American Indian" population in addition to, and as part and parcel of, a blatant strategy of genocide. These analysts would totally ignore the fact of germ warfare tactics used by the invader culture as they spread thanksgiving gifts of infested and infected blankets and clothing to the "American Indians."

It is noted that some studies have speculated that syphilis may have come from the New World encounter and was then transmitted back to Europe by invaders who raped "American Indian" females and then became infected. However, when one examines the massive population reduction of the "American Indian" populations due to infectious disease after their fatal encounter with the invaders, it becomes very clear that the masters and grand masters of deceit were very busy trying to cover their blood-stained tracks. The carriers of the plague of disease and disorder can be more readily identified. It is noted that diseases such as measles, chicken pox, typhus, typhoid fever, dysentery, scarlet fever, diphtheria, syphilis, and after 1832, cholera had devastating effects on the American Indian populations. However, research indicates that these diseases combined did not equal the adverse effects of smallpox in terms of the number of deaths, destabilization of tribes, and disruption of the entire way of life of massive populations.

---

[3] *Requerimiento.* Document written by jurist Palacios Rubios of the Council of Castille. 1510. Online Source: http://phobos.ramapo.edu/~rchristo/articles/reqmient.htm.

The toxic vibrations and sensations of the hunting and herding culture perpetuate attitudes and behaviors of sex and violence that manifest as rape, bestiality, orgies, promiscuous and reckless sex and other violations against the divine union of Man, He and She. Violations of divine order always result in disease, disorder, dysfunction and depletion of one's whole life presence. Modern day accounts of males being arrested for having sex with sheep are noted in recognized national newspapers. Research indicates that Alfred Kinsey found in his studies of human sexual behaviors during the 1940's and 1950's that some humans make a practice of engaging in sexual acts with animals. His study indicated that in rural areas, the most common form of human-animal sexual interaction involved farm animals such as sheep and calves. It is not a far reach in the imagination to recognize that the same vicious invaders who were nomadic hunters and herders descending from the Caucasus mountain and steppe region, were the same cold-blooded and beastly males who would rape a sheep just as soon as they would rape a female human. The ice-cold, deep-freeze mentality that perpetuated rape, homosexual acts, bestiality and massive practices of toxic consumption is a plague-ridden mentality.

Instead of addressing the causes of such disease and disorder, the usual approach within the death consumption culture is to offer a product or drug as a quick-fix solution. Therefore, it is no surprise that condoms were devised as a way to protect the wearer from the consequences of toxic behaviors while allowing the same toxic behaviors to continue. It is noted that in the 1600's England's King Charles II requested his physician, the Earl of Condom, to devise something to protect him from syphilis and his solution was an oiled sheath made from sheep intestine that is today known as the condom. The rampant spread of sexually transmitted diseases in the death consumption culture is a sure sign that the reproductive and sexual organs of Man, He and She, are being misused and abused within common practices of toxic relationships and toxic consumption.

### *Biological Germ Warfare or What?*

There have been many historically documented plots and schemes by those who consider themselves to be noble and righteous. The ice-cold, deep-freeze mentality has established a pattern of murder, rape, steal and take against populations of the Children of the Sun with a golden tan. From the first vicious invasions that descended from the Caucasus Mountain and steppe region, vicious invasions and attacks continue up until today in the most modern cultures of death consumption. Therefore, the plots and schemes of the ice-cold, deep-freeze mentality invariably reflect strategies for attacking and conquering either an individual or an entire targeted population. These toxic and devastating patterns continue to manifest in many attitudes and behaviors that are born and bred in the energy that is opposite of Supreme Love. As one becomes infected with the vibrations of toxic consumption, namely lust, lies, illusions, confusion, death and deadly destruction, one seeks others to infect, contaminate, corrupt, and destroy. The old saying, "misery loves company," reflects that misery seeks to multiply itself by spreading toxic consumption to others. In this way, cycles of destruction and self-destruction repeat themselves over and over until total depletion is the final stage.

The presence of sickness, disease and disorder is an indication of toxic consumption, be it intentional or unintentional. Disease and disorder is caused by the introduction of toxic substances that produce adverse effects within the body system. Toxic substances come in the form of environmental conditions; thoughts and attitudes; food substances; toxic agents such as drugs and other chemicals; bacteria; viruses; parasites and fungi. The body temple is equipped with an immune system to counteract and eliminate the presence of toxic substances and agents. However, repeated and continual toxic consumption weakens and depletes the body until it is left vulnerable and defenseless against attack and invasion. When toxic invader forces are present within the body temple, disease and disorder are the symptoms of an overall system breakdown. The breakdown of divine order eventually leads to consequences that are fatal.

Intentional toxic consumption is practiced daily by a mass majority of Man, He and She, who may admit that what they are consuming is harmful or damaging, and yet they continue. The rationalizations and justifications to support and defend toxic consumption do not prevent the consequences. The case of the worldwide AIDS crisis presents some key points that are worthy of investigation. Although there are many debates and emotional accusations surrounding the origin of AIDS, certain facts are clear. AIDS or acquired immunodeficiency syndrome is noted to be caused by a virus called HIV. By killing or damaging cells of the body's immune system, HIV is reported to progressively destroy the body's ability to fight infections and certain cancers. It is noted that people diagnosed with AIDS may get life-threatening diseases called opportunistic infections, which are caused by viruses or bacteria that usually do not make healthy people sick.

The latest statistics on the world epidemic of HIV/AIDS were published by the United Nations Programme on AIDS (UNAIDS) and the World Health Organization (WHO) in December 2004. It is reported that in 2004 an estimated 39.4 million people worldwide were living with HIV/AIDS. The year also saw more than three million deaths from AIDS, despite the availability of HIV treatments which reduced the number of deaths in high income countries. The report by UNAIDS/WHO indicated that the greatest number of people with HIV/AIDS, totaling 25.4 million people, are living in Sub-Saharan Afrika. The total number of AIDS deaths between 1981 and the end of 2003 is reported to be 20 million people.

HIV/AIDS has often been viewed as a problem that affected males, specifically homosexual males, but statistics show that the adverse effects on females is growing at alarming rates. "African American" and Hispanic American/Latina females make up less than one-fourth of all U.S. females, yet 80% of the females infected with HIV in the U.S. are reported to be African-American or Hispanic. HIV is the leading cause of death for "African American" females between the ages of 25 and 44. Research indicates that globally, females make up 60% of the 15 – 24 year olds who are HIV+. The adverse effects on the female are an indication that the hands that rock the crib are certain to pass on the adverse effects of HIV/AIDS to the next generation. At the end of 2004, there were an estimated 2.2 million children (under 15 years) around the world who were living with HIV, many of whom were infected with HIV at birth. It is noted that a large number of these infected children will not live to adulthood. So far, the AIDS epidemic has left behind an estimated 15 million orphans. Around 80% of these AIDS orphans live in sub-Saharan Afrika.

Biological warfare has long been a part of the ice-cold, deep-freeze mentality. The idea behind this kind of attack is that a weakened enemy is an easily defeated enemy, and all is fair in love and war. Science and technology within the death consumption culture have been at the service of the hunting and herding principles and practices of creating more and more efficient instruments of death and deadly destruction. There are numerous examples of biological germ warfare throughout history. The ability to swiftly kill is a badge of honor within the death consumption culture. It is noted that the ancient Romans used dead animals to contaminate their enemies' water supply. Research indicates that in the sixth century B.C., the Assyrians used a parasitic fungus called rye ergot to poison enemy wells. The fungus is noted to spread a disease called ergotism which causes gangrene and convulsions. Other findings show that around 590 B.C. Solon of Athens used black hellebore roots to contaminate the water source leading from the Pleistrus River to a city under attack. It is noted that upon drinking the water, the target populations developed violent and uncontrollable diarrhea and were thus quickly defeated. Another case in point comes from the violent and bloody Christian "holy wars" of the Crusades that lasted from 1095 to 1291. It is noted that a common war tactic during the Crusades was to catapult dead bodies infected with small pox into enemy fortresses. Further research indicates that in 1346 the Tartars had a practice of infecting the enemy by catapulting dead bodies contaminated with bubonic plague over the walls of the city of Kaffa.

In the land identified as America, germ warfare was used by the British colonists against the "American Indians" that they encountered when infected blankets spread smallpox and typhus to the unsuspecting "American Indian" populations. In 1763, British General Jeffrey Amherst is noted to have been involved in a germ warfare scheme to deliver small-pox infected blankets to "American Indians." His exact role is debated, however the clear intent of his reported attitudes and behaviors is not difficult to identify. Archived microfilm images of original handwritten letters by Lord Amherst reveal his particular attitude regarding "American Indians," "You will do well to try to inoculate the Indians by means of blankets, as well as to try every other method that can serve to extirpate this execrable race. I should be very glad your scheme for hunting them down by dogs to take place."

Research indicates that other correspondence by Amherst includes references to the "American Indians" and actions to "...put a most effectual stop **to their very Being"** (emphasis in original document). Upon close examination, a common pattern of hostile aggression, contempt, and fright and fear emerges within the ice-cold, deep-freeze mentality. Toxic attitudes and toxic behaviors are not simply the base and foundation of toxic consumption; they are the origin of violence upon the brain and the body. The violence within is marked by irritation, agitation, imbalance, inflammation, blockage, misery, aches and pains. In a state and condition of inner violence due to toxic consumption, an individual reacts explosively and projects inner disturbance on some outside circumstance or factor. Within a larger social grouping, this explosive disturbance is directed outside of the group identity at "them" or the other guy.

The ice-cold, deep-freeze mentality refuses to identify and accept responsibility for the consequences of toxic consumption. Violence upon the brain and the body is biological warfare of the most vicious degree. It is inevitable that biological and germ warfare are the wretched manifestations of a culture that is based on the principles and practices of toxic consumption.

Within the principles and practices of the hunting and herding culture, destruction of life is honored, celebrated and glorified. As one consumes of these toxic vibrations, one becomes a manifestation of the toxic vibrations, yet one tends to rationalize and justify one's own attitudes and behaviors as righteous while denouncing the other guy. The governing bodies of any social order are a reflection of the collective attitudes and behaviors of the dominating social economic group. The death consumption culture is true to form within every level and degree of its institutions. The question is not who is to blame for the rampant disease and disorder within the death consumption culture, because the blame game is an endless cycle of pointing the finger and targeting scapegoats while the problems continue. The question is not how vicious and cold-blooded plots and schemes have been the controlling force of events on the global scene. The question is not about whether covert actions exist or whether there is a secret and hidden orchestration that creates massive destruction and death upon the planet. The question is: "What exactly is the problem, and what can one do to be a part of a divine solution?"

HIV/AIDS represents a disease that touches upon many issues of toxic consumption within the death consumption culture. The issues include eugenics or targeting undesirable populations for reduction and elimination, attitudes and behaviors regarding sexual practices, scientific research and implementation of projects regarding biological and germ warfare, and the rampant proliferation of infectious diseases. Research indicates that the degeneracy theory was formulated in the early 1700's as a precursor to the eugenics movement in the U.S. and maintained a strong following until the 19th century. This particular theory maintained that the cause of such problems as sickness and disease, early death, mental illness and degeneration in offspring were the result of environmental factors that affected heredity. It is noted that masturbation, then called onanism, was presented in medical schools as the first biological theory of the cause of degeneracy. Reports state that fear of degeneracy through masturbation led a prison physician in Indiana, to carry out vasectomies on prisoners beginning in 1899. It is noted that fears regarding degeneracy resulted in an Indiana law mandating compulsory sterilization of "degenerates" which was enacted in 1907, representing the first eugenic sterilization law in the United States.

The presence of disease and disorder within the death consumption culture triggers fright and fear when one begins to feel threatened. The prospect of a plague that can strike at any moment without warning can cause massive panic and anxiety. The ice-cold, deep-freeze mentality responds to terrorizing fright, fear, panic and anxiety by seeking someone to blame, i.e. a "scapegoat." The ice-cold, deep-freeze mentality resorts to hostile aggression and targets someone to victimize. Once a scapegoat is identified, it becomes a small step to destroy or eliminate the "scapegoat." Instead of examining why a culture would be the breeding ground for disease and disorder in the first place, the ice-cold, deep-freeze mentality attempts to target populations that represent the characteristics that appear most threatening, are the most feared, are held in the most contempt, or are the most different or opposite. In this way, a particular population can be targeted and all the wrong-doings of the offending group can be projected upon the target population. By projecting one's misdeeds and errors on others, the offending group can hide in deception and begin to feel self-righteous about the "purity" or "godliness" of the group attitudes and behaviors.

## Scapegoats and Guinea Pigs

The term "scapegoat" is one of the many references to the hunting and herding practices of the ice-cold, deep-freeze mentality that have become common expressions within the death consumption culture. Therefore, the meaning of the words that derived from a culture of death consumption carry the vibrations of slaughter, enslavement and blood sacrifice in their context, reference and application. We should be reminded that a culture covers every aspect of life from the religious/spiritual practices to the deity worshipped to the commoners who practice those cultural ways. The culture defines the mental, physical and spiritual health and well-being of the disciples and followers of that culture. Therefore, a culture can be identified by its patterns of consumption. If a culture manifests rituals of blood sacrifice, slaughter, and violence, then it is a death consumption culture that can breed nothing more than the energy that is opposite of Supreme Love.

A general definition for "scapegoat" refers to one who is innocent, yet who is blamed for someone else's troubles. For example, research indicates that under the laws of Moses, the ancient ritual once observed on the Hebrew Day of Atonement (Yom Kippur) actually involved two goats. It is noted that one goat, known as "the Lord's goat," was slaughtered and sacrificed during the rites. Research further indicates that the other goat, over whose head the religious leader confessed the sins of his people, was then taken into the wilderness and allowed to escape, symbolically taking all the sins with him. Other references have indicated that both goats were slaughtered during the religious ritual. The placing of blame became a ritualized practice within the ice-cold, deep-freeze mentality, and the burden of the blame often resulted in one being targeted, cast out or sacrificed.

There are numerous theories regarding the origin of HIV/AIDS, and many suggest that the virus was introduced into the human population as a part of a biological germ warfare scheme against targeted populations. The I in I am not attempting to debate or validate one way or the other the introduction of HIV/AIDS or any other afflicting plague of the death consumption culture. The I in I have come as part and parcel of a divine intervention to salvage the sacred presence of Man, He and She. The spiritual healing of mental and physical disorders, sickness and disease is the most vital priority facing Man, He and She today, regardless of one being blonde or bald or natty, natty dread. The I in I have come to rescue Man, He and She, from the most deadly plague ever known to Man, He and She, i.e. the plague of the ice-cold, deep-freeze mentality. Therefore, whether one is a predator or whether one has been preyed upon, this most vicious and deadly disorder leaves nowhere to run and nowhere to hide.

The intent is to expose the nature of the ice-cold, deep-freeze mentality and the adverse effects of those attitudes and behaviors against the sacred presence of Man, He and She. The purpose is to identify the nature of the death consumption culture born from the ice-cold, deep-freeze mentality and the consequences of thought and reasoning that emerge from the hunting and herding values, principles and practices. The specific focus here is to show the direct correlation between mental and physical sickness and disease, and toxic mental and physical consumption.

It should be clear that those who are consumers of the death consumption culture stand as a mirror reflection of the energy that they consume. The behaviors that reflect one's consumption continue to emerge, regardless of one's intellectual claims, scholarly research, scientific experiments, religious doctrines or political agendas. Since the emergence of the ice-cold, deep-freeze mentality, there has been a driving force to maintain social economic control and dominance by any means necessary. The more an entrapped creature struggles to be free, the more deadly is the next blow inflicted by the hunter. Within the hunting and herding culture, it has long been understood that the wounded animal is the most dangerous and therefore the most feared. The more the vibrations of murder, rape, steal and take have been inflicted upon the mass populations of suntanned Children, the more those who mastermind these strategies and those who benefit from these strategies grow to fear the big payback. Within the ice-cold, deep-freeze mentality, scientific research has been used to formulate, develop and produce the means for mass destruction.

Let's take a little time and review the patterns of a mentality that would plot and scheme in a survival-of-the-fittest model where fitness is determined by possessing the ability to swiftly kill. Instead of approaching the problems and ills of the social environment with a holistic healing model, the power elite of the ice-cold, deep-freeze mentality resort to the time-honored survival-of-the-fittest model. The practices and procedures of inflicting misery, aches and pains, and the swift ability to kill remain the standard of military strategies, even in modern times. One can only be a sum total of all that one consumes. To expect anything different from a culture that perpetuates death consumption is to ignore the toxic and tragic side effects of the ice-cold, deep-freeze mentality.

One of the primary objectives in biological germ warfare is to determine the effects of the toxins on the subject. Scientific research in the death consumption culture has used animals, such as the guinea pig, as the subjects of medical experimentation. Research indicates that the experiments on infectious diseases by Louis Pasteur in Paris brought the use of guinea pigs to the wider public attention. Findings show that as a part of his research, Pasteur grew cultures of the anthrax microbes and injected these toxic agents into rabbits and guinea pigs, thereby causing these animals to become infected with the anthrax disease.

It is noted that the anthrax disease generally occurs in warm-blooded animals, particularly goats, cattle, and sheep, but it can also infect humans. A number of diseases have been introduced into the body temple of Man, He and She, as a consequence of the hunter and herder way of life that includes the intimate contact, close handling and consumption of domesticated animals. Findings show that Pasteur developed the first anthrax vaccine for livestock in 1881-82. Hence the term "guinea pig" came to be used as the term to describe a living being/creature that is sacrificed to science for experimentation. The term has expanded in the death consumption culture to include Man, He and She, who is used as the subject of scientific experimentation; hence, the term "human guinea pig" is a familiar expression of the ice-cold, deep-freeze mentality.

In reviewing the details of the Tuskegee Study, the I in I will cite a few "authorities" on this issue. First on this list is the Center for Disease Control which states that the "Tuskegee Study of Untreated Syphilis in the 'Negro' Male" was conducted from 1932 to 1972 in Macon County, Alabama. In accordance with the Center for Disease Control Tuskegee Syphilis Study profile, the study involved 600 "black" men, 399 with syphilis and 201 who did not have the disease. Researchers told the men they were being treated for "bad blood," a local term used to describe several ailments, including syphilis, anemia, and fatigue. In truth, there was a covert program to do just the opposite, and the "Negro" males did not receive the proper treatment needed to cure their illness. In fact, proper treatment was deliberately withheld along with information that would alert the men regarding the truth of their health condition. In exchange for taking part in the study, the men received free medical exams, free meals, and burial insurance.

Further research indicates that the start of the project was to analyze treatment. However, after funding ran out it is noted that the project priorities shifted. Rather than treatment of the disease, the project aim was to observe and document the degenerating and fatal effects of syphilis on "black" men under the guise of a treatment program. As a part of the experimentation process, innocent women and children were unknowingly infected by those who were misled and deceived about their condition and were denied treatment for the disease. In "Bad Blood: The Tuskegee Syphilis Experiment," James Jones reports that 62 percent of the patients admitted to the program in Macon County had congenital syphilis which means that they were born with the disease that had been passed on from their mother.[4] Research indicates that the syphilis disease had become endemic, or transmitted from mother to child in utero within the "Negro" population.

There seems to have been a total ignoring of the fact that the "African American" female was considered to be a piece of property for hundreds of years within the social order of the United States of America. Therefore, every thought and reasoning regarding the social economic position of the slave would reflect the attitude that the "black" man and "black" woman were therefore unequal or inferior to whites. No laws existed to protect the "black" woman from being raped by the "white" man. There were no laws that would punish the "white" rapist for his brutal and cold-blooded acts. In some

---

[4] *Bad Blood: The Tuskegee Syphilis Experiment.* James H. Jones. Free Press, revised edition, 1993.

circles, it was common reasoning that the slave master was actually entitled to sexually use his "property."

In fact, throughout the entire 300 plus years of slavery through the Emancipation Proclamation period and up until most recently, the "Negro" woman was used to satisfy the lust and predatory appetites of the master, his kin and friends, and others among the "white man." It mattered not whether these "white men" were unhealthy, infected, or practiced bestiality. Therefore, the forced transmission of various venereal diseases upon the "Negro" woman occurred repeatedly because of the ice-cold, deep-freeze mentality that viewed her as just another beast of prey. It mattered not that the "white man" maintained toxic consumption and ejaculated the full load of his hostile aggression and brutality into her. It mattered not that his poor and wretched state of being was a pure statement of the energy that is opposite of Supreme Love. The only thing that mattered was that being "white" was might and might made right.

If the "white" man happened to encounter the "black" woman and he lusted and craved to sexually attack her, then all he required was the brute strength, weaponry, threats or cunning to overcome her. With these factors being in place, the "African American" woman, i.e. the "Negro" female, was subject to his will, his commands or his demands. In truth and reality, it mattered not that she had her own mate and family, it mattered not if she was the daughter of a sharecropper, it mattered not if she was a house "Negro" or a field "Negro." With these known facts present, it then becomes very perplexing to review the rationale of the Tuskegee study. The idea that the "black" male had syphilis because of his promiscuous lifestyle totally ignores and denies the historical phenomena of sexual abuse practiced in theory and reality within the slavery-to-freedom system of the ice-cold, deep-freeze mentality.

In an official report, Taliford Clark of the U.S. Health Service explained why Macon County was the choice location for the syphilis experiments. "Macon County," he wrote, "is a natural laboratory; a ready-made situation. The rather low intelligence of the "Negro" population, depressed economic conditions, and the common promiscuous sex relations not only contribute to the spread of syphilis but the prevailing indifference with regard to treatment."[5] It is noted that the famous Tuskegee Institute, founded by Booker T. Washington to educate freed slaves and their descendants, relied heavily on federal funding and quickly volunteered office space and its hospital for exams and autopsies.

Another case in point that signals foul play: Findings show that in 1974, Federal District Court Judge Gerhard Gesell estimated that "over the last few years" between 100,000 and 150,000 low-income persons were sterilized under federally funded programs. Ruling on behalf of plaintiffs in a class action suit, Judge Gesell stated that "an indefinite number" of those sterilized were "improperly coerced" into accepting sterilization. Judge Gesell observed that "the dividing line between family planning and eugenics was murky.[6]" It is noted that in many cases welfare patients were told that they could lose their benefits if they did not submit to the sterilization procedure. On September 21, 1975, the New York Times Magazine reported that doctors in major cities were routinely performing hysterectomies on mostly "black" welfare recipients as a form of sterilization, a practice that came to be known among medical insiders as the "Mississippi appendectomy."

Throughout the historical readings and reviews, what stands out most profoundly are the expressed belief systems that surround the "white man's burden." The basic Darwin description of "Negro" characteristics that caused "Negroes" to be identified as the lowest species in the Darwin hierarchy were physical features, such as the size of the skull, a wide

---

[5] *The Tuskegee Syphilis* Online Source: http://www.thatsalabama.com/civilwrongs/tuskex/

[6] *Relf v. Weinberger et. al.,* U.S. District Court of D.C., March 15, 1974.

nose structure, receding chins and projecting jaws. The "Negro" population was characterized as having an excessive sexual drive which threatened the foundation of white society. A commonly expressed belief regarding "Negro" sexuality was that the sexual organs were overdeveloped and the brain was underdeveloped. A variation on that particular belief was that the "Negro" was physically well-endowed, but mentally deficient. Medical professionals of the time also expressed comments and observations that revealed thoughts and reasoning that the "Negro" populations were more prone to diseases, because of their lust and immorality, lack of stable families, and savage tendencies.

The chapter on the Tuskegee Study was considered closed in a 1997 presidential apology. For those who are unaware of the apology or who have forgotten the details of the apology, please be reminded that on May 16, 1997 former President Clinton stated "The United States Government did something that was wrong, deeply, profoundly, morally wrong. It was an outrage to our commitment to integrity and equality for all our citizens. We can end the silence. We can stop turning our heads away. We can look at you in the eye and finally say on behalf of the American people what the United States Government did was shameful, and I am sorry."[7]

The push for advancement in medical and scientific research within the death consumption culture reflects a continuing focus on the survival-of-the-fittest syndrome of the ice-cold, deep-freeze mentality. The ability to swiftly kill remains a top priority among the power elite who have occupied positions of authority within the hierarchy of the dominant social order. Therefore, resources, money and energy that could be directed towards uplifting the quality of life for massive populations by promoting mental, physical and spiritual health and well-being are siphoned off into projects

---

[7] *President Clinton's Statement.* The White House. Office of the Press Secretary. Online Source: http://www.cdc.gov/nchstp/od/tuskegee/clintonp.htm

and programs that focus on deadly destruction. In the last decade of the 20th century, it is noted that the knowledge of molecular biology has increased exponentially. The recent revolution in molecular biology has opened a new range of weapons to be manipulated by the ice-cold, deep-freeze mentality.

Research indicates that a former Dover Air Force Base commander accused military officials of using his troops as guinea pigs in illegal medical experiments under the government's controversial anthrax vaccination program. According to a report from a Delaware newspaper, *The News Journal* dated, October 10, 2004, troops at the Dover military base were injected with anthrax vaccine containing squalene, a fat-like substance that occurs naturally in the body. The report stated that squalene boosts a vaccine's effect, but some scientists say injecting even trace amounts of it into the body can cause serious illness. It is noted that government officials have acknowledged that the Department of Defense secretly tested squalene on human beings in Thailand. The report goes on to state that in a March 1999 report, the General Accounting Office accused the Defense Department of a "pattern of deception" and said the military confirmed human tests involving squalene only after investigators found out about them. It is noted that some civilian experts say squalene suppresses the immune system so that people predisposed to specific illnesses can get sick years earlier than normal. Findings show some young troops have reported illnesses usually seen by people in their 60's and 70's.

The same technology of biological and genetic engineering that has promised to save lives by providing treatment for many human diseases also threatens a pale reflection of being used to develop deadly weapons of biological warfare. Biological weapons are reported to include bacteria, viruses, and toxins that are spread deliberately in air, food or water to cause disease and death in Man, He and She, animals, or plants. Research indicates that bacteria and viruses work by entering the body, multiplying, and then overcoming the immune system. It is noted that in the past, only naturally occurring organisms and toxins were considered real threats, but recent advances in genetic engineering have created the ability to develop so-called "designer" biological toxins. A revealing indication of the energy of thoughts and reasoning behind such scientific initiatives is the term "black biology," which is used to refer to scientific and medical research on bacteria, viruses and toxins for the purpose of creating weapons of mass destruction, i.e. genetically engineered biological weapons.

Research indicates that scientists practicing such "black biology" have already created drug-resistant strains of anthrax, plague, and a highly infectious disease that causes skin ulcers and pneumonia called tularemia. It is noted that scientists have the ability to breed biological warfare agents that are far more dangerous and long-lived. Such genetic engineering of toxic substances and organisms could make them harder to detect, diagnose, and treat. Within the ice-cold, deep-freeze mentality, such toxins become very useful in military strategies of advancing political and social economic agendas.

Reports indicate that a project to unlock the mysteries of DNA, called "The Human Genome Project" has decoded the so-called alphabet of life and provided a human molecular blueprint. The decoding of the human genetic codes, manmade genes and organisms, new approaches to gene therapy, and the number of genetic engineering experiments with potentially toxic substances increase the possibility for the instruments of science to be used as the instruments of death. Within the death consumption culture, definitions of warfare include scenarios that are often labeled as "peacekeeping" efforts. Military strategies of the ice-cold, deep-freeze mentality are based in the vibrations of lust, lies, illusions, confusion, death and deadly destruction. Therefore, covert operations, assassinations, and plots and schemes to inflict harm reflect the common attitudes and behaviors of the war culture.

Research indicates that in the past decade, genetically engineered plants have been investigated as a means to produce and deliver vaccines. There are already a variety of research reports demonstrating that engineered plants can cause an immune response in Man, He and She. It is noted that several U.S. companies are using genetically engineered crops to produce industrial enzymes, growth hormones, and other potent pharmaceutical compounds. These techniques pose a serious risk to human health and the environment, especially when the pharmaceuticals are introduced into edible crops. Research findings show one example: a "contraceptive corn" developed by the U.S. company Epicyte. It is noted that Epicyte genetically engineered corn to produce an antibody that attacks male sperm cells.

Research indicates that there is a close relationship between traditional cancer virus research and biological warfare programs and experimentation. It is noted that in 1971 President Richard Nixon, as part of his War On Cancer, combined the U.S. Army's biowarfare department at Ft. Deitrich, Maryland, with the National Cancer Institute. Reports state that the army's DNA and genetic engineering programs were coordinated into anti-cancer research and molecular biology programs. Findings show that this coordinated effort also linked the governmental ties of cancer research to the Central Intelligence Agency, the Center for Disease Control, the World Health Organization, and private industry. Further findings reveal that AIDS scientific research and development in America is overseen by the Central Intelligence Agency according to the agency and the *Washington Post*.

Details of the vibrations that perpetuate survival-of-the-fittest tactics within the ice-cold, deep-freeze mentality are meant to create confusion, fright and fear. The trails of deception, misinformation and half-truths lead one deeper into a mind maze where divine solutions are unknown. Findings show that the U.S. General Accounting Office was officially ordered to investigate the theory that the AIDS-virus, HIV, had somehow resulted from virus tampering and related vaccine experiments during a fifteen-year cancer research program, the U.S. Special Virus Cancer Program, that began in the early 1960s. It is reported that their directive came from Ohio Representative James Traficant, in response to a federal complaint filed by a Cleveland lawyer, Boyd Ed Graves, who gained access to incriminating government documents. Boyd Ed Graves, director of the Common Cause Medical Research Foundation, notes that there is a growing speculation that the HIV/AIDS virus may have been developed as part of a scientific and political initiative.

> Kenyan ecologist Wangari Maathai, the first African woman to win the Nobel Peace Prize, (today) reiterated her claim that the AIDS virus was a deliberately created biological agent.
>
> "Some say that AIDS came from the monkeys, and I doubt that because we have been living with monkeys (since) time immemorial, others say it was a curse from God, but I say it cannot be that.
>
> "Us black people are dying more than any other people in this planet," Ms Maathai told a press conference in Nairobi a day after winning the prize for her work in human rights and reversing deforestation across Africa.
>
> "It's true that there are some people who create agents to wipe out other people. If there were no such people, we could have not have invaded Iraq," she said.
>
> "We invaded Iraq because we believed that Saddam Hussein had made, or was in the process of creating agents of biological warfare," said Ms

> Maathai.
>
> "In fact it (the HIV virus) is created by a scientist for biological warfare," she added.
>
> "Why has there been so much secrecy about AIDS? When you ask where did the virus come from, it raises a lot of flags. That makes me suspicious," Ms Maathai said.[8]

The holistic living truth is that a culture born and bred on toxic consumption will indeed perpetuate toxic consumption as the foundation of its social economic structure and will indeed breed toxic consumption into its citizenry. This same culture will manifest toxic consumption in its policies, procedures and social institutions and every practice and principle of its governing body. The I in I have stated for more than two generations that what you put in is what will come out and that is what will come back to you again.

Governmental records show that in 1970, the U.S. Department of Defense applied to the U.S. Senate Appropriations Committee for funding to research and develop a biological weapon that would attack the human immune system. It is noted that the request was for the development of "synthetic biological agents." In giving testimony to the Senate committee, Dr. Donald MacArthur, a U.S. Army biological warfare expert, stated: "Within the next 5 to 10 years, it would probably be possible to make a new infective micro-organism which could differ in certain important aspects from any known disease-causing organisms." Dr. MacArthur then added "Most important of these is that it might be refractory to the immunological and therapeutic processes upon which we depend to maintain our relative freedom from infectious diseases." He concluded that a feasibility research

---

[8] *"Nobel Peace Laureate Claims HIV Deliberately Created."* ABC News Online. Last update October 9, 2004. http://www.abc.net.au/news/newsitems/200410/s1216687.htm.

program to this end “could be completed in approximately 5 years at a cost of $10 million.”[9] MacArthur added in his statement: "It is a highly controversial issue, and there are many who believe such research should not be undertaken lest it lead to yet another method of massive killing of large populations. On the other hand, without the sure scientific knowledge that such a weapon is possible, and an understanding of the ways it could be done, there is little that can be done to devise defensive measures. Should an enemy develop it there is little doubt that this is an important area of potential military technological inferiority in which there is no adequate research program.”[10] Research indicates that the requested sum was granted for the proposed biological weapon research.

---

[9] United States House of Representatives. Subcommittee of the Committee on Appropriations 91st Congress, 1st Session, *Department of Defense Appropriations, for 1970, Part 5 Research, Development, Test and Evaluation*, HB 15090. JULY 1. 1969, Chairman Robert Sikes of Florida.
[10] See footnote 9.

# Chapter Two:
# Masterminding Scapegoats through Convenient Opportunism

# Chapter Two: Masterminding Scapegoats through Convenient Opportunism

## *Breeding of the Superiority-Inferiority Complex*

The control of the slave is a top priority for any slave master. To keep the slave obedient and productive, and ensure a steady supply of slave labor is a primary concern. Just like a parasite, the slave master exacts the life energy of the slave through forced labor. When the slave becomes a major nuisance, an undue burden or an unprofitable venture because of demands for freedom and civil rights and access to the wealth base of the social order that he or she labored to build, the slave becomes a threat and the slave becomes expendable.

The immune system is designed to rally in defense of the health of the body's cells to ward off the threats of toxic agents and foreign substances. The immune system can become weakened and deteriorated as a result of the constant invasions and attacks of toxic consumption to the point of depletion. Indeed, the life presence, i.e. the spirit can be depleted to the point that it appears to be broken and conquered. This is the stage of disease and disorder facing Man, He and She, within the death consumption culture. The threats and rumors of biological and chemical warfare are the symptoms that indicate that toxic consumption is running its course. The slavery mentality grew into more sophisticated principles and practices of controlling populations of Man, He and She. The belief system that is pervasive in the medical and scientific circles is just as pervasive in the political and religious circles and certainly in the educational circles where the next generations are programmed and conditioned into the attitudes and behaviors of the ice-cold, deep-freeze mentality. Eugenics, cloning, evolution, genetic engineering, DNA coding, targeting ethnic populations for biological warfare, and strategies for maintaining social economic dominance are not the issue. The energy that is opposite of Supreme Love is spread like a plague to all who tamper with toxic consumption. The enslavement of the sacred spirit presence of Man, He and She, by the energy that is opposite of Supreme Love is the issue. The biological and chemical warfare of toxic consumption is the issue. The principles and practices of mutation and degeneration are the issue.

In the final analysis, what can be seen is that the ice-cold, deep-freeze mentality is passed on through legislative, executive and judicial means. That is to say, biological and germ warfare tactics, extermination plans and genocidal research and development define themselves through acts of Congress and not merely the act of some lunatic radical run amuck in the heat of racist ideology. The political structure is symbolic of an electoral procedure of the people, for the people and by the people. In every instance, the measurement is determined by majority rule. It then stands to reason that ethnocentric ideologies held by the power elite along with the principles, morals and values of the energy consumed by the mass population are the ultimate determination of the policies and procedures. The mass population's frame of thought is in turn a direct reflection of the values, norms and principles perpetuated by the power elite and reinforced within every social institution and structure. In a governmental process where the majority rules, then that mass population, being the silent or the outspoken majority, will rule and dictate the happenings and events that control the destiny of the minority population.

If the mass majority decides that a minority group is a nuisance or threat to society, it becomes a simple act to legislate and enact executive orders or judicial procedures to eliminate that nuisance within the legal framework. The minority group can be controlled, isolated, eliminated and virtually brought to a point of extinction. A case in point is the vicious Trail of Tears that represents the removal of the "Black" Seminoles/Seminoles and other tribes from their homelands as authorized by the Indian Removal Act of 1830, initiated by President Jackson and enacted by Congress. Here is an excerpt from President Jackson's Annual Message to the 21st Congress in 1830:

> Humanity has often wept over the fate of the aborigines of this country, and Philanthropy has been long busily employed in devising means to avert it, but its progress has never for a moment been arrested, and one by one have many powerful tribes disappeared from the earth. To follow to the tomb the last of his race and to tread on the graves of extinct nations excite melancholy reflections. But true philanthropy reconciles the mind to these vicissitudes as it does to the extinction of one generation to make room for another."[11]

President Jackson goes on to ask, "And is it supposed that the wandering savage has a stronger attachment to his home than the settled, civilized Christian? Is it more afflicting to him to leave the graves of his fathers than it is to our brothers and children? Rightly considered, the policy of the General Government toward the red man is not only liberal, but generous." As a result of the "generous" policies, the suntanned population that was once the majority on this continent would be reduced through genocidal acts into a dwindling minority presence. The new invading majority would enforce its rule through acts of slaughter, infectious contamination and strategies of military might. The art of the

---

[11] *President Andrew Jackson's Case for the Removal Act.* First Annual Message to Congress, December 8, 1830. Online Source: http://www.mtholyoke.edu/acad/intrel/andrew.htm.

ice-cold, deep-freeze mentality has long been to decimate the indigenous population to a minority and then declare majority rule as the religious and righteously humane foundation of democracy. Any one who questions these foul and deplorable acts is considered to be an ungodly enemy of the state worthy of being extirpated.

From there the U.S. government went on to create the wretched saga of the Trail of Tears in 1838 based on the government's legal authority to forcibly remove all the "Five Civilized Tribes," i.e. the Seminoles, Creek, Cherokee, Chickasaw, and Choctaw. It is noted that the long, cold marches were made worse by shortages of wagons, horses, blankets and food. By the time the trail ended, it is noted that more than a quarter of the "American Indians" had died due to hunger, disease, or exhaustion. The Trail of Tears was a forced relocation program that ended in Oklahoma. Some "Black Seminoles"/Seminoles refused to leave their land and mounted fierce battles against the American army. It is reported that approximately 4,000 "Black Seminole"/Seminole warriors, under the leadership of Osceola, effectively launched guerrilla tactics from the swamplands of the Everglades with devastating effect against over an estimated 200,000 United States Army troops for many years. This Second Seminole War lasted from 1835 to 1842 and reportedly ended up costing the American government an estimated 40 to 60 million dollars.

It has been noted that the Seminoles were comprised of various Indian tribal nations who combined with Afrikan runaway slaves. Rarely is it noted in American history that the original "American Indian," i.e. the indigenous people of this land called the Americas, were suntanned Children of direct Afrikan descent. Archaeological findings show the artifacts and ruins of an ancient "Negroid" people who are called the Olmeks. Research indicates that the Olmeks are noted to have left as evidence of their existence at least twenty or more colossal heads carved in basalt stone each with pronounced

"Negroid" features, measuring eight to nine feet in height and weighing 20-40 tons. It is noted that the Olmeks are now recognized as the predecessors of the Mayan, Incan and Aztec civilizations. Studies done by researchers, such as Ivan Van Sertima, show that many of the scientific and cultural discoveries previously credited to those cultures are now recognized as originating from the Olmeks.

The Olmeks are a population of the ancient suntanned presence that has been identified by modern archaeological methods. They represent a recent emergence of the sacred presence of Man, He and She, as the original inhabitants of the planet Earth within the sacred garden culture. The fact that many researchers have now recognized the Olmeks as America's oldest civilization and Mesoamerica's "Mother and Father" Culture is simply a statement that the ice-cold, deep-freeze mentality reluctantly admits the truth only after it has become absolutely self-evident, "in your face," and blatantly undeniable.

Research indicates that the Olmeks developed the concept of zero, developed a calendar, and created a hieroglyphic writing system. Studies show that the Olmeks used the Mende script, a writing system used among the Mandinkas and other Afrikans in West Afrika. When the writings on Olmeks monuments were translated it was found that the language spoken by the Olmeks was Mende. Also, the Olmeks are credited for the creation of the first conduit drainage system known in the Americas. Research also indicates that the Olmeks and Washitaw, "black" Californians, Jamassee, Califunami and other pre-columbian "Blacks" of the Americas were part of a prehistoric trade network that began in Afrika and spread worldwide over 100,000 years ago and at various periods afterward.[12] Findings show that the intellectual achievements of the ancient "Negroid" civilizations, i.e. the

---

[12] *They Came Before Columbus.* Ivan Van Sertima, New York: 1976.

sacred suntanned Children, were influential in the subsequent Mayan, Zapotec, Mixtec and Aztec cultures.

There were later movements of populations that crossed the Bering Straits after the Ice Age meltdown. These descendants of the ice-cold, deep-freeze mentality carried with them the hunting, scavenging and herding culture. These individuals would come to be known as the "red" man and are identified as the "American Indian." Be reminded that there were many direct descendants of the "Negroid" Olmeks who are found throughout the Americas. However, due to the Trans-Atlantic slave trade one can hardly distinguish the original inhabitants of the land from those who came later on slave ships. In truth and reality, they represent one suntanned presence of the Children of the Sun. There still remain descendants of those who were born from the mixture of the original ancestors and those who crossed the straits from the ice-cold, deep-freeze. These are the various shades of brown people found in the southern areas of North America and throughout Central and South America.

The Spanish conquistadors and others changed these suntanned Children's language, their culture, their religion, and their holistic living way of life through vicious acts of murder, rape, steal and take. Many of these individuals would be called Moors by the Spanish invaders. The Children of the Sun who lost their tan who first invaded Spain had encountered "Negroid" populations whom they called Moors. The Spanish would later encounter populations of suntanned Children during their explorations and invasions of the Americas whom they called Moors, i.e. "Blacks."

These individuals were not runaway slaves; they were indeed the original occupants of the land. We should also note the Spanish conquistadors had done a very good job of mixing and mingling with many of these tribes through the official artistic expressions of the ice-cold, deep-freeze mentality, i.e. the vicious and cold-blooded art of rape, murder, steal and take. Let it be known, however, runaway slaves were welcome among their brothers and sisters who fully recognized them. It is barely noted that it was the Afrikans who showed the Europeans to this land in the first place. The I in I must note here that these suntanned Children who pointed and guided the way, did not show the Europeans to the Americas for the "white man" to exercise his rituals of lust, lies, illusions, confusion, death and deadly destruction. In truth and reality, the suntanned Children were attempting to show the Europeans that the Earth was not flat and that there were other lands across the water.

The fact that the first "white" men to arrive in the Americas were met by suntanned Children of direct Afrikan descent is strategically downplayed. The massive ruins outside of Mexico City have indeed destabilized the Caucasian strategy of perpetuating the suntanned Children of Afrikan descent as intellectually inferior and being of no significant culture. It is indeed a common practice for the ice-cold, deep-freeze mentality to know that one has encountered a people who already inhabit a land, and then either invade and claim that inhabited land as one's own or sell it to someone else without the consent of the original owner/occupants. Spain sold Florida to the United States in 1821 for a reported five million dollars. It would be akin to Britain suddenly deciding to sell America to China for a couple million pound sterlings with an occupation date of July 4, 2006 and China then telling the occupants to depart for they, the Chinese, are ready to occupy their newly purchased domain.

There are many historical accounts of division between tribal groups based on racial lines that have been orchestrated by the "white" man in furthering the cause of keeping the "Negroid" populations in their place within the lower strata of society. There are several news stories about U.S. government reparations to various "American Indian" tribes that expose the strategies of divide and rule that have played a major role in splitting tribes that were once a harmonious people into categories of “black” and “white.” A case in point: for generations the “Black Seminoles” and their American Indian counterparts had freely intermarried and expanded a colorful union of one people. Research indicates that in 1907, Oklahoma joined the United States and brought into its statehood the Jim Crow laws of the Deep South. It is noted that the state was then thrown into the ice cold pits of Deep South culture, erasing the freedoms that had been enjoyed by thousands of “blacks” and their “American Indian” families for the four previous decades. The Seminoles as well as other “American Indian” tribes became pawns in the color game of the ice-cold, deep-freeze mentality.

Suddenly, by U.S. legal classifications, it became convenient to classify the “red” man as a “white” man. The “black” man was singled out for discrimination and exclusion in the Jim Crow laws. As newly designated “white” men, the “American Indian” tribes began to adopt the same attitudes of racist ideology that continue generations later. The “Black Seminoles”/Seminoles of Oklahoma were effectively divided by the rule. As generations changed hands and the ideology of being a “white” man became stronger, a new frame of reference would emerge. In 1921, the miscegenation laws made it unlawful for “American Indians” and “Negroes” to marry because “American Indians” were now officially “white.” Oklahoma lands were “Indian Territory” held by “American Indians.” Oklahoma would experience an influx of “white” Americans migrating into the state. It became quick and easy, i.e. convenient opportunism, for unmarried “white” males to marry into controlling tribal land. Traditional thinking among many of the besieged populations became, “Either sell out, or die out.”

In 1990, the U.S. government reportedly paid the Seminole Indians of Oklahoma $56 million to compensate for Florida lands that were seized during 1823. It is noted that the “Black” Seminoles filed a lawsuit (*Davis v. United States*) against the

Federal Government and the Bureau of Indian Affairs. Here are some excerpts from the case:

> The Seminole Nation was formed after the European conquest of America. In addition to members of Native American ancestry, it also includes members of African ancestry, descendants of escaped slaves who began living among Native American groups in the then-foreign territory that became Florida. In 1823 the Seminole Nation's Florida lands were ceded to the United States by the Treaty of Camp Moultrie. Thereafter, most of the Seminole Nation's people, including those of African ancestry, were forcibly removed to what is now Oklahoma.
>
> After removal the Tribe entered into a treaty with the United States addressing the rights of its members of African descent, the "Estelusti." That treaty, which we will refer to as the Treaty of 1866, contains the following language: [I]nasmuch as there are among the Seminoles many persons of African descent and blood, who have no interest or property in the soil, and no recognized civil rights, it is stipulated that hereafter these persons and their descendants, and such other of the same race as shall be permitted by said nation to settle there, shall have and enjoy all the rights of native citizens, and the laws of said nation shall be equally binding upon all persons of whatever race or color who may be adopted as citizens or members of said tribe.
>
> Treaty with the Seminole Indians, Mar. 21, 1866, U.S.-Seminole Nation of Indians, Art. II, 14 Stat. 755, 756. Notwithstanding this sweeping language, the United States itself continued to distinguish the Estelusti from tribal members of

Native American ancestry. For instance, when the Dawes Commission in 1906 created official membership rolls for the Seminole Nation of Oklahoma, it created two rolls, one for those of Native American ancestry (the "Seminole Blood Roll") and one for the Estelusti (the "Freedmen Roll"). A member of mixed ancestry was classified in accordance with maternal ancestry. Today, these membership rolls, often referred to as the "Dawes Rolls," are authoritative evidence of tribal membership… Any person who can show descent from a person listed on either of the two rolls is recognized as a member of the Tribe. The Tribe's members are divided among 14 bands. The two Plaintiff-bands consist entirely of descendants of those listed on the Freedmen Roll. Even as tribal members, however, the Estelusti do not receive full membership benefits. Participation in some of the Tribe's programs requires a CDIB card, "the BIA's certification that an individual possesses a specific quantum of Indian blood." *Davis I*, 192 F.3d at 956.

A member of the Tribe can obtain a CDIB card by proving a specified relationship to a person listed on the Seminole Blood Roll. A person who proves the same relationship with respect to a person listed on the Seminole Freedmen Roll, however, is not entitled to a CDIB. In a letter dated October 4, 1995, the Superintendent of the Wewoka Agency of the Bureau of Indian Affairs explained this differential treatment: The Certificate of Degree of Indian Blood makes or infers no mention of Tribal Membership. The policy states that my responsibility is to certify one[']s Indian blood when acceptable proof of relationship to an individual enrolled on specific rolls of particular tribes [is presented]. [T]here are persons listed on the Freedman roll who were part Indian. As you know, the Seminole Nation follows maternal lineage, for example, if the person's mother was [F]reedman and the father was Indian by blood, the person was enrolled in the [F]reedman roll. This person was still part Indian and he/she and his/her descendants would be eligible to receive a [CDIB] Our policy is not to deny [Freedmen CDIBs], but to state that adequate proof of relationship to a person with Indian blood has been provided by them. Stated simply, if a Freedman band member or anyone else applies for a [CDIB] that cannot provide acceptable proof of relationship to a Seminole Indian by blood, they will be denied a [CDIB].

Aple. Supp. App. at 168-69. According to Plaintiffs, many members of the Dosar Barkus and Bruner Bands of the Seminole Nation of Oklahoma have been denied CDIBs under the BIA's policy. Consequently, members of the Plaintiff-bands have been excluded from participation in programs for which CDIB cards are required. Among the programs to which members of the Plaintiff-bands have been denied access are what the parties refer to as judgment-fund programs. These programs are supported by a $56 million judgment awarded to "the Seminole Nation *as it existed in Florida on September 18, 1823*," *Davis I*, 192 F.3d at 955-56 (internal quotation marks omitted; emphasis added), as compensation for the 1823 taking of its Florida lands. Before Congress released the judgment funds for the use of the Tribe, the BIA recommended that it exclude the Estelusti from participation because the Estelusti were not

> officially recognized as members of the Tribe until the Treaty of 1866.[13]

Seminole Chief Jerry Haney is reported as stating that the "black" members of the tribe are no longer welcome. Putting aside the history of 300 years of togetherness, the blood Seminoles are noted to be going by the book, that is, the government's book which records a 100-year-old census that came about as a result of the Jim Crow laws which separated the "Black" Seminoles from the rest of the tribe.

In June 2004, Oklahoma "Black" Seminoles lost a Supreme Court appeal over their claims. Reports state that the court refused without comment to consider reinstating their lawsuit against the federal government. A judge had ruled that their lawsuit could not move ahead unless the Seminole Nation of Oklahoma was part of it. But that is not possible because the tribe's sovereign status protects it from federal lawsuits. With the removal of the "Black" Seminoles from the tribal ranks of the Seminoles this concluded a saga that brought to an end the last the African and "American Indian" ties among the Five Civilized Tribes in Oklahoma. This long-strategized objective of completely disrupting the bonds of kinship between the "black" man and the "red" man would finally be realized. U.S. officials holding the old line were pleased. The ghosts of the Jim Crow legacy were pleased. The energy that is opposite of Supreme Love would appear to be the conquering force, but the ancestral spirit of the suntanned Children would indeed have the final word as the saga continues. The sacred spirit of the Olmeks, i.e. the sacred spirit of the Divine Children of the Sun, would look upon the rapid

---

[13] *Appeal from the United States District Court for the Western District of Oklahoma* (D.C. NO. CIV-96-1988-M). Filed September 10, 2003. United States Court Of Appeals Tenth Circuit. Online Source: http://www.kscourts.org/ca10/cases/2003/09/02-6198.htm.

decline of the lost and astray mind of the ice-cold, deep-freeze mentality.

In retrospect, as a result of the fierce Seminole defense against the American invasion, the Seminoles of Afrikan descent left a lasting impression that was rekindled during the American Civil War from 1861 to 1865. President Lincoln and his military strategists would reason that if the Union Army could command the allegiance and fighting power of "black" slaves as had been faced during the "Black Seminole"/Seminole wars, then the Union would be sure to defeat the Confederate army.... Convenient opportunism would again emerge. And so it was, and so it was. A new chain of thought was clearly amassing within the "black" population as well as the "white" population as the Civil War intensified. The turn of events orchestrated by President Lincoln to get the slaves to fight alongside the Union Army would indeed be the blow that led to the ultimate defeat of the Confederate Army.

The total population would see that these "blacks" were ready, willing and able to fight for freedom, just as during the "Black Seminole"/Seminole Wars. In an organized state of being, these "blacks" were a major force to be reckoned with. President Lincoln formulated a plan that inspired a majority of the slave population to revolt and join forces with the Union Army. This strategy was implemented by issuing the Emancipation Proclamation which declared the slaves in the rebel states as free. Although the Confederate army did have slaves fighting beside them, the will of the runaway slave to be free provided a far more aggressive foe.

It would stand to reason that the conclusion of the Civil War would have to produce some benefits for the "black" population as promised. Any reneging of these promised benefits could definitely spark another vibration similar to what had occurred during the "Black Seminole"/Seminole Wars. It was clear that reneging could cause a greater war and a collapse of the governmental system as orchestrated by the "white" social order. Therefore, at this point in history, one thing was clear, the "Negro" would have to be reckoned with by the "white" social order.

It was clear to government officials that these "Negro" soldiers had been key and instrumental during the war. It was also clear that these soldiers who fought in the Civil War were not about to return back to "massa" as his docile "Negro" slave. Additionally, it was clear that these "Negroes" were the workforce and the knowledge base of the agricultural system of the South in America. After the Civil War, under the provisions of the Thirteenth, Fourteenth, and Fifteenth Amendments to the Constitution and the Civil Rights Act of 1866, "Negroes" enjoyed a period when they were allowed to vote, actively participate in the political process, acquire the land of former owners, seek their own employment, and use public accommodations. However, what was clear during Reconstruction was that the master race population was not about to subjugate itself to the "Negro" being an equal or having the ability to reside freely as full citizens.

President Lincoln aptly captures the "racist" attitudes, thoughts and reasoning of his time when he speaks about the equality of the "Negro."

> I will say, then, that I am not, nor ever have been, in favor of bringing about in any way the social and political equality of the white and black races—that I am not nor ever have been in favor of making voters or jurors of negroes, nor of qualifying them to hold office, nor to intermarry with white people; and I will say in addition to this that there is a physical difference between the white and black races which will ever forbid the two races living together in terms of social and political equality. And inasmuch as they cannot so live, while they do remain together, there must be

> the position of superior and inferior. I am as much as any other man in favor of having the superior position assigned to the white race.[14]

These sentiments were again expressed clearly by President Lincoln on August, 14, 1862 when he addressed a group of free "colored" men regarding his solution of colonization to solve the "Negro problem" in the United States. Lincoln stated, "You and we are different races. We have between us a broader difference than exists between almost any other two races. Whether it is right or wrong I need not discuss, but this physical difference is a great disadvantage to us both, as I think your race suffer very greatly, many of them by living among us, while ours suffer from your presence." Lincoln went on to state, "Your race are suffering, in my judgment, the greatest wrong inflicted on any people. But even when you cease to be slaves, you are yet far removed from being placed on an equality with the white race. You are cut off from many of the advantages which the other race enjoy. The aspiration of men is to enjoy equality with the best when free, but on this broad continent, not a single man of your race is made the equal of a single man of ours." Lincoln further noted, "There is an unwillingness on the part of our people, harsh as it may be, for you free colored people to remain with us."[15]

The ice-cold, deep-freeze mentality was entirely too strongly rooted in every attitude and every behavior of this breed of man. The consequences were the eventual creation of the Ku Klux Klan and other "white" vigilante groups that

---

[14] *Sixth Joint Debate with Stephen Douglas at Quincy.* Mr. Lincoln's Speech. Abraham Lincoln. October 13, 1858. Online Source: http://www.bartleby.com/251/61.html.

[15] Excerpts from *Address on Colonization to a Committee of Colored Men delivered by Abraham Lincoln.* Washington *D.C.,* August 14, 1862. Online Source: http://www.etymonline.com/cw/lincoln.htm.

'terrorized the "black" population of ex-slaves and freed men. Strategies of genocide were a sincere reality carried out on a daily basis. Where it was formally thought and stated that the only good Indian was a dead Indian, it would come to be expressed that the only good "nigger" is a dead "nigger" hanging high from a big oak tree.

Hanging, or lynching as it was called, would be the quick-fix to any "Negro problem" that occurred. Tactics were developed to reclaim any land owned by these "Negroes." The "Negro," i.e. the Afrikan male, would be mentally, physically and spiritually castrated as the most profound terrorist tactics known were inflicted upon what remained of the "Negro," i.e. Afrikan family structure. The Jim Crow laws would reiterate the Black Codes with even more vigor and venom. Therefore, in short order, things would go back to normal under a new ideology of sharecropping. All of the political seats of authority that "Negroes" had gained during Reconstruction were simply taken away and placed back in the hands of the southern "white" authorities.

The biggest problem would be a reiteration of Thomas Jefferson's earlier concerns about the growing "Negro" population. And the question, "What do we do with these Negroes?" would remain. It was reasoned that if the Afrikans were sent back to Afrika without being under the "white" man's control via colonization, then they could become an imposing threat. The fear was that they could one day gather enough strength to resurrect and unleash the big payback. If the "Negro" population remained in America, then the possibility of revolt and rebellion remained ever present, and more importantly, the resurrection of a "black" messiah could cause an internal overthrow. It would be reasoned that Rome was destroyed from within.

Conflicts like the Seminole War and Civil War had caused the oppressed Afro-centric population to realize the power in the barrel of a gun and the fact that "white" blood ran just like "black" blood. This would make the "Negro" population very difficult to contain; therefore, calling for new strategies of lust, lies, illusions, confusion, death and deadly destruction to keep them "in their place." These very proud children of Afrikan descent had known the greatest degree of freedom prior to slavery and after having a taste of freedom again were unwilling to entertain the shackles and chains of the chattel slavery system. The desire for freedom and the will to fight for that freedom would only intensify as the "Negro" armies were called to bear arms to protect and serve the American way during World War One. The advent of World War One gave notice that there was still a need for the "Negro" population, as convenient opportunism would again emerge. However, the bloody trails of 1919 that followed the completion of World War One saw many "Negro" soldiers return back from the battlefield to encounter a greater conflict. This bloody era would leave a legacy where "black" men would hang from trees like a strange fruit as the segregation era intensified.

### *Blood Lines*

The attitudes, thoughts and reasoning that supported concepts of "white" racial superiority were deeply embedded within the mentality of the "white" population as an inheritance of the chattel slavery system. The ideology of eugenics was a direct outgrowth of the "white" male investment in maintaining his position of dominance as established by his privileged status as slave owner, slave master, and founding father who mastered the swiftest ability to kill. The cold-blooded sexual and racial attitudes that permitted him free reign to rape and enslave the "Negro" woman even as he declared her inferiority would cause deep-seated and agonizing fear as he envisioned the "Negro" man pursuing the "white" woman. There is a clear comprehension that survival of the fittest is meaningless without offspring to carry on the family name, tribal presence, physical traits, and genetic codes.

The genetic codes for "whiteness" are a mutation and degeneration of the original blueprint of Man, He and She. As a result the "white" male is unable to continue breeding his kind unless he breeds with a "white" female. The shepherds of the hunting and herding culture discovered this long ago while breeding sheep. For this reason, the children who were born from the slave relationship between the "white" male and the "Negro" female were simply looked upon as just another "Negro" and often sold to the highest bidder. On the other hand, a "black" male can continue breeding his kind regardless of the female's physical traits because his genetic codes are dominant and represent the original blueprint for Man, He and She, which has populated the entire planet in all shades of the darker hue as well as the albino. The notions of racial purity then feed on the fears of being bred out of existence. As the result of a fear of extinction, the ice-cold, deep-freeze mentality projects genocide on others.

It is noted that "blood quantum" was the phrase eugenicists used to determine if someone should be sterilized, the phrase the "Indian" agents used to determine if someone should be forcibly removed to a reservation, and it was also the phrase that Hitler used; anyone with mixed blood was "impure" and should be eliminated to improve the purity of the "white" race. The concept of eugenics involves strategies for maintaining the racial purity of the ice-cold, deep-freeze mutation. Eugenicists use social economic and legal measures to prevent the birth of children from allegedly "inferior" or "defective" parents…the target population being the Children of the Sun with the golden tan. Eugenicists support strategies to increase fertility and breeding among those identified as possessing "superior" genetic endowments…targeting the Nordic stock Germanic tribes that most closely reflect the ice-cold, deep-freeze mutation.

It is clear that a male's social position and status is anointed by the social position and status held by his female counterpart.

In other words, so long as the "white" male maintains a system that views the "white" female as virtuous, righteous and out of the reach of the "black" male, the determination will be that he is superior to the "black" male. By the same token, so long as the "white" male has total access by force, coercion, persuasion or social economic status to sexually subdue the "Negro" female, it will be a statement that the "black" male is unable to secure and protect his female. A male who is unable to secure and protect his female is unable to establish and secure his own presence. Indeed, he is a male who is breeding inferiority and a hopeless state of being.

It is indeed a glorified state of idolizing and worshipping the "white" female as superior when the Afro-centric female belittles herself to inferior status by perming and bleaching her hair, fade creaming her skin, and adopting other alterations to emulate the characteristics and traits of the "white" female. The Afro-centric female will indeed breed off of the energy of her consumption, and will therefore reproduce an inferior state of mind in the offspring. By the same token for the Afro-centric male to worship and idolize the characteristics of the "white" female while scorning and rejecting the natural and innate characteristics of the Afro-centric female is the true sign of an inferior and deteriorated state of mind. Inferiority has indeed overcome the suntanned Children, but it is not because of the "white" man's superiority; it is because of their refusal to honor their sacred origin. So long as the Afro-centric Man, He and She, continue to belittle and degrade their sacred spirit presence and continue to indulge in toxic consumption, the ice-cold, deep-freeze mentality will continue to guide them down a pathway of degeneration, mutation, genocide and extinction.

The cold-blooded idea of wiping out a people or totally subduing their presence has been a part of the ice-cold, deep-freeze mentality throughout history. These very same tactics were used in Nazi Germany where all known individuals of "Negro blood" were sterilized, where populations of those declared as the mud breed of Jewish Semitic people were exterminated, and where others were identified to be eliminated. These acts of persecution, sterilization and extermination were part of the policy actions of a governing body.

In 1945, the "Allied" forces joined together to bring down the Nazi regime and World War Two came to an end. Scientific research to formulate the atomic bomb had already been transferred from Germany to U.S. soil as defecting German scientists came together with their U.S. counterparts and a strong financial base. Germany had surrendered before the bomb was strategically prepared and Japan would become the likely candidate and the target of a most devastating experimental project. Whereas the First World War saw the introduction of many new technologies to the art of killing one's enemy, such as the machine gun, the tank, the airplane, the zeppelin and toxic gas, World War Two would introduce mass destruction in the atomic bomb.

The ice-cold, deep-freeze mentality that threatened to take total control of the planet also threatened to bring forward the force of eugenics to purify the master race. The master-race syndrome, or the syndrome of the blue-eyed blonde Nordic stock, is often seen as something that occurred in Nazi Germany. However, as one will come to find out in this text, the heartland of this master race ideology called eugenics was bred right in the United States of America. It is a documented fact that a majority of those identified as the financially elite of the American social economic order were indeed the financiers of the Nazi regime and, in fact, personally financed research projects under the auspices of eugenics. In fact, these research projects and programs continue to this very day as the same game with another name.

The feats of such individuals as Jesse Owens who won four gold medals in the 1936 Olympics had indeed challenged the ideology of a "superior" master race. Reports indicate that during the Olympic Games in Berlin, Germany, Jesse Owens broke eleven Olympic records, single-handedly crushing Hitler's eugenicized supermen. Both Hitler, who was the epitome of the eugenics movement and all his blue-eyed blonde supermen, had been put to shame by one man who represented the very racial group that they had aggressively denounced as inferior. It was clear that the returning suntanned soldiers had gained a new identity of strength during their experiences of World War Two. The U.S. government was aware of the many soldiers of Afrikan descent who were returning to this country after serving in the overthrow of a runaway ally, i.e. Nazi Germany.

While the "Negro" soldiers were busy fighting Hitler and his eugenic ideology of a master race, racist eugenics programs were vigorous and intense in America as eugenics ideologies transformed from overt to covert. After the defeat of Hitler in World War Two, the eugenics movement in mainstream America went from an overt "white" racist format to a covert "white" racist format, sometimes called "crypto-eugenics." In order for this updated strategy to take place, the scientific and intellectual approach of the cunning hunter would come into play. The covert strategy of the ice-cold, deep-freeze mentality would be a statement that would again reiterate the master-race syndrome, except this time the original population of suntanned Children would be so deceived by the appearance of change and the promise of integration and equal rights that they would be unable to see the clear and present danger. As the target prey, the suntanned Children would readily consume of the fantasies and delusions of the American Dream.

No doubt the violence and bloodshed of the mass lynchings, mob attacks and rapes coupled with economic hardship would trigger a mass movement out of the south as well as out of the rural areas and into the cities. It is noted that many "black" sharecroppers and tenant farmers fell deeply into debt or lost everything. In what became known as the Great Migration, "blacks" abandoned the farms in search of opportunity and urban jobs. Although research indicates that in

1910, fifty years after the Civil War, 89% of all “blacks” still lived in the South, and 80% of these in rural areas, it is noted that by 1960, 40% of all blacks lived outside the South, while 75% of all “blacks” lived in cities. Well-orchestrated terrorizing tactics had actually achieved the goals and objectives of ousting “blacks” off of their farmland as the southern “whites” reclaimed the former plantations.

The government would introduce social programs, food programs and nutritional guidelines that would continue to deteriorate patterns of consumption that were indeed already unwholesome even on the farms. The pyramid of food consumption would be structured so that the food choices reflected the consumption patterns that were born and bred in the ice-cold, deep-freeze mentality. Thus, the death consumption culture would be more firmly inculcated in the minds of the massive population, leading to the thoughts and reasoning that identified fresh and wholesome fruits, vegetables, seeds and nuts as snacks. In the death consumption culture food pyramid, the choice cuts of fresh kill, i.e. fish, fowl, beef or pork, would be considered as the first priority of wholesome consumption. The general population was experiencing a baby boom, and European immigration was also adding to the U.S. demographics. This gave eugenics advocates new fuel to justify birth control strategies and other population control measures, specifically aimed at the historic target group.

The suntanned Children of this culture would be in a ready-made and vulnerable position at the bottom of the social economic strata. This population had recently emerged out of the pale reflection of life during the wretched days of the three hundred years plus of slavery. The racist ideologies that upheld and maintained the chattel slavery system had been branded, beaten and forced into the deepest pits of their minds and memories. The chattel slavery vibration outlawed the concept of family, marriage, and mate responsibility. In fact, the hunting and herding mentality would inflict the breeding practices used for livestock upon the suntanned Children. The breeding practices maintained laws that perpetuated the male as a stud to service the master's needs in reproducing a stock or breed of slaves. The female was to serve as the wench, the bitch or the whore to satisfy the social economic and sexual needs of her master by reproducing more of the same, weaker and weaker every time.

### *Protecting and Serving the Ice-cold, Deep-freeze Mentality*

The "Negro breakers" would use violence, torture, brutality and humiliation to break the spirit of the slave. In the era that descended from slavery into modern day freedom, a new kind of "Negro breaker" would emerge with the official authority to protect and to serve the silent majority. The chain gang systems that were used to build the railroads throughout the country would be replaced with federal and state prison systems that would function like private businesses. The prison system has a dual purpose. It must be understood that if an individual is convicted of a felony in America, he or she loses the right to vote. Simply by having a legal system that profiles a target population for unequal treatment and unfair sentencing, an entire voting block of a population can be nullified. Additionally, the extended sentencing provides an extended free labor source and opportunities for experimentation on a target group. Imprisonment removes a perceived or potential threat and places that population into a contained and restricted environment that is designed to strip one of one's human dignity as punishment.

The legal system in the United States has an adverse effect on the "African American" population, especially the male. When one looks at federal and state legislation, inclusive of the U.S. Constitution, the Black Codes, the Jim Crow laws, miscegenation laws, segregation laws, etc., it is self-evident that the "white" racist ideologies of the ice-cold, deep-freeze mentality were the founding energies of a society that legalized human bondage. The very same founding father energies have been born and bred into the offspring. Additionally, when one examines the religious morals, values and ethics of spiritual leaders, e.g. the pope and others who historically declared racial enslavement as being ordained by god, it becomes easy to recognize the plight of the suntanned Children at this stage of their existence within the social environment.

Be reminded here that we are not just talking about the Christians; we are speaking of the attitudes and behaviors of all of those who are disciples and followers of the Father, the Son and the Holy Ghost. The father is Judaism, a religion that worships blood sacrifice through ritual slaughter; the Son is Christianity, a religion that worships the blood sacrifice through the crucifixion (and they would drink the "blood of the lamb"), and the Holy Ghost is Islam a religion that worships blood sacrifice through ritual slaughter. Their steppe brothers, the Aryan Hindus adopted the cultural patterns of the indigenous Afro-centric population in India. Although these so-called Aryan Hindus appear to have softened by a practice of vegetarianism, the dead and devitalized energy within the cooked vegetables continues to fuel the ice-cold, deep-freeze mentality laced within the religious order. As a result, more than 300 million of the Afro-centric population, i.e. the so-called "Black Untouchables," are relegated to a lower caste of inferiority as sanctioned by the Hindu god. It really doesn't matter if one picks and chooses from an Afro-centric frame of reference, i.e. Yoruba, Akan, Moorish Science, etc. So long as one is consuming of the death consumption culture, one is being fed by the ice-cold, deep-freeze mentality. The name of the game is to keep the suntanned populations tricked and divided, conquered and undecided.

As the old saying goes, "Laws are made to be broken." Prisons are made to incarcerate the law-breakers who are caught. Historically, the "African American" male could be sitting at home and be intruded upon by a law officer for any number of reasons. It is a known fact that in many instances covert strategies were and continue to be orchestrated to legally incarcerate targeted individuals or groups. Obviously, if someone of power and authority wanted another person out of the way, there are enough laws amassed to ensure that the targeted individual could definitely trip over one of them and could be charged for something, even suspicion. Even if one is charged with suspicion, one can be contained long enough to disrupt and tamper with one's life. The legal system is in place to protect and to preserve the status quo. In this way, a job could be well done "legally," leaving no one with anything to say except that procedures were followed "by the book." Within the majority of communities in America, the stigma and the stereotype is so strong that once someone says that an "African American" committed a crime, the individual is assumed guilty by racial association.

Let's be very clear here: the I in I am certainly not saying that "black" males do not commit crimes. It is clear that a lower social economic state of being in a culture that promotes the luxuries of "in-your-face" wealth also promotes greed, exploitation and criminal activities to attain those material goods. It must be understood that American history shows that the wealth base was acquired through theft, enslavement, mafia tactics, and cunning plots and schemes geared towards mass deception. It also must be understood that this has been traditionally broadcast and telecast, and taught in schools. Target populations that have historically been denied access to mainstream economic advantages would be inclined to resort to illegal means, i.e. any means available.

The constant fear is that if "African American" males are not put "in their place" and kept "in their place," they will and must indeed become sick and tired of oppressive "white" ideologies. There is dread and panic at the thought that "African American" males will one day stop being irresponsible and chaotic "boys" and grow up into men who seek revenge as is the tradition of the ice-cold, deep-freeze mentality. What the I in I am saying is that the methodologies of the ice-cold, deep-freeze mentality are geared with ulterior motives that directly link to the fright and fear created by the Nat Turners, the Black Panthers, the Mau Mau Underground and others who became sick and tired of being oppressed by "white" racist ideology.

The I in I maintain that what is required is for males, especially the suntanned male, to assume the full stature of their responsibilities as the father spirit by seeking divine spirit consciousness and providing divine guidance and divine protection to the mother spirit and their offspring. Leave the toxic vibrations of the ice-cold, deep-freeze mentality to those who claim degeneration and mutation as their birthright and work diligently to reclaim the divinity of the sacred garden culture. In this way, a divine example can be set that will eventually show all of Man, He and She, that holistic living harmony is the greatest advantage that humanity could ever acquire. Unfortunately, so many of the "African American" males are so deeply indulged in the attitudes and behaviors of the ice-cold, deep-freeze mentality and so addicted to the death consumption culture that they cannot see the vicious traps that have been laid by a cold-blooded mentality.

The I in I am quite aware that many of these brothers of skin and kin would consider the I in I too soft in directing them towards divine spirit consciousness in seeking solutions. However, if one would simply reason with a little spirit sense, one would comprehend the nature of the energy that is opposite of Supreme Love. Thus, one would comprehend the hunting patterns of sabotage, ambush and booby-traps within the death consumption culture and the ice-cold, deep-freeze mentality. With this divine clarity, one would understand the importance of regaining one's divine spirit consciousness as the masculine presence. One would then gather enough reasoning to know the necessity of providing divine guidance and protection for the feminine presence in order for there to be a forwarding of the multiplication of one's whole life self.

Remember that whoever controls the hands that rock the crib controls the nation and every generation of that nation. All it takes is to open one's eyes and look around at any city, any state or any town and one will see who is in control of the hands that rock the crib.... It is certainly not divinity. The truth speaks for itself through obesity, perms, fried and dyed heads, high-heeled and high-fashion sophistication of a superficial and artificial order, cold-blooded brotherhood and sisterhood relationships, and other self-hate factors that are fed to the offspring, i.e. children. These synthetic behaviors occur in clubs, in churches and other religious formats; social economic, and political organizations; as well as in educational institutions. Unquestionably, the Children of the Sun are equally under the absolute rule of the ice-cold, deep-freeze mentality. Although the ice-cold, deep-freeze mentality operates under racist ideologies, the mentality does not discriminate in providing equal opportunity to emerge into its toxic and vicious insanity.

The goal and objective is to establish family community and a wholesome social economic way of life. These goals and objectives are severely hampered if the "African American" male is emasculated. It is fruitless if the "African American" male is placed in the predicament of being helpless and vulnerable to the whims and commands of a historic hostile aggressor. It is unfortunate that the suntanned populations cannot comprehend that the most revolutionary act of liberation, justice and freedom is to align oneself within the holistic living way of life of the sacred garden culture.

This is the sacred spirit movement that the I in I have been promoting strongly both nationally and internationally for generations. On the other hand, there have been many movements and ideologies professing different methods of revolutionary tactics and approaches since the 1960's. These social and political movements have been clearly shown through statistical evidence and documentation throughout this text to be an absolute failure. It appears as though the sacred sons and daughters have totally assimilated the ice-cold, deep-freeze mentality of the death consumption culture and have committed themselves to suicidal extermination.

What has happened time and again with the Children of the Sun with the golden tan is that they continue to fall for the tricks and deceptions of the ice-cold, deep-freeze mentality. They simply jump from one religious order to another religious order within the death consumption culture; from one political ideology to another political ideology within the death consumption culture; from one social economic scheme to another social economic dream within the death consumption culture. The lost and astray Children with the golden tan continue to crave the vibrations and sensations of lust, lies, illusions, confusion, death and deadly destruction. Therefore, they continue to praise, idolize and worship the social orders, the political orders and religious orders that descended from the ice-cold, deep-freeze mentality. And so, what goes around or is sent around continues to come back around to the suntanned Children from the ice-cold, deep-freeze mentality over and over again while the suntanned Children expect different results.

Back in the day, there was lots of talk about undercover intelligence agents at work in the "black" community who were using divisive tactics to seek, search and destroy by any means necessary. It was also a known fact that drugs were being flooded into the "black" communities from unknown external sources. Some suspected that the very same governmental agencies that were in place to disrupt and destabilize were also the connection to the influx of illegal substances. Under the guise of protecting the existing social order which had demonstrated adverse effects on the suntanned populations, these agents were committed to an ideology that justified eliminating a perceived threat by any means necessary. It is quite clear that those who have established a pattern of violence are quick to fear the violent backlash from their instigating behaviors, because the assumption is that "the other guy" is going to behave as they would behave.

**The Seeds of Self-Destruction**

It must become very clear to the Children of the Sun that if the seeds of self-destruction are planted and nurtured within a people and if there is no change in the internal genetics of the seed, it will continue to produce the same toxic fruit to the point of total destruction. Take a little time and read the following excerpts regarding the COINTELPRO program orchestrated against the conscious-oriented among the Afro-centric population.

Keep in mind that during the time of COINTELPRO's intervention, i.e. covert invasion, into the "black" community, the term "afro" was a statement of Afro-centric beauty and statements such as, "Say it loud, I'm black and I'm proud" were common. A sense of self-love, dignity and pride were beginning to filter through the ice-cold, deep-freeze mentality that was the inherited state of mind from pre- and post-slavery. One need but look around at the suntanned populations of today to see the tragic consequences of esteemlessness both nationally and internationally.

> COINTELPRO is the FBI acronym for a series of covert action programs directed against domestic groups. In these programs, the Bureau went beyond the collection of intelligence to secret action defined to "disrupt" and "neutralize" target groups and individuals. COINTELPRO began in 1956, in part because of frustration with Supreme Court rulings limiting the Government's power to proceed overtly against dissident groups; it ended in 1971 with the threat of public exposure. In the intervening 15 years, the Bureau conducted a

sophisticated vigilante operation aimed squarely at preventing the exercise of First Amendment rights of speech and association, on the theory that preventing the growth of dangerous groups and the propagation of dangerous ideas would protect the national security and deter violence.

Many of the techniques used would be intolerable in a democratic society even if all of the targets had been involved in violent activity, but COINTELPRO went far beyond that. The unexpressed major premise of the programs was that a law enforcement agency has the duty to do whatever is necessary to combat perceived threats to the existing social and political order…The Black Nationalist program, according to its supervisor, included "a great number of organizations that you might not today characterize as black nationalist but which were in fact primarily black."3a Indeed, the nonviolent Southern Christian Leadership Conference was labeled as a Black Nationalist "Hate Group."….Under the COINTELPRO programs, the arsenal of techniques used against foreign espionage agents was transferred to domestic enemies. As William C. Sullivan, former Assistant to the Director, put it, "This is a rough, tough, dirty business, and dangerous. It was dangerous at times. No holds were barred....We have used [these techniques] against Soviet agents. They have used [them] against us. . . . [The same methods were] brought home against any organization against which we were targeted. We did not differentiate. This is a rough, tough business…." In marked contrast to prior COINTELPROs, which grew out of years of intensive intelligence investigation, the

Black Nationalist COINTELPRO and the racial intelligence investigative section were set up at about the same time in 1967.

Prior to that time, the Division's investigation of "Negro matters" was limited to instances of alleged Communist infiltration of civil rights groups and to monitoring civil rights protest activity. However, the long, hot summer of 1967 led to intense pressure on the Bureau to do something to contain the problem, and once again, the Bureau heeded the call. The originating letter was sent out to twenty-three field offices on August 25, 1967, describing the program's purpose as...to expose, disrupt, misdirect, discredit, or otherwise neutralize the activities of black nationalist, hate-type organizations and groupings, their leadership, spokesmen, membership, and supporters, and to counter their propensity for violence and civil disorder. Efforts of the various groups to consolidate their forces or to recruit new or youthful adherents must be frustrated. 89

On March 4, 1968, the program was expanded from twenty-three to forty-one field offices. 93 The letter expanding the program lists five long-range goals for the program:

(1) to prevent the "coalition of militant black nationalist groups," which might be the first step toward a real "Mau Mau" in America;

(2) to prevent the rise of a "messiah" who could "unify, and electrify," the movement, naming specifically Martin Luther King, Stokely Carmichael, and Elijah Muhammed;

(3) to prevent violence on the part of black nationalist groups, by pinpointing "potential troublemakers" and neutralizing them "before they exercise their potential for violence;"

> (4) to prevent groups and leaders from gaining "respectability" by discrediting them to the "responsible" Negro community, to the white community (both the responsible community and the "liberals" -- the distinction is the Bureau's), and to Negro radicals; and
>
> (5) to prevent the long range growth of these organizations, especially among youth, by developing specific tactics to "prevent these groups from recruiting young people." 94
>
> As Justice Brandeis declared in a different context fifty years ago: "Our government is the potent, the omnipresent teacher. For good or for ill, it teaches the whole people, by its example. Crime is contagious. If the Government becomes a lawbreaker, it breeds contempt for law: it invites every man to become a law unto himself. To declare that in the administration of the criminal law the end justifies the means -- to declare that the Government may commit crimes in order to secure the conviction of the private criminal -- would bring terrible retribution. Against the pernicious doctrine this Court should resolutely set its face. Olmstead v. U.S., 277 U.S. 439,4 85 (1927). Approximately 28% of the Bureau's COINTELPRO efforts were designed to weaken groups by setting members against each other, or to separate groups which might otherwise be allies, and convert them into mutual enemies.[16]

---

[16] *COINTELPRO: The FBI'S Covert Action Programs Against American Citizens*. Supplementary Detailed Staff Reports on Intelligence Activities and the Rights of Americans. Book III. Final Report of the Select Committee to Study Governmental Operations with Respect to Intelligence Activities. United States Senate. (under authority of the order of April 14, 1976) Online Source:

Those who make the laws within the death consumption culture however noble and well-intentioned can only reflect the energy of their consumption. What kind of order perpetuates acts of slaughter so that one may consume the dead flesh of other living creatures/beings? It is the order of those who have the swiftest ability to kill and inflict fright, fear and terror establishing themselves as the power base of a social structure. It is the order of a cold-blooded and vicious mentality that has no compassion for the prey whose blood is shed and whose life is taken. The laws of the ice-cold, deep-freeze mentality are characterized by the energy that is opposite of Supreme Love.

It should be noted that the Rockefeller family has had a peculiar relationship with eugenics which is generally defined as a systematic method of racial purging. Due to Mr. Rockefeller's popularity among the silent majority who appreciated his frame of reference, he became governor of New York from 1959 to 1973. It must also be noted that many within the "African American" community have had a peculiar relationship with marijuana, cocaine and other mind-altering drugs also known as narcotic substances that tend to make one feel momentary relief from displeasing social conditions. For this reason, the Afro-centric population was vulnerable to laws that related to street drugs, drug trafficking, and illegal drug/narcotic use. The cunning and ruthless strategies of the hunting, scavenging and herding culture allow the hunter to track the patterns of vulnerability and capitalize on the weakness of one's targeted prey so that the assault is lethal. A legal system that serves as the infrastructure of a social order founded upon the principles and practices of chattel slavery is by design an instrument of maintaining the status quo of its origin.

Research indicates that the New York state laws, enacted in 1973 and named the Rockefeller Drug Laws for then-governor

---

http://www.icdc.com/~paulwolf/cointelpro/churchfinalreportIIIa.htm.

Nelson Rockefeller, removed judicial discretion and imposed heavy sentences for drug-related crimes. A first-time offense for the possession for sale of two ounces of a narcotic substance or just simple possession of four ounces could yield 15 years to life in prison. The drug laws, based on how they were applied, became an effective tool for targeting "black" males through racial profiling. A commonly noted example of racial profiling has been called "DWB," i.e. "driving while black." The U.S. Congress made the following finding: "The use by police officers of race, ethnicity, or national origin in deciding which persons should be subject to traffic stops, stops and frisks, questioning, searches, and seizures is a problematic law enforcement tactic. Statistical evidence from across the country demonstrates that such racial profiling is a real and measurable phenomenon."[17] The ACLU (American Civil Liberties Union) addressed the issue:

> It is important to talk about the federal DEA training program because many public officials who can no longer deny the fact of racial profiling would like us to believe it is the work of rogue cops. But we are not talking about freelance cowboys here and there who violate rights. No, we are not talking about rogue cops. We are talking about rogue policy. We are talking about rogue leadership. We are talking about a national policy which is training police all over this country to use traffic violations, which everyone commits the minute you get into your car, as an excuse to stop and search people with dark skin.... In 1973, Governor Nelson Rockefeller... introduced what came to be known as the Rockefeller Drug Laws,

[17] *End of Racial Profiling Act of 2001* (Introduced in House) H.R.2074. Online Source: http://thomas.loc.gov/cgi-bin/query/F?c107:1:./temp/~c107kAhU4b:e1813.

which created draconian mandatory minimum sentences, and helped legitimize the notion of mandatory minimums that plague us today and are responsible for the escalation of incarceration in this country. Mandatory minimums were brought to us, courtesy of the drug war. The idea was that now we're really going to get tough. Now if you were caught with even a particle of a forbidden substance, you were going to go away for 15 or 20 years, and no judge could use discretion to vary that sentence. Just since 1982, the amount of federal money that is spent on drug enforcement went up from 1.65 billion to 18 billion dollars. And that doesn't count the billions of dollars that the states spent. The result? From a few hundred thousand people imprisoned in this country in local, state and federal jails, we now have close to two million people behind bars today. The bulk of that increase has been because of drug law violations, non-violent violations, possession, sale, buying.

There is a hundred-fold disparity between sentences for conviction of possession of equivalent amounts of crack cocaine and powder cocaine, despite the fact that there is no pharmacological difference in the effect it has on the body. It's a different system of delivery that creates a different feeling, but it is no more pharmacologically harmful. But the sentences are harsher for crack cocaine, which is crystallized cocaine, than it is for powder. And guess what? Most of the folks who use powder cocaine are white, and most of the folks who used crack cocaine during its heyday were black and Latino. The racial profiling reflected in traffic stops

> reflects itself in every aspect of drug law enforcement.
>
> According to the National Institute of Drug Abuse, the federal agency that tracks these things, 13 percent of all monthly drug users in this country are African-Americans. That's just about their percentage of the population. Not disproportionate. But 35 percent of those arrested for drug possession are African-Americans. 55 percent of those convicted of drug possession are African-Americans and 74 percent of those imprisoned are African-Americans. And so it is no accident that among the increases in incarceration, we find that for black women between 1987 and 1991, incarceration on drug offenses increased by 800 percent, and has continued to go up since then. Homicide is the leading cause of death among young black men aged 18 to 25, and a lot of those deaths are caused by drug trafficking.
>
> One of every three African-American men between the ages of 20 and 29 are under the jurisdiction of the criminal justice system in this country. One of every three. And in places like the District of Columbia it is one of two.[18]

Amnesty International reports that racial profiling is so pervasive that it has impacted nearly 32 million people in the United States. A year-long study conducted by the Domestic Human Rights Program of Amnesty International USA found that the unlawful use of race in police, immigration, and airport security procedures has expanded since the terrorist attacks of September 11, 2001. As documented in the 2004 report,

---

[18] *Biennial Speech.* Ira Glasser, Executive Director ACLU, June 1999. Online Source: http://www.aclu.org/DrugPolicy/DrugPolicy.cfm?ID=5040&c=82

"Threat and Humiliation: Racial Profiling, National Security, and Human Rights in the United States," the U.S. continues to use race, color, ethnicity, national origin and religion as a cause for criminal suspicion, in violation of international treaties to which it is party. Research indicates that victims of racial profiling are sometimes further victimized and fall prey to acts of police violence and brutality. This is illustrated by numerous reports Amnesty International has documented, including the case of Santiago described in the report "Threat and Humiliation." Santiago, an epileptic "black" man who wore dreadlocks, was killed because police automatically assumed that a "black" man convulsing on the floor must be on drugs. Officers reportedly forced him flat on the ground, penned a knee on his back and caused him to stop breathing. He was given oxygen, gained consciousness for a short while, was handcuffed and taken to the hospital where he died.[19]

The effects of being racially profiled and interrogated simply because one is dark-skinned or belongs to a targeted group are reported to cause feelings of being degraded, humiliated, intimidated, traumatized and unfairly persecuted. These feelings can produce reactions of fear, anxiety, contempt, resentment, bitterness and anger in the innocent victim. Those who practice racial profiling are noted to be suspicious, distrustful and oftentimes hostile based on the racial characteristics of a targeted suspect.

A 2001 Department of Justice report on citizen-police contacts in 1999 found that, although African-Americans and Hispanics were more likely to be stopped and searched, they were less likely to be in possession of contraband. On average, searches and seizures of African-American drivers yielded evidence only eight percent of the time, searches and seizures of Hispanic drivers yielded evidence only 10 percent of the

---

[19] *Threat and Humiliation: Racial Profiling, National Security, and Human Rights in the United States*. Amnesty International. Online Source: http://www.amnestyusa.org/racial_profiling/sevenfacts.html.

time, and searches and seizures of white drivers yielded evidence 17 percent of the time.[20]

The Rockefeller Drug Laws allowed the strong arm of the law to lean on the reasoning and attitudes of racial profiling to target young “black” males specifically. The sentencing guidelines of the Rockefeller Drug Laws were considered so harsh that the international human rights organization Human Rights Watch as well as other organizations and activists called for reform. Research indicates that on Dec. 7, 2004, the New York State Legislature finally voted to reform the state’s Rockefeller Drug Laws, which were noted to be the harshest in the nation, according to a study commissioned by the New York State Senate. Nevertheless, the focus remains on incarceration as a treatment for symptoms of social disorder rather than addressing corrective actions for the underlying causes of the social disorder. In other words, the social system still seeks to target a scapegoat. Under the new drug legislation, prison terms for those convicted of narcotic possession or sale have been shortened from the 15-years-to-life mandatory prison sentence to an eight-to 20-year sentence.

Research indicates that the United States has the highest incarceration rate in the world. With 5% of the world's people the U.S. holds 25% of the world's prisoners. It is noted that over two-thirds of these prisoners are “African American” or Latino.

> African Americans make up just 12% of the U.S. population but comprise 47% of the country's prison population. As of June 2002, the total number of individuals incarcerated was 2,019,234. This population consisted of: 818,900 African American males, 637,700 white males, and 68,000 Hispanic males. 1 in 10 African American males between the ages of 25 and 29 were incarcerated in

[20] Reference footnote 19.

> state or federal prisons by the end of 2001. According to the U.S. Department of Justice, nearly 1 in 3 African American males born in 2001 will go to prison during his lifetime. Young African American males are twice as likely to die and 27 times more likely to go to jail as young white males…
>
> Texas for instance, ranks number 3 in spending on prisons, while it ranked 20th for education spending. It ranks number 1 in putting citizens to death. Texas has an African American population of 11%, and an African American prison population of 44%. In Louisiana, African Americans comprise 33% of the general population, and 76% of the prison population. In Mississippi, African Americans constitute 36% of the general population and 75% of the prison population. In Illinois, African Americans make up 15.1% of the general population and 65% of the prison population. African American males make up nearly 3 out of 4 detainees in Cook County Jail located in Illinois. In addition, nearly 3 out of 4 African American males who reside in Cook County are also incarcerated in Illinois prisons or on parole. 30 to 40% of the next generation of African American males will permanently lose the right to vote if current trends continue.[21]

What is the effect of these profiles on those whose great grandfathers were slave owners, whose grandfathers wrote the Black Codes, whose fathers carried out the Jim Crow laws and who are themselves bred on racist ideologies? The gnawing guilt and deeply submerged fear that festers in the ice-cold,

---

[21] *The State of the African American Male*. Prepared by the Office of Illinois Congressman Danny K. Davis. The Wilmington Journal, October 18, 2004.

deep-freeze mentality is projected on the scapegoat, the target population. The lost and astray Children who lost their tan have left a bloody trail of murder, rape, steal and take everywhere they have invaded. Every native and indigenous population that the children who lost their tan have encountered has fallen prey to the ice-cold, deep-freeze mentality through force of violence; absolutely no population has willingly submitted to the toxic attitudes and behaviors of the lost and astray Children who lost their tan. Why wouldn't these descendants of the vicious nomadic invaders who glorified in murder, rape, steal and take be afraid of their own shadow, the shadow of their own violent and bloody heritage? It becomes easier to understand how those of the ice-cold, deep-freeze mentality who are in elite positions of power and wealth within the death consumption culture would fear what they have created, because all that they can create is a paler and more cold-blooded version of all that they have consumed.

Is it irony, is it coincidence or is it by orchestration that a targeted community was inundated by drugs? The plots and schemes of the COINTELPROs, etc., to prevent the development of a strong "black" consciousness have broken down these communities into a dilapidated state of being. The ice-cold, deep-freeze mentality continues to create cold, harsh and barren environments where drug addiction and esteemless behaviors dominate a conflict-oriented way of life. Amazingly, the very same war tactics, i.e. the drugs and toxic substances, that invaded the "black" communities during the heyday of consciousness during the 1970's were the exact same instruments used to enslave, i.e. incarcerate, the offspring of the sons and daughters of the consciousness era. It seems that what was covertly sent around to divide, conquer and destabilize the "black" community has come back around to add the final blows. The divine and sacred ancestors look upon yet another tragic plight of the suntanned Children knowing that the Most Supreme Spiritual Essence of Life will have the final say.

The 1989 case of a Central Park jogger who was allegedly attacked and raped by five teenagers caught the imagination of the ice-cold, deep-freeze mentality. The jogger was a "white" female of wealth, status and credentials within the death consumption culture; the teenagers were Afro-centric males from Harlem. What transpired in the case had more to do with the pale ghosts and goblins that live in the ice-cold, deep-freeze mentality than any question of guilt or innocence. More than thirteen years after the events of the case, a convicted rapist who was already serving a life sentence came forward to confess that he committed the crime. Findings show that DNA evidence linked him to the crime. The five men's convictions were thrown out at the district attorney's request. Imagine after these five suntanned males had been incarcerated and served their full prison sentence, the case was thrown out. After being found guilty, these suntanned males were exonerated.

Law enforcement methods of the ice-cold, deep-freeze mentality rely on the use of coercion, intimidation, threats, physical violence and deception to "break" the will of the interrogated suspect. Keep in mind that the ice-cold, deep-freeze mentality is entrenched in the historical patterns of conquering and breaking the will of those who are captured. It is no surprise that the same attitudes and behaviors would survive in the more "civilized" setting based on law and order…the law and order of the ice-cold, deep-freeze mentality. As a result, officers are indoctrinated into the mental methods of interrogation designed to get a suspect to confess. Research indicates that training manuals tell investigators, for instance, to use the physical environment to law enforcement advantage, by creating small, starkly furnished, and brightly lit interrogation rooms; they instruct in how to get in a defendant's face and invade his personal space. Officers reportedly learn how to conduct long interviews that may span three or four days, with little respect for a suspect's need for sleep, food, or bathroom breaks. Findings show that law enforcement officers may lie to suspects and these lies can be very harmful, since the suspect can, through repetition, be induced by the investigator to believe them. Studies show that some people who falsely confess do so because they internalize the repeated suggestions and scenarios of questioners.

The formula is repeated again and again within the ice-cold, deep-freeze mentality. An individual or population is targeted. Historically, the target population has been the suntanned Children. An offense is projected upon the target population with an assumption of guilt. Then the accuser sets up mental and physical factors that are designed to reinforce the projected claims. Repeated reinforcement causes a "breaking" until the captured individual or population submits to the dominant attitudes and behaviors and assumes the characteristics that have been projected.

In the Central Park case, the teenagers and their families claimed that the confessions were coerced and were the result of illegal and improper police interrogations that took place before the videotaping of the confessions. The young males maintained their innocence. The question remains: "How could these boys be convicted when there was no physical evidence to link them to the crime and their confessions were inconsistent and even contradicted each other?

The media coverage of the time captured many of the underlying fearful perceptions that linger in the minds of the lost and astray Children who lost their tan. A newspaper article by columnist Pete Hamill in the New York Post, entitled "A Savage Disease Called New York" described the perceptions of fright and fear of a "dark" menace:

> They were coming downtown from a world of crack, welfare, guns, knives, indifference and ignorance. They were coming from a land with no

> fathers… They were coming from the anarchic province of the poor.
>
> And driven by a collective fury, brimming with the rippling energies of youth, their minds teeming with the violent images of the streets and the movies, they had only one goal: to smash, hurt, rob, stomp, rape. The enemies were rich. The enemies were white.[22]

Research indicates that members of the media readily accepted and projected racially charged images that portrayed black and Latino adolescent males as guilty of committing a vicious gang rape. Sexual stereotypes regarding "black" males, stereotypes regarding drugs, crime, violence, and impoverished communities were the formula for attitudes and behaviors that pronounced the target individuals guilty by association. The predominantly "white" press covered the details of the case with a bias resulting from the ice-cold, deep-freeze mentality. It is noted that highly sensational news coverage led to increased racial tension in New York City and fueled a public outcry for the conviction of the five Afro-centric male youths. The mass perceptions of Man, He and She, within the death consumption culture have been grossly discolored by the ice-cold, deep-freeze mentality. The lynch-mob mentality was barely beneath the surface in the emotional reactions, quick conclusions and racial profiling that occurred surrounding the rape case. Even the thought of a scenario that suggested that a "white" female had been raped by "black" males was a formula for explosive fear, loathing, anger and violence within the ice-cold, deep-freeze mentality, a formula for projecting on the suntanned male what has been historically categorically committed by the "white" male. A 2003 article further exposes the attitudes that were triggered by the events of the case:

---

[22] *Who's Wilding Who?* By Mumia Abu Jamal. Socialist Viewpoint. Vol. 3, No. 2, February 2003. Online Source: http://www.socialistviewpoint.org/feb_03/feb_03_22.html.

> At the same time, middle-class white people were slowly moving back to midtown and reclaiming the symbol of the city, Central Park. Fear that ghetto crime could spoil this sanctuary struck a powerful chord, especially among the rich and the elected. Donald Trump, the real-estate magnate, would spend $85,000 on full-page ads calling for the death penalty in the jogger case: "They should be forced to suffer," Trump opined. "I want them to be afraid." Mayor Ed Koch was often quoted calling the arrested boys "monsters" and complaining that juvenile laws were too soft. Pete Hamill, looking back now, remembers a city on edge, maybe over the brink. "Aside from the savagery of the rape and the beating itself, there was a sense that the city was unraveling," he says. "That young people fueled by crack and rage, and armed with guns, were out of control."[23]

These young males became the scapegoats for those who are the benefactors of permitting, protecting and serving a social economic environment that instigates social evils against targeted populations. Even more importantly, those individuals who should have been proponents of at least having the semblance of a fair trail were the very ones who upheld the mentality of the lynch law. The Worcester's Dictionary of 1846 defines Lynch law as "an irregular and revengeful species of justice, administered by the populace or a mob, without any legal authority or trial." For the verb "lynch" the following meaning is given, "to condemn and execute in obedience to the decree of a multitude or mob, without a legal trial...." The lynch concept of old would continue to remain embedded in

---

[23] *Coloring the Central Park Jogger Case.* Lynnell Hancock. Columbia Journalism Review, Jan. 16, 2003.

every thought and every reasoning of every generation, regardless of them being blonde or bald or natty, natty dread. The adverse effects on the Afro-centric population would be horrifying when viewed from a holistic living perspective. Fortunately these suntanned sons were not tried in Texas or they may have been executed before they had the chance to be exonerated. 117 innocent people have walked off Death Row in the modern era after spending up to 33 years condemned to death.[24]

Incidents of police brutality within the death consumption culture are a symptom of the brutality that is inherent within the ice-cold, deep-freeze mentality. Repeated exposure to brutality as a target population creates a climate of fear, resentment, bitterness, anger and anxiety. These toxic vibrations and sensations have a deteriorating effect on one's mental and physical health and well-being as a part of a systematic "breaking" process. One of many cases of police brutality that came to national attention is the case of Abner Louima, a "black" Haitian immigrant. Findings show that Louima was arrested in a brawl outside a nightclub in Brooklyn, New York on Aug. 9, 1997. Officers reportedly handcuffed Louima and hauled him into the police station at which point one of the police officers claimed that Louima punched him. The court case revealed that a "white" law enforcement officer and at least one other "white" officer then dragged Louima into a bathroom at the police station. The "white" law enforcement officer reportedly took a broken broomstick and sodomized Louima while another officer held him down, and then pushed the stick into Louima's mouth, breaking two teeth. Reports state that Louima also suffered a punctured bladder and intestines.

The officers were brought to trial and were found guilty. Research indicates that in 2002, a federal appeals court tossed

---

[24] *The Death Penalty in Texas*. Texas Moratorium Network. Online Source: http://texasmoratorium.org/mod.php?mod=userpage&menu=13 &page_id=19&group=3

out the convictions of three of the four officers convicted of torturing and sodomizing Louima by claiming that prosecutors did not have enough evidence. The police officer who led the assault on Louima in 1997 is now serving a 30-year prison sentence and is not affected by the ruling.

Research indicates that on February 4, 1999, four "white" police officers in plainclothes approached Amadou Diallo, an immigrant from West Afrika, outside his apartment building in the South Bronx and shot him down in a barrage of 41 bullets. Findings show that the officers who were members of the Street Crime Unit noted that Diallo fit the racial profile of a serial rapist. The plainclothes police claimed to have identified themselves as New York police officers. Diallo reportedly reached into his jacket and pulled out his wallet. The officers claimed that they mistakenly identified the wallet and thought it was a gun. The four officers fired 41 shots, hitting Diallo 19 times. News reports indicated that no weapons were found on Diallo's body.

During the aftermath of the case, civil rights and minority groups filed a class-action lawsuit to shut down the aggressive Street Crime Unit, claiming that the unit used racial profiling and unfairly frisked thousands of young "black" and Latino men every year without cause. Findings show that a Bronx grand jury indicted the officers on charges of second-degree murder and reckless endangerment. Later a New York appellate court ordered a change of venue to Albany, New York, stating that pretrial publicity had made a fair trial in New York City impossible. On February 25, 2000, after two days of deliberations, a jury acquitted the officers of all charges.

One cannot help but remember the "good ol' slavery days" when reviewing these cases. The history of America states very clearly that when there is a crime committed against the suntanned Children by members of the "white" populace or the protecting and serving authorities of the white populace it is not abnormal for the perpetrators to be cleared of all sins in a court of law. This process of denial is a tradition within a social order that has struggled to justify, rationalize, excuse and forget the barbaric and inhumane acts of chattel slavery and racist ideologies. The scapegoat policy holds very strongly within the social economic, political and religious structure as formulated by the ice-cold, deep-freeze mentality. Although the ice-cold, deep-freeze mentality may have many different faces and different names, it remains the same game of misery, aches and pains. How long do the consequences of the ice-cold, deep-freeze mentality continue to produce disease, disorder and deadly destruction? The consequences of toxic consumption continue as long as the mental, physical and spiritual consumption patterns remain the same.

### The Breaking Process through the Divide and Rule Syndrome

The breaking process of the ice-cold, deep-freeze mentality is a strategy that has been used throughout history. The Willie Lynch theory reveals the breeding practices used for livestock that continue to be played out within the death consumption culture on the suntanned populations: "Take the stud horse, break him for limited containment. Completely break the female horse until she becomes very gentle whereas you or anybody can ride her in comfort. Breed the mare until you have the desired offspring. Then you can turn the stud to freedom until you need him again. Train the female horse whereby she will eat out of your hand, and she will train the infant horse to eat of your hand also."

The translation into human terms exposes the level and degree of vicious and cold-blooded thought that festers in the ice-cold, deep-freeze mentality, as Lynch instructs: "Take the meanest and most restless nigger, strip him of his clothes in front of the remaining niggers, the female, and the nigger infant, tar and feather him, tie each leg to a different horse faced in opposite directions, set him a fire and beat both horses to pull him apart in front of the remaining niggers. The next step is to take a bullwhip and beat the remaining nigger male to the point of death in front of the female and the infant. Don't kill him. But put the fear of God in him, for he can be useful for future breeding."[25] Historical documentation, slave narratives and eyewitness accounts of the peculiar institution called slavery within America confirm the savage acts of brutality that were inflicted upon slaves, not as an exception to the rule but as the rule of thought and reasoning bred within such a degraded system in the first place.

Therefore, the Afro-centric population in the United States of America began a greater downward spiral under the ideology of being free as granted by federal legislation. However, the fears of the Thomas Jeffersons and others of his kind were echoed in the minds of the mass populations. With the likes of Nat Turner in America and Toussaint L'Ouverture in Haiti, the mind of the ice-cold, deep-freeze mentality could not let peace be still.

The strategies of mind control would be looked upon and labeled as a successful venture as the steps to a more profound plan of population control, i.e. population reduction. It was not too difficult for the power brokers to calculate that if there was global democratic rule, then those of Caucasian stock would be the lesser minority population. And so the powerbrokers would come up with another plan, a new plan of democracy based on the racial purity of a mutated breed, a democracy that would count the majority population in a manner similar to the Constitutional 3/5 clause. The catch phrase would be the First World nations and the Third World nations. Under this plan and strategy would be born such concepts as population control, family planning, and global inoculation/vaccination programs. This strategy would be launched through divisive tactics that would include factions and inter-group conflict, social economic and political tensions, and war. The divide

---

[25] *The Making of Slave*. Willie Lynch, 1712. Online Source: http://www.northtulsa.com/willielyn.htm.

and rule game would have expanded its effectiveness as the same game with another name.

The east-west syndrome emerged into a cold war only to surface under a single social economic focus. Within this particular state of affairs there would be a profound stretch of research that developed, there would be an identified enemy, and there would be a projection of being able to accomplish one's goals and objectives before the other guy. The trap would be well set as the suntanned populations of the world found themselves divided within the camps of the east-west syndrome. While the global population of suntanned Children struggled to lay claims to fame under socialist, communist or capitalist ideologies or under one of the religious ideologies of the invader culture, their already well-controlled natural resources would be placed under a new kind of neo-colonial rule. Convenient opportunism at play.

## Foresight and Comprehensive Analysis

Beyond the shadow of a doubt, there was definitely a depletion of the whole life presence of those individuals who descended from the cold northern blizzards of the Caucasus mountain and steppe regions. Adverse environmental conditions experienced in the dank, bleak and cold caves of the last Ice Age caused deterioration in basic consumption patterns. Man, He and She, of the ice-cold, deep-freeze mentality degenerated and mutated into a scavenger and predator-like being. It is the nature of this predator/hunter mentality to identify target groups to prey upon. Additionally, the lost and astray mind of Man, He and She, seeks to point the finger at the other guy as the problem rather than looking at the toxic vibrations and attitudes that are very glaring within self.

It becomes easier to understand why a population whose characteristics are clearly the consequence of severe degeneration and mutation would target a population that represents their opposite, i.e. the sacred and blessed origin of Man, He and She. The ice-cold, deep-freeze mentality readily targets another population as inferior and unfit, based on values, norms and principles that were born and bred in the degeneration and mutation of the bleak and barren caves. If one has become pale due to the breeding of massive deficiencies within the icy whiteness of a frigid environment, what would most represent the opposite circumstance other than someone who is tanned from the solarized warmth of a vibrant and lush environment? Due to adverse environmental conditions, the natural, innately wholesome consumption patterns of the lost and astray Children of Man, He and She, degenerated and deteriorated into scavenger and predator-like consumption patterns. The biological composition of Man, He and She, clearly indicates that the scavenger and predator-like consumption patterns are indeed toxic, depleting, and fatal to the whole life presence.

It stands to reason that the characteristics of degeneration and mutation can only be maintained by breeding in the isolation of degeneration and mutation. The thing that is not reasoned with here is that breeding degeneration and mutation with even more degeneration and mutation is in fact a negative breeding pattern that will further degenerate and mutate the mental, physical and spiritual characteristics of those participants among Man, He and She. Those who suffer from the ice-cold, deep-freeze mentality have categorized the historic target group as needing to be eliminated through genocidal practices to keep from muddying the bloodlines of the master race.

The intense and isolated methodology of toxic consumption that originated in the Ice Age caves reduced these malnourished and depleted Children of the Sun who lost their tan to a degenerated and mutated state of being. It also becomes clear that as a degenerated and mutated breed of Man, He and She, these individuals amass tactics to reverse the holistic living truth and claim superiority through cold-blooded acts. As Abraham Lincoln stated during his debate with

Stephen Douglas in 1858, "…And I will say, in addition to this that there is a physical difference between the white and black races which will ever forbid the two races living together on terms of social and political equality. And inasmuch as they cannot so live while they do remain together, there must be the position of superior and inferior. I am as much as any other man in favor of having the superior position assigned to the white race." In fact, those of the ice-cold, deep-freeze mentality would indeed be superior at inflicting cold-blooded acts of lust, lies, illusions, confusion, death and deadly destruction. These lost and astray Children of the Sun who lost their tan would in fact be the amassment of an energy that is opposite of Supreme Love and would spread it like a plague throughout the planet. They would in fact be a superior breed of invaders and terrorists, and superior at the game of deception. And all would be fair in love and war.

This mutated and degenerated breed of Man, He and She, was so inflicted with mental and physical sickness and disease that they themselves would become baffled by their own deep-seated suicidal and homicidal behaviors. Hostile aggression would be a norm and seeking to search and destroy would be a way of life. Lust, lies, illusions, confusion, death and deadly destruction would be the emerging energy of every strategy and of every attack. Imagine this ice-cold, deep-freeze mentality invading a culture that honored peace, love, harmony and problem-solving through group interaction. Imagine a culture that honored the earth, the wind, the rain and the sun and every living thing and where bloodshed was the ultimate "sin." Imagine a culture that worked for generations to establish and maintain irrigation systems, a garden presence, and organized communities linked in divine oneness. Imagine a body temple and all of its internal organs and systems, functioning in divine order as a result of consuming raw and living fruits, vegetables, seeds and nuts.

Imagine what would emerge from violent invasions and intrusions by a hunting and herding culture that had total disregard for the sacred garden culture, except to fatten up their livestock to be feasted upon. Imagine the conflict of interest from the murder, rape, steal and take that would occur to destabilize the sacred family structure of the suntanned Children, replacing it with the attitudes and behaviors of the death consumption culture. Imagine the sacred garden culture being violated and viciously attacked by a savage and beastly kind of man whose ice-cold, deep-freeze mentality allowed no compassion for life, absolutely no respect for the sacred order of the feminine energy, and no respect for the relationship of any other living thing or for the environment.

Imagine the desecration that occurred and continues to occur against the suntanned populations that originated in the sacred garden culture. Imagine the god-of-the-dead syndrome of the ice-cold, deep-freeze mentality being forced upon the suntanned Children of the sacred garden culture by any means necessary. Let it be known that this was and is real, and is not just my imagination running away with me. Let it be known that the adverse effects of toxic consumption can be witnessed on a daily basis. The rampant diseases and disorders that plague Man, He and She, are a sign that the state and condition of mental, physical and spiritual health continues to rapidly deteriorate and degenerate. It stands to reason that if mutation and degeneration are consumed by a mutated and degenerated presence, then the outcome can only be the breeding of a fatal attraction to death and deadly attraction. Therefore, all who consume of the ice-cold, deep-freeze mentality are consuming of a degenerated and mutated state of being and it matters not if one is blonde or bald or natty, natty dread.

Whereas, mutation and degeneration originated in the ice-cold and dank caves of the Caucasus Mountain and steppe region, the modern day levels of degeneration and mutation occur within the lost and astray mind, regardless of rain or shine. The ice-cold, deep-freeze mentality definitely commits genocidal acts against the sacred presence of Man, He and She.

These fatal consequences affect all of Man, He and She. However, the greatest level and degree of clear and present danger, i.e. toxic and depleting adverse effects, is being suffered by the suntanned Children of the planet. What this means in reality is that a vicious and most fatal energy of toxicity is being launched against the sacred origin of Man, He and She. This toxic and vicious energy is being orchestrated by a breed of suntanned Children who mutated and degenerated, losing their tan and losing their mind to an ice-cold, deep-freeze mentality. Just as the struggle continues to counteract the adverse effects, a greater struggle to accelerate mutation and degeneration is being waged against the sacred origin of Man, He and She. The ultimate enemy and the ultimate threat to the existence of Man, He and She, is the ice-cold, deep-freeze mentality.

Hostile aggression breeds fright, fear, and terror that destabilize the thoughts and reasoning of an individual or a population. Once an enemy can destabilize the thoughts and reasoning of an individual, then the individual will immediately seek ways and means of regaining security and stability. The individual will choose methods of either fight or flight. In any case, fight or flight can be mental, physical or religious/spiritual. This fight-or-flight syndrome can manifest through toxic drugs and addictive habits, material and intellectual stuff and things, or escapism through entertainment. These are the times when the strategists of the ice-cold, deep-freeze mentality are at their very best. Quicker than a flash, toxic and depleted programs that are declared to have a soothing effect will be invented, either real or imagined, and fed to the lost and astray mind. It is no wonder that when a people or a population become destabilized, toxins such as alcohol, cigarettes, sugar, drugs or other toxic quick-fix substances are quickly provided and consumed.

If one has begun to know full well that one has control over the thought and reasoning of a population, then the next step in controlling the destiny of that population is to focus on the sexual organs and the reproductive system. Thus, the culture of the ice-cold, deep-freeze mentality will determine the level and degrees of birth and related sexual behaviors. If that controller culture determines that there is a need for larger populations among the victimized culture, this will be orchestrated through laws, rules, regulations and procedures, as well as encouraging promiscuous sexual behaviors. By the same token if the controller culture wanted to limit or reduce that population's presence, then this will be orchestrated through laws, rules, regulations and procedures promoting sterilization, contraceptive programs and other birth control methods, abortions, etc. Thus, a specific population group could be manipulated and orchestrated to produce mass numbers in order to serve as a slave labor force. A mechanized and automated labor system could reduce the need for a specific population within the ice-cold, deep-freeze mentality. There are many ways to address this kind of issue, but they all fit into only two categories. Either the solution accentuates the positive by honoring the whole life presence, or it is a solution that accentuates the negative by degrading and violating the whole life presence. Within the ice-cold, deep-freeze mentality, genocidal-like programs and schemes would be established via sterilization, imprisonment, abortions, massive birth control methods, and biological warfare programs.

In clear logic, if one has been infested with sickness and disease within the sexual organs and reproductive system, one can only breed sickness and disease, and thus a weakening of the whole life presence of the offspring is the result. Again we reiterate that toxic mental, physical and spiritual consumption is the fuel of degeneration and mutation. Toxic consumption breeds the ice-cold, deep-freeze mentality, and the ice-cold, deep-freeze mentality is the root and foundation of the death consumption culture. If one is infested with degeneration and mutation and one continues to indulge in degeneration and mutation, then one will indeed forward the multiplication of degeneration and mutation to the point of extinction.

# Chapter Three:
# Long-Lasting Biological Warfare and the Plots and Schemes of Mind Control

# Chapter Three: Long-Lasting Biological Warfare and the Plots and Schemes of Mind Control

## *Freedom of Choice*

There are many ways to implement programs of biological warfare. However, the I in I will venture to say that the most effective way to institute lasting biological warfare is to establish programs, procedures and beliefs that will cause the biological effects of destruction to be self-inflicting. In other words, the most effective way to implement long-lasting biological warfare without any guilt is to implement programs of self-destruction through mind control. Through the plots and schemes of mind control, populations can be slowly manipulated into programmed attitudes and behaviors that would cause that population to seek, to search and to destroy itself. A lack of self-esteem, self-love, and the resulting esteem deficit disorder and attention deficit disorder automatically breed mental and physical disease and disorder. The patterns of disease and disorder automatically occur when the brain is malnourished.

There is absolutely no question that toxic consumption causes depletion and error within the brain cell functions. In other words, depleted and malnourished food substances are in fact toxic. The death consumption culture perpetuates the ideology that malnutrition stems from a lack of consumption. That is to say, the death consumption culture perpetuates the idea that if one does not eat plenty, then one suffers from malnourishment. The culture of death consumption has perpetuated the idea that malnourishment results in a skinny and frail body. The culture ignores the fact the malnourishment has another signature, i.e. being overweight and obese. If one would take a look at the American population from that perspective, one would clearly understand the I in I's position on malnourishment.

It will be understood beyond a shadow of a doubt that America is suffering from massive obesity, i.e. massive malnourishment. A deceptive program is in place that breeds the idea that malnourishment is equated to thinness and frailness. This deceptive program ignores the fact that malnourishment is also reflected by obesity, and actually encourages one to consume oneself into an overweight and obese state of being. It is ignored that by chugging toxic, depleted food substances into one's system one is over-feeding a malnourished brain with toxic and depleted fuel. The toxic and depleted fuel causes further disruptions and deterioration within the remaining organs of the body temple. There is no question that obesity is a toxic and deadly killer because of the deterioration and degeneration it causes within the body temple. There is absolutely no question that obesity is a major killer, although obesity kills in many ways that are not necessarily recognized within the context of obesity. There are many adverse effects that obesity produces, such as clogged arteries which are a major cause of heart attacks and heart disease, high blood pressure, and digestive and colon disorders. Here is a quote from the World Hunger Organization that reiterates the point that the I in I have been making for the last generation:

> To be sure, there are still far too many hungry and underfed people—1.1 billion at last count. But over one billion people are now overweight and obese...Usually poor, they are succumbing in alarming numbers to the misleadingly named "diseases of affluence"—obesity, heart disease, cancer, and diabetes—that arise from changing diets, lifestyles, and economies. Chronic non-communicable diseases now cause close to 60

> percent of all deaths worldwide. Surprisingly, nearly 80 percent of these deaths occur in developing countries. Overweightness and obesity, the most glaring outward sign of the changing face of malnutrition in developing countries, increase the chances of a person falling prey to the other non-communicable diseases. According to the World Health Organization (WHO), obesity-related ailments afflict more than 115 million people in the developing world, up from essentially none two generations ago. By 2030, these diseases as a group are projected to be the No. 1 killer of poor people around the world.[26]

We have spoken in general about these disorders that are causing massive destabilization of Man, He and She, and specifically threatening the existence of the suntanned Children of this land and elsewhere upon the Earth. Now, let us take a look at individual factors beginning with the brain, and the weak and feeble state of thought that becomes prey to mind control programs. One of the key frames of reference of the lost and astray mind of thought and reasoning is to condense every thought, practice and behavior into the idea that one is thinking and deciding for oneself.

Quickly an individual will say, "I am privileged to have many choices, and this is my choice." It is as though the individual is saying, "I choose obesity," "I choose manic-depression," "I choose psychological disorders," "I choose toxic relationships," "I choose heart disease," "I choose cancer," "I choose liver disorders," "I choose toxic sexual behaviors," "I choose mutation and degeneration of my whole life presence," "I choose arthritis," "I choose prostate disorder,

---

[26] *The Changing Face of Malnutrition*. Chris Burslem. IFPRI Forum, October 2004. International Food Policy Research Institute: Washington, D.C. Online Source: http://www.ifpri.org/pubs/newsletters/ifpriforum/if200410.htm

disease and cancer," "I choose fibroid tumors and hysterectomies," "I choose sterilization programs that eliminate my physical presence and existence in the near future," "I choose not to bring forward life as divinely created, but rather to maintain the principles of selfish greediness of the I-me-my syndrome, thus refusing to be responsible for the forwarding of new life."

There are many who would in fact agree that "Yes, this is a choice," and they would insist that they are making the choice of their own free will and that no one can stop them from doing what they want to do, because it is their life. It matters not that their life causes toxic effects of hurt, harm and disease for themselves or others. For after all, clearly, a crack addict chooses to be a crack addict; and an alcoholic chooses to be an alcoholic. These choices are thought to be of one's own free will, and one insists that no influences, no circumstances, no environmental factors, and no manipulations of mind control have caused this toxic reasoning to occur. If one can believe that, then one will surely know that one is lost and astray in the mind.

### *Soul-less Food and the Politics of Toxic Consumption*

Know for a fact that one is a sum total of every energy, of all energies, that one consumes—be they mental, physical or spiritual energies. Therefore, the master programs will automatically focus on the energy that one consumes in order to influence and control one's thoughts and behaviors. The physical food that one consumes is the primary source of energy that dictates one's thoughts and one's behaviors. For example, the energy amassed in toxic consumption originates from the hunting and herding vibrations of the ice-cold, deep-freeze mentality. The offspring of the prey has no relevance to the hunter except to be consumed or marketed for consumption. The offspring of the flock has no relevance to the herder except to be consumed or marketed for consumption. The cold-blooded attitude that is necessary to be a hunter or a herder becomes an integral part of the predator-like being. These attitudes and behaviors will in fact affect any other relationship that one encounters. Consumption patterns are the primary factor in the development of a culture of sex and violence. The hunter mentality is played out in every strategy that one experiences when one consumes of the "hunted" or the "kill." These basic principles of hunting and herding hold true, whether the hunt is for sex or for violence.

Within the death consumption culture, one is an amassment of toxic consumption mentally through thoughts and reasoning, physically through the food substances of one's consumption, and spiritually through the religious practices that are in fact disorders and contradictions to the whole life presence of Man, He and She. Among those who have become masters and grand masters of the plots and schemes of deception and mind control, it has become very clear that the most effective programs of mind control are those practices that are subliminal. It is considered masterful to create a pattern of control that dictates attitudes and behaviors without the individual even knowing that the program has been installed and is running at its optimum capacity.

For example, one can take the toxic and depleted food values of "soul food" and then those foods can be epitomized as rich cultural food and can be sold to individuals as a way of life. It will matter not that these devitalized and depleted food substances were created in a very harsh environment of suffering and damnation; it will matter not that these devitalized and depleted food substances were the leftover scraps from an era of slavery; it will matter not that these devitalized and depleted food substances are the key to such fatal diseases as heart attacks, obesity and strokes. The scraps of dead flesh from pigs, i.e. pig's feet, ham hocks, chitterlings, pig ears, hog jowl, tripe, and crackling became glorified as delicacies in the slave mentality.

EXPOSING THE ICE-COLD, DEEP-FREEZE MENTALITY AND WHOLE LIFE HEALING OF SEXUAL ENERGY WITHIN THE DIVINE PARALLEL

The practice of taking the discards from the plantation house and upholding those meager bits and parts as a wholesome meal has ingrained a pattern of consuming the waste matter of the death consumption culture and calling it "finger-licking" good. The only thing that would matter is, "Mmmm, this sure is some good, ol' soul food, baby." One of the primary goals and objectives of mind control programs and systems is to be able to create practices and behaviors that cause one to become addicted to the program and the products that the program produces.

Research indicates that food-related sensitivity and allergy exerts its most profound effect on the limbic portion of the brain. The limbic area of the brain is noted to house the control centers of emotions as well as memory and body functions, including body temperature, sexuality, blood pressure, sleep, hunger and thirst. Food allergies seem to affect most of these vital functions. Food allergies are caused by the immune system's response to foreign or toxic substances that have been ingested. The allergic reaction is the basic response to toxic consumption.

An example that can help to identify this pattern of allergic reaction that leads to addiction is the toxic consumption of liquor and alcoholic beverages. Most individuals who drink alcoholic beverages, such as beer or gin, recall that during their first experience the drink was distasteful and even awful. Many experienced symptoms, such as a burning throat, unpleasant taste sensations, choking, and dizziness. The physical reactions can be taken as evidence that the liquor or alcoholic beverage has some toxic effects on the body. Despite warning signals, the individual persists in the toxic behavior over and over again. Through repetition and reinforcement toxic habits are formed. After drinking alcoholic beverages becomes a habit, the symptoms are no longer as noticeable or are simply ignored. The body grows accustomed to the taste and effects of the alcohol. Symptoms are said to be "masked" or hidden. The process of the body masking the symptoms can be considered an adaptation by the body to tolerate the poison that is consumed. The adaptation to toxic consumption takes its toll in terms of chronic body stress.

During this period of repeated consumption, adaptation becomes so strong that one can become dependent on the effects of alcohol, or in other words, addicted. One can become so accustomed to the toxic vibrations and sensations of dead, depleted and devitalized consumption that one will actually hunger and thirst for toxins. Once addicted, the individual gets cravings to consume more alcohol on a regular basis in order to avoid the discomfort of withdrawal symptoms. When the individual attempts to quit, the body craves the toxic consumption that it has been programmed to receive. The cravings become the overriding signal that dictates the individual's consumption patterns. One becomes addicted in the truest sense of the word. This is the defining syndrome of the death consumption culture that keeps the mass majority of Man, He and She, locked in the self-destructive attitudes and behaviors of the ice-cold, deep-freeze mentality.

Studies are finally beginning to expose what has been ever-present within divine spirit consciousness: the consumption of dead, devitalized and depleted food substances is toxic and addictive. For example, research indicates that casein is the curd that forms when milk is left to sour; it is the most commonly used milk protein in the food industry. It is noted that casein peptides react with opiate receptors in the brain, thus mimicking the effects of opiate drugs like heroin and morphine. Findings show that certain foods appear to stimulate the release of opiate chemicals within the brain. These are chemical cousins of morphine and heroin, and cause addictive behaviors especially when an individual is stressed, tired, angry, or alone. The food substances that were identified as having an addictive effect are sugar, animal fat, chocolate, cheese, and meat. The I in I state clearly that any consumption that is outside of the divine consumption of raw and living fruits, vegetables, seeds and nuts is toxic consumption and will cause toxic consequences.

**Buying into the Degeneration and Mutation Profile**

It is no wonder that one can witness females of the suntanned complexion and hair texture roaming the streets in massive numbers, perming their hair and dyeing their natural hair blonde. The process of perming, bleaching and blondeing serves the mastermind program of projecting artificially induced beauty standards that symbolize the glorification of mutation and degeneration. These toxic behaviors, in fact, take it a step further as an indication that these individuals feel that those imitated beauty standards are superior to the natural and innate beauty standards originated by the Most Supreme Essence of Life and Supreme Love. It is an undeniable statement by these altered individuals that they feel that the Most Supreme Essence of Life and Supreme Love made a tragic mistake in creating them. It is a statement by these individuals that they feel privileged to be able to take actions to correct the disorders, mistakes and curses of the Most Supreme Essence of Life and Supreme Love. Many will claim that they are only making a fashion statement.

Every effort was made to strip the Afrikan slaves of their connection to their original ancestry and cultural heritage. Research indicates that in the early fifteenth century, hair served as a means of communication in many West Afrikan societies. Studies reveal that many of the captured slaves came from West Afrikan tribes, such as the Mende, Fanta, Wolof, Yoruba, and Mandingo. These tribes were noted to honor the significance of natural hair in communicating age, marital status, ethnic identity, religion, wealth, and rank in the community. As a result of the wretched horror of the Middle Passage in the bowels of a slave ship these captured Afrikans would be chained, beaten, defiled, raped, and many thrown to the sharks as bait. Their hair would be covered in feces, urine, blood, lice and other parasites, and their scalps would be covered in sores. The hair of the Afrikan slave was often shaved as a way to break his or her cultural identity as well as a selling device.

Ties to tribal identification, language, and traditions were systematically broken during the enslavement ordeal. The dark presence of the "Negro" slave was degraded and violated in every vicious manner that the ice-cold, deep-freeze mentality could enact. The natural and innate beauty of the "Negro's" coarse-textured hair was looked down upon as ugly and scornful. Slave owners often described the Afrikans' hair as being "woolly" as a way of comparing the Afrikans to animals and lowering them to the status of sub-human. This treatment of Man, He and She, as livestock and property is a fundamental practice of the hunting, scavenging and herding culture of death consumption.

The Afrikan slave sought to maintain the integrity of identity in the face of the pale reflection of the ice-cold, deep-freeze mentality. However, generations of repeated abuse, degradation, rape, fright and fear, physical violence, and overall conditions of enslavement caused an adaptation to occur. Degeneration and mutation occurred due to the toxic consumption of the ice-cold, deep-freeze mentality. The "Negro" slave began to seek ways and means to become more acceptable in the eyes of the slave master. Research indicates that "Negro" slaves devised hair straightening techniques that included the hair being slicked in waves with axle grease, wrapped with string to make it straight and relaxed using concoctions of potatoes, potash, lye and heavy fat. It is noted a form of punishment that included sticking the head of a "Negro" slave into a bucket of lye solution led to the discovery that lye had a straightening effect on hair.

Sources reveal that around 75% of "African American" women regularly perm, dye or otherwise alter their natural hair. It is reported that "African Americans" spend over $400 million a year to alter the texture of their hair by stripping the natural bonds. The mass marketing campaign promotes the idea of rejecting one's natural and innate physical characteristics in order to become a more defined representation of degeneration and mutation. "African American" newspapers, radio stations, magazines and other media regularly advertise products aimed at encouraging the "African American" female to purchase perms, relaxers, texturizers, straighteners, hair dyes and bleaches and skin bleaching creams. And the next generation of "African American" girls is primed to apply "baby perms."

It ought to be a crime for such ruthless programming to be inflicted upon a child that strips away every sense of self-esteem and self-worth based on a superficial value of racist ideology. It is, in fact, a crime against nature and the sentence is often twenty years to life as the perpetrator burns, fries or dyes her hair until it falls out or until she gets cancer and it gets burned out by chemotherapy. The use of such products have a deteriorating effect, causing hair breakage, hair thinning, lack of hair growth, scalp and skin irritation, scalp damage, and hair loss. Research indicates that the FDA lists hair straighteners and hair dyes among its top consumer complaint areas.

A primary selling strategy is to appeal to the "African American" female's desire to be "dark" and "lovely" by relaxing one's hair into straightness. The idea of relaxing implies that one's hair is not "relaxed" in its natural state, but rather it is hyper-tensed, stressed and uncomfortable. Such a promotional campaign can only be successful if the mass populations have already accepted the false beauty standards of a degenerated and mutated presence. And the question is invariably asked, "Do blondes have more fun?" The "African American" female has become so entrenched in the ice-cold, deep-freeze mentality that she will actually argue that perming her hair has nothing to do with "wanting to look white." The idea of making oneself over is smoothly injected into the thoughts and reasoning of the feminine presence by promoting makeovers that turn one "glamorous." The reasoning becomes that the Most Supreme Unseen did not do a credible job during the divine process of the creation. There never seems to be a thought that the true work needs to begin inside that individual's head, inside the memory bank and those lost and astray thoughts that spark ice-cold esteemlessness.

If questioned, the individual will quickly reply, "Different strokes for different folks. This is my thing, and I'm loving it." The individual does not have the ability to reason with the holistic living truth about Supreme Love. The individual becomes totally unaccountable to the Essence of Life of which they were created. The individual falls into a deep and entrenched stage of denial, rejection and esteemlessness. The rationale and justification will be quickly shot back that "this is my choice within a free society and I have the right to do whatever I want to do."

These toxic disorders, false beauty standards, and esteem deficit disorders are fed to the children, the offspring and others who surround that individual's life presence. In such instances, that individual will quickly respond, "I had the chance to do what I wanted to do and the child has the right to do what they want to do." The individual will totally ignore the fact the child has no choice except to learn by example, for a child does not learn simply by words. Therefore, the example that is put forward to the child will breed the order of toxic programming, toxic confusion and chaos to be passed on, manifesting the same game with another name with even more misery, aches and pains.

So there are massive programs that are perpetuated on a daily basis to sell a commodity, to sell an item by any means necessary. It does not matter what the side effect is. The only thing that matters is that one continues to believe that one is making one's own choices and decisions. It is a competitive market, and in that competitive market everyone has the opportunity to create programs and schemes that will sell commodities, because all is fair in love and war. Either it is a price war, a competitor's war, or a war on poverty. Whoever can create the best jingle, whoever can create the most effective dynamics, whoever can manifest the greatest scheme of deception is the individual who will be most successful in the sales and promotion of his or her product. That is all that matters, because it is all about the bottom line. And it works.

The statistics speak for themselves. According to Target Market News, "African Americans" spent $656 billion in 2003, including $2.2 billion on alcoholic beverages, $2.5 billion on entertainment and leisure activities, and $53.9 billion on food.[27] A 1996 survey indicated that "African Americans" spent an estimated $11.3 billion on hamburgers; it is a certainty that the amount has increased based on the eating patterns of the "African American" population and the increasing number of adults and children who are overweight and obese. The next generation becomes the target as marketing campaigns aim at children in order to program them into becoming loyal consumers. Children within the death consumption culture become easy prey for the aggressive marketer to target. The majority of television commercials during prime time and children's programming encourage the consumption of sugary, salty and greasy food substances.

It is not about the mental, physical and spiritual health and well-being of the population. It is not about the holistic living way of life of Man, He and She. It is not about securing divine life standards. The statistics speak for themselves.

It is, however, about selling a product by any means necessary. Deception is one of the greatest strategies in selling a product within the death consumption culture. And so it is an automatic outcome that the greatest and most beneficial method of manipulation would be through mind control. This is why individuals pay millions of dollars for a few minute

---

[27] *The Buying Power of Black America, 2003.* Target Market News, The Black Consumer Market Authority. Online Source: http://www.targetmarketnews.com/buyingpowerstats.htm.

timeslot during special television programs that are being viewed by huge audiences. Those few minutes of exposure play a vital role in the installment of mind control. As a result, the individual walks away from a commercial, humming a jingle that leads him or her straight to the shelf of a market to make a purchase. Thus, the continuous consumption of toxic, depleted and devitalized food substances is promoted as a way of life.

There is no question that agencies, such as the Food and Drug Administration, Department of Human Services and others most certainly work in their own best interests. It is also no question that there are individuals who run these organizations and these individuals also work in their own best interests. For example, it is noted that the 28th Secretary of the U.S. Department of Agriculture (USDA) sworn in on January 21, 2005 grew up doing chores on his family's dairy farm and maintains fond memories about a way of life that he values. It is clear that his best interests are going to be a direct reflection of the hunting and herding mentality. Keep in mind that the USDA is the government agency that has had historic responsibility for guiding consumer food choices for the last 100 years in the United States. There are no and's, if's or but's about the fact that there are lobbying entities that support these agencies and these lobbyists work in their own best interests. In fact, they are called interest groups. It has become very clear that it is in the best interest of the death consumption culture to maintain massive deception by any means necessary. Those who are elected within the death consumption culture are elected to serve their constituencies who voted for them.

When one considers lobbying entities like the beef and poultry industries, the canning industries, the frozen food industries, and the leather goods industry and on and on, there is no question that these industries survive off of the ways and means of the death consumption culture. These industries are very strong lobbying groups with heads who sit in the elite bracket of the social economic strata. These industries will, in fact, continue regardless of the toxic side effects, because it is all about the bottom line. Unfortunately there are glaring contradictions within a culture that perpetuates toxic consumption in one breath and then attempts to address the health and well-being of its populations in the next. A case in point:

> …The National School Lunch Program, which gives schools more than $6 billion each year to offer low-cost meals to students, has conflicting missions. Enacted in 1946, the program is supposed to provide healthy meals to children, regardless of income. At the same time, however, it's designed to subsidize agribusiness, shoring up demand for beef and milk even as the public's taste for these foods declines. Under the program, the federal government buys up more than $800 million worth of farm products each year and turns them over to schools to serve their students. The U.S. Department of Agriculture, which administers the system, calls this a win-win situation: Schools get free ingredients while farmers are guaranteed a steady income. The trouble is most of the commodities provided to schools are meat and dairy products, often laden with saturated fat. In 2001, the USDA spent a total of $350 million on surplus beef and cheese for schools—more than double the $161 million spent on all fruits and vegetables, most of which were canned or frozen. On top of its regular purchases, the USDA makes special purchases in direct response to industry lobbying. In November 2001, for example, the beef industry wrote to Agriculture Secretary Ann Veneman, complaining that a decline in travel after September 11, along with a lowered demand for

> beef in Japan, was suppressing sales of their product. The department responded two months later with a $30 million "bonus buy" of frozen beef roasts and ground beef for schools.[28]

### *Diet-Related Diseases*

There is undoubtedly a plague of toxic and destabilizing sickness and disease afflicting the global population in general and the historic target population specifically. One may begin to wonder if the presence of massive sickness and disease is fitting a pattern of adverse effects that has plagued the historic target population. One may begin to wonder if the social economic conditions are such that will indeed breed a depleted physical standard of health as well as a depleted mental standard of health within the historic target population. The way of life that has been amassed within the death consumption culture serves as a toxic breeding ground for many diseases and disorders. Research indicates statistics that approximately 1.5 to 2 million Americans die every year of heart attacks, cancer, strokes, etc. According to the American Heart Association (AHA) statistics, there are 53 million Americans with cardiovascular diseases, which include arteriolosclerosis, high blood pressure, and strokes.

Findings show that the U.S. spends $1.4 trillion dollars per year on health. It is clear that a large portion of this trillion dollar spending goes towards paying the pharmaceutical companies in a standard pattern of the death consumption culture. The standard treatment methods deal with relieving symptoms rather than actually addressing and correcting the cause of the problem. The consumption of dead, devitalized and depleted food within the death consumption culture is the problem that must be addressed.

---

[28] *USA: Unhappy Meals.* Barry Yeoman. January 6, 2003. Mother Jones. Online Source: http://www.corpwatch.org/article.php?id=5609.

The living conditions of many urban dwellers, regardless of social economic status, reflect the harsh, cold and insensitive environment of the ice-cold, deep-freeze mentality. The living conditions within poverty-stricken areas provide a particularly depleted and toxic environment within the death consumption culture, although the dominant social order prides itself on being elite and sophisticated. The historic target population, by design, remains within the social economic constraints of a social order that was born and bred on a deliberate and intentional division between the have's and the have not's.

The primary factor of mind control is that a habit is created, a repeated pattern that establishes ways of performing. The focus is on the female, the hands that rock the crib. As the norms and values begin to become acceptable and familiar, even if at a later time the adverse effects are exposed, it will not matter, because one will have formed a habit, an addiction and a conditioned response that is very difficult to break. The program will be in place, the habits will be in place, and the individuals will continue to perpetuate the same old patterns.

The social order will continue to reinforce the toxic habits. For example, the fast food restaurants may begin to offer salads, but the memories, images, smells and habits of toxic consumption that have been well-programmed will eventually pull one back into a familiar eating pattern that has been reinforced through massive advertising campaigns for years and years, since one's childhood. As long as one can be kept as a paying customer, one will be likely to revert at the counter one day and order a little depleted snack to go with that salad. A little snack that continues to grow bigger and bigger as the salad grows smaller and smaller until one begins to echo new lyrics to the old familiar tune of, "Hold the lettuce, hold the tomatoes…"

Reports indicate that although "African American" males are among the most seriously affected by diet-related chronic diseases, they have the lowest consumption of fruits and vegetables overall, eating an average of only 3.1 servings a day of the nine recommended by federal nutrition policy. Even with the 3.1 servings of fruit and vegetables that are consumed, it is very doubtful that the whole life substance of the fruits and vegetables is even present. The dead and devitalized substances of cooked and processed fruits, vegetables, seeds and nuts are somehow mistaken for whole life nutrition. It is somehow reasoned that substances, such as commercially processed tomato ketchup, apple turnovers, and steamed vegetables qualify as the natural composition of the plant-based nutrition. It is such a shame to see massive populations of Man, He and She, living such toxic deceptions while being overrun with disabling and life threatening sickness and disease.

The financial investments of the death consumption culture are a guarantee that any changes that are made to address the alarming rates of obesity and diet-related diseases will be cosmetic changes at best. Research indicates that the food industry generates annual revenues of $900 billion dollars, has an advertising budget of around $30 million dollars and employs over 12 million people as the United State's largest private sector employer. Please don't forget that power concedes nothing without a struggle, especially the power to control your mind of thoughts and reasoning. The cosmetic changes of an industry that spends millions of dollars on advertising and generates billions of dollars in consumer spending means that business as usual within the death consumption culture will remain heavily invested in toxic consumption. In fact, there is great resistance within the death consumption culture to even make minor changes that might affect the bottom line.

Studies have shown that the standard American diet is high in animal by-products, cooked and otherwise processed foods, and thus high in total fat, animal fats, saturated fats, hydrogenated fats, trans fatty acids and cholesterol, low in fiber, and low in plant-based foods. Dietary cholesterol is noted to be found only in meats, poultry, eggs, seafood and dairy products which causes an increase in blood cholesterol and contributes to plaque build-up in the arteries or coronary artery disease. And, these animal by-products are noted to be the primary source of saturated fat. The standard American diet is also high in processed sugars and refined carbohydrates. Research indicates that the main dietary factors associated with cancer risk are high fat or alcohol intake, high salt diets and low fiber intakes. Cancers that are noted to have been linked to diet include those of the mouth and throat, stomach, large bowel, pancreas, liver, gall bladder, lung, breast, uterus, ovaries and prostate.

The toxic patterns of consumption are so familiar and routine within the death consumption culture that they are not even considered mind control programs. Toxic consumption is viewed as simply being the way of life that one remembers from childhood, from family tradition, from school days and from the very beginning of man's existence as the story goes. The death consumption culture will never create a program that identifies the mainstay commodities as unhealthy or toxic. The compromise within the death consumption culture has always been that one can maintain toxic consumption by balancing it with a little wholesome intake. Therefore, one's toxic habits can remain undisturbed in practice while one righteously preaches moderation in principle. Nevertheless, the consequences of disorder from the "reduced" toxic consumption will still remain in effect, and the toxic programs will still produce adverse effects.

A case in point is the Surgeon General report that smoking is hazardous to one's health. Cigarette smokers are still puffing. Those who stopped smoking often found that they simply acquired another addiction of toxic consumption to replace the smoking habit. The tobacco industry still managed to maintain massive profits. Research indicates that the United States Justice Department charges that under the Racketeer

Influenced and Corrupt Organizations Act (RICO), cigarette companies have deceived the public for decades in an effort to sell their products. In 2004, a Washington Post article reported that the U.S. government accused the nation's largest tobacco companies of conspiring over the past 50 years to deceive the public about the proven dangers of smoking to protect billions of dollars in profits the industry earned from cigarette sales. According to the article, the Justice Department contends that the six largest tobacco companies conspired to commit fraud under a racketeering law that was originally designed to punish criminal gang leaders.[29]

It is noted that nearly 500,000 Americans die each year from smoking-related illnesses. The individual becomes so addicted to the habit, whether it be alcohol, tobacco, other drugs, depleted food substances, cocaine or whatever, that the idea of stopping actually causes distress. In such circumstances, the adverse effects of toxic consumption are denied or simply endured as the price for satisfying one's addictions and cravings. Those of the ice-cold, deep-freeze mentality find ways and means to rationalize, justify, and accommodate their addictions to toxic consumption. Within a culture of toxic consumption, one can usually find a support group, peer group or interest group to join in the maintenance of one's toxic addictions.

There are social addictions that control one's attitudes and behaviors. For example, football games are a primary part of a way of life within the death consumption culture. Football epitomizes the whole idea of rivalry, competition, inflicting pain and hostile aggression against an adversary. There is little chance that the coaches and the team owners are going to stop encouraging the football players to eat the flesh of slaughtered animals. The reason for their consumption of these toxic and

---

[29] *U.S. Trial Against Tobacco Industry Opens.* Carol D. Leonnig. Washington Post, September 22, 2004, page A03. Online Source: http://www.washingtonpost.com/ac2/wp-dyn/A38583-2004Sep21?language=printer

depleted food substances is to maintain the vibrations and sensations of the "killer instinct" on the field. In the meantime, the spectators are encouraged to drink alcoholic beverages and consume the same devitalized and depleted food substances that make the athletes famous. In fact, consuming toxic, dead and devitalized food substances becomes a social event that is expressed at tailgate parties, sports bars and in the comforts of home. The mental, physical and spiritual health of the athlete is not a long-term concern. The major concern is that the players score and the team wins. The mental, physical and spiritual health of the paying audience is not a major concern. The major concern is that tickets are sold and that televised games have a large viewing audience.

### *Pharmaceutical Solutions*

The solution for toxic consumption within the culture of the ice-cold, deep-freeze mentality is an increase in the availability of pharmaceutical treatments. One can then take a pill to alleviate the symptoms of indigestion; one can take a pill to numb the signals of pain; one can take a pill to suppress one's appetite so that one can binge later; one can take a pill to heighten one's aggressive sexual behaviors; one can take a pill for whatever ails one. The term "diet-related disease" actually sidesteps the acknowledgement that one's overall consumption patterns determine one's overall state of health and well-being. Consumption refers to one's mental, physical and spiritual energy intake. There is really only one solution that addresses the adverse effects of toxic consumption. The solution is to cease and desist from toxic consumption. The program is deeply embedded within the death consumption culture that will not even allow one to consider a life beyond the death consumption culture.

The reasoning of the ice-cold, deep-freeze mentality is that one should not be willing to give up all of one's toxic addictions—maybe a few, but certainly not all. And those few will be replaced as the same game with another name under the guise of being "lite," "sugar-free," "low-fat," or "low-carbs." The deep thing about this analysis is that it runs along the same course as the previous example regarding salads in the fast food chains. The program is run so that eventually one's habitual taste sensations will carry one right back to the mainstay product. You see, the masterful mind control programs are well in place to cause the individual to shutdown all reasoning and "go for the gusto." The concepts of balance and moderation are usually presented as an argument in defense of toxic consumption. Some individuals continue to feel that the choice is theirs to make, regardless of the massive amount of programming that has actually determined their values, tastes, cravings and addictions.

One can actually feel that one should balance one's consumption with an equal proportion of dead and devitalized food substances on par with raw and living fruits, vegetables, seeds and nuts. The majority feels that one should balance one's consumption with a variety of dead and devitalized food substances and include a salad as an appetizer and fruit as a dessert. Still, there are many others who feel that a balanced diet is one where one holds the lettuce and holds the tomatoes when consuming the food substances that serve as a constant reminder of "how the west was won," i.e. rape, murder, steal and take, kill to serve the gentleman's will.

The ability to mastermind programs, plots and schemes is a money-making venture that causes the massive populations of Man, He and She, to consume of toxic, depleted and devitalized products. Those who produce and manufacture those products will continue to be predators pursuing the lost and astray mind. With all the commercial resources and advertising dollars geared towards promoting symptom-treating drugs, it is no wonder that Man, He and She are more inclined to pop a pill than work at making divine lifestyle changes.

The drug industry is a multi-billion dollar industry that has built itself from scratch by producing wonder drugs that have adverse effects. The individual conditioned to "take two pills and call in the morning" has more concern with momentary relief than any possible long-term consequences. What began as corner drugstores has become one of the most profound economic mechanisms of the western world. Additionally, by having medical doctors tied into the prescription concept as a major incentive for capital gain, it is no wonder that self-healing is pushed far in the background. A report by the American Medical Student Association states that for most of the past decade, the pharmaceutical industry has been the most profitable industry in the United States. The report indicates that in 2002 the combined profits for the ten drug companies in the Fortune 500 grouping ($35.9 billion) were more than the profits for all the other 490 businesses put together ($33.7 billion). Persuading patients to take prescription drugs is a very lucrative business.

Worst of all, in the death consumption culture, the major social economic programs are geared around treating symptoms rather than resolving problems. The I in I have heard many individuals say that it requires too much discipline and too much time to deal with self-healing techniques. In fact, making lifestyle change does not seem to be a priority except in the most critical conditions and states. Even then, lifestyle change becomes the very last alternative as a last ditch effort to avoid the graveyard.

In most instances when one is suffering from sickness and disease, the norm is to seek out a quick-fix solution. Most individuals tend to look for a solution that will require the least amount of change in his or her addictions or habits. As a result, the mass majority of individuals who are suffering from sickness and disease tend to become over-the-counter drug addicts instead of attempting to work with nature. As most individuals have come to realize, either through personal experience or from general observation, drugs are the priority treatment for disease and disorder within the death consumption culture. Within the mainstream of a culture that prides itself on the consumption of dead and devitalized food substances, there is a definite connection between devitalized consumption patterns and treatment modalities.

Within this general medical framework, drug therapy is used to treat a wide range of mental and physical disorders. Unfortunately a pattern of thinking has emerged within the death consumption culture where a pill, tablet, or capsule is considered a quick-fix for health problems that actually stem from lifestyle disorders and toxic consumption. Nevertheless, the ability to take a pill to mask or relieve troublesome symptoms keeps many individuals passively repeating the same unwholesome patterns of consumption with only a few minor changes. Within the death consumption culture, the biological, ecological, and social systems are malfunctioning in grave disorder, and there is only one solution that is the divine solution.

Let us take a look at some general health statistics regarding the historic target group, i.e. "African Americans" and see how well the toxic mental programming has worked to promote self-destructive consumption patterns.

### *Health Disparities in the Death Consumption Culture*

"The success or failure of any government in the final analysis must be measured by the well-being of its citizens. Nothing can be more important to a state than its public health; the state's paramount concern should be the health of its people," Franklin Delano Roosevelt is quoted as saying. It is noted that President Roosevelt's appointment of a "black cabinet" of prominent black leaders to advise him and his inclusion of such prominent black activists as Mary McLeod Bethune gave weight to the appearance that the Roosevelt administration was responsive to "black" peoples' needs. Findings show that the actual practices of these special acts and programs served to maintain the racial status quo rather than address the real ills of discrimination. President Roosevelt is noted to have claimed that if he supported legislation which threatened the South's racist order, then he would lose the votes of Southerners in Congress, votes that he needed.

Time and time again throughout the history of the death consumption culture the appearance of change or a "new deal" serves to re-package the same game with another name. Treating the surface symptoms of disorder can soothe and pacify temporarily, but a disorder that is left uncorrected will fester under the superficial treatment and will intensify to erupt at a later time in a full blown, acute crisis. The health of any system, then, can only be assured and secured through corrective actions by the affected individuals that establish wholesome and whole life consumption patterns. These whole life consumption patterns must affect every realm of one's mental, physical and spiritual existence.

Let us examine some health statistics that present a telling profile of toxic consumption patterns as an instrument of biological warfare.[30] We remind the reader that although biological warfare can be implemented as a government's military tactics; biological warfare can also be self-inflicted through the acts of toxic consumption. According to the 2002 U.S. Census statistics, those who are identified as "black" or "African American" constitute approximately 13.3 percent of the American population—approximately 38 million individuals. It is noted that the U.S. Department of Health and Human Services created the Office of Minority Health in 1985 as a result of the *Report of the Secretary's Task Force on Black and Minority Health,* which revealed large and persistent gaps in health status among Americans of different racial and ethnic

---

[30] Statistical information compiled from the Office of Minority Health, Center for Disease Control, The National Center for Health Statistics, Congressional Black Caucus Foundation and the American Cancer Society.

groups. The Center for Disease Control and Prevention created their own Office of Minority Health in 1988 in response to the same report. Congress passed the "Disadvantaged Minority Health Act of 1990" in order to improve the health status of underserved populations, including racial and ethnic minorities.

Findings reveal that current information about the biological and genetic characteristics of minority populations does not explain the health disparities experienced by these groups compared with the "white" population in the United States. These disparities are noted to be the result of the complex interaction among genetic variations, environmental factors, consumption patterns and specific social behaviors. It is noted that infant mortality is used to compare the health and well-being of populations across and within countries. Even though it is reported that the nation's infant mortality rate is down, the infant death rate among "African Americans" is still more than double that of "whites." Infant mortality among "African Americans" in 2000 was noted to have occurred at a rate of 14.1 deaths per 1,000 live births which is more than twice the national average of 6.9 deaths per 1,000 live births. Studies show that this widening disparity between "black" and "white" infants is a trend that has persisted over the last two decades.

Research indicates that heart disease death rates are more than 40 percent higher for "African Americans" than for "whites." The death rate for all cancers is 30 percent higher for "African Americans" than for "whites." For the "African American" males, the prostate cancer rate of incidence is more than double that for "whites." The prevalence of diabetes among "African Americans" is about 70% higher than among "white" Americans. The rate of homicide for "African Americans" is six times higher than that for "whites." "African American" males have a life expectancy 7.1 years shorter than other racial groups. 40% of "African American" males die prematurely from cardiovascular disease as compared to 21% of "white" males. "African American" males experience disproportionately higher death rates in all the leading causes of death.[31]

***Top Two Killers: Cardiovascular Disease and Cancer***

Cardiovascular disease, primarily heart disease and stroke, cause more deaths in Americans of both genders and all racial and ethnic groups than any other disease. It is also one of the leading causes of disability in the United States. Cardiovascular disease is reported to cost an estimated $300 billion annually as measured in health care expenses, medications, and lost productivity due to disability and death. Overall, it is noted that minority and low-income populations have a disproportionate burden of death and disability from cardiovascular disease. "African Americans" are reported to have the highest rate of high blood pressure of all groups and tend to develop it younger than other groups. It has been noted that education and social status do not serve as a security blanket against the adverse effects of heart disease, hypertension and strokes. It is noted that in general these diseases cross every spectrum of the social order.

Research indicates that cardiovascular disease ranks as the number one killer of "African Americans," claiming the lives of more than 37% of the more than 285,000 "African Americans" who die each year. It is noted that about four in every ten "African Americans" have cardiovascular disease while one in three "African Americans" has high blood pressure or hypertension. "African Americans" between the ages of 45 and 55 have four to five times the stroke death rates of "whites," according to the National Institute of Neurological Disorders and Stroke. Heart disease and cancer combined account for nearly half (48.6%) of all deaths among "African Americans" nationally.

---

[31] Statistical information compiled from the Office of Minority Health, Center for Disease Control, The National Center for Health Statistics, Congressional Black Caucus Foundation and the American Cancer Society.

Cancer is reported as the second leading cause of death in the United States, causing more than 500,000 deaths each year. The chances of having cancer in a lifetime are said to be 45 percent for men and 41 percent for women. The American Cancer Society's Annual Cancer Report states that "almost half of all people who get cancer will die." Overall, "black" men are noted as having a 40 percent higher death rate from all cancers compared to "white" men, and they are twice as likely to die of prostate cancer as white men. Nationally, statistics indicate that "African American" women die at a 20 percent higher rate than white women from cancer. Although deaths caused by breast cancer have decreased among "white" women, findings show that "African American" women continue to have higher rates of mortality from breast and cervical cancer.

Findings show that males in "African American" populations also have more cancers of the lung, prostate, colon, and rectum than do "white" men. The American Cancer Society reports that lung cancer rates are 47% higher among "African American" men than "white" men and the death rate is 36% higher in "African American" men than "white" men. Overall, it is noted that "African Americans" have more malignant tumors and are less likely to survive cancer than the general population. Research indicates that the death rate for all cancers combined is still about 30% higher for "blacks" than for "whites." Public health experts have found that a third of U.S. cancer deaths are due to poor diet, excess weight, and a lack of physical activity.

### *Diabetes and Obesity*

Findings show that more than 17 million Americans have diabetes, and over 200,000 people die each year of related complications. Diabetes is a group of diseases described by high levels of blood glucose resulting from defects in insulin secretion, insulin action, or both. Approximately 13 percent of all "African Americans" are reported to have diabetes. It is estimated that about 730,000 “African Americans” have diabetes but do not know they have the disease. On average, “African Americans” are noted to be twice as likely to have diabetes as “white” Americans of similar age. Death rates for people with diabetes are noted to be 27 percent higher for “African Americans” compared with whites.

Research indicates that the “African American” population has the highest prevalence of overweight females at 78 percent and obese females at 50.8 percent while 44 percent of “African American” males are considered overweight and 24 percent are obese[32]. A new study released by the University of Chicago Children's Hospital finds that television shows geared toward “African American” audiences have more overweight characters and 60 percent more food commercials than shows that attract a general audience. Findings indicate that obesity is a condition that poses an important risk factor for four of the six leading causes of death in this country—heart disease, certain cancers, stroke and diabetes.

Research indicates that “African Americans” tend to be more allergic than other groups. Findings show that researchers think that one common factor may be the level of a protein in the blood that is used by the body to help identify foreign invaders that the immune process is designed to attack. What this means is that the immune system of many of the suntanned population is on constant alert to ward off the presence of foreign and toxic substances that have been consumed. The practices of depleted, devitalized, and toxic consumption cause reactions of irritation, degeneration and mutation.

It is reported that more than 24 percent of all asthma deaths are among “African Americans.” Research indicates that the asthma attack prevalence rate among “African Americans” was

---

[32] Statistical information compiled from the Office of Minority Health, Center for Disease Control, The National Center for Health Statistics, Congressional Black Caucus Foundation and the American Cancer Society.

more than 31 percent higher than that for "whites." Asthma deaths among children increased 188 percent between 1980 and 1993, according to the Center for Disease Control, and in 1993, "African Americans" in this age group were 4 to 6 times more likely to die from asthma than "whites."

### *Functional Insanity and Dysfunctional Insanity*

One in two Americans is diagnosed with a mental disorder each year, including 44 million adults and 13.7 million children. Since 1980, reports indicate that suicide has doubled among young "black" males in America. Moreover, it is noted that from 1980 to 1995, the suicide rate among "African Americans" ages 10 to 14 increased 233%, compared to 120% among "whites" of that same age group. Studies show that "African Americans" are over-represented in high-need populations that are particularly at risk for mental illnesses:

- People who are homeless. While representing only 12% of the U.S. population, African Americans make up about 40% of the homeless population.
- People who are incarcerated. Nearly half of all prisoners in State and Federal jurisdictions and almost 40% of juveniles in legal custody are African Americans.
- Children in foster care and the child welfare system. African American children and youth constitute about 45% of children in public foster care and more than half of all children waiting to be adopted.
- People exposed to violence. African Americans of all ages are more likely to be victims of serious violent crime than are "whites." One study reported that over 25% of African American youth exposed to violence met the

> criteria for having post-traumatic stress disorder.[33]

It is a tremendous history that makes up the vibrations, the energies, the thoughts and the reasoning that have emerged out of the ice-cold, deep-freeze mentality. It is amazing for there to be social orders that profess scientific genius and the ability to amass extreme wealth in a social economic environment dominated by the greed of specific breeds and their disciples and followers. Even more so, it is amazing that within the land mass governed by the specific breed there would be massive populations that were enslaved and traumatized by a cold-blooded mentality.

For those suntanned Children who survived the vicious raids of madness and insanity where rape would be the norm, lost and astray minds would be born within the same cold-blooded mentality as the rapist. The murderous father spirit of the lost and astray Children who lost their tan emerged from the ice-cold, deep-freeze. Those who were born and bred of this ice-cold, deep-freeze mentality would continue to feed off of this cold-blooded mentality and would continue to rationalize and justify the plight of insanity.

In spite of the homicidal and suicidal plights of those who consume of the death consumption culture that feeds the ice-cold, deep-freeze mentality, there would continue to be a steadfast worship of the energy that is opposite of Supreme Love. The lost and astray Children who lost their tan are so intoxicated by the cruel and vicious maddening insanity that they have inflicted upon others, it would seem that they are obsessed with the idea that others will inflict the same insanity back upon them. As a result, there are major plots and schemes

---

[33] *Mental Health: Culture, Race, Ethnicity – Supplement.* 1999. U.S. Department of Health & Human Services. Office of the Surgeon General. Online Source: http://www.mentalhealth.org/cre/default.asp.

being orchestrated to institute various plans of genocide and annihilation of those of the suntanned skin.

Historic reality is emerging as the entire planet comes to understand that the Children of the Sun with the golden tan originated from the divine presence of Man, He and She. The Afrikoid man is, in fact, the original Man, He and She. In fact, the dominant Afrikoid gene pool is the primary reason why the ice-cold, deep-freeze mentality pushes eugenics and other doctrines of "white" racist ideology. As we have noted within this document, the primary fear is that the mutated breed can only be maintained by breeding with a mutated kind. The gene pool of "whiteness," i.e. mutation from the original context is so weak that any Afrikoid genetic mix will dominate. Unfortunately, the sick and insane minds of so many who orchestrate the triggers of mass destruction would call these dominant traits of nature pollution. Therefore, insane and hideous reasoning would develop within genocidal plans to wipe out the dominant presence of the original mothers and fathers of Man, He and She.

The ice-cold mentality would create such massive deceptions of insane fantasies and delusionary realities that it would be too steeped, too deep into the plague of insanity to work its way out of the mind maze. Every piece of historic reality would point to the fact that the origin of Man, He and She, is the Afrikoid, the sacred spirit presence of the Divine Children of the Sun with the golden tan. This is undoubtedly the holistic living presentation of Man, He and She. Those children who lost their tan are the result of an ice-cold and cruel, vicious entrapment within the ice-cold, deep-freeze of the last Ice Age. There is a total and absolute refusal to acknowledge that the lost and astray Children who lost their tan mutated and degenerated, mentally, physically and spiritually. The mental mutation definitely gave birth to the ice-cold, deep-freeze mentality. The cold, harsh, cruel, insensitive mentality of the ice-cold, deep-freeze is, in fact, the massive insanity of mutation and degeneration that is causing chaotic disorder upon the planet today. The primary factor of the massive disorder stems from the inability to identify and acknowledge the problem so as to be able to find a divine solution. This insanity spreads like a plague and has infested all of those of skin and kin who continue to be disciples and followers of the death consumption culture.

The ice-cold, deep-freeze mentality creates the vibrations of masterminding weapons of war and destruction, of breeding ways and means of being the top dog and having the ability to dominate over others. In the position of dominance within the ice-cold, deep-freeze mentality, one declares oneself superior regardless of the human errors that have been bred inside of one's mental, physical and spiritual gene pool. Yes, the ice-cold, deep-freeze mentality is a weapon-breeding social order that functions by dealing with the surface and superficial presentation of what a thing looks like. Within this kind of mentality, one does not attempt to heal as one would do inside of the sacred garden culture. Within the sacred garden culture, the focus is on consuming the herbs and the foods of the gardens of the trees of life as a way to maintain holistic mental, physical and spiritual healing. The sacred garden culture would have no existence within the death consumption culture. Divine spirit consciousness would have no existence within the ice-cold, deep-freeze mentality. Both the sacred garden culture and divine spirit consciousness can only exist within a divine parallel. The death consumption culture that feeds the ice-cold, deep-freeze mentality exists within the energy that is opposite of Supreme Love.

This mutated and degenerated mentality breeds a social order that deals with treating the symptom of a problem. Massive wealth is created by the constant treatment of symptoms where individuals spend their entire life sick and afflicted with mental, physical and spiritual disease and disorder. Every generation born off of this mentality continues to breed the same insanity over and over again while expecting different results. To imagine that one is able to experience self-healing is just not the reality within the ice-cold, deep-freeze mentality. In fact, one treats to treat, and the result is that those who perpetuate the treats to treat continue to amass major profits.

When one really thinks about it, what is the value of the profit if one is not able to have a peaceful coexistence upon the planet? What is the value of the financial gains if one is in constant terror, fright and fear, living in paranoia, because this is exactly what one has inflicted upon others? It becomes the reality that this type and kind of social order will breed mental illness. In fact, mental illness is the root and foundation of the social order within the death consumption culture. In the midst of this toxic environment, one would not even recognize the level and degree of mental illness that actually exists. It would not be reasoned that the dead and devitalized food substances of the death consumption culture breed mutation and degeneration within the DNA of Man, He and She. It is a sign of mental illness for Man, He and She, to consume of the death consumption culture.

Consumption of dead, devitalized and depleted energy in fact breeds continuous disorder; it breeds manic insanity; it breeds physical disease. Again, we repeat, these mental and physical disorders are merely the symptoms of gene mutation and degeneration. However, so many of Man, He and She are well-indoctrinated and well-invested in the hideous culture of death consumption. The death consumption culture will continue to move in the fast lane.

Anyone who refuses to go along with the programs of the ice-cold, deep-freeze mentality will be seen as out of synch and will, in fact, be scorned, ridiculed and declared insane. Additionally, one can become so intoxicated with the fantasies and illusions of the death consumption culture that one will become delusional and non-functional. What we are talking about here is that there are two points of emergence: the first is the origin of Man, He and She, the holistic living presence of

Man, He and She within the sacred garden culture, perpetuating divine spirit consciousness. This first presence is the reflection of the optimum thought and reasoning in divine order. Then, there is the ice-cold, deep-freeze mentality that is bred of an energy that is opposite of Supreme Love and that is fed by the death consumption culture. It is clear that this vicious mentality is born and bred in a mind maze and feeds the insanity of death consumption. However, within this mentality the condition of insanity is simply accepted as reality. Such vibrations as drinking alcohol, smoking cigarettes, taking drugs, consuming coffee, candy, soft drinks and other toxic treats are known to have adverse effects. To knowingly consume of these toxic substances over and over again while expecting anything other than disease and disorder is to practice insanity. Consuming of dead, devitalized and depleted substances such as barbequed baked, or fried animal flesh or boiled, baked or roasted fruits, vegetables, seeds and nuts over and over again while expecting anything other than disease and disorder is to practice insanity.

The death consumption culture has no way or means to address this vicious and cold-blooded mental, physical and spiritual disease and disorder. The lost and astray mind that consumes of the death consumption culture suffers absolute disconnection from divine spirit consciousness. Within this, the mental disease and disorder must be addressed. Let us take a few moments and see how the governing order of the most dominant nation on the planet is gearing itself to address mental disorder. The following information is to inform and educate regarding your presence:

> NAMI (National Alliance for the Mentally Ill) calls on federal, state and local leaders to immediately take affirmative steps to implement mental health screening for children and adolescents. This position is consistent with the

recommendations included in President Bush's New Freedom Commission report on mental health that calls for mental health screening in child-serving settings.[34]

The final omnibus spending bill includes $20 million in new funding for the Bush Administration's "Mental Health Transformation" proposal to support state planning efforts to implement the 2003 New Freedom Initiative Mental Health Commission Report. This is less than half the $44 million that President Bush had requested (and that had been supported by the Senate).

A separate effort to prevent funds under this initiative (also known as State Incentive Grants) from being used to support mental health screening of children under age 18 was rejected…[35]

An attempt by Rep. Ron Paul, R-Texas, to add language to the omnibus spending bill in Congress to require parental consent for any mental-health screening done to children with federal money has failed.

The language was proposed to blunt the effect of a program proposed by the New Freedom Commission on Mental Health, which President Bush established in 2002. The New Freedom Initiative recommends screening not only for

---

[34] *Mental Health Screening Will Save Lives.* NAMI (National Alliance for the Mentally Ill). January 19, 2005

[35] *NASP Legislative Update.* NASP (National Association of School Psychologists). December 10, 2004. Online Source: http://www.nasponline.org/advocacy/legisup121004.html

children but eventually for every American.[36]

Recently, the Association of American Physicians & Surgeons (AAPS) criticized a move by the U.S. Senate to join with the House in funding the New Freedom Initiative because it involved the mandatory psychological testing of every child in America without the consent of parents. Other critics say the bill violates the Fourth and Tenth Amendments to the Constitution.[37]

The model for the New Freedom initiative is the TMAP, which stands for the Texas Medication Algorithm Project - that's right, the state that George used to govern, a project that first saw the light of day during his time in office there. TMAP promotes the use of the new, and more expensive, antidepressants and antipsychotic drugs, such as Zyprexa (olanzapine), which is Eli Lilly's best selling drug. It grossed $4.28 billion in 2003, with 70 per cent of the revenues paid for by government agencies such as Medicare and Medicaid." Critics say the plan protects the profits of drug companies at the expense of the public.[38]

---

[36] *Attempt to Stop Mandatory Mental Screening Fails.* WorldNetDaily November 24, 2004. Online Source: http://www.mindfully.org/Health/2004/Mandatory-Mental-Screening24nov04.htm.

[37] *Big Brother in Your Medicine Cabinet* by Jordanne Graham. Intervention Magazine. Sunday, November 28, 2004. Online Source: http://www.interventionmag.com/cms/modules.php?file=article&name=News&op=modload&sid=930.

[38] *The New Freedom Initiative (US): Ready to Be Tested?* Robin Good. July 16, 2004. Online Source: http://www.masternewmedia.org/news/2004/07/16/the_new_freedom_initiative_us.htm.

Within the death consumption culture there is functional insanity and dysfunctional insanity. Functional insanity simply refers to those who are able to function within the insane attitudes and behaviors that are the dominating norms of the status quo. Those who are not able to function within the insanity that is established as the dominant governing order of the status quo are considered to be dysfunctional and insane. Mental health is an extremely important factor if Man, He and She, is to survive upon this planet. In fact, the thought and reasoning of a population, of the governing order of a people, of a global society must move to a state of divine spirit consciousness. Man, He and She, must move to a state of recognizing that a population cannot grow and emerge into a peace-loving and harmonious people if functional insanity is the leading force. It is absolutely not possible as long as the functional insanity and the dysfunctional insanity continue to trade places with each other, depending on who is in control of the weapons of mass destruction.

We are witnessing functional insanity and dysfunctional insanity on a global level. We see the plague of the ice-cold, deep-freeze mentality spread into every land, among every Man, He and She. It matters not if one is blonde or bald or natty, natty dread. The plague infects all who indulge in the ice-cold, deep-freeze mentality. It affects all who consume of the death consumption culture, regardless of categories of "race," creed or color. There are those who function in insanity with the dominant ability to swiftly kill. There are those who function in insanity as the supporters, disciples and followers of those who have the ability to swiftly kill. Then there are those who are dysfunctional in their insanity, yet they plot and scheme on ways to get on top, to get control of the ability to swiftly kill.

This totally insane order of the war culture maintains gods created in their own image and continues to threaten the mental, physical and spiritual presence of the holistic living existence of Man, He and She. Unquestionably, the social order is facing massive challenges of physical sickness, disease and disorder as a result of consuming of the death consumption culture. By the same token the social order is suffering massive spiritual sickness, disease and disorder. This spiritual disease and disorder is a result of consuming of the death consumption culture. Unquestionably, the social order is suffering from massive mental sickness, disease, and disorder as a result of consuming of the death consumption culture. The thoughts and reasoning are out of whack, because Man, He and She, continues to indulge in the ice-cold, deep-freeze mentality.

# Chapter Four:
# Violating the Sacred Presence of Man, He and She: Tracking Sexual Disorders and Diseases

# Chapter Four: Violating the Sacred Presence of Man, He and She: Tracking Sexual Disorders and Diseases

### *Sexualization*

Sexual disorder and promiscuous behavior are just another part of the social values within the death consumption culture. The energy that is opposite of Supreme Love, is ingrained as the way of life within every sub-culture and alternative lifestyle of the death consumption culture. In fact, as it is in a culture of disorder Man He and Man She actually come into union for all the wrong reasons. In most cases they have already tampered with and intercoursed themselves to the point of saturation. In fact, Man He after his numerous explorations is ever on the prowl for another conquest. The thrill of pursuit becomes the main attraction of the dating games, and conquest becomes a challenge. The greater the challenge, the greater the energy applied only to be disappointed, because behind the pubic hairs lies the same physical presentation. The male player finds this out in disappointment and frustration as the spoils of victory are short-lived. It is as though one is searching for a different shaped vagina, maybe sideways or upside down or some other mutation or degeneration from the natural presence of Man She. In truth and reality, Man, He and She, has been following the ice-cold, deep-freeze mentality for so long that their sexual encounters are just another phase of foreplay with deception.

Some males have grown to believe that any time they get an erection; they must stick their penis somewhere. It reminds one of the old saying, "A stiff dick has no conscience." By the same token many a female has grown to believe that any time she sees an erect penis or the appearance thereof, it is a sign that the male is attracted to her, "turned on," and really wants her. With the right words at the right time in the right place, that female will open herself like the Nile Valley. The terrible thing is that the only knowledge that the female will have is that which is provided by the male in question. The male will tell her whatever it takes to get it in. It will not matter to him if he or she has a venereal disease, or if she is ovulating. The only thing that will matter is getting another notch on his belt and the thrill of victory

Within the various social orders, gangs, cliques and old boy's clubs of the death consumption culture, Man He is actually encouraged to practice his manhood on some innocent or unsuspecting female. He is actually encouraged to sow his oats through acts of sex and violence that play out in whorish vibrations, promiscuity, and prostitution. As the Caucasian male often claims, prostitution is the world's "oldest profession." It stands to reason that prostitution and rape were born and bred in the harsh and cruel lifestyle of the Caucasus Mountains and steppe region of Northern Europe.

The instant gratification of conquest keeps the male on the prowl since some females have somehow become more expressive in their stimulation or have become convincing actresses in expressing their stimulation. Many males feel victorious when the acts of sexual intercourse show signs of reward as the conquest is accompanied by the oohs and ahhs, hollers, screams and shouts of a submitting female. The male basks in the thrill of victory and looks down upon the female as the conquered in the agony of defeat with thoughts such as, "Whoa, I'm bad, pumping it to her; wearing it out." These inflated thoughts don't have much to do with anything except ego, and moments later, weeks later, he is on the prowl again. Some other unsuspecting feminine presence becomes his next prey and a victim of circumstances. All it takes to inspire the predator-like pursuit is a smile, a new dress style and the appearance of the female being hot and wild.

When the female is not able to perform up to the male's expectations or imagination, she is dismissed as being dull, disappointing, inexperienced or uptight. The female is often exposed to teachings and attitudes that make her feel a sense of guilt or a sense of shame about her glorious temple. The male on the prowl will simply continue his search. Sometimes, the male will be on the prowl for a super freak to act out his wildest fantasies, sometimes he may be on the prowl for a virgin to break in. Regardless, the mission remains the same: to seek, search and destroy another victim of prey by leaving another damaged female as the spoils of victory and the agony of defeat. The cold-blooded nature of the death consumption culture is, in fact, merely a manifestation and an enactment of the energy that is opposite of Supreme Love.

It is clear that Man He has been dishonoring the mother spirit, the gateway of life, and thus dishonoring the ancestral presence of the Most Supreme Seen and Unseen. It is no excuse that these dishonoring practices against the feminine presence are learned behaviors that emerged out of the ice-cold, deep-freeze mentality. It is no excuse to state that one's ancestors spent 300 hundred years enslaved by a system that outlawed the suntanned Man, He and She, from establishing a sacred union. It is no excuse that the sacred sons and daughters were inflicted with the cold-blooded mentality that emerged out of the ice-cold, deep-freeze 6,000 years ago. It is no excuse to state that there are no conscious women around, and relationships are just too much trouble. Excuses only serve to keep one entrapped in the mind maze of confusion within the ice-cold, deep-freeze mentality. In every instance, these kinds of excuses serve to propagate prostitution, homosexuality and other deviant behaviors as males seek an easy way out rather than to live up to the divine obligations to the mother spirit. Any male who does not take his divine duties, obligations and responsibilities to provide divine guidance and protection for the feminine presence does not deserve the attention, devotion or nurturing vibration of any feminine presence.

It must be understood that the mother spirit or the feminine presence will nurture the energy that is brought to her. The only way that she can possibly nurture anything other than the death consumption culture of the ice-cold, deep-freeze mentality is for the holistic living way of life of the sacred garden culture to be brought to her. If the feminine presence is presented with the option of a holistic living way of life of the sacred garden culture and she then decides that her choice is the ice-cold, deep-freeze mentality of the death consumption culture, her personal choice is hers. The best thing for Man He to do in a case like this is to move out of harm's way instead of continuing the pursuit, because "she is so fine." Man, He and She, must come to know that beauty is the inner essence instead of the outward presentation of fashion, style and glamour or any of the other beauty standards of the death consumption culture.

The standard pattern is that the masculine presence who thinks that he is of consciousness continues the same pursuit patterns with a little cultural conscious style added to his game plan. In every instance that one can imagine, the results are the same, and the relationship finds its way to the same kind and type of dead end. In order for the masculine presence to be in divine order, he must receive the divine guidance of spiritual leadership. Unless that spiritual leadership is within a holistic living way of life of the sacred garden culture where the principles, morals and practices of divine consumption of raw and living fruits, vegetables, seeds and nuts is the way of life, the masculine presence in question will perpetuate disorder. So many times, the masculine presence will claim a vibration of righteousness and being holier than thou. However, in truth and reality, he is simply playing the same game with another name while seeking the glory of fortune and/or fame.

## CHAPTER FOUR: VIOLATING THE SACRED PRESENCE OF MAN, HE AND SHE: TRACKING SEXUAL DISORDERS & DISEASES

So long as the female is only offered some other game with another name within the death consumption culture of the ice-cold, deep-freeze mentality, it must be clearly understood that she has never been confronted with any other option except the status quo that is consistently brought to her. At every point, one must check oneself to see if one truly represents the holistic living way of life of the sacred garden culture before using the feminine presence as one's scapegoat. It is easy to find a scapegoat and say that there are no good women or conscious women in one's territory. In truth and reality, these justifications and rationalizations are an indictment against oneself as a masculine presence. Since the mother spirit nurtures what is brought to her, it really means that there are no good men or conscious men in one's territory.

The way of life that degenerated and mutated in the ice cold caves of the Caucasus Mountains and steppe regions was a recent occurrence upon the planet, yet it has contaminated and disrupted massive populations of Man, He and She, to the point of utter ruin and despair. The violent and degraded relationships that emerged in the ice cold caves of the deep-freeze vibration established the patterns of sexuality that continue to be perpetuated in modern times. The violent and degraded relationships of the ice-cold, deep-freeze environment are the birthplace of the energy that is opposite of Supreme Love.

The vicious brutality of the pale conquering invaders was smeared in the blood of rape and impregnated in the females who were dark and lovely within the vast regions of the sacred garden culture. The original and divine image of the suntanned father of the planet was destroyed and replaced by the cold-blooded warlord, a lost and astray son, who returned with a blood-lusting vengeance for deathly deceit. Because of the first acts of disobedience and disorder among the lost and astray Children, the divinity of Man, He and She, was defiled through acts of toxic consumption. As a result, the sexuality of

Man, He and She, was defiled among any one who tampered with the energy that is opposite of Supreme Love. All points of exploration from within the culture that resulted from the first disorders of toxic consumption can only reflect more disorder and toxic consumption.

The sexuality of the ice-cold, deep-freeze mentality can and does include every deviant performance that emerged in the dank and bleak caves of the deep freeze, including bestiality, homosexuality, sadism, masochism, bondage, domination, rape, necrophilia, frenzied orgies and every strain of sex and violence imaginable. The vibrations and sensations of humiliation, shame, degradation, receiving pain as pleasure, inflicting pain as pleasure, violation, force and brutality echo from the dank and bleak caves of the deep-freeze experience. Such sexual expressions reflect the disconnected, numb, lost and astray appetites of lust, lies, illusions, confusion, death and deadly destruction. It is absolutely essential to distinguish the toxic vibrations encountered within the death consumption culture from the whole life vibrations of Supreme Love originating from within the sacred garden culture.

Sexual perversions of the deep freeze mentality are conditions in which an individual receives sexual pleasure, excitement, gratification, stimulation and/or orgasm through acts of toxic consumption. Toxic consumption of a sexual nature refers to interactions, encounters, relationships and associations that are based on vibrations and sensations outside of the Supreme Love vibration. Many of the sexual perversions are enacted based on arousal impulses that can result from pain, distress, humiliation, force, indulgence in pornography, prostitution, molestation, imposing one's sexual aggression on someone who does not consent, and engaging in activities with inanimate objects, children or animals.

Many who are prone to sexual perversions feel an uncontrollable urge to engage in toxic acts and may become obsessed with sexual acts that induce stimulation. The sexual offenders and sexual predators of the death consumption culture are the public representatives of the sexual perversions that are part and parcel of the ice-cold, deep-freeze mentality. Those who participate in sexual perversions are noted to experience guilt, depression, shame, isolation, emotional impairment, and feelings of being naughty, nasty and dirty. It is absolutely essential to distinguish the toxic vibrations encountered within the death consumption culture from the whole life vibrations of Supreme Love originating from within the sacred garden culture.

### *The Nomadic Vibration in Male Female Relationships*

Within the death consumption culture, Man He quickly grows tired and bored with the feminine presence, because every impulse is inspired by the nomadic lure of newness and the unexplored territory in acts of conquest. And so Man He grows tired not only from the acts that he has just overindulged in, but also from the idea of settling down with family responsibilities. The feminine presence begins to calculate that so long as she can keep the male in between her thighs, then she can keep control of him and he won't abandon her. Her attempt to use feminine charms and sexual skills as a vice grip, as a device of control, may succeed temporarily. However, the male grows tired and restless, because every stimulation in the death consumption culture is geared towards promoting and getting something new—a new car, a new suit, a new pair of shoes, a new drug, or a new toxic food substance.

The death consumption culture is all about the vibration of novelty, newness, and wandering from one new adventure to the next, instead of a vibration of stability and long-term cultivation. The lost and astray mind is a wandering vibration that constantly seeks distractions and amusements in the steady pursuit of adventure. Restlessness in the search for new thrills just over the horizon or a new relationship just down the road is definitely not the same vibration as having the motivation to participate in the cultivation and enrichment of self, of family and of divine social economic family community. The cycles of growth and development within the sacred garden culture are a renewing and invigorating process of advancement, mentally, physically and spiritually. It should be comprehended and understood that until one has mastered maintaining and securing what one has produced; one is actually producing with a short-term focus or selfish goals and objectives that cause errors. When one produces in error, the errors produce disorder. In error, one will produce experiences and toxic relationships, causing adverse effects that will show up later in life.

There are times when an individual may find himself or herself in a wrong relationship for all the wrong reasons. Oftentimes, this is because of one's earlier stages of ignorance, mis-education, fantasized perceptions, misinformed direction and lack of divine guidance. As one begins to move into divine spirit consciousness, one may realize that the relationship that one has been maintaining is actually in contradiction. Quite frequently, the two individuals involved have been moving in entirely different directions from the onset and have actually been maintaining the relationship for sexual or social reasons that are inadequate. If and when one finds oneself in this type of predicament, one must not hide in denial. When Man He or She recognizes these contradicting differences, he or she must face the fact that the relationship either has to come into divine oneness, or it must be released. As one emerges into divine spirit consciousness, one will learn to let go of that which one does not really have in the first place.

Once one has let go of a toxic and disorderly relationship, i.e. a relationship in contradiction, one must realize that there is a need for a time to heal from the scars and wounds regardless of how unaffected one may appear to be. Any healing process requires de-toxing. Only after a cleansing or de-toxing process can one expect to be able to move into an upward spiral of mental, physical and spiritual consciousness. If this healing process is ignored or taken for granted, one will simply build the next relationship on a toxic and depleted foundation that will eventually lead to system breakdown and the breeding of the scapegoat mentality.

### ***Sexual Violation and the Conquest Syndrome***

The lust-oriented conquest mentality within the lost and astray mind of Man He perpetuates the misuse and abuse of the feminine spirit. Vibrations of exploration and curiosity have been distorted to appear as if one is merely on an adventurous journey into unknown territory. Lust can be defined as the corrupted urges and impulses to gratify one's physical appetites, cravings, and hunger. Lust is the vibration that emerged in the ice-cold caves as deprivation, starvation and a complete disconnection from spirit presence set in. Ravenous hunger and the frenzied search for something to devour caused physical appetites and momentary gratification to become the overriding authority in the deep-freeze caves. The hunt for physical gratification was the quick-fix treatment for the disorders of the ice-cold cave. The vibrations of the ice-cold cave remain today in the attitudes and behaviors of many of Man, He and She.

In truth and reality, the lost and astray mind is one that reflects the vibrations of "seek, search and destroy" for the purposes of conquest and consumption. This scenario of conquest is played out in every arena of life, most especially in the masculine spirit. Man He is on a lustful crusade against Man She. The unknown territory of what lies beyond the pubic hairs of a particular female causes Man He in modern times to function much like the wandering and plundering nomads who emerged from the ice-age deep freeze. The fierce and warlike nomads herded animals and roamed from place to place as ruthless raiders seeking conquest and booty. The booty is any valuables, belongings and property seized by the violence, robbery and theft of the invading forces. In fact, the booty of plunder and pillage give an added incentive to join in campaigns of conquest.

Principles and practices of warfare and hostile aggression are the hallmark of a way of life that is fueled by the slaughter and consumption of livestock. Many of Man He still engage in the attitudes and behaviors of the hunter, herder, nomad, warrior, cave-clan mentality. The battle cry, "To the victor goes the spoils," can still be heard in modern times from males who are winning athletes on the game field or the males on Wall Street who close the deal.

In the more intimate settings, victory to the modern male is often when his rap and his appeal convince the female to surrender to his advances and she becomes the spoils. The female was the spoils of the traditional death consumption culture as the most brutal and fierce male dominated by acts of violence, and she remains the spoils of today. And sexual intercourse is considered by many of Man He to be the act of final conquest. It comes as no surprise how the violent and degrading act of rape is a common act within the death consumption culture. Taking by force, coercion, the tricks of deception and acts of terror are the standard code of operation within the ice-cold, deep-freeze mentality.

Slaughter and consumption of hunted and herded animals formulate the vibrations of the ice-cold cave-clan way of life, a way of life that is the origin of the death consumption culture. The use, abuse, and destruction of another living creature for one's personal gain are fundamental in the death consuming mentality. The level of insensitivity and cold-blooded relationships between Man He and Man She is a direct reflection of the death consumption way of life. The hunting and herding tribes of the steppe regions were born of the cave mentality of deprivation, hostile aggression and violence that marked the harsh, cold and cruel environment of the ice-age deep freeze.

The act of licking the sweet juice of a mango would form the definition of pleasures within the sacred garden culture. In the deep-freeze caves, the act of licking the blood from the bones of a slaughtered animal formed the definition of pleasure within the cultural references of the lost and astray Children who lost their tan. To this very day, commercials advertising the sizzle and smell of charred remains are used to entice the appetites of the lost and astray mind.

The brutality, cruelty, and ruthlessness of the nomad tribes are legendary. Nevertheless, the vicious acts of warlord invaders are often glorified as great military strategies throughout the history of the death consumption culture. The perpetuation of the conquest mentality is echoed in a quote attributed to Julius Caesar as he returned from bloody victory in Asia Minor, "*Veni, Vidi, Vici* (I came, I saw, I conquered)." The same conquering vibration of his expression could be applied to the overthrow and possession of Egypt or his bedding of Cleopatra, the Egyptian queen.

Man She within the death consumption culture is devalued to the role of a sex partner. Whether she is simply the object of lust, a sex symbol or the hot fantasy projected in the lost and astray mind of Man He, she receives and nurtures the waste matter of toxic consumption in every cold-blooded attitude and behavior that Man He brings to her. There is a blatant ignorance of the fact the Man, He and She, is a sum total of the energy that one consumes. There is even more ignorance regarding the fact that the energy of what Man He ejaculates into Man She is a sum total of what will come back to Man, He and She, again. So long as there is the toxic value that all is fair in love and war, then lust, lies, illusions, confusion, death and deadly destruction will be the outcome of the relationship between Man, He and She.

## EXPOSING THE ICE-COLD, DEEP-FREEZE MENTALITY AND WHOLE LIFE HEALING OF SEXUAL ENERGY WITHIN THE DIVINE PARALLEL

To begin a divine analysis of the sexual behaviors of Man, He and She, one must consider the original and divine presence of Man, He and She, within the sacred garden culture. One of the primary reasons why it has taken so long for the western culture to acknowledge the whole life value of the feminine presence is because too often the feminine presence is viewed as a sidekick who came by the way as an afterthought. For far too long the female has been viewed as inferior to the male and as the weaker sex. The ice-cold, deep-freeze mentality can not reason with the fact that Man She is a divine part of the whole presence of Man just as Man He is a divine part to the whole presence of Man. When evaluating strength and weakness, the lost and astray mind can not reason that the value of strength that is equated with the male is entirely different from the value of strength equated with the female. However, in truth and reality, what else should be expected from a mutated and degenerated mind of thought and reasoning that is fed by a culture of mental, physical and spiritual deprivation?

The male of the ice-cold, deep-freeze mentality has been quite busy in his vibrations of rape, conquest, and control. The invading male took no time to consider the victims upon whom he preyed. The feminine presence has long been a victim of the ice-cold, deep-freeze mentality as the first domestic violence occurred in the dank and bleak caves. As a result, death consumption cultural behaviors regarding sexuality continue to be steeped in sex and violence, and the vibration of lust. The mainstay of the culture that practices hunting, scavenging and herding, is the stimulation received from violation, slaughter and the consumption of dead flesh.

The sexual behaviors of the feminine presence have become defined in terms of the cold-blooded hunting and herding male who invaded the sacred garden culture as a vicious nomadic warlord. This vicious invader emerged from the Caucasus Mountains and steppe regions as a malnourished and brutal cave dweller. The lost and astray Children who lost their tan in each historical instance of invasion, relied on some variation of kill, rape, burn and pillage to enslave and subdue massive populations of Man, He and She, who were herded like sheep for capital gain. The female of the nomadic tribes was treated like a whore with utter disregard, like excess baggage to be used and discarded, while the nomadic male violently enforced his blood-lusting will to kill, rape, burn and pillage.

Sexual violation and the conquest mentality go hand in hand through the bloody history of the death consumption culture. The spirit presence was completely submerged in the physical sensations and vibrations of starvation, death consumption, and the threat of being consumed or devoured as the weaker sex or being slaughtered or abandoned as excess baggage. Sexual encounters would be contaminated by fright, fear, misery, aches and pains as the energy that is opposite of Supreme Love festered in the feminine presence. By tracking the energy that is opposite of Supreme Love, it becomes clear how the female became just another piece of flesh to devour in the lost and astray mind of the death-consuming male. The dominant male would degenerate into a masculine presence who abandoned his divine duties, obligations and responsibilities that called for him to provide divine guidance and protection for the feminine presence. Instead the dominant male of the ice-cold, deep-freeze mentality would express care and concern as self-preservation through acts of killing and the consumption of dead flesh.

The social norms and values of the death consumption culture have attempted to mask the violent and brutal sexual origins of those who descended from the deep-freeze experience. All those who have assimilated and integrated into that ice-cold, deep-freeze mentality carry the mark of those beastly, violent and brutal origins. Concepts of chastity, vows of celibacy, and serious hang-ups regarding sexuality are several responses to sexual disorder within the ice-cold, deep-freeze mentality. Religious restrictions that attempt to control the "carnal nature" and lustful appetites that are rampant within the death consumption culture often lead to sexual perversions where individuals engage in covert activities.

Vibrations of violation and corruption serve to feed the toxic addictions of so many within the ice-cold, deep-freeze mentality, even as one prays to a deity for forgiveness. Religious taboos against sexuality have served to keep the female entrapped in vibrations of shame, guilt and disgust at her own body. Within many religious orders, the female is devalued, sex is viewed as sinful, and the body is considered to be the source of temptation. The image of a virgin mother is upheld to be worshipped. By the same token, the celibacy vows of a religious order are highly publicized and revered as a symbol of righteousness. Nevertheless, those in the religious hierarchy are exposed as hypocrites after years of engaging in the homosexual raping of young children behind closed confessional doors of pious deception.

### *Pornography: Toxic Sexual Consumption*

Once force and violation became the normal means to secure a meal and satisfy one's appetite, the use of force and violation to satisfy one's sexual appetites followed close behind. If the female did not cooperate or submit, the ice-cold, deep-freeze mentality revealed an undeniable pattern of take by force. The female was not physically able to fend off the sexual aggression of the dominant male, and she would be taken by force, used and abused to suit his sexual pleasures. After repeated violations, the female would begin to equate being overpowered and sexually violated with her position in life in the death consumption culture. As she reasoned with survival in her harsh and cruel environment, the female became cunning in her attempts to secure herself and her offspring by teasing and appeasing the dominant male. Being physically beaten, sexually assaulted, and treated like an object of possession became the ongoing experiences of Man She in her deep-freeze relationship with Man He. The death consumption culture continues to perpetuate this vibration with acts of domestic violence, sexual slavery, female infanticide (killing baby girls), rape and prostitution.

As the suntanned female was repeatedly raped and enslaved by the invading warlords of the ice-cold, deep-freeze mentality, the structures of the sacred sisterhood societies were dismantled. The defining elements of the glorious suntanned feminine presence were corrupted with the ejaculation of wretched filth and toxic decay that festered within the energy that is opposite of Supreme Love. The violation and corruption continued with social economic and religious rape, murder, steal and take that occurred from offspring who fed on the toxic mentality and dominated the mother spirit presence of the sacred garden culture.

As the masculine presence lost control of his divine characteristics of providing divine guidance and protection, the suntanned daughter was lowered to the status of concubine, whore, and mammy to the death consumption culture. Her fate was to be used and abused and treated like hell. She would learn to glorify in the stench of the death consumption culture smell. With her sexuality sold on an auction block, she would be traded and consumed like livestock. Her sense of divine sisterhood relationship would be ripped and torn apart, and replaced with envy, jealousy and greed and a broken heart. She would learn to compete for favors while nurturing the death consumption culture, thus rejecting the sacred garden culture. This would reduce the feminine presence to a lowly state of being and disconnect her from the divine knowledge, wisdom and understanding of her sacred and divine mental, physical and spiritual presence. Understanding that the feminine presence nurtures what is brought to her, one can begin to understand the present dilemma of Man, He and She. The sacred mother spirit, left without protection, is presently reduced to a position of nurturing the death consumption culture and going forward to multiply it in her offspring.

The deep-freeze male used his penis as an instrument of aggression, becoming aroused and stimulated by brutal acts of dominating the female and imposing his will. As a result, repeated episodes of degradation, humiliation and submission to violence were run over and over again within the feminine presence. These constant re-runs for generations after generations would cause the memory bank to become a storehouse of violent stimulation. The violent stimulation would be nurtured in every offspring born from the harsh, vicious and cruel relationships of Man, He and She, within the ice-cold, deep-freeze mentality. The toxic stimulations of fright, fear, physical force, and pain became entangled with the vibrations of sexual arousal in the lost and astray mind of Man, He and She. In fact, the toxic vibration of using physical force to control others and subdue prey manifested an entire syndrome of sex and violence that festers in the norms and values of the death consumption culture today. It becomes clear how acts of murder, rape, steal and take define a code of attitudes and behaviors that descended with the vicious invaders from the Caucasus Mountain and steppe region and all the disciples and followers of the death consumption culture.

The toxic vibrations of the energy that is opposite of Supreme Love fester throughout the history of the death consumption culture in every ugly form and fashion. Research indicates that the origin of the word, pornography, is drawn from the Greek word *porne* said to mean female captive, slave or prostitute and the word *graphos* said to mean writing or drawing. Be reminded that the Greece of old was originally a suntanned community long before the vicious invasions of the ice-cold, deep-freeze mentality caused the formulation of new and toxic concepts and new terms to define the toxic behaviors that these cold-blooded invaders brought with them. Thus research indicates that the origin of the word pornography links visual images of women with the concepts of conquest and bondage. In pornography, either the woman is shown submitting to lustful male aggression or she is portrayed as highly aroused and enticing lustful sexual advances. Pornography, including child pornography, is big business in the death consumption culture.

The mother spirit will in fact multiply the energy of the environmental attitudes and behaviors that are ejaculated into her. Repeated exposure to images and acts of degradation, humiliation and submission cause one to become increasingly desensitized to the toxic images and acts. Under such circumstances, one begins to crave even more toxic stimulation like a drug addict. It is possible for a female to become so desensitized and disconnected as a result of exposure to pornography, sexual violation, and violence that she becomes conditioned to experience a stimulation response from acts of humiliation and degradation. Within the death consumption culture, it is not unusual to hear of females who become sexually aroused from being called degrading names during sex or "being treated like a whore."

Degrading images of the feminine presence as a sexual object are glorified in the death consumption culture media, such as movies, magazines, commercial ads, music videos and even sports events. These degrading images are then upheld by young females who flaunt their sexuality and practice dressing, talking and acting like the latest "hot and wild" sex symbol. The basic projection is that "she's gotta have it" by any means necessary, and she doesn't care who it is. When the going gets tough she simply makes a "booty call," although some disguise it as going out on a date.

Within the death consumption culture, the female has been conditioned to seek the sexual attention of a male as an indication of her worth and appeal as a female. The sexual attention that the male has been conditioned to give a female within the death consumption culture is based on the lustful vibrations of many pornographic fantasies. More and more, the female within the death consumption culture is integrating and assimilating many of the sexual predator attitudes and behaviors of the ice-cold, deep-freeze mentality. This cold and insensitive approach that the female adopts is usually the result of a damaging or abusive encounter where her trust factor has been mishandled by a male.

What happens to the female who has been violated, damaged or abused is that she develops a numb layer of emotional scar tissue, and instead of being sensitive, caring, and nurturing; she turns cold, angry and calculating. Different levels and degrees of damage involve issues of security and trust based on relationships with males in her life. Without the divine guidance and divine protection of the masculine presence, the female is vulnerable to predatory advances and attacks; she is also easily corrupted by the toxic influence of a male with whom she has developed an emotional bond. In fact, Man She can become a He Man's worst nightmare overnight if she is improperly treated.

Whoever controls the hands that rock the crib controls the nation and every generation of that nation. Following the lost and astray mind back into the dank vibrations of the ice-cold, deep-freeze mentality is tantamount to diving into a cesspool of toxic waste, overflowing with stench and rot, covering one from head to toe. The lost and astray mind can only lead one into being lost and astray.

While feminists shout and protest about male domination and the abuses of the patriarch, mothers continue to give birth to the same mentality of toxic consumption in He and She. While females complain about not being able to establish a committed relationship with a male, they continue to support false beauty standards and addictive social habits of I, me, my that nurture the invading nomadic warlord approach to relationships. For every complaint that the female may lodge against the macho-male syndrome of brute force and cold-blooded emotions, she still dreams and aspires to some variety of status, influence and/or wealth within the death consumption culture.

As long as one continues to participate in any aspect of the death consumption culture, one will experience disorder. Sexual disorders and relationship disorders will simply be one more consequence of one's toxic consumption, and toxic disorder is all that one will go forward to multiply.

## Orderly Systems of Disorder

There are critical issues that directly impact the overall health and well-being of Man, He and She, upon the planet. How does one find order within a disorderly system that perpetuates an energy that is opposite of Supreme Love? How does one find order within the death consumption culture? The answer is blunt and simple: In truth and reality one cannot find order within the death consumption culture except to find an order of death consumption and the consequences that it has upon its consumers and its victims. Within the death consumption culture, one can find an orderly process of leading the cows, chickens and pigs to the slaughterhouse. One can find an orderly process of harnessing the chickens in organized egg production. In and around November, one can find an orderly process of plucking and packing turkeys to be delivered for consumption as though it was the turkey's mission in life.

Religions within the death consumption culture establish orderly mass and orderly sessions with the rabbis, imams, priests and preachers. Religious practices have an orderly script to follow so as to declare a slaughtered creature as being blessed for consumption. These orderly systems include practices of declaring slaughtered creatures as kosher or a blessing or hilal by a designated head person. One can find an orderly system of hospitalizing the sick and afflicted where hospitals are a dominant institution, more prominent and widespread than organic crop farms. And then there is the orderly system of preparing for death through the pre-purchase of plots, caskets, dress attire and final funeral arrangements. And then there is the orderly system of burial. In fact, it is unquestionable that the death consumption culture is a very orderly system of disorder that maintains the vibrations and sensations of an energy that is in truth and reality the opposite of Supreme Love. When one examines the death consumption culture and its adverse effects on the mental, physical and spiritual health and well-being of Man, He and She, then one is able to identify the death consumption culture as a massive system of disorder.

The death consumption culture is a culture based on the consumption of dead and devitalized food substances where disease and disorder have become a natural and innate pattern of behavior. The death consumption culture is a culture that perpetuates the consumption of dead and devitalized food substances. These dead and devitalized food substances include animals and animal by-products, such as chickens, cows and fish; and consuming of fried, baked, and boiled potatoes, soy beans and other vegetation and dead and devitalized fruit products and by-products. Dead and devitalized consumption also includes chemical substance abuse, drug and alcohol addictions, and other forms of toxic entertainment to create a "feel-good" vibration. Dead and devitalized consumption promotes deviant sexual behaviors, sexual disorders, and promiscuity. The death consumption culture is founded on principles that have made dead and devitalized consumption part and parcel of every institutional framework, i.e. social, political, economic and religious systems.

Medical and pharmaceutical organized structures function as major components to validate and justify the death consumption culture as a way of life that is widely accepted and appreciated by all those who participate in it. Therefore, as a participant within the death consumption culture, one must come to fully realize truth and consequences. Indeed, one has rights and privileges to consume as one chooses in accordance with the laws, rules and regulations of the death consumption culture.

Based on the nature of toxic consumption, the values, attitudes and behaviors within the death consumption culture reflect toxicity. Therefore, within such a framework, toxic reasoning can and does easily emerge. For instance, if prostate massage is administered as an acceptable therapeutic healing practice, then within the death consumption culture a degenerated practice would develop to parallel any wholesome vibrations. A deviant practice would develop, such as declaring that the prostate is being massaged through anal sex. The more absurd such toxic acts and behaviors are within the principles and practices of the sacred garden culture, the more appealing and tempting toxic consumption appears within the mind of the energy that is opposite of Supreme Love.

The nature of the death consumption culture perpetuates the vibrations and sensations of masterful and deceitful programs. The justifications and rationalizations of the death consumption culture serve to excuse and promote behaviors that are totally out of synch and out of harmony with the divine oneness of Man, He and She. Such toxic reasoning is even used to perpetuate tendencies of a homosexual nature or down-low syndromes that make a mockery of the divine and natural state of divine union between Man, He and She.

If one takes a simple look at the reproductive system of Man, He and She, and the debilitating and deadly consequences of such afflictions as prostate disorder or fibroids, it will become absolutely clear that degeneration is self-evident and mutation is the prolonged factor. As anyone who is familiar with vehicles can attest, low-grade fuel results in lowered performance. Likewise, depleted fuel for the cells results in dysfunction and error. Indeed, when the codes of divine order are broken in one's consumption, then the codes of divine order are broken from the smallest cell to the largest bodies until disorder becomes the norm. When disorder becomes the norm, an initial mutation will appear to be the standard pattern. Unfortunately, degeneration will cause a further deterioration until the mass of the body begins to show the signs of rampant disease, disorder and mutation.

The genetic changes that are a consequence of consuming depleted and devitalized energies are a deviation from the divine genetic order that maintains wholesome health and well-being within the wholly temple of Man, He and She. The genetic disorders that trigger the cancerous growth of cells are a result of toxins in the system.

Living cells will continue to replicate and perform based on genetic codes that are decreasing in vital information for cell function until cellular breakdown occurs. When cellular breakdown occurs at a threshold level then organ and system breakdown occur. When system breakdown occurs, the crisis is a time for further breakdown to the point of depletion or a breakthrough of divine intervention. Living systems were created to eliminate damaged (and, hence, potentially harmful) cells through a self-destruct and disposal mechanism: identified as programmed cell death, or apoptosis. When disorder continues to a critical level, the self-destruct mechanism is activated and one experiences the symptoms of disease and disorder. This self-destruct mechanism can be activated under many different circumstances. Although a general theory of adaptation highlights mutation as a natural selection process, adaptation in the death consumption culture is a degenerating proposition.

The reasoning of natural selection is that the most necessary traits for the survival of a species are those genetic codes that dominate over time. Therefore, within the death consumption culture, mutations have occurred to preserve traits that are best suited to the consumption of dead and devitalized food substances, i.e. scavenger and predatory vibrations, aggression, conquest attitudes and behaviors. These "survival-of-the-fittest" traits may appear to have the upper hand until the inherent consequences of death consumption begin to accumulate in the system and trigger the self-destruct mechanisms. War, sex and violence, homicide, suicide, crimes and hostile aggression are signs of the self-destruct mechanism kicking in. The consequences of indulging in the death consumption culture are played out through the adverse and fatal conditions of prostate disorder, fibroids, relationship disorders, sexually transmitted diseases, cancer, diabetes, obesity, heart attacks, strokes, AIDS, Alzheimer's disease, manic depression, psychosis, etc. It does not matter if these diseases are intentional or accidental. It does not matter whether these diseases are the result of biological warfare or heredity. Within the life cycle of the species of Man, He and She, that time of reckoning is at hand.

Research within the death consumption culture is based on an entirely different set of morals, values, attitudes and behaviors than the original divine model of Man, He and She. Scientific research and advances in genetics and biology within the death consumption culture reflect the toxic thought and reasoning of the ice-cold, deep-freeze mentality. The primary principles of the ice-cold, deep-freeze mentality begin with the assumption that non-melaninated traits are superior and that melaninated traits are inferior. Such assumptions contradict all divine reasoning within a solar system where the sun is a supreme presence of whole life energy.

It should be clear to reason that mutation and degeneration that reflects a depletion of melanination is the direct consequence of solar deprivation, i.e. a deprivation of whole life energy. It would then stand to reason that depraved, mutated and degenerated thinking would automatically manifest from the severe state of deprivation experienced in the ice-cold deep freeze. It would stand to reason that these predatory behaviors would be the adopted norm by all those who surrendered to the forces of deception.

The non-melaninated children degenerated into deadly predators who master in the ability to swiftly kill, control and dominate. This domination caused a toxic wave of thought and reasoning to emerge. Thus, religious and scientific theories and ideologies that define the existence of Man, He and She, would, in truth, be a reflection of the ice-cold, deep-freeze mentality. More importantly, research would be conducted on the model of disorder and dysfunction of toxic consumption with the premise that toxic consumption is the original design of Man, He and She. Those of melanination have then been following the laws, rules and regulations of mutation and degeneration rather than the divine order of the sacred garden culture which manifested the original blueprint of Man, He and She. As a result, prostate disorder, and many other diseases and disorder, are rampant among "African American" males and females. In a social environment where toxic and depleted consumption patterns automatically breed massive sickness and disease in the general population, the "African American" is becoming an endangered species.

It would seem that the suntanned Children would have already ceased and desisted from following this toxic model since the consequences continue to be so grave and fatal. The toxic consequences of the ice-cold, deep-freeze mentality have been equally as devastating on the lost and astray Children who lost their tan. The dominant culture claims the spoils of conquest and continues to fantasize about the power to control and the swift ability to kill. These lost and astray Children who lost their tan gut through anxiety-ridden, stressed and paranoid sufferings with a business-like smile, feeling they at least have the upper hand within the death consumption culture. For this reason, come hell or high water, these lost and astray Children who lost their tan find it of the utmost importance to maintain the status quo.

The status quo satisfies the toxic ego of the lost and astray Children who lost their tan as well as their disciples and followers. The ice-cold, deep-freeze mentality causes one to project a sense of self-esteem when in truth and reality one is actually struggling to protect a superficial and unstable self-image that is the result of low self-esteem and massive insecurities. In other words, within the ice-cold, deep-freeze mentality the surface image is everything. It matters not what the holistic living truth is. Therefore, the ice-cold, deep-freeze mentality reflects glamour and deception; it reflects the stereotypes, biases and distortions of the lost and astray mind. Within this toxic reality, the outer appearance is more important than the whole life substance. For example, a multi-shaped veganically grown tomato with optimal nutritional values would be rejected and discarded whereas a perfectly round genetically engineered tomato with far less nutritional value would be admired and quickly sold in almost any public market.

There is no Supreme Love for divine order within the ice-cold, deep-freeze mentality; there is however an overblown, cocky and arrogant behavior that appears as the opposite parallel to supreme self-love. As a result of mental disorder, the lost and astray Children who lost their tan and their disciples and followers maintain a spiteful, vengeful and hateful attitude regarding the divine and original presence of Man, He and She. When the ice-cold, deep-freeze mentality claims godliness and holiness, it is truly referencing a god of war, jealousy, envy, greed and spite. Therefore, divine righteousness is lost within the opposite parallel where righteousness becomes deceptive behaviors that exonerate the mutative and degenerative manifestations of the death consumption culture.

Somewhere within the toxic reasoning of the ice-cold, deep-freeze mentality it is sensed that this vibration of thought is leading Man, He and She, to a fatal conclusion. This is why within the religious texts of the death consumption culture, i.e. the hunting and herding culture; there is a clear projection of mass destruction via the apocalypse or Armageddon syndrome. These are the reasons that the death consumption culture manifests life after death fantasies, such as a non-Earth heaven. With this kind of toxic reasoning in place, the lost and astray mind functions just as the mutated and degenerated breed did in the ice-cold, deep-freeze experience. In other words, there is absolutely no divine order regarding one's sexual behaviors within the ice-cold, deep-freeze mentality. As for the hostile and aggressive mind, anything goes, and all is fair in love and war.

The whole life order of Man, He and She, is to function in a matehood relationship that inspires the forward multiplication of Man, He and She. Yet, within the ice-cold, deep-freeze mentality, sexually deviant behaviors are the agenda that reflect the ice cold caves where the dominant male ruled. Within this dominant rule, the dominant male took out his sexual aggression on any male or female under his domination. As the dominant macho male syndrome moved deeper into the herding vibration, the same degenerated principles applied to the animals that were herded. The hunting and herding male of the ice-cold, deep-freeze mentality took out his sexual aggression on sheep, cows, horses or any other animal under his domination and control. With no hygienic values, concerns or care, this male would attack others with vengeance and hostile aggression. He would rape, murder, steal and take while spreading the vicious and cold-blooded mental and physical diseases and disorders that were picked up along the way.

The simple matter of fact is that this ice-cold, deep-freeze male would misuse his sexual organs and then pass these toxic vibrations on into the reproductive system of the feminine presence. The bottom line is that out of mutation and degeneration would be bred a death consumption culture and the toxic sicknesses and diseases that were its consequences. Disciples and followers who assimilated, degenerated and began to worship the religious orders and the deceptions of this ice-cold, deep-freeze mentality would have their own personal reward. The disciples and followers would be rewarded with even more toxic and afflicting side effects than those who were the original carriers of the toxicity.

When one takes a look at the devastating mental, physical and spiritual disease and disorder afflicting the suntanned Children, it becomes self-evident that the adverse effects are life-threatening and degenerative. It is therefore very harmful for the suntanned Children to continue upholding the attitudes, behaviors and values of the ice-cold, deep-freeze mentality. It must be understood that a sacred few among Man, He and She, must take the position of providing divine guidance. It should be clear that only those with the least amount of investment and ties to the death consumption culture hold the greatest opportunity for throwing off the yoke of the ice-cold, deep-freeze mentality.

It is, in fact, harmful for all of Man, He and She, to continue to uphold values where mutation and degeneration are exonerated and the divine presence of Man, He and She, is considered to be inferior. The fatal attraction to the deceptions and toxic reasoning of the ice-cold, deep-freeze mentality pose the greatest threat of self-destruction ever known to Man, He and She. Therefore, in order to secure the holistic living presence, it is necessary for every Child of the Sun to be aware of the subliminal and obvious traits, characteristics and symptoms of the ice-cold, deep-freeze mentality and the culture that it breeds. In order to solve any problem, one must first be able to identify the problem. Let us examine the truth and the consequences of the diseases and disorders afflicting the sexual organs and reproductive system of Man, He and She.

## Man He: Diseases and Disorders of the Sexual Organs

One of the most prevalent health concerns that the male faces in the death consumption culture is prostate disorder and malfunction. According to the American Prostate Society, four out every five men develop prostate disorder and malfunction in the United States. One of the most common prostate disorders is called prostatitis, which is inflammation and soreness of the prostate.

Prostatitis is reported to cause millions of males to suffer prostate discomfort and pain each year. One of the generally accepted causes of prostatitis is often identified as bacterial infection. Prostatitis strikes more men than either prostate cancer or prostate enlargement. Commonly recognized symptoms of prostatitis are the frequent urge to urinate, difficulty in starting to urinate, a burning sensation when urinating, dribbling, frequent nighttime trips to the bathroom, and pain.

Research indicates that bacteria that cause prostatitis are likely to enter the prostate from the urethra by backward flow of infected urine into the prostate ducts or from rectal bacteria. It seems that prophylactics are totally excluded in the research. How can one ignore the facts that so-called rubbers or condoms contain various chemical powders, lubricants, spermicides, and are be made of dead animal membranes as well as other irritants and materials? These materials can cause toxic consequences commencing at the head of the penis and working all the way back through to the prostate and beyond.

What one can conclude from these findings is that the masculine presence must be very careful, conscientious and protective of where he sticks his penis. Additionally, one must be conscientious about what or who comes in contact with one's penis. If one is dealing in toxic oral relationships where infections, sores, or other toxic bacteria are present then the toxins can be transmitted back through the urethra of the penis. By the same token, if one is having oral sex with someone who consumes of dead and devitalized food substances, i.e. toxic consumption, bacteria can be transmitted. Imagine having an oral sex encounter with someone after they have just finished consuming of dead and devitalized flesh, laden with the parasites and bacteria of rigor mortis. Imagine the toxic effects of anal sex when all that toxic energy is coming out the other end. Imagine the suffering, hell and damnation that toxic consumption breeds.

Within the death consumption culture, it is said to be a common occurrence for the prostate gland to become enlarged as a man ages. As most research indicates, the prostate goes through different phases of growth and development as the male matures. Prostate growth within itself cannot possibly be considered a disorder. We must be clear that what is normal and natural within the death consumption culture is not a reflection at all of the normal and natural state of being of Man, He and She. The very nature of the death consumption culture is based on the consumption of toxic and depleted substances. Toxicity and depletion are the root causes of disorder and disease. Therefore, growth of the prostate would have to be considered as a natural and normal process unless this enlargement is in fact an outgrowth of consumption disorder.

Within the death consumption culture, hormonal changes, mutation and degeneration are triggered by toxic consumption. Toxic consumption comes in many forms including, the down-low formula of promiscuous relationships. Toxic consumption also includes dead and devitalized substances; which range from artificial flavors, coloring and smells; preservatives; chemical additives; cooked/devitalized fruits and vegetables; pesticide-ridden products; hormone/steroid-injected dead animal flesh; bleached, processed and denatured white sugars and starches; fatty and greasy fried substances; and the list goes on within the death consumption culture.

Health statistics reveal that more than half of all males over the age of 50 within the death consumption culture experience symptoms of an enlarged prostate. As the prostate enlarges, the layer of tissue surrounding it stops it from expanding, causing the gland to press against the urethra like a clamp on a garden hose. The bladder wall becomes thicker and irritable. The bladder begins to contract even when it contains small amounts of urine, causing more frequent urination. Eventually, the bladder weakens and loses the ability to empty itself. Urine remains in the bladder. The narrowing of the urethra and partial emptying of the bladder cause many of the problems. Effects of prostate enlargement vary from almost unbearable misery to minor annoyance, and varying degrees in-between which may adversely affect a male's ability to perform sexually.

Facts and figures from the National Prostate Cancer Coalition state that, on average, one American male in every six is at a lifetime risk of prostate cancer. "African-American" males have a 60 percent higher risk of getting prostate cancer than "white" males and have twice the risk of dying from it. In fact, findings show that "African-American" males have the highest rate of prostate cancer in the world and the lowest rate of survival. Prostate cancer is caused by one of many forms of toxic consumption. Several studies have shown a link between prostate cancer and diets that are high in animal fat and meat.

**Toxic Sexual Attitudes and Behaviors**

So long as one approaches male sexuality in only physical terms one is limited to the vibrations of lust or sexual appetite with no regard for divine stimulation and going forward to multiply divinity in one's relationships. As a consequence, the emptiness and confusion of toxic relationships can, over time, numb and diminish one's natural desires. One either seeks artificially induced stimulation through pornographic, promiscuous or deviant activities and falls into the addictive vibrations of lustful encounters, or one becomes totally inactive, impotent and frustrated. Toxic relationships breed contempt, conflict, dishonesty, bitterness, anger and stress, and all of these vibrations can cause impotence in the male.

Engaging in relationships where there are psychological and sexual hang-ups regarding the body and physical expressions can cause attitudes and behaviors of withdrawal and depression. Libido disorders are affected by one's concepts of manhood. In a society that perpetuates the consumption of dead and devitalized food substances, sex and violence are the basics of a way of life. Concepts of manhood will therefore reflect the syndrome of sex and violence as defined by social norms and values. The male is then conditioned within mental programs of sexual predator attitudes, brute force, domination and disregard for being accountable for one's actions.

Within the lustful vibration of the sex-and-violence syndrome, the more urgent, aggressive and forceful the male performs the greater his excitement and satisfaction. The thrill is often heightened by engaging in acts that are considered forbidden, naughty or nasty. While the thrill is heightened, the feelings of shame or guilt add to the sexual tension. For example, when a male encounters a female, the newer his sexual conquest and the more vivid his fantasies about the unexplored abilities of his sexual partner, the more passionate and intense the male becomes. A male can therefore be very stimulated by a female during the first few weeks of their relationship and can then move to the point of little or no stimulation or impotency in short order after an extended period of aggressive behavior. As the fantasies, false presentations, and great performances wear thin, the male may develop a wandering eye for the next conquest. The male may show little or no desire or regard for the female and will quickly shun attachments or commitments once the sexual dazzle has worn off. In fact, the male's psychological perception of the female in question could actually cause a turn-off and weakening of the male's libido response.

The lost and astray mind of the male can be highly stimulated by fashion, style, and appearance while quickly sinking into a state of near impotency when the appearance begins to change. Based on the superficial appeal of physical appearance and fantasized circumstances, the male so easily reneges on his responsibilities to give divine guidance and protection to the female once he has "been there and done that." When the challenges of being responsible arise, the male is quick to justify the reasons for his rapid departure. Loss of sexual interest and loss of libido are often cited as factors in relationship decline. The sense of attraction or appeal fades away, and the thrill is gone as the object of one's affection can turn into the object of one's deepest contempt.

It is, in fact, a natural behavior in divine order for the female to be stimulated. The male, once the giver of tender and adoring Supreme Love vibrations within divine union, has actually caused a horrifying neglect and abuse of the female temple by becoming a giver of lustful abuse, misuse, and ego gratification. Female stimulation definitely brings a sacred and more receptive vibration to the union which, in fact, serves to inspire the male libido to even greater heights. Divine stimulation is an experience within the whole life energy that accentuates the reciprocation of Supreme Love vibrations between Man, He and She. The intensity of divine stimulation causes every sensation and vibration of lustful pursuit and superficial stimulation to absolutely pale by comparison.

In spite of popular notions to the contrary, when one examines the extended anatomy of the penis, it is clear that the male is the giver within the sexual encounter. When one examines the inverted anatomy of the vagina, it is clear that the female is the receiver. However, within a culture of sex and violence, the male is portrayed as the conqueror and to the victor goes the spoils. The male will then pride himself on "getting some" and "tearing it up." In truth and reality, the female opens up to receive the male and she, the female, actually gets some, i.e. semen and sperm. The male gives it up, i.e. semen and sperm, which represent the essence of his whole life energy.

Due to the mental conditioning of individuals within an oversexed society that thrives on lust, the female can put pressure on the male to perform with a "come-and-get-it" attitude. The female places demands upon the male to perform sexually based on the same mental programs that promote superficial physical encounters. As the male stalks his next prey, the female poses and postures to attract the attention of a desirable male. When the physical appearance of the female begins to change because she becomes pregnant or she is no longer that new and vibrant experience, the male's sense of sexual attraction may shift or shatter. The toxic mental programs in male-female relationships perpetuate disorder. If Man, He and She, do not understand the natural and innate behaviors of sexuality as it relates to maturity, pregnancy, and childbirth, then lust, lies, illusions, and confusion will breed massive relationship disorder.

The natural response within the male that is signaled by a female's pregnancy indicates a decrease in sexual activity but an actual increase in the male's presence of divine guidance and protection as she nurtures the emerging spirit within. It is clear within nature that there is already a birth within the womb and there is no need for further ejaculation at that time. The forward multiplication of divinity in the offspring is a strong desire and attraction for the male within divine order.

Within the culture of disorder, the female who becomes fat and frustrated may experience the complete turn-off of the male who is programmed to pursue the glamour-girl image of an artificial beauty standard. The female who finds herself impregnated by a male may find herself alone as he wanders away from his masculine responsibilities in favor of the roaming vibrations of the "love-them-and-leave-them," ice-cold, deep-freeze mentality.

The spiritual responsibility of the male is completely lost within the culture of disorder. Likewise, the spiritual dimensions of divine union are completely lost. As a result, the relationships of Man, He and She, are debased and degraded to their lowest possible level. Desirability within the culture of disorder is often limited to physical terms of appearance, money or status. The female often measures her worth by how well she holds the attention of a male based on levels and degrees of sexiness, sex appeal and sexual activity. The male measures his manhood by how many females he has deceived, conquered and abandoned in his search for the perfect fantasy lover. All of these different toxic vibrations emerge in the mind because sexuality is looked upon with lust and machismo rather than as a natural and innate function of manifesting divine union between Man, He and She. The male libido is under constant threat and attack because of the reciprocating nature of the toxic energy that the male ejaculates which comes back to him and those of his state of mind.

## Man She: Diseases and Disorders of the Sexual Organs

Vaginitis is a term used to describe any disorder that causes swelling or infection of the inner vagina area. Vulvitis is a term that is used to specifically refer to inflammation of the external vaginal area, which includes the inner and outer lips, the clitoris and the entrance to the vagina. When the natural balance of bacteria in the vagina is disturbed, it is reported that some types of bacteria die off while others multiply, causing a condition that is identified as bacterial vaginosis. Bacterial vaginosis is said to refer to a vaginal infection caused by an imbalance of bacteria. A brief survey of health references indicates that there are many different kinds of infections that result in irritation of the vagina and the area surrounding the opening to the vagina, and many of them are categorized as sexually transmitted diseases (STDs). Sexually transmitted diseases refer to diseases identified as being caused by bacteria and viruses that are usually transmitted by sexual activity with an infected person.

Cervicitis is identified as being an inflammation and irritation of the lining of the cervix. Cervicitis is most often noted as being an infection that is caused by a sexually transmitted bacteria or virus. However, in a few cases it has been noted that cervicitis may be caused by injury, exposure to chemicals, such as douches and contraceptive spermicides, or from a foreign object that is inserted into the vagina, such as a latex condom or a forgotten tampon. Common infections of the cervix are said to include Chlamydia and gonorrhea.

If left untreated, studies indicate that cervicitis may lead to pelvic inflammatory disease, infertility, spontaneous abortion, cervical cancer, ectopic pregnancy or other complications during the delivery of a baby. Ectopic pregnancy is noted as a life-threatening condition in which a fertilized egg grows outside the uterus, usually in a fallopian tube. Research findings identify increased risk factors for cervicitis that include having sexual relations at an early age, engaging in high-risk sexual behavior with many partners, or having a history of sexually transmitted diseases.

Vaginal yeast infections are one of the most common causes of vaginitis according to reports from the National Women's Health Resource Center. Most women—reportedly as many as 75 percent—are said to experience at least one vaginal yeast infection, and it is further indicated that many women will have two or more during their lifetime. A kind of fungus called Candida is said to cause vaginal yeast infections. According to research, yeast is present within the vaginal environment and normally maintains a balance with other organisms. However, when balance is lost, yeast overgrowth is noted to occur. Hormonal changes reportedly can affect the acidity of the vagina and lead to yeast overgrowth.

Semen allergy is identified as being a rare but often-misdiagnosed condition that can reportedly masquerade as a common yeast infection or herpes infection. Studies indicate that some females are allergic to proteins in semen. Although research indicates that many of the proteins associated with the semen allergy are believed to be common proteins found in all semen, it is noted as a possibility that an individual can be allergic to a protein that is unique to another individual. One wonders if the allergic reactions are actually caused by reactions to the toxins within an individual's semen.

Pelvic inflammatory disease (PID) is a general term that identifies an infection of a female's upper genital tract which includes the uterus, fallopian tubes, and ovaries. Findings indicate that bacteria can move upward, from a female's vagina or cervix into her fallopian tubes, ovaries and uterus, causing infection. Many types of bacteria can cause pelvic inflammatory disease, but bacteria found in two common sexually transmitted diseases—gonorrhea and Chlamydia—are reported to be the most frequent causes of PID. Untreated, PID is said to cause scarring, long-lasting pelvic pain, internal abscesses, which are pockets of pus that are hard to cure, and other serious consequences. PID can also reportedly cause damage to the fallopian tubes and infertility. Findings show that untreated PID is most likely the leading cause of infertility in the United States. Studies indicate that each year in the United States, more than one million females experience an episode of acute PID, with the rate of infection highest among teenagers. PID is reported to be two to three times more common in "black" females than "white" females.

According to research, fibroids are the most common form of tumors diagnosed in the female reproductive system. Fibroids are growths in the walls of the uterus. According to some estimates, "African American" females are three times more likely to be diagnosed with fibroids, and fibroids tend to be larger and occur at an earlier age in "African Americans." By their late 40s, more than 80 percent of "African American" females and nearly 70 percent of "white" females have developed benign uterine fibroid tumors, according to a study conducted by the National Institute of Environmental Health Sciences.

Clinical reports and research findings point to the fact that many fibroids contain genetic mutation in the codes for the muscle cells of the uterus. Most reports indicate that many females may have fibroids and have no noticeable symptoms depending on the size and location of the fibroid. However, it is also noted that some females with fibroids may experience mild to severe pelvic and abdominal pain, excessive and prolonged menstrual bleeding, bleeding between periods, frequent urination, lower back pain, and pain during sexual intercourse. Fibroids can cause reproductive problems such as infertility, miscarriage, and early onset of labor during pregnancy.

According to the National Center for Health Statistics, approximately 600,000 hysterectomies are performed each year, and 60% are due to uterine fibroids. A hysterectomy is the surgical removal of a female's uterus. Hysterectomies are done through a cut in the abdomen or a cut in the vagina. The National Women's Health Information Center reports that the hysterectomy is the second most common major surgery among women in the United States while the most common major surgery that women have is cesarean section delivery. Studies published in medical journals estimate that 20 to 40% of hysterectomies cannot be justified on any established criteria. Based on statistics, about one third of women in the United States have had a hysterectomy by age 60. Hysterectomies occur in 30–40% of women over age 40, and are three times more likely to be present in "African-American" females than in Caucasian females.

Endometriosis is a painful, chronic disease that affects 5½ million females and girls in the U.S. and Canada and millions more worldwide, according to the Endometriosis Association. The disease is said to occur when certain cells develop outside of their normal location inside the uterus. Findings indicate that these misplaced cells respond to the menstrual cycle in the same way as those lining the uterus, causing the tissue that grows to shed blood at the time of menstruation. However, instead of flowing out of the body through the vagina, the blood shed by the misplaced cells is said to have no way of leaving the body. Reportedly, the resulting internal bleeding can lead to chronic inflammation and the formation of scar tissue.

Areas commonly affected by endometriosis include the ovaries, fallopian tubes, the area between the vagina and rectum, the outer surface of the uterus and the lining of the pelvic cavity. Some of the adverse effects of endometriosis are noted to be infertility, repeated miscarriages, and low resistance to infection.

Cancer can arise in the female sexual and reproductive system affecting the vagina, cervix, uterus, fallopian tubes and/or ovaries. Studies indicate that in cancer the cell starts dividing haphazardly, making millions and billions of copies of itself. This process is a reproduction of mutated cells. The out-of-control cell is said to take up the nourishment needed by other cells, depriving them so the cancer can continue to grow. These quickly growing cells are said to clump up and form what is called a tumor. Research findings indicate that if the tumor is confined to a few cell layers, for example, surface cells, and it does not invade surrounding tissues or organs, it is considered benign. However, if the tumor spreads to surrounding tissues or organs, it is said to be malignant, or cancerous. When cancerous cells break away from the original tumor, travel through the blood or lymphatic vessels, and grow within other parts of the body, the process is identified as metastasis. It is this capacity for spread and invasion that is noted as making cancer so deadly and dangerous.

In the United States, cancer of the uterus is the most common cancer of the female reproductive system, according to the American Cancer Society. Research indicates that uterine cancer is the fourth most common cancer and the eighth most common cause of cancer death in women in the United States. Although uterine cancer rates are reported to be higher among "whites" than "blacks," "black" females are nearly twice as likely to die from uterine cancer as "white" females.

Only within recent years have studies appeared that indicate a growing recognition that mutations (damage or defects) to DNA can alter important genes that regulate cell growth. The American Cancer Society reports that individuals may inherit a defect in certain genes that normally help repair damage to DNA and if these repair enzymes are not working properly, damage to DNA is more likely to persist and cause cancer formation.

### *Sexually Transmitted Diseases of Man, He and She*

Sexually transmitted diseases are identified as diseases that are caused by a virus, bacteria, parasite or fungus and that are spread from person to person primarily through contact with the sexual organs. Research indicates that there are more than twenty different sexually transmitted diseases that have been identified. It is noted that sexually active teenagers, young adults and others who have multiple sex partners, i.e. promiscuous relationships, are most at risk of contracting a sexually transmitted disease.

Many sexually transmitted diseases may show no noticeable signs of a person being infected. As a result, an individual can be infected with a sexually transmitted disease and not be aware that he or she is carrying the disease. Males, especially, are noted to be capable of spreading the disease to sexual partners without showing any symptoms and without knowing that they are infected. Studies reveal that an estimated 200 to 400 million people worldwide are infected with sexually transmitted diseases. According to the U.S. Department of Health and Human Services, in the United

States more than 13 million people are newly infected each year and more than 65 million people are infected with an incurable sexually transmitted disease.

As medical science has become more focused on diagnosing infectious diseases, the list of identified sexually transmitted diseases continues to grow. As promiscuous and irresponsible sexual activity continues to spread through patterns of toxic relationships between Man, He and She, the spread of such diseases will continue to increase. Many of the symptoms of sexually transmitted diseases may not be visible or obvious during encounters of casual sex. The female receives ejaculation fluids that travel her entire reproductive tract making her both vulnerable to infection and susceptible to becoming a carrier of infection.

Research findings confirm that the greater the number of partners an individual has within sexually promiscuous relationships, the greater the risk of infection from any sexually transmitted disease. Studies indicate that because the cervix of teenage girls and young females is not fully matured, they are at particularly high risk for infection if sexually promiscuous.

Findings show that sexually transmitted diseases are a leading cause of infertility. In fact, it is noted that untreated STDs may be the leading cause of infertility among "African-American" women, because of the high rates of infection in "African American" communities. STDs like Chlamydia and gonorrhea can lead to pelvic inflammatory disease (PID), which can prevent conception by causing scarring in the fallopian tubes. Research indicates that Chlamydia, gonorrhea and PID are all much more commonly occurring in "African-American" females than in females of other populations. The Centers for Disease Control and Prevention report that the incidence of Chlamydia is nine times higher in "African-American" females than in "white" females, and 76 percent of all cases of gonorrhea occur among "black" females.

Chancroid is identified as being a highly contagious bacterial infection that both males and females can get. It is a disease said to be found primarily in developing and "Third World" countries, but cases are continuously diagnosed in the United States. Chancroid is said to spread through contact with another person's chancroid sore or ulcer during vaginal, anal, or oral sex. Chancroid is said to begin with a small bump that becomes an ulcer within a day of its appearance. Reports indicate that approximately half of the infected individuals will develop enlargement of the lymph nodes that are located in the fold between the leg and the lower abdomen. Symptoms are said to include painful ulcers, swollen lymph nodes, draining lymph nodes and abscesses which are collections of toxic matter identified as pus.

Infections due to Chlamydia are reported to be the most common bacterial sexually transmitted diseases in the U.S. today. Chlamydia is a bacterial infection that is transmitted through sexual contact with an estimated 4 to 8 million new cases occurring each year according to reports. Studies show that among adults, Chlamydia is transmitted during vaginal or anal sexual contact with an infected partner. It is noted that Chlamydia can also be passed from an infected mother to her baby during vaginal childbirth.

Chlamydia is known as a "silent" disease because reportedly about three quarters of infected women and about half of infected men have no symptoms. In women, untreated infection can reportedly spread into the uterus or fallopian tubes and cause pelvic inflammatory disease (PID). Women infected with Chlamydia are also noted to be up to five times more likely to become infected with HIV, if exposed.

Genital and anal warts are also known as venereal warts and are identified as being caused by a virus. Health experts estimate there are more cases of virus infection that causes genital warts than any other sexually transmitted disease in the United States. According to the American Social Health

Association, approximately 5.5 million new cases of sexually transmitted genital wart virus infections are reported every year. Studies indicate that as many as one in five American adults has a genital wart virus infection and that there are nearly 100 different strains of the virus. Some strains have been associated with cancers of the cervix, anus, and genital skin. Genital warts are described as being soft, moist, or flesh colored and are noted to appear in the genital area within weeks or months after infection. It is noted that if an individual is infected but has no symptoms, the virus can still be spread to sexual partners and complications from the virus can still develop.

Though genital warts can be treated, medical sources clearly state that none of the available treatments are a cure for genital warts, because the virus can remain in nearby skin after treatment. It is noted that because the virus can lie dormant in the cells, in some cases warts can return months or even years after treatment. Left untreated, genital warts can grow into skin sores, causing bleeding, pain or itching, and other complications.

Approximately 400,000 cases of gonorrhea are reported to the U.S. Center for Disease Control and Prevention each year in the United States. The most common symptoms of gonorrhea are noted to be discharge from the penis and painful or difficult urination. Gonorrhea rates are 30 times higher in “African Americans” than in “whites” according to statistics from the Center for Disease Control. Gonorrhea bacteria are said to be able to grow in the warm, moist areas of the reproductive tract, including the cervix, uterus, and fallopian tubes, and the urethra. The bacteria is also said to be able to grow in the mouth, throat, and anus.

Symptoms may include inflammation of the reproductive system, rectum, or mouth, depending on where the infection is located. In men, gonorrhea causes, a painful condition of the testicles that can lead to infertility if left untreated. Untreated gonorrhea in women can reportedly develop into pelvic inflammatory disease. If a pregnant woman has gonorrhea, it is noted that she may give the infection to her infant as the baby passes through the birth canal during delivery, and this can cause blindness, joint infection, or a life-threatening blood infection in the baby.

One of the most widespread sexually transmitted diseases is herpes, affecting both males and females. Genital herpes affects an estimated 60 million people in the United States. Approximately 500,000 new cases of this incurable viral infection are reported to develop annually. Genital herpes is said to be caused by sexually transmitted viruses called herpes simplex virus or HSV. There are reportedly two types of HSV, and both can cause genital herpes. HSV type 1 is noted as most commonly infecting the lips, causing sores known as fever blisters or cold sores, but it also can infect the genital area and produce sores. It is noted that the major symptom of herpes infection is blisters or open sores in the genital area that may be preceded by a tingling or burning sensation in the legs, buttocks, or genital region. HSV type 2 is noted as the usual cause of genital herpes, but it also can infect the mouth. Research findings indicate that as many as one out of every five people in the United States is infected with the virus that causes genital herpes, and only about 20% of those who are infected know they have it.

According to reports, people often get genital herpes by having sexual contact with others who do not know they are infected or who are having outbreaks of herpes without any sores. A person can have an outbreak and have no visible sores at all. A person with genital herpes also can reportedly infect a sexual partner during oral sex. After the virus has finished being active, it is said to then travel to the nerves at the end of the spine where it stays for a while. If a woman has her first episode of genital herpes while she is pregnant, she can reportedly pass the virus to her unborn child and may deliver a premature baby. According to reports, half of the babies infected with herpes either die or suffer from damage to their nerves. It is noted that a baby born with herpes can develop serious problems that may affect the brain, the skin, or the eyes.

Syphilis is a persistent, highly infectious STD that can have devastating consequences. It is caused by bacteria which can live almost anywhere in the body and spread rapidly. Research indicates that the rate of syphilis is 30 times higher in “African Americans” than in “Caucasians.” The Center for Disease Control reports that cases of primary and secondary syphilis in 1999 had the following race or ethnicity distribution: “African Americans” 75 percent, whites 16 percent, Hispanics eight percent, and others one percent. Syphilis reflects one of the most glaring examples of racial disparity in health status. According to reports, Syphilis is passed from person to person through direct contact with a syphilis sore. Sores are noted as occurring mainly on the external genitals, vagina, anus, or in the rectum, and can occur on the lips and in the mouth. Findings indicate that transmission of the organism occurs during vaginal, anal, or oral sex.

It is said that most people with syphilis infection have no recognizable symptoms. Many people infected with syphilis reportedly do not show any symptoms for years, yet remain at risk for late complications if they are not treated. If symptoms are experienced, they are noted to include rashes, especially on the palms of the hands and soles of the feet. Reports indicate that painless, open sores called chancres can appear on the penis, the anus, inside or outside the vagina, on the mouth or lips, or on any skin exposed during sex. The syphilis bacteria can infect the baby of a woman during her pregnancy. Depending on how long a pregnant woman has been infected, findings indicate that she may have a high risk of having a stillbirth (a baby born dead) or of giving birth to a baby who dies shortly after birth.

If left untreated, syphilis can cause blindness, brain damage, paralysis, heart disease or death. About 30–40% of infected people are reported to progress to the final stage of syphilis. The person may no longer be contagious, but the bacteria reactivate, multiply, and spread throughout the body, damaging the heart, eyes, brain, nervous system, bones, and joints. Research indicates that the damage is irreversible.

Trichomoniasis is identified as being an infection caused by a single-celled parasite called Trichomoniasis vaginalis that affects both males and females, although symptoms are said to be more common in females. The World Health Organization estimates the worldwide prevalence of trichomoniasis is 170 million, which is greater than that of gonorrhea or Chlamydia. The Center for Disease Control states that trichomoniasis is the most common curable sexually transmitted disease in young, sexually active women. Statistics from the CDC indicate that an estimated 7.4 million new cases occur each year in women and men. Incidence of trichomoniasis in the United States is said to be higher in females than males.

Studies indicate that most people with trichomoniasis do not show symptoms. According to reports, the parasite rarely causes symptoms in men, and re-infection of women by untreated partners can occur.

Trichomoniasis is said to be almost always spread through contact with an infected person during vaginal sex. Research findings indicate that unlike most sexually transmitted diseases, trichomoniasis can survive for some hours outside the body on infected objects and can be transmitted by sharing bodily fluids, contaminated bedding, damp towels and sheets, and toilet seats.

Hepatitis B is a virus that is said to cause inflammation of the liver. Hepatitis B is reported to be 100 times more infectious than HIV infection. Research indicates that chronic

Hepatitis B can cause liver cell damage, which can lead to scarring of the liver and cancer. It is estimated that 5,000 people die each year in the United States due to the complications of cirrhosis and liver cancer as a result of Hepatitis B. Approximately two-thirds of the Hepatitis B cases were noted to be transmitted through sexual contact. Hepatitis B is transmitted through direct contact with blood, semen, or vaginal secretions. According to Centers for Disease Control and Prevention, it is estimated that 1.25 million people in the United States have chronic Hepatitis B.

Research indicates that there are different types of the virus called HIV. It is noted that most individuals have HIV-1, but there are many strains or types; and a person can become infected with more than one strain. According to reports, HIV attacks the body's immune system, which is the body's natural defense system against disease, by destroying one type of blood cells that helps the body fight off and destroy germs, and eliminate disease. In the body, HIV invades these cells, makes copies of itself, and kills the healthy cells. Then the body can't fight germs anymore. When HIV takes over enough cells or causes serious infections, a person is then said to have AIDS. Research indicates that HIV is spread through some of the body's fluids: blood, semen, vaginal fluids, and breast milk. HIV is noted to pass from one person to another by having sex (vaginal, anal, or oral) with a person who has HIV; sharing needles with a drug user who has HIV; during pregnancy, birth, or breastfeeding if a mother has HIV, and getting transfusions of blood with HIV.

Findings show that “African American” and Hispanic American/Latina women make up less than one-fourth of all U.S. women, yet account for more than three-fourths (78%) of AIDS cases. HIV is the leading cause of death for “African American” women between the ages of 25 and 44. “African Americans” accounted for over half of the new HIV diagnoses reported in the United States. The Center for Disease Control reports that the leading cause of HIV infection among "African-American" men is sexual contact with other men, followed by injection drug use and heterosexual contact; the leading cause of HIV infection among "African-American women" is heterosexual contact, followed by injection drug use.[39] Reports state that sixty-two percent of children born to HIV-infected mothers were "African American."

The National Cancer Institute cited a number of health factors which expose an overall deteriorating state of "African-American" males in a culture that is based on the consumption of depleted and devitalized food substances:

> Overall, African American males have the highest cancer incidence and mortality rates, as well as the highest rates for certain cancers of any ethnic or racial group; they have the highest rates of prostate cancer and high blood pressure in the world; they are twice as likely as white men to develop diabetes; they develop diabetes and high blood pressure earlier in life than other men, and are more likely to suffer serious side-effects from these diseases; they have higher mortality rates from heart disease and obesity than other ethnic groups.[40]

Within the death consumption culture, the glaring consequences of death consumption have become such a dismal proposition that confronting toxic consumption patterns

---

[39] *HIV/AIDS Among African Americans.* Centers for Disease Control and Prevention. Online Source: http://www.cdc.gov/hiv/pubs/Facts/afam.htm.

[40] *HHS and NCI Launch National Campaign to Address Diet-Related Diseases Affecting African-American Men: Major Campaign Urges Men to Eat 9 Servings of Fruits and Vegetables a Day to Reduce Chronic Disease Risk* Press Release. National Cancer Institute. U.S. National Institutes of Health. Online Source: http://www.cancer.gov/newscenter/pressreleases/9ADay/print?page=&keyword

is inevitable. In order to address these issues of disease and disorder in a whole and complete manner, one would have to get this population of Man, He and She, to cease and desist from practicing the attitudes, behaviors, the addictions, habits and way of life that have been maintained to create this deteriorating state of being. However, changes in one's attitudes and behavior are one of the biggest challenges that one could face, because one becomes addicted to the toxic consumption patterns of the ice-cold, deep-freeze mentality. Many can not even imagine leaving the addictive and "glamorous" lifestyle of the death consumption culture. After all, within the ice-cold, deep-freeze mentality it is not about what the thing is, but rather what it looks like. It is not about the actual harm that the substance abuse causes, but rather it is about the appearance of being with the social groove or with the "in" crowd or "wild and reckless." When one is appealing for popular acceptance, it is totally forgotten that misery loves company.

The present state of strained relationships between Man, He and She, is a tragic reflection of the absence of Man He as the divine guiding and protecting presence for Man She. The imbalance in the numbers of Man He to Man She, most especially among suntanned males, is creating a desperate and despairing circumstance where Man She is unable to have her basic needs met. A situation of desperation in the mother spirit of Man, He and She, serves as a critical warning. It is clear that the predatory system that evolved from the deep-freeze experience is a mutated and degenerated system of disorder.

As one considers the system of disorder and the statistics that relate to that system of disorder, one thing is very apparent. It is very apparent that the male-female relationships and the pattern of family structure bred within the system of the ice-cold, deep-freeze mentality do not work for Man, He and She, most especially the "African American" male and female. In fact, this system of disorder cannot possibly work for anyone who is focused on the divine order of a holistic living way of life. Another thing that is very apparent is that the suntanned male, most especially the "African American," is on the brink of destruction while breeding self-destruction as a result of assimilating and maintaining the values of the death consumption culture.

In real terms, the suntanned male, most especially the "African American" male, has become an endangered species. And if that is the tragic case, what is to happen to the suntanned female, most especially the "African American" female? Is she to sit and wait and hope that a vicious system of disorder will suddenly change and that a male savior will appear to rescue her from despair and loneliness? Is she expected to make divine and holistic living change without the divine guidance and protection provided by Man He? Or is Man She of the suntanned or "African American" stock to focus on establishing a She/She relationship to substitute for the divine order of Man, He and She?

These are very serious questions that Man, He and She, must begin to divinely reason with as they are called by the universe of the Most High Essence of Life and Supreme Love. Man He is called to play a greater role in masterminding a sense of order, a sense of divine corrective action. The masculine presence is called on to deliver a greater sense of divine guidance and protection. He is called upon to come up with a divine solution to a very critical and serious problem for Man, He and She, in general and most especially for the "African American" Man, He and She, and their offspring.

# Chapter Five:
# Lust, Lies and Illusions

# Chapter Five: Lust, Lies and Illusions

### *Adverse Affects*

We have identified the depleting and dilapidated sicknesses and disease that have come about as a result of consuming, breeding and assimilating a culture of dead, devitalized and depleted physical food substance, mental food substance, and spiritual/religious food substance. In other words, we have identified the adverse effects of toxic consumption that have occurred against the divine presence of Man, He and She. In identifying the weak, depleted and fatal consequences that have arisen from this toxic consumption pattern, it has become very clear that Man, He and She have moved far away from the sacred garden culture of their origin. There is a clear indication that the suntanned Children who most reflect their original presence are suffering the most fatal and the most depleting consequences. Although the consequences are spread far and wide, the level and degree of mental, physical and spiritual mutation and degeneration that is being manifested upon the suntanned Children is actually threatening the existence of the divine, sacred and original presentation of Man, He and She. It is quite clear that this fatal tragedy would have grave consequences on the planet and would be a most devastating loss of the most precious piece in the "human" puzzle.

We are talking about the massive acceptance, support, integration, assimilation, and association with the values and the norms of a culture born and bred out of murder, rape, enslavement, steal and take. The death consumption culture holds the same toxic philosophies and values regarding sex and violence, as well as the food substances that are consumed. Clearly, we are talking about a hunting, scavenging and herding culture that historically found it very difficult to delineate between suntanned Man, He and She, and livestock. Historically the patterns of hunting, scavenging, herding, enslavement, and the domestication of Man, He and She, have been similar to the hunting, scavenging, herding, enslavement and domestication of livestock. We are referring to cultural values and norms that inspire the lost and astray among Man, He and She, to live in delusions and fantasy, hallucinations about life as they vicariously relate to each other from the stimuli of toxic programming, movie dramas, and cinematography creations that reflect the full manifestation of a culture of sex and violence and toxic consumption patterns.

The most startling point that has been brought up is that a specific group of Man, He and She, continue to suffer massive adverse effects that are totally and absolutely disproportionate to the overall population. The social economic environment has a philosophy that has declared racism to be an outlawed policy. And so it was, and so it is, and so it continues to be. It is clear that this social economic, political and religious structure was based, rooted and founded on racist ideologies and principles that inherently bred adverse effects against the very nature of the suntanned population. And so it was, and so it is, and so it continues to be. It is also clear that this genetic lineage of the suntanned Children has suffered the consequences of massive raids and attacks that originated from the Caucasus Mountain and steppe regions. And so it was, and so it is, and so it continues to be. Therefore, for well over 6,000 years the sacred garden culture has been under siege and attack, murder, rape, and theft leaving a bloodstained track. And so it was, and so it is, and so it continues to be.

When we look into more modern times, it becomes very revealing that when the Arab/Muslim jihads were launched against the sacred garden culture, severe damage had already been inflicted by other invading forces of the ice-cold, deep-freeze mentality. And so it was, and so it is, and so it continues to be. What the Arab/Muslims did was to add severe gashing blows to a wound desperately trying to heal. Thus, the continuous sieges and attacks from the cold-blooded and vicious jihad warlords and their disciples and followers drastically weakened the infra-structures of the sacred garden culture. The glory of the sacred garden culture and the divinity of the original Man, He and She, would fall to the point of basic collapse. And so it was, and so it is, and so it continues to be.

Upon and after this basic collapse, the cold-blooded mentality of the Islamic jihads would replace a once glorious infra-structure with its own social religious order. And so it was, and so it is, and so it continues to be. These vicious, violent raids of social economic opportunists dressed in the doctrines of religious order had indeed struck a blow of fatality to the sacred garden culture. In fact, these Arab/Muslims were simply a reflection of the mentality that descended from the Caucasus Mountain and steppe regions. And so it was, and so it is and so it continues to be.

With vicious odds working against them, the last vestiges of the Divine Children of the Sun with the golden tan would be shattered and scattered in the trans-Atlantic slave trade. From the onset, the vicious and cold-blooded mentality that descended from the ice-cold, deep-freeze would not be able to reason with divine spirit consciousness. As a result, the lost and astray Children who lost their tan could not reason with the sacred and glorious presence of the suntanned Children. Why then would the suntanned Children feel that these murderous raping and enslaving Christian invaders who orchestrated the Trans-Atlantic slave trade were any different? They would simply be another pack of the same gang with a different name, playing the same game with a different picture frame.

If only the suntanned Children could have known and comprehended the deadly behavior patterns of Christopher Columbus against the Taino population...If only the suntanned Children could have comprehended the Portuguese invasions of Angola, the Congo, etc.…If only the suntanned Children could have comprehended the methodologies of the Pope and other leaders of the Christian order...If only the suntanned Children could have comprehended King James and the strategies behind his version…If only the suntanned Children could have comprehended the plots and schemes of colonialism…If only the suntanned Children could have comprehended the plots of Reconstruction…If only the suntanned Children could have comprehended COINTELPRO…If only the suntanned Children could comprehend the nature of the ice-cold, deep-freeze mentality before it is too late.

The suntanned Children would be at a crossroads, facing a plague that descends from the historic raids of murder, rape and theft with no options in the death consumption culture. However, there would be those who would see an option and who would begin to live out that option on a daily basis. The primary option taken by the mass majority of the suntanned Children would be to integrate and assimilate into the death consumption culture by adopting the ice-cold, deep-freeze mentality. This would however intensify the problem and make the matters worse due to the laws of competition in the ice-cold, deep-freeze mentality.

It would somehow be forgotten that the basic law of the ice-cold, deep-freeze mentality is survival of the fittest. It would somehow be forgotten that competition is somehow equated to war and that war is competition. The second basic law of the ice-cold, deep-freeze mentality is that all is fair in love and war. The principle of every basic law within the ice-cold, deep-freeze mentality would be based on lust, lies, illusions, confusion, death and deadly destruction. Therefore, every problem within the ice-cold, deep-freeze mentality would be geared towards treating the symptoms of the problem, rather than seeking to heal from the problem.

It then stands to reason that the energy that fuels the ice-cold, deep-freeze mentality is in fact the energy that is opposite of Supreme Love. Divine solutions would therefore be impossible to reason with within the ice-cold, deep-freeze mentality. Divine spirit consciousness would be necessary to implement a plan of sexual healing, and divine spirit consciousness would not be possible within the death consumption culture that feeds the ice-cold, deep-freeze mentality. And so it was, and so it is, and so it continues to be. The suntanned population would be in a hex of a fix, facing massive physical disease, a fatal dose of mental disorder, spiritual disorder, and massive incarceration. The age old question that was, that is, and that continues to be echoes a vibration: "How do we handle the 'Negro' problem?" We will look back into history and see how a founding father of the United States responded to this question as it was, as it is, and as it continues to be. Thomas Jefferson stated that:

> Deep rooted prejudices entertained by the whites; ten thousand recollections, by the blacks, of the injuries they have sustained; new provocations; the real distinctions which nature has made; and many other circumstances, will divide us into parties, and produce convulsions which will probably never end but in the extermination of the one or the other race.[41]

## Enslavement

Out of the rubble and despair of bloodbaths, rage and rape that followed the Arab Muslim takeover of Egypt, the Trans-Saharan slave trade would be born. This would be the dominant slave trade, providing the supply for the demand of that time. The Trans-Saharan slave trade preceded the Trans-Atlantic slave trade. What would come to be known as the

---

[41] *Notes on the State of Virginia.* Query 14: Laws. Thomas Jefferson, 1781. pp. 264-270. Online Source: http://etext.lib.virginia.edu/toc/modeng/public/JefVirg.html.

Trans-Atlantic slave trade was officially anointed in 1452 when Pope Nicholas V issued *Dum Diversas,* a bull, i.e. major papal decree, authorizing the Portuguese to reduce any non-Christians to the status of slaves. In 1455, Pope Nicholas V issued *Romanus Pontifex*, a bull, i.e. major papal decree, granting the Portuguese a perpetual monopoly in trade with Afrika. Studies reveal that in 1493, Pope Alexander VI issued the *Inter Caetera* proclamation, which created a line that divided territories in the Americas and Caribbean between the Catholic powers of Spain and Portugal. It is noted that everything to the west, which included most of the Americas, was "handed over" to Spain, and everything to the east, Brazil and all of Afrika, to Portugal. Since they were trading basically the same people, i.e. the Children of the Sun with the golden tan, this agreement was seen to be fair and just in the eyes of the Christian god.

Therefore, those who were already in the trade and experts on the ordeal of slavery, i.e. the Arab Muslims, would now have a trading partner of skin in the trade of the suntanned Children of kin. And so, as a basically collapsed sacred garden culture was traded over to the financial partners of the Christian culture, a new era of Trans-Atlantic slave trade would be installed. Make no mistake about it, the Trans Atlantic slave trade was a lucrative business deal. The founding fathers of this business deal had simply completed collective bargaining with the keepers of the Trans-Saharan slave trade. Just for the record this particular collective bargaining had been initiated during the earliest invasions of Egypt, when in 641 A.D. Cyrus, the Roman Christian Patriarch of Alexandria, signed a treaty with Arab Muslims giving them control of Egypt in return for tributes. Therefore, two invader forces came together to make an agreement on the ancestral land of the suntanned Children when the land was not theirs to give or receive. The vicious attack on the Nubian Empire by the Christian invaders as well as the Muslim invaders is still manifesting activities of conflict and confusion today in the Sudan, the land of the ancient Nubian Empire. Thus continues the great divide that is still being pursued at the cost of the Nubian population in the Sudan and elsewhere.

Let us make it very clear here the point that the I in I am bringing forward. In no uncertain terms, both the Arab Muslim, i.e. Islam, and the Roman Catholics, i.e. Christians are born off of the same invader father vibration represented by Judaism. In no uncertain terms, those who call themselves Semitic and Aryan in modern times are the descendants of the ice-cold, deep-freeze mentality. In no uncertain terms, this ice-cold, deep-freeze mentality has spread like a plague and has many disciples and followers, regardless of them being blonde or bald or natty, natty dread. When one reasons in search of divine clarity, one must ask, "Where did this most fatal, toxic and devastating mentality emerge from?" As the I in I have stated throughout this text, this vibration emerged from the ice-cold, deep-freeze. Let us take a few moments and reason with details of the emergence of this ice-cold, deep-freeze mentality. Let us trace the roots and foundation of the cold-blooded, vicious and cruel energy that is opposite of Supreme Love.

### *Tracing the Roots of the Ice-Cold, Deep-Freeze Mentality*

Philosophies of deception run rampant within the ice-cold, deep-freeze mentality. It should be crystal clear here that all of Man, He and She, originally descended from the sacred garden culture presence of the Divine Children of the Sun with the golden tan. We must understand that there has been a very gruesome, hostile, toxic, negative and depleted path of blood trails that has manifested from the ice-cold, deep-freeze mentality of the death consumption culture. It is quite clear that the lost and astray Children who lost their tan represent a reversal in the evolutionary process of Man, He and She, due to mutation and degeneration.

This reversal is best comprehended by realizing this fact: a person is the sum total of all that he or she consumes, mentally, physically and spiritually. Therefore, in order for one to mutate to the complete opposite of one's original presence, it stands to reason that one would have to consume of an energy completely opposite of one's original consumption patterns. Consuming this opposite energy would create opposite attitudes, behaviors and values. Therefore, the origin of Man, He and She, within the divine presence of a sacred garden culture would be reversed to an opposite condition and state of being, reflecting consumption patterns that are opposite. Instead of the raw and living fruits, vegetables, seeds and nuts that grow from the harmony of earth, wind, rain and sun, one would begin to consume of self, i.e. one would begin to consume of flesh and bones of blood and skin. Not only would this opposite consumption reverse the thought processes, it would reverse the chromosomes and every cell in the body as well as causing mutation and degeneration in the DNA.

The end result of this mutation and degeneration would be completely opposite of one's original and divine presence. This opposite state of being would automatically cause a severe deprivation in self-esteem and severe deficiencies in one's mental, physical and spiritual self. The opposite energy would then be defined as the energy that is opposite of Supreme Love. Over time this mental, physical and spiritual deprivation would create values, attitudes and behaviors that would reflect the mentality of the depleting environmental factors. The lost and astray Children who lost their tan mutated and degenerated in an ice-cold, deep-freeze environment. As a result, the values, attitudes, and behaviors of these individuals reflect an ice-cold, deep-freeze mentality.

The reversal occurred due to hardship, deprivation, and malnutrition in one of the most barren and bleak kind of environmental situations that Man, He and She, has had to endure. The mere fact that Man, He and She, survived such an ordeal is a credit to the tenacity of the life presence and reflects the ability to make drastic changes for the sake of survival. It is self-evident that once one has survived, it is not only necessary, but it is absolutely essential, to make drastic changes to correct the mutation and degeneration suffered in the ice-cold, deep-freeze mentality. However, if one becomes steeped in denial and massive deception that targets scapegoats, one will simply continue an even more fatal stage of mutation and degeneration.

Worst of all, those individuals with the ice-cold, deep-freeze mentality would seek to spread this deteriorating disease to everyone whom they encountered and would hold their values of being a superior culture to be self-evident. It is absolutely amazing that one would have the ability to declare massive mutation and degeneration as superior unless one is referring to a superior state of corruption and insanity personified. As a matter of fact, the harsh and cruel conditions of the cave caused Man, He and She, to revert to a scavenger and predator state of being. The conditions of the ice-cold, deep-freeze experience were a catastrophe in every sense of the word.

The ice-cold, deep-freeze experience was not within the divine order of Man, He and She, and the results speak for themselves. The offspring who survived in the caves became dead-flesh-consuming scavengers and predators. There is no time left to glorify in the toxic and depleted consumption patterns that created such a cold-blooded, cruel and callous mentality. Deception created a way of life of lust, lies, illusions, confusion, death and deadly destruction; a way of life that has been earmarked by murder, rape, steal and take; a way of life where the master gardeners became master predators.

Within the ice-cold, deep-freeze experience, the keepers of holistic living truth would degenerate into masters and grand masters of deception. One who began by holding all things dear within the earth, wind, rain and sun relationship would degenerate into one who is in constant conflict and opposition with nature and every living thing. As a result, one who began by honoring the supreme presence of life would degenerate into one who honors and glorifies slaughter and death. Man, He and She, must become consciously aware of the insidious attitudes and behaviors of the ice-cold, deep-freeze mentality. There is no advancement in a social order that perpetuates the savagery of slaughter, except the advancement of inhumanity and bloody atrocities. There is no brilliance in the cold-blooded acts of violence that define the war culture of the mutated and degenerated breed. There is no intelligence in a culture that perpetuates syndromes of war, vengeance, greed and blood sacrifice, except the depleted intelligence of a degenerated way of life. It must clearly be comprehended that gross madness, insanity, and vicious, cruel violation have befallen Man, He and She, ever since the ice-cold mutation and degeneration occurred.

One may give the rebuttal that for all of its depravity and deprivation, the death consumption culture appears to have overtaken the sacred garden culture. However, if one begins to take notice of the destruction and self-destruction that is part and parcel of the ice-cold, deep-freeze mentality, one will better understand the cycle of time that Man, He and She, is now upon. A culture that originated in the vibrations and sensations of lust, lies, illusions, confusion, death and deadly destruction will multiply those vibrations to their logical conclusion.

On the other hand, a culture that originated in the vibrations and sensations of Supreme Love and the whole life energy will multiply those vibrations from the Most Supreme Unseen to the Most Supreme Seen. In other words, slaughter and death represent a concluding energy that curses life. Equally, honoring life as the Supreme Seen presence divinely connected to the Most Supreme Unseen presence represents an everlasting emergence process from the seed to the root to the fruit to the seed. The sacred spirit of the Divine Children of the Sun has never been extinguished.

There is no way one can maintain the toxic deceptions of the ice-cold, deep-freeze mentality and the accompanying vibrations of "white" supremacy without receiving the due consequences of the toxic consumption. It is quite clear that these types of expressions and ideas are nothing more than a reflection of a cold-blooded, cruel and callous energy, i.e. the energy that is opposite of Supreme Love. The toxic reasoning of the ice-cold, deep-freeze mentality has perpetuated social, economic and religious orders of massive deception; social economic and religious orders of cold-blooded, brutal murder. The gods of war, jealousy, vengeance, greed and spite are the projections of individuals who sank into the toxic waste of their own struggles within the ice-cold, deep-freeze experience. The god mythologies of the mutated and degenerated breed represent their state of disconnection and alienation from the divine order of the sacred garden culture.

There is no glory in the fantasies, illusions and deceptions of the lost and astray mind clouded by the whiteness of ice and snow that freezes one into a numb state of being. The lost and astray mind cowered in the shadows of chilling caves during desperate and desolate generations of breeding the ice-cold, deep-freeze mentality. All that was born in the ice and the snow was a cold-blooded indifference to the pain and suffering of one's prey as slaughtering to survive became the ways and the means of the death consumption culture.

One must come to comprehend that nothing short of reemerging into the sacred garden culture, nothing short of re-aligning with the Supreme Love spirit of the Most High Essence of Life, nothing short of honoring one's holistic living presence can repair the damage of indulging in the vibrations and sensations of the ice-cold, deep-freeze mentality. The first presence of Man, He and She, i.e. the Divine Children of the Sun with the golden tan, represented all that was essential in the attainment of a most high state of being. Anything short of honoring that sacred model can only lead to further deprivation, further deterioration and further levels and degrees of insanity. It must be comprehended that the ice-cold, deep-freeze mentality is the death consumption culture and that the death consumption culture is the energy that is the opposite of Supreme Love.

One is a sum total of all that one consumes, mentally, physically and spiritually, and one can be no more than that energy which one consumes. When one consumes of the energy that is opposite of Supreme Love, one is multiplying lust, lies, illusions, confusion, death and deadly destruction. One must cease and desist from consuming of the death consumption culture. One must cease and desist from consuming of the ice-cold, deep-freeze mentality. There must be a massive purging of the mental, physical and spiritual self, regardless of one being blonde or bald or natty, natty dread. Regardless of the level and degree of the mutation and degeneration that one has suffered, one must come to comprehend and honor the Most Supreme Spiritual Essence of Life. One must come to comprehend the most supreme spiritual presence of the glorious mother and father spirit of the Divine Children of the Sun with the golden tan.

On a daily basis, the mass majority of Man, He and She, continue to honor the cold-blooded, cruel, callous and deceptive vibrations that originated in the Ice Age devastation. It is quite clear that those lost and astray Children who were caught and entrapped in the cold-blooded vibration of the cave-dwelling days found themselves battling for life both day and night, especially with the previous occupants of those caves, i.e. the cave bears. When one begins with the caves as the origin of Man, He and She, one is actually reversing the whole life presence of Man, He and She, into a decadent, dead and devitalized conceptual existence. One must understand that the individuals who glorify in the mutations and degeneration are suffering from post-traumatic stress syndromes of the ice-cold, deep-freeze mentality due to generations and generations of toxic consumption. The invading father of the ice-cold, deep-freeze mentality has ejaculated the toxins of the energy that is opposite of Supreme Love into any presence encountered, be it male or female, man or animal.

**Life in the Caves**

It has been stated that the cave man, as the origin of the "white" man, spent 95% of his time in the caves during the deep freeze periods. It is clear that the cave dwellers were not spending their time studying the dynamic relationship of earth, wind, rain and sun within the natural life cycle or learning about the healing qualities of fresh herbs within the garden. The lost and astray Children who lost their tan were deteriorating to the level of a mentality that reflected constant fright, fear, deprivation, hunger and freezing cold. As a result, the lost and astray Children who lost their tan had no culture of value to offer the sacred garden culture. The consumption of slaughtered animals and the vile practices of murder, rape, steal and take were all that the nomadic populations carried with them when they departed the caves.

It should be quite clear that the lost and astray Children who lost their tan were crouching inside those cold echoing caves doing everything they could do to survive. The mutated and degenerated breed ate of the dead whether one dropped dead or whether it got to a point where someone or something targeted as weaker was killed to be eaten. Malnutrition caused severe deficiencies in the brain. The life-threatening conditions of fighting for basic survival day to day caused severe mental disturbance and disorders. Long periods without sunshine in the gloomy and dim caves caused imbalances in the natural body rhythms. Whatever remained of an intellectual reasoning process deteriorated into toxic emotional reactions. The maturity, wisdom, and stability of the sacred garden culture were replaced by the insensitive, selfish, and brutish attitudes and behaviors of the death consumption culture.

There would be a tremendous and urgent struggle for warmth; there would be a tremendous and urgent struggle for power and control; there would be a tremendous and urgent struggle to just make it through one more day. It does not require complex reasoning to comprehend the nature of the environment where the lost and astray Children lost their tan. The context of the loss resulted in a devastating setback in the mental, physical and spiritual development of Man, He and She. The prolonged exposure to ice and snow caused severe damage. Man, He and She, lost connection with self-dignity, self-respect, and self-esteem in the ice cold caves. Man, He and She, lowered themselves to the consumption of foul and putrefying flesh, be it human or animal. As a result, these mutated and degenerated children would breed foul and putrefying thoughts and behaviors against both man and animal, and every living thing.

We must have compassion for the plight of the lost and astray Children who lost their tan, but this compassion should not extend beyond another moment. For it is quite clear that the toxic reactions of the mutated and degenerated breed have violated and degraded the whole life presence of Man, He and She. The vicious, cold-blooded and cruel Children who lost their tan became bloodthirsty predators and vicious nomads who learned to glorify in their toxic behaviors.

The lost and astray Children who lost their tan deteriorated into hunters and herders in the perpetuation of the death consumption culture. It should be clear that what one can inflict upon an animal, one will find within reason to inflict upon another human being, because one is using the same reasoning of violation and violence. Within the ideology of the survival of the fittest remember that all is fair in love and war, and anything goes to satisfy one's own personal I-me-my syndrome of selfish greed.

Let us review the populations that occupied the northern regions of the planet prior to the last major Ice Age. Offshoots of the sacred and original family of man who were descendants of the sacred garden culture have been archaeologically traced on a migration from their southern homeland, what is now called Afrika. The physical traits of these original populations reflect the melaninated relationship with the sun. DNA tracking indicates that there have been population movements around the planet that originated from out of Afrika occurring over a wide span of time.

The suntanned populations traveled by land and by sea to the northern areas of the planet, including what is now called Europe, inclusive of France, Britain, Germany, Scandinavia, Switzerland, Central Europe, Bulgaria, etc. It is difficult for a mind that has been entrenched within the ice-cold, deep-freeze mentality to fathom that the earth was populated by the Afrikoid suntanned populations as the original and divine presence of Man, He and She. It is also difficult for those of the ice-cold, deep-freeze mentality to realize and comprehend that the sacred garden culture is the original and divine way of life of Man, He and She.

The most ancient movements of the suntanned populations will herein be identified as Kwasunic tribes that reflected the sacred garden culture and a holistic living way of life. The various scientific labels and names that have been assigned within the death consumption culture do not reflect the vibration and divine presence of these original Children of the Sun with the golden tan. The assumption of the ice-cold, deep-freeze mentality is that the death consumption culture is the first way of life of Man, He and She. The assumptions of the ice-cold, deep-freeze mentality are in error.

## Ancient Movements of the Kwasunic Tribes

The movements of the Kwasunic tribes radiated out from the continent of Afrika, spreading the seeds of the sacred family of Man, He and She, i.e. the suntanned Children. Again, we must note that the Divine Children of the Sun with the golden tan were not only dispersed throughout Europe; they populated the entire planet. The presence of the sacred spirit of Man, He and She, is beyond the chronology of the lost and astray mind. Reports reveal that a human skull was discovered in 2001 at Dmanisi in the Republic of Georgia and the estimated age is said to be 1.8 million years old. The fossils suggest that early humans moved out of Afrika hundreds of thousands of years earlier than previously thought by many archaeologists, historians and researchers. The age and skeletal characteristics of the Dmanisi skulls link them to the early humans who lived in East Afrika during the same time period. It is also noted that a complete skull found in Kenya, dated at 3.5 million years old, is believed to represent a newly discovered early human. An article in a 2002 issue of the journal *Nature*, announced the discovery of a 7-6 million year old hominid skull in the Djurab Desert of Chad, Central Afrika. This is reported to be oldest-yet discovered hominid fossil. These fossil findings are added to the unquestionable evidence that was signified by the 1974 discovery of the 3.2 million year old skeletal remains of Queen Mother Zebeka in Ethiopia, archaeologically identified as Lucy.

Successive waves of movement out of Afrika resulted in the suntanned populations of the Kwasunic tribes establishing an ancient presence upon the planet that has been lost and forgotten by the ice-cold, deep-freeze mentality. The faintest whisper may still be heard in the folk myths and lore of a garden paradise. Periods of glaciation or freezing cold in the northern regions of the planet created an environment where Man, He and She, would be forced to either retreat or succumb to the harsh and barren conditions. The encounters within the various Ice Age cycles would isolate populations inside the freezing zones, and mutation would occur based on temperature, environmental conditions, consumption patterns, and sun exposure. Many of these suntanned populations would begin to mutate in the ice-cold northern regions, many survived for periods of time before becoming extinct, leaving behind fossil remains as evidence of their existence upon the planet. It is, in fact, only because of the ice-cold, deep-freeze that occurred within the northern regions of the planet during the most recent Ice Age that there even exists a new breed of Man, He and She identified as the Caucasian, i.e. the "white" man.

Research indicates that human skulls have been found that belong to a particular tribe of Kwasunic people who traveled from the original birthplace of Man, He and She, i.e. the sun-filled regions now called Afrika, to enter the northern regions of Europe about 60,000 to 50,000 years ago. Findings show that these suntanned "Negroids" were the presence of modern Man, He and She, at a time when earlier populations of mutated breeds still existed in northern regions of the planet. Various names have been assigned to this population by archaeologists who uncovered the remains. All that can be projected by the ice-cold, deep-freeze mentality is another version of the death consumption culture.

These Kwasunic people, archaeologically identified as the Grimaldi Negro carried with them a distinct language, art and tools. By identifying stone implements, carvings, figurines, utensils, and fossils, it is clear that this population of suntanned Children was widely dispersed throughout Europe as recently as 50,000 years ago. Some of the more significant sites have revealed the presence of distinctive "Negroid" black goddess figurines. Research indicates that in ancient cultures upon the planet even in what is referred to as "Old Europe" black was the color of fertility and abundance, like the rich black soil of the Nile and other river valleys. It is noted that white on the other hand was the color symbolic of death.

Research indicates that Venus figurines that depict the feminine presence have been found throughout Europe, from western France, to western Russia. The age of the Venus figurines covers a time span from 27,000 years ago, to 20,000 years ago. The mother goddess figures, sometimes called Venus figurines, have been found carved in stone, ivory and wood, and also crafted of clay. The most famous Venus figurine, the "Venus of Willendorf," was found in an area of Willendorf, Austria. However, the Venus of Willendorf is only one small portion of the diversity of all the figurines found through out Europe. These figurines are important to clearly indicate the Afro-centric populations that occupied Europe prior to the mutation and degeneration era. It should also be clearly indicated that those children who were stuck in the frozen glaciatic ice of the deep freeze had not been released from the ice cold caves that imprisoned them. These figurines and findings indicate clearly who were the original mothers and fathers of those children who mutated and degenerated in the deep freeze.

The main point of bringing these figurines in is that there must have been a horrifying occurrence that would cause Man, He and She, to lose focus on the honor of the divine union of the father and mother spirit to reverse to the point where they would uphold a male god figure. It is very difficult to comprehend how the mother spirit, i.e. the sacred feminine presence could have been down graded so low when she is, in fact, the key to the multiplication of life. What this means is that the children who mutated and degenerated actually degenerated into worshippers of the dead instead of worshippers of life. This is demonstrated by the fact that he who had the swiftest ability to kill would be exalted to the status of a god. Amazingly, from the time of the mutation up until the present, the feminine presence of the Children of the Sun who lost their tan has held the position of inferior, weak, and feeble. The feminine presence within the ice-cold, deep-freeze mentality would no longer hold the position of honored mother spirit as she was originally created.

This same cold-blooded mentality, i.e. the ice-cold, deep-freeze mentality has indeed spread throughout the planet and has reduced the feminine presence to her lowest term. Until the mother spirit has been exonerated to the level, degree and status that she held within the ranks of the Divine Children of the Sun with the golden tan, the planet will continue forward into doom and gloom. When we think about the divine resurrection of the sacred feminine presence we must focus on the resurrection of the sacred origin of Man, He and She, i.e. the mother spirit of the Divine Children of the Sun with the golden tan. The Black Goddess or Black Venus, as she has been called, i.e. the suntanned feminine presence, is the key to divinity, the key to the resurrection of divinity. It must be comprehended that Mother Earth is the birthplace of the raw and living energy manifested by her divine relationship with the sun.

It is not surprising that the ice-cold, deep-freeze mentality would interpret the "black" goddess figurines as representing "a bisexual, self-fertilizing woman" which would equate to their image of a male war god who had no feminine mate. The divine union of the sacred father spirit and sacred mother spirit has been completely forgotten within the ice-cold, deep-freeze mentality. Likewise, the ice-cold, deep-freeze mentality is unable to reflect or manifest anything but the horrors of the Ice Age mutation and degeneration as the social environment. Simply look at the death consumption culture and one will see the origins of mutation and degeneration played out as a modern way of life.

Evidence shows that prior to the most recent Ice Age the other populations of the Kwasunic tribes mutated in Ice Age cycles, and remained relatively isolated in the northern regions of the planet. Names have been given to these mutated and degenerated descendants. One name that has been given is the Neanderthal who is said to have existed somewhere between 200,000 to 30,000 years ago. The Neanderthal man represents the emergence of the mutated and degenerated breed who adapted to survive in the cold and harsh environment that was widespread throughout the northern regions of the planet. This mutated and degenerated population lived through and adapted to the most violent extremes in climate that Man, He and She, has been able to survive. Research indicates that the remains of one breed of the mutated and degenerated populations were discovered in Duesseldorf, Germany in the Neander Valley in 1856.

The mutations have been identified by scientific laws of eco-geographic adaptation, i.e. changes that occur based on environmental conditions. For example, the physical traits of those who dwell in an extremely cold environment over a period of time are distinguishable from those who inhabit a warm and sunny environment. The physical adaptations to extreme cold are noted to be a higher body volume which would indicate a thick and stocky build; this compact physical form is noted to help the body conserve heat better. The genetic traits for the ice-cold, deep-freeze mutation include shorter extremities such as short limbs and short fingers that have less surface area to keep warm; broad chests, stocky and thick build. Research indicates that physical adaptations for extreme cold favor short round compact body types. Those who have mutated traits for cold climate adaptation are noted to have narrow nostrils and longer nasal passages. Long and narrow nasal passages would allow one to warm and humidify the cold, dry air of Ice Age Europe before it reached the throat and lungs. It is also noted that pale skin is less susceptible to cold injury.

Findings show that the average height of the mutated population that has been identified as Neanderthal was about 5 feet. It is noted that the body type of these cave dwellers were most likely thick and stocky with thick legs. Findings show that Neanderthals had low brow ridges, and their front teeth were larger than modern humans. Research indicates that Neanderthal characteristics were adaptations to the cold, dry climate during the Ice Ages in what is now Europe. It is noteworthy that for all the focus on brain size, and cranial capacity as a sign of intelligence the cave-dweller population called the Neanderthal had an average brain size which was reportedly larger than the brain of the modern human.

The original presence of Man, He and She, which migrated from Afrika represented physical traits that reflected a warm solarized environment. It is noted that dark pigments increase in species that live in warm and sunny environments. It is also noted that when a species inhabits a warm environment there is usually a lower body mass, meaning there is less bulk or thickness, and the body type can be described as having a longer and leaner physical appearance.

Much of the European land mass would resemble a tundra environment during the Ice Age. A tundra is defined as an extremely cold environment. Research indicates that tundra winters are long, dark, and cold, with average temperatures below freezing for six to ten months of the year. It is noted that the temperatures are so cold that there is a layer of permanently frozen ground below the surface, called permafrost. Vegetation in the tundra is adapted to the cold and has a short growing season. Mosses, sedges, and lichens are noted to be common, while few trees grow in the tundra. The shortage of vegetation in the frozen regions during the Ice Age would mean that populations would make a drastic change in their consumption patterns. The sacred garden culture would have no place in the ice-cold, deep-freeze experience. When one begins to reason with the entire way of life that was lost in the bitter and extreme cold of the northern European regions, one can begin to sense the tremendous deprivation of the death consumption culture.

## Caveman Consumption

The ice-cold, deep-freeze mentality was born in the throes of malnutrition. Every possible state of lack and deficiency that could be imagined was experienced outside of the sacred garden culture. As a result, the lost and astray Children who lost their tan have an immense and gnawing mental base of insecurity, powerlessness and fear. Thus, it becomes easier to recognize the toxic reactions of violence, domination and enslavement as the festering symptoms of a deeply impoverished and depleted state of being. However, since the lost and astray Children who lost their tan have raped, slaughtered, stolen and deceived their way into a power base of social economic, political and religious control, the most impoverished and depleted mentality to emerge upon the planet, i.e. the ice-cold, deep-freeze mentality, is upheld as superior.

Archaeological findings at the cave site of Moula-Guercy in southeastern France since 1991 have uncovered evidence that, not only did the mutated and degenerated breed called the Neanderthals survive by eating dead animal flesh; the Neanderthals were also cannibals. Findings show that the remains of deer bones and human bones at Moula-Guercy had the same kind of cut and slice marks in a butchering pattern. Findings indicate that a group of Neanderthals removed the flesh of at least six individuals before breaking their bones apart with a hammer and anvil to remove the marrow and brains. The archaeologists stated:

> We interpret these data to indicate that the hominid and deer carcasses were butchered in a similar way, with the objective being the removal of soft tissues and marrow. An inference of cannibalism is therefore warranted for Moula-Guercy level XV. We find no evidence that modifications to the hominid or deer bones from Moula-Guercy represent any form of mortuary ritual for either species.[42]

The mutation of Man, He and She, from a garden dweller to the deteriorated state of cave dweller was a humiliating process of degeneration and toxic consumption. In addition to

---

[42] *Neanderthal Cannibalism at Moula-Guercy, Ardèche, Franc.* Online Source: http://cas.bellarmine.edu/tietjen/Human%20Nature%20S%201999/neanderthal_cannibalism_at_moula.htm

grave malnutrition and toxic consumption, the cave dwellers also had to contend with the first inhabitants of the ice cold caves. Research indicates that the cave bears, Ursus spelaeus and their cousins Ursus deningeri, were fierce, 20-foot long versions of Grizzly bears with huge teeth and razor sharp claws. Findings show that until Neanderthals appeared on the scene in Europe and the Mid-East, these giant beasts infested the caves from sea level to altitudes near 10,000 feet. The evidence suggests that the cave dwellers did not simply use caves for occasional shelter, but inhabited them continuously, or at least seasonally, for millennia. Studies reveal that cave bears inhabited caves in Europe from about 300,000 to 15,000 B.C., disappearing by the end of the last ice age.

Violence was an ongoing experience within the ice cold caves amid freezing temperatures. Defending against large hungry animals on the prowl was a constant battle to secure one's shelter. The ability to swiftly kill secured one a space to sleep at night and a meal to eat. The violence directed in self-defense to protect oneself from an attacking animal became the same violence directed in attack against man and animal perceived as a threat or a possible prey. The violence and bloodshed grew to include Man, He and She, against Man, He and She, where it had once been unknown and unthinkable to commit such atrocious acts.

The mutated and degenerated tribes of the ice-cold, deep-freeze all are common descendants of the dead-flesh-eating cave-dwellers who emerged with the hunter, scavenger, herder way of life. It should be noted that caves lack natural light, and therefore support species which are adapted to living in the dark. The populations who degenerated and mutated in the ice-cold, deep-freeze are noted to have decreased pigmentation, consumption patterns that are based on dead flesh and fluids of the dead, solar deprivation and an adaptation to the dark. The more one is deprived of sunshine the more pallid and destitute of color one becomes. Such a pale appearance has been described as corpse-like.

The environment of the Ice Age caves would be a breeding ground of pollution and contamination. The cave-dwellers would wallow in the stench and filth of human waste, the smoke and soot of burning fires, the odors of dirty bodies covered in decayed animal skins, and the infestation of parasites, bacteria, fungus and virus. The mere fact that these lost and astray Children survived this experience is a testament to the most sacred original and divine presence of Man, He and She.

For a very long time, the deceptions, misinformation and errors of the Caucasian breed of man have projected the Caucasian as the superior stock of man. There has been a desperate attempt to keep the errors of Caucasian reasoning as secret and unknown as possible. Numerous ruins throughout the planet, artifacts and fossils show clearly and beyond a shadow of a doubt that all of mankind descended from the sacred presence of Man, He and She, i.e. the Divine Children of the Sun with the golden tan a.k.a. "Negroid/Afrikoid." It is also self-evident that the Divine Children of the Sun with the golden tan ascended from the sacred garden culture which is completely opposite from the deception that man descended from a hunting, scavenging, and herding culture.

Research indicates that there have been many dramatic climate changes over the last 100,000 years upon the planet Earth which would have caused major changes in the populations of affected areas based on the availability of food and shelter. The last major Ice Age is noted to have peaked in severity 20,000 years ago and ended around 10,000 years ago. It has been noted that the mutation that resulted in the lost and astray Children of the Sun who lost their tan, i.e. the "white" man occurred somewhere during this last Ice Age period. The emergence of the mutated and degenerated breed of the ice-cold, deep-freeze reflects a recent and tragic disruption in the history of Man, He and She. Let us look at some of the modern experiences that have occurred in frigid climates with depleted food supplies. These examples should give one an idea about what happened during the more severe conditions of cold and food depletion during and after the last Ice Age.

As we have moved into a time presence, there have been many fantastic tales, or should I say fantastic deceptions about the great and mighty warlords of civilization. Hitler and others have talked much about the brilliant intelligence of the Aryan stock. It has even been inferred that this breed and stock of man is unquestionably the highest point of evolution and superiority of mankind. When one glorifies in a war culture, it is most likely that murder, rape, steal, take and the swift ability to kill will define superiority. What we shall do is look at the breeds that were born of the ice-cold, deep-freeze mentality. We will define the glorious culture that has been identified as superior, i.e. the death consumption culture.

### *Tracing the Blood-Stained Trail of Mutation and Degeneration*

Please let us be reminded here that there is only one true race of Man, He and She upon the planet, i.e. the Divine Children of the Sun with the golden tan. Any other breed represents either the direct degeneration and mutation of the ice-cold, deep-freeze or a population that has mixed or inter-bred with the lost and astray Children who lost their tan. This mixed breeding can occur either mentally, physically or spiritually or all of the above. In any case, the holistic living truth is that Man, He and She, is either of the sacred origin, i.e. the Divine Children of the Sun who manifest within the sacred garden culture, or they are a mutated and degenerated breed. The degeneration and mutation of the Children of the Sun with the golden tan occurred in the ice-cold, deep-freeze and resulted in the death consumption culture of hunting, scavenging and herding.

There are those who are the direct descendants of the ice-cold, deep-freeze mentality. There are those who have become disciples and followers of the ice-cold, deep-freeze mentality.

Collectively, these lost and astray Children of the Sun pose a very deadly threat against the holistic living presence of Man, He and She. Contrary to popular beliefs as projected by "white" racist ideology, the frigid ice-cold environment retards rather than accelerates the development of any living thing. Therefore, it must be clear that the degeneration and mutation that occurred among those lost and astray Children who lost their tan in the ice-cold, deep-freeze began as a long, drudging and slow process. However, the spreading of this vicious and cold-blooded plague of the ice-cold, deep-freeze mentality has been swift, widespread and most devastating among the suntanned Children.

Let us also be reminded that the majority of inter-breeding from the earliest times onward were not voluntary acts, but rather the consequences of brutal, and cold-blooded rape by the invading nomadic tribes of the ice-cold, deep-freeze mentality. In this way, the original blueprint of the suntanned man resulted in offspring that came to reflect the melaninated shades of man and the lesser shade identified as "white."

The various theories of the ice-cold, deep-freeze mentality have projected a philosophy that superiority is measured by cranial capacity and brain size. According to this deceptive reasoning, the Neanderthals would be considered as far superior to those identified as modern man based on the size of their head and brain.

The Neanderthals became extinct and indeed were superior killers. However, in measuring intelligence by cranial capacity it is clear that there are other factors to consider. A most vital point here is that when caught in an ice-cold environment the body tends to become bulky in order to maintain enough mass to keep the internal organs warm. It would then stand to reason that those lost and astray Children who lost their tan in the ice-cold, deep-freeze would have big heads to house a big and bulky mass of brain tissue. It should be noted that within a warm environment the body mass is less, including the cranium. However, when reasoning with divine spirit consciousness and the maintenance of the whole life presence, it is quite apparent that this cold-blooded lost and astray mind of Man, He and She, identified as the "white" man has taken a short period of time to virtually annihilate the divine presence of Man, He and She. The big, bulky-brained being that descended from the ice-cold, deep-freeze remains headstrong on perpetuating lust, lies, illusions, confusion, death and deadly destruction.

It is scientifically stated that Man, He and She, use only a small percentage of their brain capacity. The key issue is: What is the purpose of the brain's function? If Man, He and She, continue to use the brain to perpetuate lust, lies, illusions, confusion, death and deadly destruction, what difference does the size make except in determining the level and degree of damage and destruction one is capable of inflicting upon oneself and others? The issue regarding brain size is pointless. Are we to believe that the reason for the establishment of an atomic bomb is because those who developed the bomb have bigger brains, and therefore they created a bigger means of destruction against the other guy? Just to figure out how to use the brain to its fullest capacity poses a challenge. It is insidious and insane to perpetuate the idea that a people who lost their natural melanination in 20,000 years of continuous, freezing cold lost only their suntan. It is quite apparent that the mutated and degenerated breed of the ice-cold, deep-freeze mentality lost all of their connection to divine spirit consciousness.

Why are these so-called big-brained people so anxious to accelerate extermination, i.e. genocidal, plans against the original suntanned Children? How can this breed of lost and astray Children who lost their tan who declare themselves as Aryan consider themselves as superior to all other "white" men as well as the men of color? It is clear that nature will take care of this matter, and that is what those of the ice-cold, deep-freeze mentality seem to fear the most. If, in fact, these Aryans, i.e. "white" men, are so superior, then they do not have to worry, because the dominant genes will determine the outcome of a natural encounter between the children who lost their tan and the Children of the Sun with the golden tan. It is clear that those who have the greater loss will be endowed with their missing link. This has been the primary factor that gave birth to eugenics and "white" racist ideology. The Children of the Sun who lost their tan have somehow come up with an excellent scapegoat. It doesn't seem to bother them that they are targeting the sacred father and mother of Man, He and She. An excerpt from *The Passing of the Great Race* by Grant Madison states:

> A rigid system of selection through the elimination of those who are weak or unfit—in other words social failures—would allow us to solve the whole question in one hundred years, as well as enable us to get rid of the undesirables who crowd our jails, hospitals, and insane asylums. The individual himself can be nourished, educated and protected by the community during his lifetime, but the state through sterilization must see to it that his line stops with him, or else future generations will be cursed with an ever-increasing load of misguided sentimentalism. This is a practical, merciful, and inevitable solution of the whole problem, and can be applied to an ever widening circle of social discards, beginning always with the criminal, the diseased, and the insane, and extending gradually to types which may be called weaklings rather than defectives, and perhaps ultimately to worthless race types.[43]

---

[43] *The Passing of the Great Race.* Grant Madison. Chapter Four: The Competition of the Races. 1916. Online Source: http://www.africa2000.com/XNDX/madgrant04.html

Clearly the pale minds of the ice-cold, deep-freeze mentality continue to evaluate superiority based upon the power-elite syndrome and the swift ability to kill instead of the ability to perpetuate a divine life presence. Let us review one of many samplings of this reasoning:

> The theological expression of eugenics is called Beyondism, a term coined by world-renowned psychologist Raymond B. Cattell, professor emeritus at the University of Illinois. Based on evolutionary theory, Beyondism teaches that the brightest and wealthiest should inherit the earth; anything less leads to the survival of the unfit and the demise of civilization. Honored recently by his students as one of "the 20th century's most influential behavior scientists," Dr. Cattell explained to an audience of leading American psychologists that "much of mankind is obsolete...What we are finding is we don't have the brains to understand" our problems and "the only real advance in science... is going to occur through breeding for brain size..."[44]

These individuals of great intellect are perpetuating the most vicious and cruel form of selfish greed known. With all of the true intellect of the global sphere at their disposal, these lost and astray Children have not shown the capacity to lead the planet toward honoring the sanctity of all living things, both plants and animals. The lost and astray Children have not shown the leadership capacity to maintain clean and wholesome water and food supplies, clean air, clean industrialization or a peaceful co-existence. In order to know

---

[44] *Human Cognitive Abilities Conference,* University of Virginia, Charlottesville, Sept. 22-24, 1994.

where someone is going, it becomes very vital to know from whence one came.

**The Mutated and Degenerated Breed**

Let us trace a few of the tribal families that the modern lost and astray Children who lost their tan off sprang from. Herodotus, known as the "Father of History," wrote of a nomadic tribe of invaders called the Scythians. The Scythians or steppe people were a warring breed that carried the violent vibrations of the ice-cold, deep-freeze mentality. Findings show that the Scythians represented the portion of the Nordic population which continued to inhabit south Russia and grazed their flocks of sheep and herds of horses on the grasslands. Research indicates that these tribes emerged from what is now known as the European Russian steppe, north of the Caucasus Mountains during the latter half of the seventh century B.C.E.. The Greek historian Herodotus wrote about the death consumption culture of these bloodthirsty invading hordes:

> Now the Scythians blind all their slaves, to use them in preparing their milk. The plan they follow is to thrust tubes made of bone, not unlike our musical pipes, up the vulva of the mare, and then to blow into the tubes with their mouths, some milking while the others blow...The milk thus obtained is poured into deep wooden casks, about which the blind slaves are placed, and then the milk is stirred round....Such is the reason why the Scythians blind all those whom they take in war; it arises from their not being tillers of the ground, but a pastoral race.
>
> The Issedonians [a nomadic tribe from the Ural Mountains] are said to have the following customs. When a man's father dies, all the near relatives bring sheep to the house; which are

sacrificed, and their flesh cut in pieces, while at the same time the dead body undergoes the like treatment. The two sorts of flesh are afterwards mixed together, and the whole is served up at a banquet. The head of the dead man is treated differently: it is stripped bare, cleansed, and set in gold. It then becomes an ornament on which they pride themselves, and is brought out year by year at the great festival which sons keep in honour of their fathers' death.

...Each year a hundred and fifty wagon-loads of brushwood are added to the pile, which sinks continually by reason of the rains. An antique iron sword is planted on the top of every such mound, and serves as the image of Mars: yearly sacrifices of cattle and of horses are made to it, and more victims are offered thus than to all the rest of their gods. When prisoners are taken in war, out of every hundred men they sacrifice one, not however with the same rites as the cattle, but with different. Libations of wine are first poured upon their heads, after which they are slaughtered over a vessel; the vessel is then carried up to the top of the pile, and the blood poured upon the scymitar. While this takes place at the top of the mound, below, by the side of the temple, the right hands and arms of the slaughtered prisoners are cut off, and tossed on high into the air. Then, the other victims are slain, and those who have offered the sacrifice depart, leaving the hands and arms where they may chance to have fallen, and the bodies also, separate...

In what concerns war, their customs are the following. The Scythian soldier drinks the blood of the first man he overthrows in battle. Whatever number he slays, he cuts off all their heads, and carries them to the king; since he is thus entitled to a share of the booty, whereto he forfeits all claim if he does not produce a head. In order to strip the skull of its covering, he makes a cut round the head above the ears, and, laying hold of the scalp, shakes the skull out; then with the rib of an ox he scrapes the scalp clean of flesh, and softening it by rubbing between the hands, uses it thenceforth as a napkin. The Scyth is proud of these scalps, and hangs them from his bridle-rein; the greater the number of such napkins that a man can show, the more highly is he esteemed among them. Many make themselves cloaks, like the capotes of our peasants, by sewing a quantity of these scalps together. Others flay the right arms of their dead enemies, and make of the skin, which stripped off with the nails hanging to it, a covering for their quivers. Now the skin of a man is thick and glossy, and would in whiteness surpass almost all other hides. Some even flay the entire body of their enemy, and stretching it upon a frame carry it about with them wherever they ride.

The skulls of their enemies, not indeed of all, but of those whom they most detest, they treat as follows. Having sawn off the portion below the eyebrows, and cleaned out the inside, they cover the outside with leather. When a man is poor, this is all that he does; but if he is rich, he also lines the inside with gold: in either case the skull is used as a drinking-cup. They do the same with the skulls of their own kith and kin if they have been at feud with them, and have vanquished them in the presence of the king. When strangers whom they deem of any account come to visit them, these skulls are handed round, and the host tells how that these were his relations who made war upon him, and how that he got the better of them; all this being looked upon as proof of bravery.

Once a year the governor of each district, at a set place in his own province, mingles a bowl of wine, of which all Scythians have a right to drink by whom foes have been slain; while they who have slain no enemy are not allowed to taste of the bowl, but sit aloof in disgrace. No greater shame than this can happen to them. Such as have slain a very large number of foes, have two cups instead of one, and drink from both…

…On this procession each tribe, when it receives the corpse, imitates the example which is first set by the Royal Scythians; every man chops off a piece of his ear, crops his hair close, and makes a cut all round his arm, lacerates his forehead and his nose, and thrusts an arrow through his left hand. Then they who have the care of the corpse carry it with them to another of the tribes which are under the Scythian rule, followed by those whom they first visited.

In the open space around the body of the king they bury one of his concubines, first killing her by strangling, and also his cup-bearer, his cook, his groom, his lacquey, his messenger, some of his horses, firstlings of all his other possessions, and some golden cups; for they use neither silver nor brass. After this they set to work, and raise a vast mound above the grave, all of them vying with each other and seeking to make it as tall as possible.

When a year is gone by, further ceremonies take place. Fifty of the best of the late king's attendants are taken, all native Scythians- for, as bought slaves are unknown in the country, the Scythian kings choose any of their subjects that

> they like, to wait on them- fifty of these are taken and strangled, with fifty of the most beautiful horses. When they are dead, their bowels are taken out, and the cavity cleaned, filled full of chaff, and straightway sewn up again....The fifty strangled youths are then mounted severally on the fifty horses. To effect this, a second stake is passed through their bodies along the course of the spine to the neck; the lower end of which projects from the body, and is fixed into a socket, made in the stake that runs lengthwise down the horse. The fifty riders are thus ranged in a circle round the tomb, and so left.[45]

If one truly does not have the imagery of this ordeal, the simplest thing is for one to imagine a circus and a merry-go-round. The historian Cornelius Tacitus was commissioned by the Romans and served to record the war culture of the time. His *Histories* captured the ice-cold, deep-freeze mentality of 68-69 A.D. and the vibrations of violence and violation that stand as the hallmark of the death consumption culture. The atrocious acts of bloody massacre and destruction are the common bond of the warrior/soldier throughout the history of the ice-cold, deep-freeze mentality. Imagine the devastation and horror that befell the Children of the Sun with the golden tan when they came face to face with the mutated and degenerated breed that glorified in killing and feasting upon the slain of the wild hunt. The following account describes a representative invasion scene:

> Forty thousand armed men burst into Cremona, and with them a body of sutlers and camp-followers, yet more numerous and yet more

[45] *The History of Herodotus*. Book Four. Herodotus. 440 B.C.E. Online Source: http://classics.mit.edu/Herodotus/history.4.iv.html.

abandoned to lust and cruelty. Neither age nor rank were any protection from indiscriminate slaughter and violation. Aged men and women past their prime, worthless as booty, were dragged about in wanton insult. Did a grown up maiden or youth of marked beauty fall in their way, they were torn in pieces by the violent hands of ravishers; and in the end the destroyers themselves were provoked into mutual slaughter. Men, as they carried off for themselves coin or temple-offerings of massive gold, were cut down by others of superior strength. Some, scorning what met the eye, searched for hidden wealth, and dug up buried treasures, applying the scourge and the torture to the owners. In their hands were flaming torches, which, as soon as they had carried out the spoil, they wantonly hurled into the gutted houses and plundered temples…. and nothing was forbidden.

For four days Cremona satisfied the plunderers. When all things else, sacred and profane, were settling down into the flames, the temple of Mephitis outside the walls alone remained standing, saved by its situation or by divine interposition. Such was the end of Cremona, 286 years after its foundation….I have the very highest authority for asserting, that there was among the conquerors such an impious disregard of right and wrong, that a private cavalry soldier declared he had slain his brother in the late battle, and claimed a reward from the generals. The common law of humanity on the one hand forbade them to reward this act of blood, the

> necessities of the war on the other forbade them to punish it.[46]

Research indicates that the Celts were a sprawling population of vicious nomadic invaders who murdered, raped and pillaged throughout central and northern Europe from about 800 B.C.E. to 400 C.E. According to Diodorus Siculus in his 1st century *History (Bibliotheca Historia)*, the Celts were noted to cut off the heads of the slaughtered enemies in the same way that the hunter nails up the stuffed head of slaughtered animals as a trophy:

> They cut off the heads of enemies slain in battle and attach them to the necks of their horses. The blood-stained spoils they hand over to their attendants and carry off as booty, while striking up a paean and singing a song of victory; and they nail up these first fruits upon their houses, just as do those who lay low wild animals in certain kinds of hunting. They embalm in cedar oil the heads of the most distinguished enemies, and preserve them carefully in a chest, and display them with pride to strangers, saying that for this head one of their ancestors, or his father, or the man himself, refused the offer of a large sum of money. They say that some of them boast that they refused the weight of the head in gold; thus displaying what is only a barbarous kind of magnanimity, for it is not a sign of nobility to refrain from selling the proofs of one's valour. It is rather true that it is bestial to

---

[46] *The Histories.* Tacitus. 109 C.E. Online Source: http://classics.mit.edu/Tacitus/histories.1.i.html

> continue one's hostility against a slain fellow man.[47]

According to the geographer Strabo (64/63 B.C.E. to 21 C.E.) who recorded his travels in his extensive *Geography,* the Celts practiced other kinds of human sacrifice:

> Again, in addition to their witlessness, there is also that custom, barbarous and exotic, which attends most of the northern tribes—I mean the fact that when they depart from the battle they hang the heads of their enemies from the necks of their horses, and, when they have brought them home, nail the spectacle to the entrances of their homes….But the Romans put a stop to these customs, as well as to all those connected with the sacrifices and divinations that are opposed to our usages. They used to strike a human being, whom they had devoted to death, in the back with a sabre, and then divine from his death-struggle. But they would not sacrifice without the Druids. We are told of still other kinds of human sacrifices; for example, they would shoot victims to death with arrows, or impale them in the temples, or, having devised a colossus of straw and wood, throw into the colossus cattle and wild animals of all sorts and human beings, and then make a burnt-offering of the whole thing.[48]

We should note that the Druids were the religious leaders of the Celtic tribes, similar to a pope or rabbi or imam or pastor

---

[47] Celts. Wikipedia. The Free Encyclopedia. Online Source: http://ms.wikipedia.org/wiki/Celt.

[48] *The Geography of Strabo.* Strabo. Book Four: Celtica. Online Source: http://www.maryjones.us/ctexts/classical_strabo4.html

or brahmin. The mutated and degenerated breeds of the ice-cold, deep-freeze mentality have maintained a consistent pattern of sex and violence throughout the history of the death consumption culture. Research indicates that the practices and principles of the vicious war culture included acts of ritual homosexuality among many of the cold-blooded invading nomadic tribes as noted in the Heruli who were reportedly a Germanic people from Scandinavia during 268 to 568 A.D.:

> Precursors to the berserkers of the Vikings, the Heruli would attain states of ecstasy called *wodnysse* in Old English, or literally "Wodan-ness," madness inspired by Wodan, the raging wolf-god....According to Procopius, bishop of Caesaria, the Heruli practiced a warrior-based, ritual homosexuality. In his *De Bello Gothico*, Prokopios is scandalized by the fact that "*kai miis ouch hosias telousin, allas te kai andron*" (Greek), or "and they have sex contrary to the ends of divine law, even with men" (VI. xiv. 36)... the homosexuality practiced by the Heruli was ritualistic and initiatory in nature, for "pederasty was practiced in connection with the transition from youth to manhood" in the early Germanic "men's societies (Männerbünder)" as well as being common to all Indo-European cultures....Ritual, warrior-based pederasty [homosexuality between older male and male youth] seems to have been common to all Indo-European peoples; variant forms of ritual homosexuality are well-documented and were particularly institutionalized in Sparta, with the nearly invincible Sacred Band of Thebes,

> among the Dorians and Athenians, the Scythians, the Celts, and others.[49]

Each of these vicious and degenerated offspring tribal groups maintained a hunting, scavenging, and herding culture and vigorously perpetuated the ice-cold, deep-freeze mentality and the death consumption culture. These cold-blooded tribes populated the region that is today called modern Europe. They continued their mutated and degenerated ways as the base and foundation for every social economic, political and religious order that emerged within the death consumption culture. These blood-lusting tribes and their war god religious beliefs evolved into the modern religious culture of Judaism, Christianity, Islam and Hindu. Their mastery was in war, hunting, animal husbandry and enslavement with murder, rape and theft as their entertainment.

> The nomadic Aryans, after destroying the Dravidian Indus Valley civilization, introduced primitive practices like sati, bride-burning, human sacrifice, cannibalism, etc. Another such primitive Aryan custom was the horse-sacrifice, referred to in Sanskrit as `Ashwamedha', which, along with other Hindu filth like the Vedic human sacrifice (purushamedha), Widow-burning (sati) and Female Infanticide, is fully sanctioned and enforced by those `sacred' texts, the Vedas.... The Vedic Ashwamedha sacrifice was, even in the later post-Vedic period, an act of great pride for Aryan kings. It signified the acceptance of a king in the circle of greater kings. This ritual involved the sacrifice of a horse as well as beastiality, and is hence a true depiction of ancient Hindu Aryan manners. The

---

[49] *Heruli*. Wikipedia. The Free Encyclopedia. Online Source: http://en.wikipedia.org/wiki/Heruli

following description of the Asvamedha, [ Bar ] as given in the Shatapatha Brahmana 13.5.2.1-10 (translation from [ Text ]) fully describes the filthy acts that the Hindu Chief Queen had to perform with the horse -

"A cloth, an upper cloth, and gold is what they spread out for the horse, and on that they 'quiet' him. When the sacrificial animal has been quieted, the (king's) wives come up with water for washing the feet - four wives and a maiden as the fifth, and four hundred women attendants. When the water for washing the feet is ready, they make the chief queen (Mahishi) lie down next to the horse, and they cover the two of them up with the upper cloth as they say the verse, 'Let the two of us cover ourselves in the world of heaven', for the world of heaven is where they 'quiet' the sacrificial animal. Then they draw out the penis of the horse and place it in the vagina of the chief queen, while she says, 'May the vigorous virile male, the layer of seed, lay the seed'; this she says for sexual intercourse.[50]

Acts of killing within the ice-cold, deep-freeze mentality have been to known to cause a frenzied kind of adrenaline rush and thrill which reflects the emotional excitement of the energy that is opposite of Supreme Love. The toxic stimulation of violence can lead to acts of brutality that represent the same vibrations and sensations that emerged in the ice-cold, deep-freeze caves. The cave-dwellers would devour the still-warm raw flesh of the slain animal with their pulse still racing from the acts of slaughter. The collective memory within the ice-cold, deep-freeze mentality holds the violence of killing, the

[50] *Asvamedha: Vedic Horse Sacrifice.* Babu Rao. Dalitstan Journal, Volume 2, Issue 6, Dec. 2000. Online Source: http://www.dalitstan.org/journal/hindutwa/htv000/asvameda.html.

violence of death consumption and the violence of brutal sex acts as the perverse pleasures of the death consumption culture. The war culture gives license to the warrior/soldier/law enforcement officers to act out hostile aggression with the approval of the social order.

The nightmarish atrocities committed in the heat of battle are imprinted in violent impulses within the genetic codes of the mutated and degenerated breed. Research indicates that the symbolism of the predatory wolf is common in early nomadic invader cultures. As carnivorous hunters and vicious warriors, the violent strain would be reinforced within the ice-cold, deep-freeze mentality. These roving bands of violent and brutal males are the tradition of the lost and astray Children who lost their tan, a tradition of ruthless warlords, bloodthirsty warriors, killing-frenzied wolf packs and cold-blooded hunters. This should make it clearly understood that within the death consumption culture one who has the swiftest ability to kill has the swiftest ability to instigate fright and fear through murder, rape, steal and take. Therefore, to impose one's will is a statement of superiority within the ice-cold, deep-freeze mentality.

One can certainly see the traces of these degenerated bloodlines and the ways and means of those who evolved from the pagan practices of the original war culture. The principles and practices of slavery, caste systems and blatant racist ideologies against the original Man, He and She, i.e. the Children of the Sun with the golden tan are the tragic inheritance of the ice-cold, deep-freeze mentality.

All of the regions that had not been stricken by the ice-cold, deep-freeze were still populated by the Kwasunic tribes. This includes parts of Europe—west, central, and east—that were not snowbound, the areas that are called Asia that were not snowbound, and all the glorious homeland of Man, He and She, now identified as Afrika. The lands of the Children of the Sun with the golden tan, i.e. the Kwasunic tribes, expanded across the continent to areas today identified as the Middle

East, inclusive of Iraq, Iran, Armenia as well as India, China, etc. The invasions of the mutated and degenerated breed against the sacred garden culture spread a plague of the ice-cold, deep-freeze mentality. The toxic patterns and practices of violence, slaughter and death consumption are the blood-stained trail that the tribes of the lost and astray Children who lost their tan inflicted upon the original and divine culture of the planet Earth, i.e. the sacred garden culture.

We note here an oxymoron. The brutal nomadic tribes who invaded from the ice-cold, deep-freeze became classified by the social orders that they invaded, destroyed, and claimed. The languages that they learned to speak reflected the suntanned populations that were invaded and conquered. These warring bands carried the tainted bloodlines of the violent cave dwellers into the regions of the planet that had not suffered the devastation of the ice-cold, deep-freeze. The constant waves of vicious rape, murder, steal and take inflicted by the lost and astray Children who lost their tan contaminated the sacred garden culture with the plague of the ice-cold, deep-freeze mentality.

The off-spring of this toxic breeding between the mutated and degenerated clans of the ice-cold, deep-freeze and the suntanned populations of the sacred garden culture resulted in tribal characteristics that have been identified as Semitic. The Semitic language is said to be an Afro-Asian language. Prior to the arrival of these nomadic hunter and herder tribesmen who descended from the degeneration and mutation of the ice-cold, deep-freeze, the Afro elements of the languages referred to the "Negroid" people who occupied that land. Equally, the Asian elements of the languages referred to the "Negroid" people who occupied that land. What this means is that the Semitic tribes spoke a "Negroid"-"Negroid" language, or an Afrikoid-Afrikoid language. Any way one turns it, the fact remains that the original populations of the planet were the Children of the Sun with the golden tan.

It also means those identified as Asians speaking an Asian language actually spoke a "Negroid" language. However, this in no way excludes the fact that these invader tribes brought with them toxic and hostile speech patterns and language expressions that epitomize the ice-cold, deep-freeze mentality. The holistic living truth is that the original language structure called Sanskrit is a "Negroid" language from a "Negroid" people occupying a "Negroid" land. The vicious, cruel and cold-blooded rapists and thieves who invaded that land and who presently identify themselves as Aryan are nothing more than yet another example of the ice-cold, deep-freeze mentality. Let us examine the attitudes and behaviors of these mutated and degenerated predators on the prowl.

## Contaminating the Sacred Garden Culture

What were the effects of the repeated vicious invasions by nomadic tribes who unleashed the ice-cold, deep-freeze mentality upon the suntanned populations? These tribes were known to be bloodthirsty both literally and figuratively. In fact, among many of them consuming blood was a part of their religious rites. They had dominant male warrior rituals that glorified war and violence and showed no respect or honor for the female. The vibration was truly, "Eat, drink and be merry, for tomorrow we die." War and finding ways to seek advantage over others were instilled within the ice-cold, deep-freeze mentality. Among these nomadic tribes, the vibrations of "I, me, my" were born as selfish greed dominated every attitude, behavior and action. In fact, war, the battlefield and the total annihilation of the other guy was a sport and a thrilling event that seemed to inspire the life patterns of every young male among these vicious, heartless and cold-blooded predators on the prowl. The religious practices that remained consistent among every identifiable tribal group that emerged from the ice-cold, deep-freeze reflects the ideology of an autonomous god of war, vengeance, jealousy, greed and spite. This god complex epitomized the way of life that they lived.

The ideology was "submit or die" and in most cases, it was "submit and die."

The general vibration of hunting, scavenging and herding was the reflection of their nomadic lifestyle. It was a way of life regardless of whether it was animals or populations of Man, He and She. The consistent raids and rape and torturing and brutal murders would leave a lasting imprint in the minds of all of those born off of this vibration. The ideology of this cold-blooded beast-like mentality would spread like a plague in the womb of every mother who carried the toxic seeds of the cold-blooded and ruthless ice-cold, deep-freeze mentality. And so, in the case of those who would be identified as Semites, as well as those who would be identified as Asians, i.e. Chinese, etc., the breeding of this torturing and cold-blooded energy would begin to change the color and the face, as well as the attitude and behavior of massive populations of "Negroid" people. This hostile and deadly aggression would cause the Children of the Sun with the golden tan affected by this toxicity to lose focus on the divine presence and divine spirit consciousness. Although many of these nomadic Children of the degenerated and mutated breed would begin to amalgamate back into a melaninated state, they would maintain the cold-blooded, heartless and insensitive worshipping patterns and ways of life of the ice-cold, deep-freeze mentality.

Glorious communities that maintained a holistic living presence within a sacred garden cultural environment would succumb to the vicious and hostile forces of the ice-cold, deep-freeze mentality. Many populations would become extinct, while many others would lose their garden culture distinction altogether. Even among those who descended off of this nomadic vibration, there would be a built in driving vibration to honor the degenerated and mutated father vibration of the ice-cold, deep-freeze experience. Among these newly emerging tribes descending from the nomadic movements of populations would emerge a pattern of worshipping and glorifying the paleness of degeneration and mutation as well as upholding and forcing the war gods of this pale vibration upon all whom they encountered. And this would occur to this very day. Make no mistake about it, the dominant religious orders of today are nothing more than a mirror reflection of the ice-cold, deep-freeze mentality disguised under the deceptions of love while maintaining the principle that all is fair in love and war. It has been noted that many of these invader tribes were cannibalistic. But then, why wouldn't they be? They ate the flesh of animals, and the patterns of bloodshed and cannibalism from the caves simply continued.

As these vicious hordes would gather through time, they would begin to adapt picked and chosen lifestyle patterns found within the sacred garden culture communities. They would begin to wash and wrench these patterns taken from the bloodshed of ancient people and regurgitate them in the formulas of the ice-cold, deep-freeze mentality. A case in point is the glorious suntanned population found in the area presently identified as India. An entire garden culture population was wiped out and their massive irrigation system destroyed. Many of the leaders of the invader tribes would become deified and worshipped up until today. Let us not forget that the mutated and degenerated breed of the ice-cold, deep-freeze mentality prospered by creating a god in their own image. What the I in I am saying here is that if the god is created in the image of the lost and astray mind, i.e. a racist god of vengeance, jealousy, greed, spite and war, then it would make sense that all the disciples and followers would uphold a racist ideology of vengeance, jealousy, greed, spite and war…These values would become the expressions of love, righteousness and the desire for peace and godliness within the lost and astray mind.

Among a specific invader tribe, was found a warlord who was called Indra. It has been noted that in the un-deified presence of Indra, he was that bloodthirsty leader of several savage "Aryan" tribes that invaded the Indus Valley, i.e. India.

He is historically noted to have led the annihilation of the indigenous suntanned Harappan civilization and transformed the Indus Valley into a scorching desert. Here is an excerpt from a well-respected research source, the Dalitstan Journal:

> Everywhere in the racist Vedas we find Indra praised for his extermination of non-Aryans, or `anaryas' -
>
> "Indra, the slayer of Vrittra, the destroyer of cities, has scattered the Dasyu (hosts) sprang from a black womb." (RgV. II.20.6) (Muir I.174)
>
> The singers mention "the black skin, the hated of Indra," being swept out of heaven (RgV.IX.73.5)
>
> "Indra protected in battle the Aryan worshipper, he subdued the lawless for Manu, he conquered the black skin." (Rg.V. I.130.8) (Ann.114 )
>
> The sacrificer poured out thanks to his god for "scattering the slave bands of black descent", and for stamping out "the vile Dasyan colour." ( Rg.V. II.20.7, II.12.4) (Ann. 115) [51]

The collection of texts that might be labeled "Hindu scripture" consists of millions of lines of text written over thousands of years in several languages and are known as the *Vedas*, the holy writings of India. Violence and sexual perversion penetrates even the most orthodox scripture and represent a pattern of sex and violence that is definitely of the ice-cold, deep-freeze mentality. The *Brhadārankyaka Upanishad*, for instance, condones rape:

---

[51] Dalitstan Journal, Volume 2, Issue 5, October 2000. Online Source: http://www.dalitstan.org/journal/dalitism/dal000/indra_mm.html
*See also The Holistic Living Truth About Supreme Love Book One*, p. 240, High Priest Kwatamani.

> Surely, a woman who has changed her clothes at the end of her menstrual period is the most auspicious of women. When she has changed her clothes at the end of her menstrual period, therefore, one should approach that splendid woman and invite her to have sex. Should she refuse to consent, he should bribe her. If she still refuses, he should beat her with a stick or with his fists and overpower her, saying: "I take away the splendor from you with my virility and splendor" (6.4.9, 21).

Upon his death, Indra was deified into the "Aryan-influenced" Hindu religion and remains as a god of worship well-installed by the lost and astray minds of the ice-cold, deep-freeze mentality. We should note that among the tribesmen of these so-called "Aryans," i.e. the Nordic and Germanic tribes, the supreme god of their mythology is called Odin. Research indicates that Odin represents battle and warfare and was considered as the bringer of victory. It is noted that the god was believed to lead a host of the slain and was associated with the concept of the "Wild Hunt." Findings reveal that Odin demanded human sacrifice. In tribute to Odin, male slaves, and males of each species were sacrificed and hung from the branches of trees. It was common to sacrifice a prisoner to Odin prior to or after a battle. The rites particular to Odin were sacrifice by hanging, impalement upon a spear, and burning. From the chattel slavery era into the freedom era, there were so many suntanned Children who were hanged from trees during mob celebrations of the ice-cold, deep-freeze mentality.

For those without the knowledge, the I in I bring to you the fact that prior to the Ice Age, during and after the Ice Age, the populations of what was described as "Old Europe" were "Negroid," England notwithstanding. The I in I remind you that there were many invasions into "Old Europe" inclusive of England that completely changed the face of the population through time. The Nordic tribes were primary invaders. Among them were Vikings who encountered these "Negroid" populations. The reason we mention these historical notes is because the individuals who were the offspring of these invasions were of this Nordic and Germanic stock. And these happen to be the same individuals who forwarded to the newly discovered land of America to become the slave owners and plantation owners of the deep south and elsewhere.

Others who epitomize the nomadic behaviors are individuals such as Ghengis Khan, Ivan the Terrible, Atilla the Hun, and Tamerlane. These individuals glorified the thrill of the hunt and the kill, and declared war culture to be the ways of their most ancient ancestors. These individuals are known to have actually worshipped the thrill of the kill and the blood spill. Such practices as drinking the blood of the defeated from their skulls used as cups, mounting skulls into pyramids, and other hideous behaviors of deep-freeze insanity simply highlighted a way of life. One thing that the nomadic tribes were famous for was tying a human being between two horses and pulling the human being apart. Additionally, another great thrill of the nomadic horsemen was to tie individuals to the back of the horse and drag the individuals to death. This sounds familiar where individuals have been chained behind vehicles and dragged to death on the paved streets of America (*a specific incident, Jasper, Texas, 1998*). And the I in I note that the individuals dragged to death in all incidents reported and unreported happened to be "Negroid." There are far too many to mention, and if we were to begin mentioning these citings, it would cause a severe interruption in the purpose and focus of this text. So the I in I leave it to you to determine if this, too, is "just my imagination running away with me."

### *Little White Lies and Other Pale Deceptions*

Unquestionably, the garden culture community of the suntanned Children has suffered vicious and destabilizing nomadic invasions by the lost and astray Children who lost their tan. The vicious nomadic invasions have caused a major conflict upon the planet. These vicious nomadic invasions perpetuated an opposing way of life. This opposing way of life is definitely a conflict of interest to the Children of the Sun with the golden tan and the sacred garden culture community. The pale, nomadic hunter, scavenger and herder culture has historically attacked and invaded the stable and flourishing suntanned garden culture communities. This has been the pattern of the encounter since the initial departure of the lost and astray Children who lost their tan from the mutating environment of the ice-cold, deep-freeze. The mutated and degenerated breed departed the caves as carnivorous hunters and scavengers who eventually became wandering predator-like wolf packs of nomadic invaders.

The Kwasunic cultures that honored the fertile "black" mother earth as the garden presence in union with the masculine life energy of the sun were destabilized by the war cultures of the ice-cold, deep-freeze mentality. In every instance, the root and foundation of collapse would be spearheaded by the raids, rapes and invasions inflicted by the degenerated and mutated breed of the ice-cold, deep-freeze mentality. Additionally, all of the surrounding communities that were occupied by the Kwasunic tribes, such as England, France, Portugal, Spain, Rome, Greece, Turkey, and Iran were attacked and invaded. All of the regions that are now considered Eastern Europe suffered these same kinds of attacks of raids, rape and invasion. For mental clarity, we remind you that all the above mentioned areas of Europe and elsewhere were "Negroid" prior to the mutation. Therefore, as one can envision the lost and astray Children who lost their tan were very busy functioning like rabid predators on the prowl. The mutated and degenerated Children were slaughtering long-term garden communities as a way of life. This way of life was supported by a violent religious mythology perpetuated by a male war god.

And so, in desperate attempts to escape the pale hordes of vicious invaders, the Children of the Sun with the golden tan became displaced populations on the run, pushing further and further south. The death-worshipping nomadic tribes would eventually occupy all of the Old Europe land mass and would commence their onslaught of the ancient kingdoms of the ancestral origin of Man, He and She. The ancient Kwasunic tribes of areas called China would be relentlessly assaulted with the bloody and brutal attacks by the nomadic invader tribes that emerged from the ice-cold, deep-freeze caves. After repeated raids of horrifying rape and slaughter these tribes would inject the ice-cold, deep-freeze mentality into the indigenous suntanned populations forming a breed that would come to be known as Mongols.

The entire mental, physical and spiritual presence of each and every garden culture community would fall victim to the harsh and cruel conditions of raging rape and brutal slaughter inflicted by the lost and astray Children who lost their tan. It must have been noticed that the lost and astray Children who lost their tan did not re-appear in their offspring born from these encounters with the original presence of Man, He and She. Clearly, these mutated and degenerated Children must have realized that the suntanned Children were the more dominant physical presence of Man, He and She. This must have eventually introduced the idea that the dominating physical traits of the suntanned Man, He and She, must undoubtedly relate to a more sacred, a more whole, a more supreme, and a more ancient presence.

The encounter with the suntanned presence of the Kwasunic tribes deeply threatened the world view of the pale nomadic invaders who came to hold a vengeful hatred and abiding fear of the Children of the Sun with the golden tan.

This intensely hostile fear and hatred emerged as a result of realizing that any mixture with the suntanned Children would never reproduce whiteness again. It had taken 20,000 years of being ice-bound for the lost and astray Children to lose their tan, their mind, and their divine spirit presence. It would be impossible for them to reason beyond the pale emptiness that they had come to reflect. Within the ice-cold, deep-freeze mentality, darkening of the offspring was viewed as a fate worse than death unless it served momentary goals and objectives.

The brutal savagery of the Aryan tribes polluted what is today called northern India and unleashed an arsenal of death and deadly destruction upon the indigenous suntanned inhabitants referred to as Dravidians. The caste system forms a rigid hierarchy that is based on the mutated and degenerated breed at the top and the suntanned populations at the bottom as established by the vicious invading hordes of the lost and astray Children who lost their tan. The social religious doctrine of this pale breed that descended from the ice-cold, deep-freeze created the idea that it was more permissible to breed with a cow or another animal than it is to breed with the lowest caste, i.e. the "black" untouchables of the Dravidian seed:

> An adulterer shall be made to pay the highest amercement if he has had connection with a woman of his own caste; for adultery with women of a lower caste, the second amercement; the same (fine is ordained) for a bestial crime committed with a cow. He who has had connection with a woman of one of the lowest castes, shall be put to death. For a bestial crime committed with cattle (other than cows) he shall be fined a hundred Karshapanas. *Visnusmrti* 5:40-44.

Although the Semitic tribes were the offspring who resulted from the lost and astray invaders mixing with the suntanned Children, the Semitic tribal allegiance remained with the hunting, scavenging and herding culture brought forward by the invader father.

It is no wonder that there is such a conflict between the blue-eyed-blonde conceptual vibration of the Nordic and Germanic tribes and the so-called "mud races" that they fear will pollute their purity, i.e. the purity of mutation and degeneration. The racial identity of the mutated and degenerated breed has been violently imposed throughout the brief history following the last Ice Age emergence of the lost and astray Children who lost their tan. Grant Madison was popularly recognized as an advocate of racial hygiene and a champion of the Nordic racial classification as detailed in his book *The Passing of the Great Race:*

> This is a purely European type, and has developed its physical characters and its civilization within the confines of that continent. It is, therefore, the Homo europaeus, the white man par excellence. It is everywhere characterized by certain unique specializations, namely, blondness, wavy hair, blue eyes, fair skin, high, narrow and straight nose, which are associated with great stature, and a long skull, as well as with abundant head and body hair. This abundance of hair is an ancient and generalized character which the Nordics share with the Alpines of both Europe and Asia, but the light colored eyes and light colored hair are characters of relatively recent specialization and consequently highly unstable.
>
> The pure Nordic race is at present clustered around the shores of the Baltic and North Seas, from which it has spread west and south and east in

> every direction…The centre of its greatest purity is now in Sweden, and there is no doubt that at first the Scandinavian Peninsula, and later the immediately adjoining shores of the Baltic, were the centres of radiation of the Teutonic or Scandinavian branch of this race.
>
> The population of Scandinavia has been composed of this Nordic subspecies from the beginning of Neolithic times, and Sweden today represents one of the few countries which has never been overwhelmed by foreign conquest, and in which there has been but a single racial type from the beginning….Southern Scandinavia only became fit for human habitation on the retreat of the glaciers about twelve thousand years ago and apparently was immediately occupied by the Nordic race. This is one of the few geological dates which is absolute and not relative. It rests on a most interesting series of computations made by Baron DeGeer, based on an actual count of the laminated deposits of clay laid down annually by the retreating glaciers, each layer representing the summer deposit of the subglacial stream.[52]

The reasoning of the ice-cold, deep-freeze mentality concludes that the damage and deterioration sustained in the ice cold caves was actually the supreme environment to grow and develop the highest qualities of mental, physical and spiritual presence. The purity of the mutated and degenerated breed reflects the depth of isolation in the extreme ice cold over prolonged periods, resulting in mental and physical consumption patterns that focus on slaughter and dead flesh.

---

[52] *The Passing of the Great Race.* Chapter Three: European Races in History. Grant Madison. 1916. Online Source: http://www.africa2000.com/XNDX/madgrant04.html.

Indeed the oppressive hardship of simple survival consumed all of the energy of the lost and astray Children who lost their tan. The tentative and uncertain food supply of the mutated and degenerated breed meant that every meal became a matter of life and death. These mental pressures, stresses and tensions do not promote harmonious, peaceful and gracious relationships. Therefore, the ice-cold, deep-freeze mentality has been identified by its original and consistent patterns of murder, rape, steal and take. The ice-cold, deep-freeze environment was an extreme abnormality that caused an extreme and deadly abnormality to form within the collective body of Man, He and She.

## Invasion and Displacement of the Sacred Suntanned Presence

In regard to invasions by the nomadic tribes, it would be sinful if the I in I did not make mention of the masterful defense waged by ancient Kemet to keep these savage and beastly hordes in check. The Sphinx would not be enough to continue to scare off the cold-blooded invaders of the ice-cold, deep-freeze mentality. A specific nemesis of ancient Kemet was the sheep herders who would later become known as the ancient Semitic tribes. Although there was a strong attempt to bring these lost and astray Children into a community setting, they refused to relinquish the toxic behaviors of the ice-cold, deep-freeze mentality. Instead the Semitic tribes became more deeply engrossed in lust, lies, illusions, confusion, death and deadly destruction. Their pattern of behavior earned the Semitic tribes a reputation for being shrewd storytellers who could project deceptions as truth. Additionally, they were notorious for being conniving and greedy while maintaining a constant plot to control the wealth base of others. In other words, the Semitic tribes upheld the glory of the ice-cold, deep-freeze mentality while smiling innocently.

There have been so many efforts to transition the lost and astray Children who lost their tan into a more humane, compassionate and sensitive presentation of Man, He and She. Osiris and Isis were great leaders of pre-historic Kemet who were later venerated to the status of deities. They represented the masculine and feminine presence of the sacred suntanned Children. Osiris, would exemplify the efforts of the suntanned rulers to civilize the barbaric and nomadic invaders who were the descendants of the ice-cold, deep-freeze mentality. It has been stated in countless ways that the great king Osiris sent out delegations among the savage and brutal hordes in an attempt to halt this emerging death culture. These vicious and merciless killers were hunters, scavengers and herders who glorified in flesh consumption, including human. It has been noted that Osiris would make every effort to teach these pale ones to consume from the sacred garden culture and to relinquish the cold-blooded and beastly mentality that they had acquired in the ice-cold caves of mutation and degeneration. These delegations were acknowledged as going out among the savage populations to make every attempt to transition them from the ice-cold, deep-freeze mentality into the garden culture.

The great suntanned rulers would give instructions to build temples as learning centers. The structures of many of these learning centers, i.e. pyramids, would remain standing until today. The original pyramids were the creation of stable, settled suntanned communities of the sacred garden culture at a time when the mutated and degenerated breed was moving from being lost and astray in the caves to being lost and astray, wandering with the herds as nomadic hordes. The Divine Children of the Sun with the golden tan were builders who left their signature in the great pyramids or mounds with a pyramid shape that have stood the test of time and have been often imitated but never duplicated. Research indicates that there are literally hundreds of pyramids of various styles scattered over the Earth, in Europe, Afrika, the Middle East and Far East,

Southeast Asia and South Pacific, and in North and South America.

Clearly, Osiris's efforts to rescue these lost and astray Children fell on deaf ears. By the time ancient Kemet was called ancient Egypt, military strategies had to be established in every corner to defend against the constant waves of vicious invasions from settled and unsettled nomadic offspring who were bred from the ice-cold, deep-freeze mentality. As time would pass, new bands would formulate identified as Indo-European. These invading tribes had conquered Greece, Rome and other areas previously occupied by the suntanned Children. So the Ethiopian people of the lands identified as Kemet, Egypt, Nubia, the Indus Valley/India, and Mesopotamia would be deeply impacted and would face collapse as garden culture communities.

Needless to say, by the time ancient Kemet, i.e. ancient Egypt, was finally overthrown, the degenerated and mutated breed had disrupted and destroyed the life of hundreds of millions of suntanned populations that once flourished within a sacred garden culture. Gaining control of Afrika, the land of the Ethiopian man, would certainly not bring an end to this cold-blooded, war-oriented invasion culture. This would only be the beginning of a new world order perpetuated by the ice-cold, deep-freeze mentality. And so, the sacred garden culture of the Divine Children of the Sun would degenerate into massive chaos, spearheaded by religious fanaticism of the war gods of holy wars, crusades, and jihads. The principles, morals and values of the death consumption culture would be forced and coerced into the lives of the suntanned Children by any means necessary. The divine process of fruits being one's meat would be replaced with blood and bones, guts and skin. The divine relationship of Man, He and She, and the family community would disintegrate under the pressure of harsh and cruel violence from deadly social, religious and political deceptions.

### *The Way of Life in the Little Ice Age*

Studies indicate that a period called the Little Ice Age affected Northern Europe between 1150 A.D. and 1460 A.D. and a continuing cold climate between 1560 A.D. and 1850 A.D. that brought dire consequences to its population. Findings show that the colder weather impacted agriculture, health, economics, social strife, emigration, and even art and literature while having a detrimental affect on the health of Europeans. Research indicates that during The Great Famine of 1315-1317 A.D., millions in northern Europe would die over an extended number of years. Research shows that the period of famine was marked by extreme levels of criminal activity, disease and mass death, infanticide, and cannibalism.

Chronicles of the period reveal that by the time the famine ended many individuals were so weakened by diseases such as pneumonia, bronchitis, tuberculosis, and other sicknesses, and so much of the seed stock had been eaten, that it was not until 1325 A.D. that the food supply returned to somewhat stabilized conditions. A historical review of medieval Europe in the 13th century shows that these populations formed a very violent culture where rape and murder were common affairs. It is then understandable why criminal activity had become a plague during the famine and why most individuals had no thought about resorting to any desperate means to feed themselves or their family.

Massive epidemics of infectious diseases swept through Europe for generation and after generation. A plague commonly referred to as the Black Death ravaged Europe from 1348 to 1351 and is noted to have killed at least 33% of the world's population of the time or about 27 million people. Study findings reveal that before the Black Death plague epidemic in 1348, Europe had more people than the agricultural system could support. It is noted that the European population was already suffering from poor hygiene and housing, and many were seriously malnourished. Research indicates that the outbreak of the Plague was accelerated by a total absence of sanitary conditions. For instance, it is noted that the dead were heaped in piles, where rats and dogs fed on the infected corpses and the cycle of infection was extended. It is further noted that the domesticated animals were kept in close quarters with the people.

Research indicates that the major killers of humanity throughout recent history—smallpox, influenza, tuberculosis, Salmonella, malaria, plague, measles, and cholera—are diseases that evolved from diseases of animals. It is noted that those of the hunting and herding culture began to live closer to and spend more time with livestock and pets, the germs from these animals were transferred to humans. Upon infecting humans, the bacteria, viruses, and parasitic worms spread either by direct contact through the air, polluted water and food, or by indirect contact through blood-sucking insect carriers of disease such as fleas, and lice. The bacteria and viruses not only evolved to feed off the nutrients provided by the human body, but also developed means to spread between potential victims.

Reports state that the streets were barely wide enough for a single cart to pass, and the streets were covered with garbage and excrement. It is noted that the people of Europe rarely bathed. The hunting and herding culture crowded into cities with populations of domesticated animals and the bacteria from the animals, animal feces, human sewage, garbage, the dead flesh consumed and scavengers created a toxic environment, rife with disease and disorder.

For many, many generations in Europe, the environment was a plague-ridden and life-threatening breeding ground for massive epidemics of infectious disease that killed millions and millions of people. The Bubonic Plague of 1665, the cholera epidemic, the influenza outbreak of 1918 which reportedly killed 20 to 40 million people, smallpox, yellow fever, syphilis, mumps and other diseases ravaged the populations of Europe. Research findings state that even into mid-nineteenth century

European cities were reservoirs of disease because of the presence of garbage, poor hygiene and lack of sanitation.

How did the ice-cold, deep-freeze mentality respond to the toxic environment? The same thoughts and reasoning that emerged in the dank, bleak, cold and barren caves of the ice age period were simply intensified in the modern era of the ice-cold, deep-freeze mentality. The destruction and devastation of disease continued to be the way of life within the death consumption culture.

The entire period of the little ice age offers a miniature reflection of the environmental conditions of the ice-cold, deep-freeze. Research indicates that the barren growing conditions and resulting famine killed millions, and poor nutrition decreased the stature of the Vikings in Greenland and Iceland. It is noted that cool, wet summers led to outbreaks of an illness called St. Anthony's Fire which caused whole villages to suffer convulsions, hallucinations, gangrene and rottening of the extremities, and even death. Historical accounts reveal that the food base was severely weakened by the cold climate and freezing weather conditions. The storages of grain were said to become tainted, because cool, damp conditions can cause grain to develop a fungus known as ergot blight that ferments and produces a drug-effect similar to LSD. Research indicates that malnutrition led to a weakened immunity to a variety of illnesses. It is noted that in England, malnutrition aggravated an influenza epidemic of 1557 to 1558 A.D. in which whole families died. In fact, findings indicate that during most of the 1550's, deaths outnumbered births in Europe. It is also noted that the Black Death (Bubonic Plague) was hastened by malnutrition all over Europe.

These devastating occurrences were the result of a so-called little ice age. Imagine what the full-scale ice-cold, deep-freeze did to the Children of the Sun with the golden tan during the last major Ice Age. It is no wonder that the lost and astray Children who lost their tan, their mind and their divine spirit consciousness became afflicted with the ice-cold, deep-freeze mentality. It is no wonder that there is such a vicious, cruel and cold-blooded personality that has given birth to the death consumption culture. It is no wonder that there have been such vicious and cold-blooded genocidal plans against the populations of the suntanned Man, He and She.

The ice-cold, deep-freeze mentality is rooted in the toxic attitudes and behaviors of sex and violence. The validation for the ice-cold, deep-freeze mentality is instigated and maintained through the institutions of race and religion. The race vibration has constantly been one of color, where the pale mutation of the ice-cold, deep-freeze mentality has been perpetuated as the most evolved characteristics of Man, He and She. Thus, it has been declared that the "white" man, i.e. the Caucasian or Nordic stock is in fact the more evolved, and, therefore, the superior race of man. There has been a total and absolute ignorance and ignoring of the sacred and most blessed fact that Man, He and She, was created in the most supreme image of the Most High Essence of Life and Supreme Love. It has been totally disregarded that Man, He and She, is the glorious manifestation of the earth, the wind, the rain and the sun. Within that glorious manifestation, Man, He and She, was given a golden tan to relate to the solar system that houses the planet Earth. And so with absolute disregard for the divine presence of Man, He and She, and their sacred solarized origin, the ice-cold, deep-freeze mentality has perpetuated a vicious energy of hate, war and strife within the order of a concept declared as "white racism."

# Chapter Six:
# Breeding A Pale Reflection of Life

# Chapter Six: Breeding A Pale Reflection of Life

## Modern Scientific Methods of Justifying the Ice-Cold, Deep-Freeze Mentality

All of the natural behaviors of the ice-cold, deep-freeze mentality would be in place, and out of these attitudes and behaviors would be born a scientific instrument of deception called eugenics. Eugenics would in fact be the new instrument of the ice-cold, deep-freeze mentality used to perpetuate the energy that is opposite of Supreme Love. The practices and principles of breeding were familiar territory to the shepherds of the hunting and herding culture. Such terms as purebred which refers to an animal with 100% of the bloodline from the same breed comes from the language of those who herd, hunt and slaughter animals. The breeding practices for sheep are described in terms of color codes. It is noted that according to the breeding practices white is a not a color, but a cell mutation causing the absence of color that turns off the color gene for brown or black to create "no color" or white.

Farming and animal husbandry sources note that the only method of ensuring white offspring is to start with two white parents. In other words, it takes mutation or the absence of color to breed mutation or the absence of color. Add a little color in the mix, and the whole process changes. This is the reasoning behind racist ideology that is bent on projecting mutation as superior. Be reminded here that a black sheep can produce any color, including the albino. However, there is no guarantee that albinism will occur, because albinism or the absence of color is only produced by mutation within the genetic structure.

To shed more light on this subject, the I in I find it necessary to bring forward a related research project. In 1998, a scientific research team at Thomas Jefferson University in

Philadelphia succeeded in turning several all-white mice black by using an experimental "gene repair" technique that repairs a genetic mutation. Findings show that the technique they used corrects a single alteration, or mutation, in a gene responsible for skin color in mice. The defective gene failed to produce an enzyme involved in making melanin, the agent which changes the color of skin. It is reported that not only did the cells turn black during the experiment, but the scientists showed for the first time that such changes are both permanent and can be passed to offspring.

Interestingly enough, the thought and reasoning of the hunting and herding way of life appears in the common terms of the ice-cold, deep-freeze mentality. The term “black sheep” is defined as a member of the group/family who is regarded as a disgrace, an embarrassment, a troublemaker, the bad one or one who doesn’t fit in. A similar term is *bête noire,* which is French for "black beast" meaning something disliked or feared. The term “black cattle” refers to any cattle that is raised for slaughter in distinction from a dairy cow.

## Concepts, Theories and Systems of Eugenics

Modern thinkers who reason from the ice-cold, deep-freeze mentality oftentimes declare that genocide is the way to rid the planet of any reminders of Man, He and She’s original presence. Research indicates that Francis Galton (1822-1911), cousin of Charles Darwin, was an English scientist who coined the word *eugenics* which he defined as “the study of agencies under social control that may improve or impair the racial qualities of future generations, whether physically or mentally.” Be well aware that the concept of eugenics involves controlling the reproduction of specific populations of Man, He and She. When one investigates the background of an individual, quite often one can identify the circumstances that cause one to project specific attitudes, behaviors, and ideologies.

Research indicates that during one of his many excursions where Galton patronized prostitution, he contracted a venereal disease that reportedly led to his own sterility. Research also indicates that Galton was devastated by his inability to have children with his wife, and after years of non-productivity and depression, founded the modern eugenics movement. It has been noted within the eugenics concept that certain populations of Man, He and She, are more fertile and more prone to reproduction. The general concern that is expressed by many advocates of the eugenics frame of thought is that the "white" population is facing diminishing returns. Meanwhile it is noted that those of the darker hue continue to multiply to the point where dark-skinned domination would become inevitable. Eugenics can be seen as a manipulated strategy to guarantee that the "white" population will continue to dominate even in the face of global democratic concepts of majority rule.

The basic strategy of the dominant "white" population has been to covertly promote their ideologies through biased interpretations under the guise of scientific research. This scientific research maintains an appearance of promoting goodwill and the betterment of humanity while strategizing the subjugation and neutralization of targeted populations. In this way, the dominant "white" population is able to fortify itself by capitalizing on the social and economic vulnerabilities of the targeted population. Therefore, an individual such as Francis Galton, who could produce no children, would appear to have a noble concern for the good of mankind regarding issues of overpopulation and inferior breeding.

There are many different methods that have been used to perpetuate population control concepts. In each instance, the bottom line of population control relates to genocidal elimination via extermination, sterilization, abortion, incarceration, medication, mis-education, and infectious contamination. Many may have the idea that genocide must involve recognizable methods, such as the overt use of violence, bloody massacres and wide-scale murder in order to exterminate a breed of Man, He and She. However, genocide can be accomplished in much more subtle and covert ways that will keep the targeted population complacent, passive and idle in a false sense of security while the eugenics programs are being run.

When one refers to acts of genocide, one must address issues of birth and reproduction, for without offspring there is no future generation of one's genetic profile. Therefore, if a breed becomes sterile that breed will surely vanish into extinction. If a breed does not bear children that breed will fade into oblivion. A noted eugenics spokesperson addresses the issue:

> Under existing conditions the most practical and hopeful method of race improvement is through the elimination of the least desirable elements in the nation by depriving them of the power to contribute to future generations. It is well known to stock breeders that the color of a herd of cattle can be modified by continuous elimination of worthless shades, and of course this is true of other characters. Black sheep, for instance, have been practically destroyed by cutting out generation after generation all animals that show this color phase, until in carefully maintained flocks a black individual only appears as a rare sport.[53]

The reasoning becomes slack within the ice-cold, deep-freeze mentality when one must consider the damaging effects of mutation and degeneration that caused a hunting, scavenging, and herding culture to destabilize the sacred garden culture. It stands to reason that when a breed mutates

---

[53] *The Passing of the Great Race.* Chapter Four: Competition of Races. Grant Madison. 1916. Online Source: http://www.africa2000.com/XNDX/madgrant04.html.

and degenerates to the point that it is no longer able to maintain the genetic identity of its original presence that breed will sooner or later be identified as an error. The mutated and degenerated genetic profile will face the self-correcting mechanisms of the whole-life system. The manifestation of cancer cells serves as a model for what happens when error, i.e. mutation and degeneration, occurs in cell reproduction. Cancerous growth is a sign of disorder and a threat to the integrity of the body temple. If one seeks to survive the malignant invasion, one will have to correct the errors in cell reproduction that created the cancerous presence in the first place. The whole life system is designed to neutralize the presence of toxic agents through self-correction as an act of self-preservation.

Only with a heavy dose and steady infusion of whole life energy, mentally, physically, and spiritually, can the errors in the reproduction cycle be reversed and corrected. The I in I have been stating for generations that what you put in is what will come out, and that is what will come back to you again. The unseen mysteries that generate the life cycle of the seed are a basic understanding granted to the Divine Children of the Sun with the golden tan within the divine spirit consciousness of the sacred garden culture. The wisdom of honoring the earth, the wind, the rain and the sun is a basic comprehension within a way of life rooted in divine consumption. The Divine Children of the Sun with the golden tan exist in a most high state of being through the whole life practices and principles of divine consumption, i.e. mental, physical and spiritual consumption of whole life energy. Anything less than divine order, any deviation from divine order, any reversal of divine order will result in grave and tragic errors in reproduction. And so it was, and so it is, and so it continues to be.

It is clear that massive errors have occurred upon the planet as a result of the ice-cold, deep-freeze mentality that is fueled by the death consumption culture. How are the errors addressed within the ice-cold, deep-freeze mentality? How are the errors addressed within the death consumption culture? The solutions themselves are an indication of which energy is being consumed, for there is only the whole life energy of Supreme Love and its opposite parallel, i.e. the energy that is opposite of Supreme Love.

The ability to decipher the presence of the energy that is opposite of Supreme Love is a sign of intelligence that the lost and astray Children who lost their tan lost in the ice cold caves. The ability to experience the vibrations and sensations of Supreme Love was also lost in the ice cold caves. The disciples and followers of the death consumption culture are stuck in a pattern of mental paralysis that is the social, cultural, political and religious heritage of the ice-cold, deep-freeze mentality. The scientific know-how of the death consumption culture is limited by the superficial reasoning capability within the ice-cold, deep-freeze mentality. Likewise, the religious/spiritual enlightenment is limited by a consciousness that has been frozen within the constructs, definitions and attitudes of the ice-cold, deep-freeze mentality. It is definitely time to get down to the real deal and remove the facades and disguises that have kept the face of mutation and degeneration shrouded in false claims and deception for generations and generations.

It is no surprise that there would emerge a "white" supremacist Neo-Nazi group that advocates eating raw and living fruits, vegetables, seeds and nuts. Amazingly, there are those within these various organizations who have actually attended lectures and presentations by the I in I and have purchased the texts of the I in I concerning divine consumption. It is not surprising that there are those who have taken the original documents and re-written the message from a perspective that totally ignores the divine origin of Man, He and She, within the sacred garden culture. The Divine Children of the Sun with the golden tan are a horrifying and perplexing thought to these lost and astray Children who have lost their tan.

These lost and astray Children who lost their tan reluctantly acknowledge that sunny Afrika is the motherland of Man, He and She, and that the "Negroid" represents the original presence of Man, He and She. While acknowledging that dark-skinned populations thrived in sunny environments as the original inhabitants of the planet, it can also be reasoned that the sacred garden culture was located in a sunny, warm region. The consumption of raw and living fruits, vegetables, seeds and nuts within the sacred garden culture is recognized as being an entirely different way of life than encountered within the ice-cold, deep-freeze experience of the death consumption culture.

Nevertheless, within the same heartbeat these individuals accelerate their death consumption patterns through declarations that the "Negroids" must be exterminated to prevent the muddying of the "white" race. Therefore, these individuals continue to uphold mutation and degeneration while rejecting the origin of their sacred presence as Man, He and She. Imagine the twisting turmoil that breeds contradiction, denial and rejection of the sacred principles of life. Imagine the conflict and confusion of lust, lies and illusions that explode within the thought and reasoning of these "white" personalities. (For a more detailed definition of white, please reference *Book Three* of the *Holistic Living Truth About Supreme.)*

The physical consumption of raw and living fruits, vegetables, seeds and nuts will become an even easier and more acceptable option for the "health conscious" as the death consumption culture continues to take its toll. It is possible to be "health conscious" and still remain within the ice-cold, deep-freeze mentality. It is possible to practice an "alternative," "healthy" lifestyle or a "spiritual" lifestyle and still remain within the ice-cold, deep-freeze mentality. One could even remove oneself from the urban madness and retreat to a secluded and sunny natural setting and still remain within the ice-cold, deep-freeze mentality. And one's offspring will still inherit the genetic degeneration and mutation of lust, lies, illusions, confusion, death and deadly destruction.

Indeed it will take more than food consumption; it will take divine consumption to emerge into divine spirit consciousness. Divine consumption is consumption for the brain, the body and the spirit. Divine consumption is the consumption of whole life energy as formulated within the sacred garden culture of the origin of Man, He and She, i.e. the Divine Children of the Sun with the golden tan. It is impossible to achieve divine spirit consciousness without having total and absolute humility to the sacred garden culture of the Divine Children of the Sun with the golden tan. It is not possible for divinity to emerge upon the planet without the presence of the Divine Children of the Sun with the golden tan. It is not possible for there to be Divine Children of the Sun with the golden tan unless these divine ones exist within the sacred garden culture.

Many will attempt to imitate, fabricate and claim possession of divinity and a holistic living way of life as the lost and astray mind has done ever since its emergence out of the ice-cold, deep-freeze. However, there is an energy of existence far, far beyond the lost and astray mind. The original errors of mutation and degeneration from the ice-cold, deep-freeze will definitely self-correct. The divine consumption pattern can not be transplanted and does not exist anywhere in the ice-cold, deep-freeze environment of the death consumption culture. Physical consumption of whole life energy is only part of the vital equation. The cause and effect of mental consumption is clearly too advanced for the ice-cold, deep-freeze mentality to reason with. This deficiency in reasoning is shown in the "big-brain" intelligence tests that measure every manner of trivia and convoluted computations yet have not even begun to identify or comprehend the basic formula of life: divine union, divine consumption and going forward to multiply divinity in the offspring.

Outside of the divine formula, everything that manifests will result in disorder, chaos, death and deadly destruction as has been witnessed during the brief but tragic history of the death consumption culture. Outside of the divine formula, every thought, every reasoning, and every analysis is distorted by the ice-cold, deep-freeze mentality. Outside of the divine formula, genetic codes degenerate and mutate as a result of consuming the energy that is opposite of Supreme Love. Outside of the divine formula, the brain's ability to function becomes a weak and feeble reflection of the original and divine presence. As a result, big brains have caused big problems on a global scale and consequently spend massive energy and resources digging deeper holes to cover the holes that have already been dug.

The ice-cold, deep-freeze mentality continues to be exposed for the violent, cold-blooded, selfish, harsh and cruel, vicious mentality that it is. It is noted that Galton's concepts of racial superiority became very popular in Europe as well as in the United States. Galton's racial grading scale of intelligence conveniently manipulated and orchestrated to position the hunter, scavenger and herder of the ice-cold, deep-freeze environment at the top of the hierarchy of life. The suntanned Children of the garden culture as the scapegoats were positioned at the bottom of Galton's hierarchy. Eugenics actually served as a system of thought to rationalize and justify the behaviors of the mutated and degenerated breed and glorify the ice-cold, deep-freeze mentality that it inflicted upon the suntanned populations of the planet. Eugenics serves to feed and reinforce the ice-cold, deep-freeze mentality that orchestrated the murder-rape-steal-and-take approach to "advanced" human relationships. Eugenics reflects the same toxic mentality that proudly instituted systems of slavery, colonialism, etc. and made it a duty, obligation and responsibility to perpetuate such systems for the "good" of all mankind. The tragic irony is that the mutated and degenerated breed has completely forgotten its sacred origin as offspring of the suntanned Children. As a result, the ice-cold, deep-freeze mentality can only glorify in the caves and sink into deceptions about the splendid results of that cave-dwelling, ice-cold, deep-freeze ordeal.

There are many plans to reduce the presence of targeted populations within the ice-cold, deep-freeze mentality. These plans are often disguised under the cover of addressing population explosions that threaten available natural resources. These concerned projections state there are too many people and not enough space and resources to sustain them. Therefore, it is reasoned that certain populations need to be eliminated. Nevertheless, there are individuals who own more than 10,000 times the land and resources than they could ever use in several lifetimes. Research indicates that the world's richest countries, with 20 per cent of global population, account for 86 per cent of the natural resource consumption; whereas the poorest 20 percent of the global population account for just over 1 percent of natural resource consumption. It is noted that a child born today in an industrialized country will add more to natural resource consumption and pollution over his or her lifetime than 30 to 50 children born in developing countries.

Clearly, there must be an ulterior motive behind these noble-sounding population control claims that are proposed by the vanguards of the wealthy elite. The general thought and reasoning among many is that a genocidal plan of action, i.e. a method of reducing and controlling a targeted population, is necessary. However, the consensus seems to be that there should be some kind of covert method of carrying it out. There are historical records that reveal that thoughts and reasoning regarding genocide have actually been in place in the United States and elsewhere within the first-world mentality.

## Charges of Genocide

Research indicates that the United States was accused of committing genocide against "African Americans" in 1951 when a petition entitled "We Charge Genocide" was submitted to the United Nations Genocide Convention. It is reported that William L. Patterson and Paul Robeson, both members of the Civil Rights Congress, which had drafted the petition, presented it to a United Nations delegate in New York. Although this issue of an anti-genocide policy was presented to the United Nations, the United States refused to take action so as not to jeopardize the United States' integrity in policies and activities regarding its domestic affairs with the "African American" population, specifically, and others in general. The U.N. Genocide Convention first introduced in 1945 was a measure to combat the kinds of practices and procedures that formulated in Nazi Germany under Adolf Hitler.

The genocide policy in the Nazi regime was established to achieve racial purity based on concepts of Nordic "Aryan" bloodline, in other words, "white" racism. These policies would directly affect minority groups, specifically those of the darker hue. Additionally, these policies targeted the mentally and physically disabled even among the majority population. One of Hitler's first directives when he came into power was aimed at the mulatto children of African-German descent. It is noted that in *Mein Kampf*, published in 1924, Hitler stated that he would eliminate all the children born of African-German descent because he considered them an "insult" to the German nation.[54] By 1937, every identified mixed race child in the Rhineland area is said to have been forcibly sterilized to prevent further "race polluting" as Hitler termed it. It is also noted that one of the first new laws passed by the Nazis in 1933 was "The Law for the Prevention of Genetically Deformed Offspring" which was enforced by a program of

---

[54] *Mein Kampf*. Adolf Hitler. Online Source: http://www.hitler.org/writings/Mein_Kampf/mkv1ch11.html

sterilization. The mentally retarded would also become a target.

Research indicates that so-called “Hereditary Courts” were set up all over Germany to hold sterilization hearings in order to consider cases of individuals reported, often by the family doctor. The Nazis adopted policies of euthanasia, i.e. doctor-ordered killings, to support the sterilization program. Persecution, sterilization, and extermination were the methods used to reduce massive populations of those identified as undesirable. Targeted groups were considered to be inferior, impure, and unfit. The most noted group to be affected by the adverse actions of the Nazi party were the German Jews. German Jews as a group had maneuvered themselves into a strong political and social economic position in Germany and were targeted for imprisonment and extermination based on the projected belief that there was a Jewish-Communist conspiracy. Although the German Jews declared themselves as Caucasians, they were considered to be an impure stock and therefore in the ranks of those of a darker hue.

In reviewing the book *Mein Kampf*, it is clear that Adolf Hitler and the German Nazi party were implementing a plan called eugenics. Eugenics has been a major concept in promoting programs of sterilization, reproductive restrictions and population control. Eugenics is a term that gained popularity in Nazi Germany to define Nordic “Aryan” racial purity and racial superiority. Although eugenics became a viable concept in the Nazi Germany ideology of a master race, the concept of eugenics is noted to have gained its strength in the United States during the early 1900’s. Some common definitions of eugenics include using principles of genetics to “improve mankind,” using methods of controlled selective breeding, and methods of breeding that only allow carefully chosen individuals to reproduce. The catchword here is “mankind.” Those who formulated the terms, concepts and definitions of eugenics, specifically earmarked the Nordic

"Aryan" stock as the superior stock of "mankind" that needs to be preserved. Eugenics introduced thoughts and reasoning to justify acts of involuntary sterilizations, genetic manipulation, race segregation and imprisonment. Research indicates that elements of the eugenics philosophy were established as U.S. national policy through forced sterilization laws and segregation laws, as well as marriage restriction laws, and anti-miscegenation laws.

Research shows that the word "miscegenation" was coined in a pamphlet printed in New York City in late 1863, entitled "Miscegenation: The Theory of the Blending of the Races, Applied to the American White Man and Negro." The idea that was commonly expressed by many "white" racists of the deep south of the past and elsewhere into today reveals a fear that if the races were mixed through inter-breeding then offspring would no longer be "white" and the "white" race would be destroyed. Sources confirm that one important strategy intended to discourage the practice of "race-mixing" was called the one-drop theory, which held that any person who had even "one drop" of Afrikan "blood" must be considered as "black."

The I in I guess that what most of these brilliant minds could not reason with at the time was that based on the one drop theory the entire planet of Man, He and She, would be classified as "black," i.e. "Negroid" of Afrikan descent...even those lost and astray Children who lost their tan in the degeneration and mutation of the ice-cold, deep-freeze. It is noted that interracial marriage was prohibited by state laws, and upheld as constitutional by the U.S. Supreme Court in *Pace v. Alabama* (1883). Research indicates that the decision was not overturned until the United States Supreme Court ruled in *Loving v. Virginia* (1967). At that time, findings show that 16 states still had laws prohibiting interracial marriage. For your information, it was not until the year 2000, that Alabama, the last state upholding these laws finally overturned its laws, banning interracial marriage. It should be noted that 40% of the Alabama voting population voted to keep these laws intact.

One of the most effective covert methods of the eugenics movement has become the sterilization programs. Findings show that since 2002, five states—Virginia, Oregon, North Carolina, South Carolina and California—have publicly apologized to individuals who were forcibly sterilized under laws in effect from the early 1900's until the 1970's. It is reported that thirty-three states enacted such laws in this period, and about 60,000 women and men were sterilized. There was a legal framework of support for eugenics that even reached the U.S. Supreme Court. In *Buck v. Bell*, the case of forced sterilization that went all the way to the Supreme Court in 1927, Supreme Court Justice Oliver Wendell Holmes wrote, "It is better for all the world, if instead of waiting to execute degenerate offspring for crime, or to let them starve for their imbecility, society can prevent those who are manifestly unfit from continuing their kind...Three generations of imbeciles are enough."

Hitler viewed the United States as a model of eugenics at work and in the book *Mein Kampf,* Hitler quoted U.S. eugenic ideology and openly expressed a comprehension of eugenics in the U.S. As he wrote, "Of course, it is not our model German Republic, but the United States." Programs of eugenics and genetics experiments conducted by Nazi Germany researchers are noted to have been financed in collaboration with major U.S. corporate philanthropic organizations, such as the Rockefeller Foundation. John D. Rockefeller and other prominent U.S. multi-millionaires, including Andrew Carnegie of the Carnegie Institute, Kellogg of Kellogg's cereal, the Harriman Family, and others are noted to have provided a considerable wealth base to finance research projects and programs of the American eugenics movement.

Eugenics has been very prominent within the death consumption culture and has left an inheritance for the many offspring of the ice-cold, deep-freeze mentality.

> After 60 years of inattention and even denial by the U.S. media, newly-uncovered government documents in The National Archives and Library of Congress reveal that Prescott Bush, the grandfather of President George W. Bush, served as a business partner of and U.S. banking operative for the financial architect of the Nazi war machine from 1926 until 1942, when Congress took aggressive action against Bush and his "enemy national" partners.
>
> The documents also show that Bush and his colleagues, according to reports from the U.S. Department of the Treasury and FBI, tried to conceal their financial alliance with German industrialist Fritz Thyssen, a steel and coal baron who, beginning in the mid-1920s, personally funded Adolf Hitler's rise to power by the subversion of democratic principle and German law.
>
> Furthermore, the declassified records demonstrate that Bush and his associates, who included E. Roland Harriman, younger brother of American icon W. Averell Harriman, and George Herbert Walker, President Bush's maternal great-grandfather, continued their dealings with the German industrial baron for nearly eight months after the U.S. entered the war...The unraveling of the web of Bush-Harriman-Thyssen U.S. enterprises, all of which operated out of the same suite of offices at 39 Broadway under the supervision of Prescott Bush, began with a story that ran in the New York Herald-Tribune on July

30, 1942. By then, the U.S. had been at war with Germany for nearly eight months.

"Hitler's Angel Has $3 Million in U.S. Bank," declared the headline. The lead paragraph characterized Fritz Thyssen as "Adolf Hitler's original patron a decade ago." In fact, the steel and coal magnate had aggressively supported and funded Hitler since October 1923, according to Thyssen's autobiography, I Paid Hitler. In that book, Thyssen also acknowledges his direct personal relationships with Adolf Hitler, Joseph Goebbels and Rudolf Hess.

After the "Hitler's Angel" article was published Bush and Harriman made no attempts to divest themselves of the controversial Thyssen financial alliance, nor did they challenge the newspaper report that UBC was, in fact, a de facto Nazi front organization in the U.S.

Instead, the government documents show, Bush and his partners increased their subterfuge to try to conceal the true nature and ownership of their various businesses, particularly after the U.S. entered the war…On October 20, 1942, under authority of the Trading with the Enemy Act, the U.S. Congress seized UBC and liquidated its assets after the war. The seizure is confirmed by Vesting Order No. 248 in the U.S. Office of the Alien Property Custodian and signed by U.S. Alien Property Custodian Leo T. Crowley.

In August, under the same authority, Congress had seized the first of the Bush-Harriman-managed Thyssen entities, Hamburg-American Line, under Vesting Order No. 126, also signed by Crowley. Eight days after the seizure of UBC, Congress invoked the Trading with the Enemy Act again to

> take control of two more Bush-Harriman-Thyssen businesses - Holland-American Trading Corp. (Vesting Order No. 261) and Seamless Steel Equipment Corp (Vesting Order No. 259)…
>
> The documents from the Archives also show that the Bushes and Harrimans shipped valuable U.S. assets, including gold, coal, steel and U.S. Treasury and war bonds, to their foreign clients overseas as Hitler geared up for his 1939 invasion of Poland, the event that sparked World War II…
>
> After the seizures of the various businesses they oversaw with Cornelis Lievense and his German partners, the U.S. government quietly settled with Bush, Harriman and others after the war. Bush and Harriman each received $1.5 million in cash as compensation for their seized business assets.[55]

Prescott Bush is the patriarch of a family line that has produced two presidents of the U.S. and his offspring have held very prominent positions of power that ranged from the head of the Central Intelligence Agency to governorships of two major states.

By the end of World War II, in the wake of the many atrocities, it became clear that Hitler took the thoughts and reasoning of the American eugenics movement and applied them as the "final solution." The term genocide was coined in 1946 by Raphael Lemkin, an international lawyer at the Nuremberg War Trials which took place after World War II. Lemkin, it is reported, lost all of his family in Nazi concentration camps. The Convention for the Prevention and the Punishment of the Crime of Genocide was voted into

---

[55] *Bush-Nazi Link Confirmed.* James Buchanan. The New Hampshire Gazette. October 10, 2003. Online Source: http://georgewalkerbush.net/bush-nazilinkconfirmed.htm

existence by the General Assembly of the United Nations in 1948. After stating in Article 1 that genocide is a crime under international law, the Convention laid down the following definition: "any of the following acts committed with intent to destroy, in whole or in part, a national, ethnical, racial or religious group, as such: a) killing members of the group; b) causing serious bodily or mental harm to members of the group; c) deliberately inflicting on the group conditions of life calculated to bring about its physical destruction in whole or in part; d) imposing measures intended to prevent births within the group; or e) forcibly transferring children of the group to another group."

In 1951, Resolution 260 A (III) established genocide as a crime under international law. We note here that the United States was not one of the countries to ratify the Genocide Convention of the United Nations. The strategy of not ratifying the anti-genocide policy of the United Nations was a profound statement of the kind of thinking and reasoning at work among the U.S. authorities and the silent majority. The primary concern of U.S. government officials was that signing the document would reflect the contradictions of state, federal and local policies, procedures and behaviors that could be interpreted as genocidal. It should be clear that the U.S. had its own peculiar problems related to the "African American" population, specifically, and other groups of a darker hue in general. Instead of ratifying policies that could find them guilty, U.S. officials simply rejected ratification until exceptions were made that allowed the U.S. to determine whether their own policies, practices and procedures should be considered genocide or not.

After many delays and much fanfare, the Genocide Convention was finally ratified by the U.S. President Reagan who signed a ratification of the Genocide Convention in 1988, 44 years after its inception. The thought and reasoning behind this ratification at this particular time would clearly point to the fact that President Reagan and the Republican party were in the disfavor of the "African American" community due to a lack of support of civil rights issues; and they were in disfavor of the Jewish community due to Reagan's political visits to Germany during V-E day (victory in Europe) ceremonies. President Reagan was also under investigations in 1985-86 for the Iran-Contra terrorist issue. It should be noted that a presidential election was on the horizon.

This is a statement that the United States promotes democratic rule. The policy of democratic rule merely states that whatever the attitudes and behaviors of the dominant population, once voted upon, become, the policy. Majority rule determines governmental policies which the set the codes of behavior within a way of life. Vote-counting and voting policies have always been in the hands of the control group among the dominant population. For example, slavery in America was legal; and the slave was denied the right to vote. Slave-owners in the south, however, were given the political advantage of the so-called 3/5 Clause in which slaves counted as a fraction of voting representation under the slave-owner's control. The 3/5 Clause was a political negotiation by the southern slave-holding states to achieve more voting power in the national legislature. The voting clout of this slave clause is said to be the margin that put Thomas Jefferson in the White House and allowed the southern slave-holding states to not merely continue, but expand, slavery. Having the right to vote would come to represent freedom, and controlling the outcome of the minority vote would become a political strategy to make an ostracized people feel like they were a part.

It is noted that the enslavement of Afrikans was a common practice in the North American English colonies for 168 years before the U.S. Constitution was drafted in 1787. Although slavery existed all across colonial America, by 1804 most Northern states, finding that slavery was not profitable for them, had effectively abolished the institution. In the South, however, especially after the 1793 invention of the cotton gin, the institution of slavery grew, becoming a vital part of southern economy and an accepted way of life by the founding fathers who penned the U.S. Constitution.

Keep in mind that we are talking about the formidable creation of the cotton gin and not the patenting of it. U.S. laws prohibited black inventors from obtaining a government patent for their products. Any patenting had to be done by a "white" man, thus, assuring that all inventions were officially tagged and credited to the designated "superior" breed instead of the designated "inferior" breed. This prohibition would be a legal way to reinforce and justify racist ideologies of superiority for all future references. The thoughts and reasoning that first manifested such a degrading and dehumanizing practice as slavery were well established, the governing legal document of the land. The rationalizations and justifications are still in place within the lost and astray mind of Man, He and She to this day. It seems that within the death consumption culture it is difficult to comprehend that acts of violation and the use and abuse of Man, He or She for one's personal gain is a full-fledged allegiance to the energy that is opposite of Supreme Love. The selfish and greedy motives, prejudices, errors in reasoning, and overt and covert racism are self-evident in the base and foundation of a social order that glorifies the rhetoric of democracy and freedom for all while practicing slavery.

It is unquestionable that the dominant male of the deep-freeze mentality continues to plot and scheme in the most cunning ways to maintain the top position as the overseer of a dog-eat-dog social order. The lust for political and social economic control dictated the thoughts and reasoning of the southern slave mentality. Legal structures, reinforced by the thoughts and reasoning of devitalized and depleted consumption, supported slavery. Economic structures, reinforced by the thoughts and reasoning of devitalized and depleted consumption, supported slavery. And religious structures, reinforced by the thoughts and reasoning of devitalized and depleted consumption, supported slavery by reaping the benefits of economic gains.

***Lactose Intolerance***

Every social economic, political and religious strategy served to secure the racial purity ideology of a mutated and degenerated breed of Man, He and She, entrenched in the ice-cold, deep-freeze mentality. Within this ideology, the natural instinct of those of the ice-cold, deep-freeze mentality was to launch research and development projects and programs that could determine methods of termination. It would become logical reasoning for those of the hunting and herding attitudes and behaviors that the perpetuation of inferior and depleted food substances would be part and parcel of the mutated and degenerated breed's consumption and had, in fact, caused the mutation and degeneration in the first place.

It became very clear that those of the darker hue would be less tolerant of this toxic consumption pattern and that their immune system would not tolerate a prolonged relationship with the consumption patterns of the hunting and herding culture. The consumption of toxic and depleted substances causes digestive disorders as well as other disorders. One example is lactose intolerance in "African Americans." Reports indicate that lactose intolerance is the inability to digest the carbohydrate lactose, a component of animal milk (cow, sheep, and goat) and many dairy products that contain this milk. Although there have been major initiatives within the death consumption culture to promote cow's milk and dairy products from the associations of cow herders, many individuals, especially "African Americans," are not genetically designed to digest the fluid by-products of cows, sheep and goats. In fact, research indicates that most adults of a darker hue around the world are lactose intolerant, clearly making this a normalized adult condition.

The perception of lactose intolerance as resulting from a deficiency actually reflects the norms and values of the ice-cold, deep-freeze mentality. Drinking cow's milk is deeply ingrained within the ice-cold, deep-freeze mentality. It is as though it is ordained by god. As a matter of fact, research indicates that the ancient Nordic myths identified the first living being as Ymir, a giant who was born out of ice and suckled by a cow. Rather than evaluating the principles and practices of drinking another species of mammal's milk well past the age of weaning, the prevailing assumption within the death consumption culture is that drinking cow's milk is necessary. Babies are naturally and innately born with the ability to digest their mother's milk. and as they get older the body prepares to receive the proper and essential food for that particular species. Human breast milk is designed for human babies and cow teat milk is designed for cow babies. Only the ice-cold, deep-freeze mentality would lock a female in a stall and steal her milk to drink.

Findings show that when undigested lactose reaches the colon, the bacteria in the colon turn the lactose into gas and compounds that promote the movement of water into the colon. Research indicates that 90 to 95% of "African Americans" are not able to digest lactose, and if they persist in consuming such foreign food substances the adverse effects may range from abdominal pain and bloating, excessive gas, cramps, nausea, diarrhea, etc. It is noted that there is a relationship between the frequency of lactose intolerance in a population and whether or not that population has a history of being involved in intensive dairy farming. Findings show that high levels of the enzyme lactase are found in Northern European populations with a long history of dairy farming, and low levels of the enzyme lactase are found in those populations whose ancestry were not traditionally dairy farmers.

It is noted that most individuals are born with adequate levels of lactase to be used during early childhood breast-feeding of mother's milk. The only way that excessive lactase can be produced is if there are errors or mutations within the system due to long-term lactose consumption which causes mutation in the system. This long-term lactose consumption will cause error or mutation in enzyme production that results in a physical tolerance although producing other adverse effects. The genetic breeding for death consumption is a result of the mutation and degeneration that continues to deteriorate the whole life system of Man, He and She.

The death consumption industry promotes toxic and depleted substances as main sources of nutrition. Multi-million dollar campaigns are waged to produce ads, commercials, jingles, slogans, and government agency reports to keep consumers hooked into the death consumption model. The whole life choice of raw and living fruits, vegetables, seeds and nuts is not truly considered within the thoughts and reasoning of the ice-cold, deep-freeze mentality. Raw and living green vegetables, such as broccoli, kale, collard greens and turnip greens are an excellent source of calcium, and sunshine is an excellent source of vitamin D. Add raw and living seeds and nuts to this model and Man, He and She, is fortified for life. The sacred garden culture relied on the fruits of the trees of life and the harmonious relationship of earth, wind, rain and sun to provide the whole life fuel for divine consumption. The acts of imprisoning, breeding, and taking the mother's milk away from her babies are the vibrations of the hunting and herding culture of the ice-cold, deep-freeze mentality. This ice-cold, deep-freeze mentality clearly breeds the enslavement of livestock, as sheep, cows, goats, and so on, and the enslavement of livestock, as Man, He and She.

The hunting, scavenging and herding culture of the ice-cold, deep-freeze mentality has exalted slaughter to the status of a religious practice. Research indicates that so-called ritual slaughter is slaughter done according to the religious requirements of either the Jewish or Muslim religious faith. Findings show that during ritual slaughter the animal is slaughtered by having its throat slit with a razor sharp knife while it is fully conscious. Shackling and hoisting is noted to be a method of slaughter restraint in which a fully conscious animal is shackled with a chain around its back leg and hoisted into the air. Several sources describe the process where the animal hangs upside down prior to slaughter. Findings show that often, nose tongs are used to pull the head back to allow the throat to be fully extended for cutting. It is no wonder that such terms as "cutthroat" have emerged within the hunting, scavenging, and herding culture of the ice-cold, deep-freeze mentality. Laws, rules and regulations such as the 1902 Humane Methods of Livestock Slaughter Act are an indication of the ice-cold, deep-freeze mentality that can easily identify acts of slaughter as humane; it is only a small step in such toxic reasoning to be able to justify the acts of murder, rape, steal and take and even invoke the name of one's deity as the sanctioning authority. Research indicates that shackling and hoisting came into widespread practice when the U.S. Pure Food and Drug Act of 1906 stipulated that, for sanitary reasons, an animal cannot be slaughtered on the ground and fall into the blood of another slain animal.

Findings show that shackling and hoisting of conscious animals was later outlawed as inhumane in the United States by the Humane Slaughter Act of 1958. However, reports indicate that kosher slaughter was specifically exempted from this ban. Research indicates that today about 50% of veal calves and 100% of sheep and lamb are still being shackled and hoisted. Furthermore, the kosher slaughter ritual of hanging an animal upside down and slitting its throat is the primary killing method used for most countries outside of the United States. Even furthermore, sources for meat industry workers warn of the dangers of being kicked in the head by violent and scared animals as they are dying. Reports also noted the distress of the slaughtered animals as measured by the levels of stress hormones in the animal carcass once it has died.

Findings show that there is a debate among some who are concerned about the animal's welfare as it is hanging upside down before slaughter, and their recommendation is that the practice of hanging live cattle and calves upside down should be eliminated. Their solution to the problem is that ritual slaughter should be conducted using modern upright restraining equipment to hold the animals "comfortably" during the killing process. Clearly, it is impossible for Man, He or She, who consumes of the death consumption culture to reason with a sense of righteousness and divine order. Instead of the argument being one that provides the consumption of plant-based foods as an alternative to perpetuating more slaughter, the lost and astray mind of the ice-cold, deep-freeze mentality simply finds more modern and refined ways to implement and justify murder and deception. So, the blood spilling disciples and followers of the ice-cold, deep-freeze mentality continue to feast as a beast of prey on the flesh of another as they perpetuate the hunting and herding behaviors of the death consumption culture.

It is clear that the bottom line is using the flesh of another to satisfy one's own personal agenda and justifying these acts as religious rituals, i.e. godly. History shows that whether it is human or animal, the bottom line is the cash value on the stock market.

### *Sterilizing Pets*

The act of enslaving animals as pets for one's personal companionship issues or control issues is a pattern that is born and bred out of the hunting and herding culture, where "Mary had little lamb whose fleece was white as snow, and everywhere that Mary went the lamb was sure to go." Acts of domination, possession, and control are fundamental to the ice-cold, deep-freeze mentality. We are reminded that Little Bo-Peep lost her sheep and can't tell where to find them. And we are also reminded, "Baa, baa, black sheep have you any wool? Yes, sir. Yes, sir, three bags full. One for my master, one for my dame, and one for the little boy who lives down the lane." The I in I note that the black sheep in question was not necessarily a black sheep or a black person but rather was the outcast of the English family at the time, i.e. the working class or peasantry who suffered heavy taxation by the royal and noble classes of the social order. The nobility was made up of lords, ladies, dukes and duchesses. We are reminded again that "the lord is my shepherd, and I shall not want." We note that in this verse, lord was considered a title of aristocracy and an indication of land ownership in England; therefore, the lord was the keeper, protector, and ruler of the land, i.e. the landlord.

The shepherd is the keeper of the sheep and the one who oversees the slaughter. Research makes it very clear that in the hunting and herding culture the pet lamb served as the "petting" lamb for sexual activities and then was served as the meal. It is no coincidence that pet is defined as an animal kept for amusement or companionship, a favorite object of affections, and the act of embracing and fondling with sexual passion. As should be clear, within the chattel slavery system, pets were kept, but these pets were Man, He and She, with a golden tan, most notably the Afrikan female. As a matter of fact the ice-cold, deep-freeze mentality has reduced the sacred suntanned daughter from the Mother of the Earth to the Whore of the death consumption culture.

The fertility and breeding practices of the Afrikan female have been a primary social economic focus of the death consumption culture. There are many ways that the target population is adversely affected. The key method of inflicting adverse affects on the population of any species is to adversely affect the production of life among that species. Within the death consumption culture, it has been proven that it does not matter whether it is a pet, livestock or Man, He and She, the control mechanisms are determined based upon the wants, desires or the needs of the controlling population. For example, city dwellers and officials of the American population decided that domestic cats and dogs were producing too many of their kind, and causing an overload of unwanted responsibility.

The most logical solution that the ice-cold, deep-freeze mentality could come up with to address population control was to surgically sever the reproductive system from the sexual organs of the pet animals, i.e. spay and neuter surgery. An alternate method used is oral contraception that is administered regularly in the food most favored by the animal. The reasoning of the lost and astray mind is that if the pet cannot breed and reproduce then the animal shelters won't get overcrowded and the unwanted animals will not have to be killed. So specific species, cat or dog, could then be kept as a purebred and as a playmate or toy of sort to be displayed and be viewed by spectators in dog shows or cat shows. There was no worry about them reproducing. Only the studs or the prize bitches of these dogs or cats would be kept in captivity to breed. The toxic reasoning continues that if these methods are not in place, local governments will have to install massive plans of extermination of these unwanted burdens on society. Just as the death consumption culture deals with the unwanted animal population, so does the lost and astray mind of the ice-cold, deep-freeze mentality deal with the unwanted human populations. It is no wonder that in the societies that are manipulated and controlled by the ice-cold, deep-freeze mentality, there have been massacres, exterminations, and mass ethnic purgings.

There are many glaring examples of these types of circumstances: 1) The bloodbath era from slavery to "freedom" throughout the Americas that served to profile the Afro-centric population with hangings, executions and other methods of killing, persecution, and control; 2) the slaughter and germ warfare encounter experienced from the time of welcoming the "white" man to this blessed land up until today when the suntanned natives of America have been weakened, depleted and exterminated to the point of virtual mass extinction with some tribes completely wiped out; 3) the exterminations and genocidal programs that took place in Nazi Germany that targeted undesirable populations, such as Semitic Jews and Afro-centric populations among others; 4) the tribal wars and exterminations in the French- and German-influenced territories of Rwanda and Burundi, home of the Hutus and Tutsis; 5) the Apartheid massacres, exterminations, and control programs established and run by the South African "white" racist regime; 6) the germ warfare tactics of spreading infectious diseases, massacres and forced displacement in Australia, reducing the "Negroid" aborigine populations by an estimated 90%; 7) the systematic elimination, extermination and social economic oppression of nearly 300 million "Negroid" Dalits by the "Aryan" populations under the guise of the Hindu caste system in India; 8) the dropping of the atomic bomb on the innocent populations of Hiroshima to force absolute surrender to the military control of the U.S. after the conclusion of World War Two; 9) the Arab Muslims strategizing and carrying out systematic genocidal plans to control the oil resources and the land base of the "Negroid" populations of Sudan, that has already resulted in over two million deaths and four million displaced. The undertone of this conflict bears a similar pattern to historical conflicts of the ice-cold, deep-freeze mentality where the Semitic Arab-controlled Muslim religion clashes for control against the "Aryan"-controlled Christian religion. And to the victor goes the spoils.

These attitudes and behaviors of massacre, extermination, and genocide grow out of the ice-cold, deep-freeze mentality that has been played out on the mass populations of suntanned Children and anyone closely affiliated with the suntanned Children. The different kinds of population control programs and their adverse effects would be targeted at any political or social economic group that is seen as a threat to the master race. The constant threat of disease and death that had caused a fixation within the ice-cold, deep-freeze mentality would formulate a new strategy of thought and reasoning.

The strategy of controlling the spread of germs would be re-focused into a strategy of useful weapons of warfare as the concepts of biological germ warfare became solidified in the ice-cold, deep-freeze mentality. The strategy would be in place, the philosophy would be in place, the ideology would be in place, the social economic order would be in place and the mechanisms of population control would be well-ingrained within the ice-cold, deep-freeze mentality of the death consumption culture.

### *Blue Blood*

Within the death consumption culture, a breed of Man, He and She, positioned themselves as the power brokers, the wealthy elite and movers and shakers of a way of life that was born and bred on the consumption of depleted and devitalized energies. The blue bloods as they called themselves have maintained a position at the top of the social economic hierarchy of the death consumption culture. Through the historic invasions and bloody trails of murder, rape, steal and take, those who benefited from the spoils and booty and privileges of conquest showed little to no compassion for the plight of Man, He and She, specifically for the suntanned Children.

The term "blue blood" is said to come from the Spanish expression *sangre azul,* referring to the pale skin of those in Spain who maintained and honored the bloodlines of the vicious Celtic invader tribes that attacked the "Negroid" inhabitants known as Basques in 300 B.C. Research in DNA tracking indicates that the Basques had migrated to Spain as Children of the Sun with a golden tan from what is now called East Afrika about 50,000 years ago. The Celts were noted to be fierce and war-like invaders who maintained the ice-cold, deep-freeze vibrations of murder, rape, steal and take and left offspring bearing the genetic traits of the pale invader father.

A lineage of Spanish families in Castile descended from the breeding practices of these Celtic invaders and the rewards of conquest established positions of wealth and social status for those who were classified as pure bred through assimilation over generations.

The paleness of their skin was held as the sign of pure breeding. By the time the "Negroid" Muslim Moors from North Afrika attacked Spain, the superiority of the ice-cold, deep-freeze mentality had been well inbred in the thoughts and reasoning of the mass population. The phrase *blue blood* came to refer to the blood which flowed in the veins of the oldest and most aristocratic families in Castile based on the paleness of their skin and the traceable genetic line to the ice-cold, deep-freeze mutation and degeneration. The phrase was taken over into English in the 1830's and is still used to define the wealthy elite families of a privileged class within the death consumption culture.

So, to avoid the stigma of actually working for a living, men and women protected themselves under large-brimmed hats and parasols. Research indicates that having pale skin was a sign of gentility, aristocracy, and high class. It is noted that for hundreds of years in Europe and Asia, many men and women did whatever they could to achieve that whiter shade of pale by applying white powders to their skin made from lead oxide or arsenic. Additionally, it is noted that some Elizabethan women in Europe sought to highlight their pale white skin by painting over the veins on their foreheads with blue paint.

The blue blood populations have had an on-going relationship with the conquest and enslavement vibrations of the death consumption culture as they are positioned in a social economic class that has historically profited from the slave labor of others to build their wealth base. To relinquish the thoughts and reasoning that maintain the vibrations of murder, rape, steal and take requires an absolute rejection of the death consumption culture. For the blue bloods, such a rejection would mean releasing the so-called social economic privileges of using and abusing the resources of others for one's own personal gain. The act of death consumption reinforces the mentality that taking the life of a living creature to feed oneself is sanctioned as a way of life. Therefore, the reasoning also follows that, within the death consumption culture, as one diminishes the life presence of someone else; one gains a greater position in life. The vibrations of parasite, predator and vampire all have the same familiar pattern within the death consumption culture. Power concedes nothing without a struggle.

We must become very clear that the mentality that descended from the cold and dank caves as the ice-cold, deep-freeze mentality continues to roam the earth with dead and devitalized thought and reasoning. The vibrations and sensations that created the blue-blood mentality also manifested the ideology of eugenics, i.e. a way to cleanse and purify the race via orchestrating programs against those whom they identified as inferior breeds. The lost and astray mind has actually focused on maintaining and honoring the bloodlines of the mutation and degeneration that descended from the ice-cold, deep-freeze. Instead of seeking to reclaim the original state of divine order as created within the sacred garden culture, the lost and astray mind has erected entire systems of scientific and intellectual reasoning based on the assumption that death consumption, mutation and degeneration are a superior state of being.

The mutated and degenerated breed of Man, He and She, has claimed itself as the superior breed and the super race among Man, He and She. The principles and practices of the culture that was born and bred on hostile aggression and toxic consumption are exalted as the superior culture. The glorified death consumption culture is celebrated by the lost and astray mind as the superior model of social order. The attitudes and behaviors that were manifested from the lust, lies, illusions, confusion, death and deadly destruction of the energy that is opposite of Supreme Love are praised as the superior model of Man, He and She. The morals and values of blood sacrifice, deities of war and vengeance, and the concepts of good and evil are worshipped and idolized as the superior religious and spiritual orders within the death consumption culture. It would be a waste of time to expect the powers that be within the death consumption culture to concede anything at all even with a struggle.

Using the trickery and deceit of a concept called evolution, the cunning and conniving minds of the ice-cold, deep-freeze mentality would perpetuate the ideology that Man, He and She, has evolved to a higher state within the death consumption culture. This higher state is in fact said to be represented by the mutation and degeneration of the descendants of the ice-cold, deep-freeze vibration. The mental, physical and spiritual characteristics of mutation and degeneration are identified within the death consumption culture as the traits of superiority. Even within that so-called higher state, those who are darker in hair color, eye color, or skin color are considered to be inferior to those of the blondest hair, the bluest eye and the palest skin. It is often ignored by the lost and astray mind that environment, consumption patterns and exposure to the sun are factors that have a direct affect on the physical appearance of skin, hair and eye color. By the same token, it is often ignored that the original DNA blueprint of Man, He and She, is encoded for the dominant expression of melanination with a darker hue simply because the Divine Children of the Sun with the golden tan reflected a divine and harmonious relationship within the solar system.

### *Color Tones of the Solar Relationship*

The brilliant minds of deception totally ignore the fact that Man, He and She, was created in divine order within a sacred garden culture. Man's natural and innate relationship with the earth, wind, rain and sun and the fruits of the trees of life is reflected within a golden, sun-drenched birthplace as opposed to the frozen and barren environment of the ice-cold, deep-freeze caves. The brilliant minds of deception totally ignore the fact that a prolonged relationship with the sun results in increased melanination, so that radiant color tones of the skin, eyes and hair can harmonize in a solarized relationship. Life within a sun-filled environment would be maintained by the consumption of the abundant green leafy plants and colorful varieties of luscious fruits, vegetables, seeds and nuts that grow freely in tropical and sub-tropical regions.

The anatomy and physical traits of Man, He and She, would clearly reflect a suntanned presence as encoded in the original DNA blueprint of each and every living cell. The divine food of the raw and living fruits, vegetables, seeds and nuts would be the natural outgrowth of the sacred garden environment. The whole life system would be genetically encoded to recognize, receive, and assimilate the nutritional components of the raw and living fruits, vegetables, seeds and nuts as the essential fuel for optimal cellular function. The harmonious functioning of the whole life system would be a direct reflection of the harmonious relationship within the earth, wind, rain and sun as each cycle and system of whole life energy reflects the harmony of the greater whole. The vibrations and sensations of this harmonious relationship are the divine order that is encoded as the original DNA blueprint of Man, He and She within the sacred garden culture.

The consumption of dead animal flesh, bones, blood, skin and gristle is completely outside of the divine order of the sacred garden culture. Death consumption actually feasts on vibrations of killing, bloodshed, and the depleted remains of destruction. Although there are some animals who function as beasts of prey, Man, He and She, in divine order is not a beast of prey or a scavenger. Death consumption was born and bred in the ice-cold, deep-freeze mentality of the lost and astray Children because of severe and grave errors in thought and reasoning and a complete disconnection from divine consumption. As a result, death consumption causes severe and grave mutation and degeneration, mentally, physically and spiritually. The consequences of mutation and degeneration are now being fully witnessed in the death consumption culture.

The patterns of hostile aggression, murder, rape, steal and take are the genetic markers of death consumption. The depleted energy of death consumption is the opposite of Supreme Love, because it reflects vibrations that negate a whole life presence in order to feed a parasitic and depleted life presence. Thus, patterns of murder, rape, steal and take are all that can be reproduced within the energy that is opposite of Supreme Love. It must become clear that if one is not able to reason within divine spirit consciousness, then one is reasoning from the vibrations and sensations of an energy that is opposite of Supreme Love. Therefore, it becomes understandable that the lost and astray mind of Man, He and She, and all of the disciples and followers of the religious orders and social institutions of death consumption honor a culture of depletion and devitalization.

It becomes understandable that the lost and astray mind of Man, He and She, would seek to go forward and multiply the cold-blooded vibrations of lust, lies, illusions, confusion, death and deadly destruction. It would matter not whether these disciples and followers are blonde or bald or natty, natty dread. It becomes understandable that the lost and astray breed of Man, He and She, would perpetuate a superior-race syndrome based on the mutation and degeneration of the ice-cold deep-freeze. Those suntanned Children who were murdered, conquered and enslaved by this vicious and brutal invading vibration would then be labeled as inferior. The lost and astray mentality would completely reverse the divine order of creation and would attempt to take that which was last, i.e. the emergence of the mutation and degeneration that descended from the Caucasus mountain and steppe region and place it as first, i.e. a superior breed of Man, He and She.

The theories of evolution within the death consumption culture would devise a race in which the mutated and degenerated breed finished first and therefore won the race as grand champions. The blue bloods would perpetuate the death consumption culture motto that might makes right and the golden rule, namely, those who control the gold make the rules. Being in the position of grand master thief and top dog in the dog-eat-dog hierarchy, one must remain on constant alert to defend against rivals, adversaries and competitors who seek to be the top dog. Therefore, the very vibration of the death consumption culture serves to create overt and covert acts of terror, intimidation, coercion, aggression, war tactics and military offenses.

The side effects of this aggressive attitude of maintaining one's elite position in the hierarchy of control creates conditions of division and strife through such tactics as racial tensions, religious conflicts, and class and caste systems. Make no mistake; issues of race are at the root of all thoughts and reasoning formulated by the dominant elite of the death consumption culture. Spoken and unspoken claims of racial superiority are used to justify every policy of domination, education and scientific formulation within the death consumption culture. We must remember that the death consumption culture was born and bred in the mutation and degeneration of the ice-cold deep-freeze that caused the lost and astray Children to lose their tan in the first place. Thus, rather than honoring the holistic living truth about the sacred presence of Man, He and She, the lost and astray mind of the ice-cold, deep-freeze mentality seeks to validate and maintain the principles, morals and values of disorder.

By the same token, religious tensions are used to justify a position of domination and control. Religious rhetoric glorifies acts of invasion, murder, rape, steal, take and enslavement as righteous and noble acts within the eyes of one's deity or god, while victory in war conveys a sign of approval within the self-serving god syndrome. Then there is the issue of class and caste systems which serve as a buffer zone to keep the mass population distracted by social and economic struggles to reach the top. In this way, a security blanket is established by promoting the ideology that anyone can reach the top if one simply works hard enough. Therefore, each class is protective of the class above while looking down on the class below as shiftless, lazy, and lacking the motivation and drive to excel. The master orchestration here is that each individual is invested within the death consumption culture system and will seek, search and destroy to maintain the status quo by any means necessary.

The lost and astray mind is able to consume all of the characteristics and values that have maintained this destructive, cruel, cold-blooded and callous vibration that manifests murder, rape, steal and take and turn these vicious acts into glorious moments where all is fair in love and war. The lost and astray mind upholds these cold-blooded, cruel, and insensitive frames of reference and declares that these acts are for the advancement of mankind as the will of god. Such acts of murder, rape, steal and take are declared as honoring god in holy wars or jihads or honoring god to serve the blood of the lamb or honoring god to advance the causes of the righteous. As for the father, the son and the holy jihad, or the holy ghost, slaughter would be a kosher act, a blessed act or a halal act so long as the hunted and herded animal is slaughtered in a ritualized and authorized manner, and/or is blessed by verbal ceremonies prior to consumption. Just as these ceremonies take place with animals, so do they take place with Man as soldiers slaughter, hunt and herd their fellow Man, He or She, during the battles of war and invasion.

The rationalizations and justifications for maintaining the attitudes and behaviors born from mutation and degeneration have bred a mindset that has no compassion for anything except the I-me-my way of life. The errors of death consumption would be programmed into the reproductive system. The errors of death consumption would be programmed into the DNA. The errors of death consumption would be stimulated and ejaculated in the sexual organs of Man, He and She, as they multiply the energy of lust, lies, illusions, confusion, death and deadly destruction. With a smile and a grin, the lost and astray mind would bask in the flaming passions of the energy that is opposite of Supreme Love. It would be only natural that the blue blood mentality of the super class or elite class of the death consumption culture would seek to inter-breed to maintain the highest concentration of that which they have become.

**The Social Hierarchy of Paleness**

Within the social hierarchy of the death consumption culture, there is a race to move on up to the height of death consumption where the fewest numbers of individuals amass the greatest amount of resources and the power to control. If one dares to look from divine spirit consciousness, one will see that the blue-blood mentality functions as a most vicious and deadly parasite on the back of Man, He and She. The blue-blood mentality of the death consumption culture functions on greedy self-interest and delusions of superiority which allow those of the blue-blood mentality to willingly sacrifice the health, well-being and security of mass populations for personal gain. The blue bloods have in fact dictated the patterns of social interaction in each level of the class hierarchy of the death consumption culture. Therefore, it is possible for the blue-blood mentality to be practiced and upheld regardless of one's bank account and pedigree, and regardless of one being blonde or bald or natty, natty dread. It is even possible to see suntanned Children assimilating, integrating and adopting the affectations, attitudes and behaviors of the blue-blood syndrome. In fact, each class within the social economic structure of the death consumption culture seeks to suck a little deeper into the vibrations and sensations of lust, lies, illusions, confusion, death and deadly destruction in order to emulate, assimilate or associate with the greedy lifestyles of the rich and famous in the elite upper class. It is clear that those who have succeeded the most within the death consumption culture have actually perfected the principles and practices of death consumption.

Therefore, if one was given the opportunity within the death consumption culture to breed into the upper class, it would be seen as a privilege and honor. By the same token, the other classes within the social order consciously and unconsciously work to support the status quo with the hope that acquiring more things and stuff will grant them a taste of the blue-blood life. For example, if a popular high-priced fashion designer who caters to the blue bloods happens to create a trendy style that costs thousands of dollars, this style is then widely promoted in glamorous magazines and exclusive boutiques. Females of lesser financial means will save their hard-earned dollars to purchase a lower priced imitation just to experience the air of status, sophistication, and class that is projected by the chic and elite jet set. Credit cards, lay-away plans and other means of financial extension keep the consumer base of the death consumption culture chasing the material rewards that are displayed by the blue bloods. Offspring are reared on commercials and advertisements that keep one focused on purchasing the next new commodity, merchandise, product, gadget and goody from the industries of the death consumption culture. The basic needs of food, sunshine and tender loving care are completely overshadowed or ignored by the appetites, lusts, and cravings for the blue-blood way of life. Unfortunately, the blue-blood way of life is reserved for only a few of the few within the death consumption culture, and the doors to enter those bastions of wealth, power, and control are locked tight, regardless of any rhetoric to the contrary.

The guarded bloodlines and bank accounts of the oldest and bluest blood families have been well-established for several generations as consolidation of wealth and a global economic strategy have emerged on the world scene. The key to this phenomenon is that the educational institutions, the scientific institutes, the religious orders, and the economic systems were actually systems born and bred off of the mentality of the ice-cold deep-freeze. The breeding of mutation and degeneration has caused a clear pattern of sex and violence, i.e. a pattern of murder, rape, steal and take to emerge on a global scale as the dominant social economic strategy. The pattern of murder ensures that those who maintain the swiftest ability to kill will be the controlling force of the death consumption culture. Great military might then relies on the ability to amass massive populations who are willing to fight and die under the banner of one's god and country. Every institution within the death consumption culture will then focus to some degree on perpetuating the vibrations of hostile aggression, violence, conflict and war to ensure that willing soldiers are bred in every generation.

The pattern of rape ensures that those who control the hands that rock the crib will control the nation and every generation of that nation. The vibrations of rape can manifest in many forms of coercion, persuasion, force, and violence to dominate the sexual organs, reproductive systems and breeding practices of massive populations. The attitudes and behaviors of rape then become a defining pattern in the relationships between males and females within the death consumption culture. Issues of population control, genocide, infertility, homosexuality, prostitution, sexual perversions, abortion, birth control, pornography, domestic violence, child abuse, and rape are common vibrations and sensations within the death consumption culture. Controlling the attitudes and behaviors of massive populations regarding sexuality and reproduction ensures that the hands that rock the crib are completely destabilized, and therefore bound, by the energy that is opposite of Supreme Love. The breeding of loyal workers and loyal consumers will then be assured for generations to come.

The pattern of steal and take ensures that the strong and mighty in war will feel righteous and superior. Also, the thieving mentality has absolutely no qualms about claiming ownership and reaping the benefits of that which was stolen. The rewards of the thievery are then honored and glorified in the death consumption culture. The vibrations of steal and take allow the lost and astray mind to feast on the dead body and wear the skin of a slaughtered animal and feel nothing but the pleasure of death consumption. The steal and take vibration allows the lost and astray mind to brutally enslave a population of Man, He and She, lower that population to the status of property like livestock and sit on the porch sipping mint juleps while the "darkies" labor in the field creating a wealth base for the slave master and his "white" offspring. This wealth base is then passed on as an inheritance to later generations of blue bloods who pride themselves on a well-deserved lifestyle. How quick and convenient it becomes to erase history and forget how grandpa got his wealth. In truth and reality, the only thing that matters is that grandpa got the wealth and it must be maintained by any means necessary. The steal and take vibration creates thoughts and reasoning to justify and rationalize vicious acts of violation by claiming superiority. Therefore, the lost and astray mind has offered excuses for slavery, colonization, etc. by claiming that a superior and righteous breed of man simply sought to civilize the "savage heathens" and "darkies." Dominating the darker populations could then be viewed as a burden, i.e. "the white man's burden."

The mutated and degenerated breed has stepped completely outside of their true evolution as Man, He and She, by perpetuating the attitudes and behaviors of the death consumption culture. In finding themselves outside of the original DNA blueprint of Man, He and She, those of the ice-cold, deep-freeze mentality have resorted to massive deceptions in order to deny the holistic living truth about their emergence as a result of mutation and degeneration. For some, it seems easier to swallow deception rather than to consume the holistic living truth about Supreme Love. This is especially so when one is confronted with the horror of one's toxic attitudes and behaviors, and the acts of murder, rape, steal and take that have been committed by the energy of one's allegiance. Instead of being disgusted by the violence, brutality and abuse that was practiced by the mutated and degenerated invaders and *conquistadores*, many of the descendants of the ice-cold, deep-freeze mentality glorify in the vicious, cold-blooded and warlike behaviors.

The genesis of the death consumption culture then signifies the genesis of deception. Genetic deterioration has occurred as a direct result of the consumption patterns of the ice-cold, deep-freeze mentality while the deception is perpetuated that mutation and degeneration did, in fact, breed a superior race and stock. The truth of the matter is that if the warring cave clans had not been able to escape the ice-cold deep-freeze and encounter other populations to slaughter, they would have eventually extinguished themselves. Regardless of the deceptions that have been perpetuated, murder, rape, steal and take are not the signs of an advanced and divine order.

Every social economic gain within the death consumption culture reflects the vibrations and sensations of murder, rape, steal and take. It only stands to reason that the laws, rules, regulations and procedures of the death consumption culture in no way relate to the natural and innate presence of Man, He and She. The laws, rules and regulations of the death consumption culture can only relate to the lost and astray thoughts and reasoning which bred a culture of murder, rape, steal and take and the energy that is opposite of Supreme Love. As a matter of fact, criminal activities are bred within the death consumption culture, both those crimes which are sanctioned by the governing bodies and those which are outlawed. The violations of divine order occurred when the lost and astray Children indulged in death consumption, and the violations were an indication that chaos and disorder would manifest upon the planet Earth. It is no wonder that the death consumption culture expends a great deal of energy in creating laws, financing a police force, tracking down criminals and maintaining prisons. The nature of the death consumption culture is crime and punishment. Few seem to comprehend that the real crime is death consumption and the punishment is self-inflicted, i.e. mental and physical sickness and disease and relationship disorders.

The claims of superiority by the mutated and degenerated breed are based on the assumption that the death consumption culture represents a superior civilization. Descendants of the ice-cold deep-freeze encountered the Divine Children of the Sun with the golden tan and could not comprehend the presence of the sacred garden culture. Certainly, the dark radiance of the original Children must have seemed alien and otherworldly to the nomadic tribes that had escaped the dank and bleak caves. Certainly, the lost and astray Children had no recollection of their melaninated origin after spending generation after grueling generation degenerating and mutating while battling the ice-cold, deep-freeze environment and each other.

### *Melanin: The Supreme Energy Conductor, Lost, Denied and Opposed*

The lost and astray Children did not recognize the suntanned presence of the Divine Children of the Sun. The mothers and fathers of the family tree of Man, He and She, were forgotten. There was no recognition of divinity, because divine spirit consciousness had been lost. The intricate, refined and harmonious social structures of the sacred garden culture were lost in the dank and bleak caves of the ice-cold, deep-freeze experience. There was no recognition of divine consumption, because the divinity of consuming from the fruits of the trees of life had been lost. There was only recognition of the power to murder, rape, steal and take.

The suntanned presence of Man, He and She, was violated through bloody onslaughts of murder, rape, steal and take. For further information, please reference *The Holistic Living Truth About Supreme Love, Book One, Book Two* and *Book Three* by this author. The spread of the energy that is opposite of Supreme Love brought a rapid deterioration of the whole life presence of Man, He and She. For generations upon generations, the sacred seed of life remained dormant within the wholly temple of Man, He and She. The vibrations and sensations of lust, lies, illusions, confusion, death and deadly destruction caused obstruction and blockage, preventing a resurrection of the sacred presence.

There was no recognition of the innate powers of melanination, because melanination had been lost. Melanination has resulted in every shade and hue of Man, He and She; however, long term mutation and degeneration for many, many generations in the ice-cold, deep-freeze caused a severe lack of melanination. Instances of mutation and degeneration can be seen in individual cases in modern time where a condition called albinism results in a lack of melanin caused by a genetic error in particular enzymes. Individuals with albinism are noted to have inherited genes that do not produce the usual amounts of melanin. Scientific findings show that there are different degrees and types of albinism, but a general trait is the lack of melanin. Research indicates that the lack of melanin usually results in very pale skin and light yellow hair. It is noted that although some individuals with albinism have reddish or violet eyes, most have blue eyes; and some have hazel or brown eyes.

The incidents of albinism represented the emergence of a pale breed of Man, He and She, into the vast and richly diverse gene pool of the Divine Children of the Sun with the golden tan. Within the sacred garden culture, any child born with a difference, including the pale ones, were not ostracized or discriminated against for every suntanned father and mother comprehended the variety and splendor of the garden. Regardless, of the differences, the child was still a son or a daughter. This honoring of life in all of its various forms remains a sacred principle within the holistic living way of life.

Remnants of this welcoming vibration continue to this very day, which is why Jews, Arabs and other Semites, immigrants, those declared as "poor white trash," radicals, outcasts, and others of this nature among the "whites" have always felt welcome in the "African American" communities. However, once these groups get on their feet within the social order, the welcoming vibration does not extend to the "Negroid" population. The hippies become yuppies and so on. The reasoning for this phenomenon is that the mothers and fathers of humanity are instinctually aware of the fact that every child on this planet descended from their melaninated gene pool. Regardless, of one being blonde or bald or natty, natty dread, every lost and astray mind will one day have to answer to mama and daddy. These are the reasons why the "African American" community has never understood how the "white" slave owners who fathered children with their "Negroid" slaves could then turn around and sell their own children into slavery. One would wonder if melanin would make that much of a difference in one's thoughts and reasoning. The ice-cold, deep-freeze mentality is clearly identified by the attitudes and behaviors of marginalizing, outcasting, persecuting, excluding and exterminating those who are "different." One thing is for sure, these toxic attitudes and behaviors are infectious and have, in fact, spread like a plague among the suntanned Children. As a result, the same kinds of attitudes and behaviors that the slave master displayed regarding his slave-born children are, in fact, the assimilated attitudes and behaviors of so many "African American" males.

Those born of albinism or paleness within the sacred garden culture would uphold the suntanned presence of their divine origin, and they would mate with those of a darker hue as a matter of course. As a result, the offspring of those pale ones would maintain and express the genetic codes of melanination as the birthright of their sacred ancestry. It is only within the ice-cold, deep-freeze mentality that differences became the cause for division. Vibrations of separation, alienation, conflict and strife based on a lack of harmony and a lack of unity within self is another identifying characteristic of the ice-cold, deep-freeze mentality. It is only within the ice-cold, deep-freeze mentality that the suntanned presence is looked upon as scornful and inferior.

It is apparent that within the ice-cold, deep-freeze experience the Children of the Sun with the golden tan did indeed produce children of albinism. However, due to the nature of the harsh, cold and cruel environmental conditions, it is also clear that the child of albinism would have a greater chance of surviving the severe lack of solar presence. Adaptations to the ice-cold, deep-freeze environment would cause the circumstances where albinism would be advantageous to survival. The fact is that the more melanin Man, He and She, has, the more sunshine Man, He and She, requires. Over a period of time, it is very clear that the suntanned Children started to mutate and lose their tan in the ice-cold, deep-freeze environment. These mutated Children began a strong in-breeding process among themselves. For the first time there was an in-breeding of mutation and degeneration. In fact, there was an in-breeding of the ice-cold, deep-freeze mentality and all of the populations of the planet Earth are still suffering from the consequences thousands of years later.

The tragic difference is not about color tones of black or white; the tragic difference is about the toxic consumption that occurred as a result of Man, He and She, degrading their consumption patterns to that of a predator and scavenger. Be very clear, the ice-cold, deep-freeze mentality is a pale reflection of toxic consumption. The physical characteristics of paleness have emerged time and time again from within the genetic pool of the original suntanned population of Man, He and She. The presence of paleness or lack of color has been identified in many breeds of animals where conditions of albinism result in "white" animals. What the sacred garden culture comprehended millennia ago in the ancient teachings and ways of a holistic living way of life has only recently been uncovered within the scientific research of the death consumption culture. For example, in 2003, a study of rickets in children presented the reasoning of environmental adaptation that would cause the suntanned Children to mutate into Children of the Sun who lost their tan.

> In terms of human evolution, the original Africoid [Afrikoid] races required minimal substrate and storage of vitamin D in the tropical environment. Under excessive exposure to sunlight and ultraviolet-B radiation, pre-vitamin D is photoisomerized to biologically inert isomers. In the ice-age environment, white skin was better adapted to vitamin D production. In a frigid northern climate, with many sunless days and shorter hours of daylight, dark or black skin became a liability. Inbreeding within the albinoid group, which continually heightened the albinoid characteristics, made the development of this new human stock possible.[56]

It has been biologically noted that when a baby is first born the eyes are often blue, because melanin production generally increases during the first year of a baby's life.

---

[56] *Vitamin D and Rickets.* Ze'ev Hochberg. Pediatric Endochrinology, Rambam Medical Center, Haifa, Israel, 2003.

Remember, the infant has not had any direct sunlight exposure during its time in the womb. The exposure of the iris/eye to light has the effect of stimulating the production of melanin in those who have the genetic codes for a more dominant melanin expression. Therefore, one is able to recognize that during its most immature state of birth a newborn baby's eyes are very pale and often blue. As anyone who has witnessed will note, a newborn's skin color is a light pale tone. One may have also noticed that the hair on a newborn is thinner and finer regardless of parental characteristics.

As every master gardener has observed, cold weather retards growth as seen in the growing patterns of plants during the cold season just as warm weather expedites growth. As a matter of fact, freezing temperatures can slow the activity and growth of plants or seeds into a dormant state of being, just as warm temperatures can expedite the plant's production of seeds. The activities of living cells are retarded by cold temperatures. Enzyme functions are retarded by cold temperatures. It becomes very simple to understand that as babies were born in the ice-cold, deep-freeze vibration, the child's melanin development would remain dormant and in an immature state due to lack of solar stimulation. The I in I must note that melanin affects the brain, the body and the spirit presence of Man, He and She.

If the status of solar deficiency is maintained for a prolonged period, generation after generation, it is understandable that there would be genetic errors that would eventually mutate the DNA codes. Additionally, research indicates that when body temperatures fall below 98.2 degrees the enzymes in the body's systems of Man, He and She, are not able to function at their most efficient state. Inadequate enzyme activity can also lead to mutation and degeneration in DNA coding. Exposure to the prolonged periods of the ice-cold, deep-freeze and frigid body conditions, lack of solar energy stimulation, the toxic consumption patterns that resulted from scavenger and predator behaviors, and the degeneration from divine spirit consciousness to the ice-cold, deep-freeze mentality caused immeasurable damage, disorder and retardation in the lost and astray Children of the Sun who lost their tan.

The scientific research of the death consumption culture is only beginning to explore what the sacred garden culture has comprehended for millennia: Out of darkness comes life. Research indicates that melanin is one of the most important materials involved in the birth and evolution of living matter. For example, studies conducted by Italian chemist, Rodolfo Nicklaus indicate that the discoveries of some physical and chemical properties of the melanin, i.e. the black materials, like electroactivity, superconductivity, communication between tissues, the capacity of organizing the cells, and the capacity of transporting metals, water and gases, make these biological materials much more essential than could be thought. Melanin is said to be an energy conductor that transfers sound and electricity in the cells.

It is noted that melanin absorbs sunlight in the outer layer of the skin, protecting the inner layers. Melanin has often been projected as simply blocking out the ultraviolet rays of the sun; however, the fact that melanin absorbs or consumes sunlight energy is often down-played. Melanin is a powerful energy transmitter clearly identified as being present in brain cells as well as the rest of the cells of the body. It stands to reason that melanin is vital to the whole life growth and development of Man, He and She. A deficiency of melanin, a vital energy conductor, will formulate into cell mutation and degeneration. Some of the noted health benefits of sunlight energy include helping to regulate many body processes, stimulating the pineal gland, stimulating production of red blood cells, increasing the oxygen content of blood, and many other benefits. A heavily melaninated individual absorbs quantities of sunlight energy via melanin, and a depletion of sunlight would understandably create symptoms of deficiency. One example of solar deficiency is reported to affect the brain and cause a condition called Arctic hysteria, which is reported to affect Inuit and other Arctic dwellers. Artic hysteria is said to be characterized by alterations in consciousness, memory loss, psychomotor seizures and other symptoms typical of epilepsy. It is now becoming clear that this black matter called melanin is activated by solar energy and is a natural and sacred phenomenon in the whole life presence of Man, He and She.

The I in I am sure that these are some of the reasons why the lost and astray Children who lost their tan also lost their memory of divine spirit consciousness as well as lost their memory about the sacred garden culture presence. Clearly, there was a great suffering of brain damage as can be indicated by the general lack of ability to experience compassion for the whole life presence. Fortunately, these are errors that can be corrected in time through the sacred acts of divine consumption. What the majority of Man, He and She, must realize is that the lost and astray Children who lost their tan suffered severe mental, physical and spiritual damage.

We must note that the ice-cold, deep-freeze mentality does indeed spread like a plague to every disciple and follower of the death consumption culture, regardless of the presence of melanin. We also note that in these modern times, the ice-cold, deep-freeze mentality breeds off of and feeds off of the death consumption culture. Therefore, toxic, devitalized and depleted food substances cause mutation and degeneration even in the sunshine. Devitalized and depleted food substances cause errors in the body's cellular system in a similar manner as a deficiency of melanin will adversely affect the body temple. In absolute terms, devitalized and depleted cells cause mutation in the DNA. However, cells that already mutated appear to have more tolerance for devitalized and depleted food substances. In truth and reality, what appears to be physical tolerance in the body produces adverse effects in the brain cells.

## EXPOSING THE ICE-COLD, DEEP-FREEZE MENTALITY AND WHOLE LIFE HEALING OF SEXUAL ENERGY WITHIN THE DIVINE PARALLEL

When one is consuming whole life energy of the solarized spectrum through divine consumption, one is able to maintain the vibrations of whole life energy within the living cells. It is a difficult fact for the lost and astray mind to comprehend and accept that the lack of divine consumption causes mutation and degeneration in ways that have yet to be acknowledged. First and foremost, the comprehension of divine consumption is beyond the grasp of the lost and astray mind. It is amazing that so many debates have been waged about the intelligence of a so-called superior race that was born and bred on malnutrition, toxic consumption and massive deficiencies. It is also amazing that the lost and astray mind continues to congratulate itself on its genius and wit in masterminding a lifestyle rooted in lust, lies, illusions, confusion, death and deadly destruction. Depleted and devitalized consumption occurred over an extended period of time during the ice-cold, deep-freeze experience which caused the lost and astray Children to experience severe genetic deterioration.

It is nearly impossible for the lost and astray mind to track the energy that is opposite of Supreme Love and comprehend that the vibrations and sensations from the ice-cold, deep-freeze are the same vibrations and sensations experienced today within the death consumption culture. The lost and astray mind is prone to shallow and superficial analysis and lacks the full ability to perceive that, although the details have changed, the vibrations of lust, lies, illusions, confusion, death and deadly destruction remain the same. The offspring are repeating the same deteriorating vibrations of toxic mental, physical and spiritual consumption again and again. Some may say that things are getting worse; however, it is simply the same old death consumption cultural games with another name. In fact, it is the same game of misery, aches, and pains played over and over again, although some seem to expect different results. Divine reasoning suggests that mutations that cause one to adapt to a harsh, cold and barren environment for generations and generations do not represent the optimal functioning for the whole life system even though the organism is able to survive. Specifically, the way of life that originated in the ice-cold, deep-freeze environment is by no means the optimal way of life. Unquestionably, the lost and astray Children who lost their tan were subjected to the harshest, coldest and most barren conditions for human survival. As a result, these lost and astray Children of the Sun who lost their tan produced the harshest, coldest and most barren culture, i.e. the death consumption culture. Out of these cold and barren conditions, was born the ice-cold, deep-freeze mentality.

**The Dog-Eat-Dog-Mentality**

In truth and reality, there has been a use of everything else except divine reasoning within the lost and astray mind. There has been a constant use of terror, fright and fear, hostile aggression, murder, theft, rape, and enslavement as the principles and practices of the ice-cold, deep-freeze mentality. These are the signs of the times of the lost and astray mind. These are the signs that alert Man, He and She, to the fact that the holistic living truth about Supreme Love has been reversed within the death consumption culture. Worst of all, at this point in time, simply comprehending that the holistic living truth about Supreme Love has been reversed is not enough. All of the disciples and the followers of the death consumption culture, be they blonde or bald or natty, natty dread have aligned with death consumption. The mass population of Man, He and She, is so deeply invested in death consumption that they are too crippled and intoxicated to apply any divine reasoning.

The lost and astray mind is programmed to focus on rewards, favor, and the privileges of assimilating and integrating into the upper classes of the death consumption culture. The dog-eat-dog mentality perpetuates the vibrations of every man for himself and the declaration that there exists a deity or god who stands for the righteous cause of advancing death consumption. Thoughts and reasoning that conclude that all is fair in love and war create a climate where one's personal wealth base is exalted as being a reward for devotion to either the political, educational, social, economic and/or religious order of the death consumption culture. Therefore, the fact that some individuals have accumulated such massive amounts of wealth in the midst of so many who have not may lead many to the conclusion that wealth is indeed a reward, a gift, a blessing and a mark of distinction that makes one superior to others.

Amassing capital by any means necessary in order to gain financial wealth would automatically translate into a major pursuit and priority within the death consumption culture. Becoming a member of the privileged class has formulated many dreams within the death consumption culture. And anybody can have a dream. From there, all this individual has to do is learn how to communicate politically correct as well as how to keep business affairs undercover, and all will be fair in love and war. Once financial wealth is established, one immediately begins to praise one's god for the deliverance of the abundance. One begins to gloat in individual egotism and project oneself as a master of success and achievement. In many instances, the focus becomes establishing a family line that will be glorified as being within a privileged class of the death consumption culture. This occurs regardless of whether one's wealth is ill-gotten gains from corrupt means or at the expense of innocent and unsuspecting populations.

One must be well aware that divine reasoning is a major conflict of interest to the lost and astray mind. Divine reasoning will only be met with fire and flames and hostile aggression fed by anger and bitterness. If one has the nerve to acknowledge anything beyond the massive deception that is being perpetuated within the death consumption culture, the lost and astray mind will simply tune out or immediately refer to a context of death consumption. It only stands to reason that selective breeding of the blue-blood mentality would intensify the lost and astray thoughts and reasoning in the offspring. It would only stand to reason that selective breeding would also be considered a means to produce a more elite model of Man, He and She. The whole vibration of the elite few conquering, enslaving and profiting from the many is a direct inheritance of the vicious and cruel invasions against the sacred garden culture by those who descended in raiding bands from the ice-cold, deep-freeze environment. In truth and reality, the entire death consumption culture is actually nothing more than the vibrations and the sensations inherited from the descendants of mutation and degeneration.

We have examined the mental heredity of these mutated and degenerated descendants. The vibrations of murder, rape, steal and take have been transmitted into the reproductive system and housed within every sperm and each egg of Man, He and She, contaminated by this ice-cold, deep-freeze mentality. Regardless of conversation, regardless of boastful claims of sophisticated intellect, regardless of any pretentious gestures, the fact remains that mutation and degeneration are the result of depleted and devitalized consumption. So long as the lost and astray mind of Man, He and She, continues to claim mutation and degeneration as superior, deterioration will continue into self-destruction. So long as the lost and astray mind continues to worship and idolize the mutated and degenerated standards of beauty, then lust, lies and illusions will continue into self-destruction. So long as the lost and astray mind continues to perpetuate the social economic and political agenda of the death consumption culture, then confusion, death and deadly destruction will continue into self-destruction.

It is the divine duty, obligation and responsibility for a sacred few of Man, He and She, to work on the side of the divine parallel. There is absolutely a divine parallel to death consumption. There is absolutely a divine parallel to the death consumption culture. There is absolutely a divine parallel to the energy that is opposite of Supreme Love. There is absolutely a divine parallel to the elite and privileged class of the blue bloods. There is absolutely a divine parallel to the superior-race syndrome. There is absolutely a divine parallel to the ice-cold, deep-freeze mentality. The divine parallel exists, because it is the original and divine state of being of Man, He and She, upon the planet Earth. Keep it in the forefront of your mind that the death consumption culture, the energy that is opposite of Supreme Love, and the mutation and degeneration of the lost and astray Children are recent errors in the whole life presence of Man, He and She.

The errors of death consumption unleashed disorder and disease upon the planet in short order. One may trace the historic invasions of the descendants of the ice-cold, deep-freeze and gain a sense of the vicious, brutal and cold-blooded acts of murder, rape, steal and take that were perpetuated again and again against the suntanned presence of Man, He and She. However, there is one thing that one will never ever find within the death consumption culture. One will never ever find the sacred garden culture while wallowing in the confines of the energy that is opposite of Supreme Love. As a matter of fact, many will claim that the sacred garden culture is legend, myth, utopia or wishful thinking. Some have actually come to believe that the sacred garden culture is a paradise that one can experience after one dies and go to heaven. Some think that angels fly over the sacred garden culture in white wings, and others think that dark-eyed virgins await them.

What all this means is that when those offspring of the ice-cold, deep-freeze mentality encountered the sacred garden culture, they saw it as a paradise, yet a paragon that they could not comprehend. The savage and brutal way of life that had been maintained in the northern cold since the Ice Age would be unleashed with savage brutality against all inhabitants of the sacred garden culture. In fact, this beastly mutated and degenerated breed of Man, He and She, would unleash this attack on nature itself and any living thing that was encountered. The depth of mutation and degeneration within the seed of the ice-cold, deep-freeze mentality would fester in the most cunning and conniving ways imaginable. There exists no such thing as compassion for anything that does not serve the personal desires of the individual who descends from this cold-blooded vibration. In fact, there remains absolutely no acknowledgement of one's sacred ancestral presence or any prerequisite that will guide one back into the sacred vibrations of divine spirit consciousness. It is very clear that those of the ice-cold, deep-freeze mentality and all of their disciples and followers have given all of their devotion and allegiance to that side of the parallel that houses the death consumption culture. It is equally clear that the contamination has spread like a plague, encompassing a mass majority of Man, He and She, regardless of one being blonde or bald or natty, natty dread. Ironically, those who are not fully aligned face the threats of destruction by the carriers of the seed of the ice-cold, deep-freeze mentality.

Notwithstanding all of this, there is a parallel to the death consumption culture, i.e. the holistic living way of life of the sacred garden culture. Yes, this is, in fact, the life consumption culture, a culture where life is for the living. Although the toxic and depleting energy of the ice-cold, deep-freeze mentality has destabilized and disrupted the foundation of the sacred garden culture, a sacred resurrection is in order. It becomes an absolute necessity that a first family or royal family among Man, He and She, must emerge. The role of this royal family is to embody the sacred presence of the Divine Children of the Sun. The royal family must establish a divine social economic family community that is rooted in the glory of the sacred garden culture. A sacred few are called to become totally focused and dedicated to the divine origin of Man, He and She, and the sacred glory of their divine presence upon the planet Earth.

The Divine and Sacred Few must cease and desist from perpetuating the murder-rape-steal-and-take attitudes and behaviors that are entrenched in the death consumption culture. One must begin to understand that massive mental, physical and spiritual disease and disorder will continue to have a breeding ground so long as the mind of Man, He and She, remains lost and astray in the ways and means of the ice-cold, deep-freeze mentality. The Darwin theories and others of that kind are held in high esteem within the lost and astray mind. Even when evidence begins to spring up all over the planet that reveals the origin of Man, He and She, as the Divine Children of the Sun with a golden tan, the holistic living truth would be ignored. Even when the evidence shows that the Divine Children of the Sun with the golden tan originated within a sacred garden culture environment, there would be orchestrated distortions and distractions and the holistic living truth would be ignored. The deep-seated vicious and cold-blooded mentality simply rejects the holistic living truth about Supreme Love and replaces it with more of the same attitudes and behaviors of distortions and distractions.

Worst of all, because of a deep-seated desire to be accepted within a privileged class and a deep-seated desire to integrate and assimilate into the status quo of the death consumption culture, the lost and astray mind becomes even more entrenched in the death consumption culture. When one examines the consequences of this deep-seated entrenchment; the massive obesity, heart attacks, cancer, diabetes, strokes, prostate disorder, toxic relationships and so on; one wonders why an individual would continue to pledge allegiance to death consumption. It appears as though toxic addictions to the things and stuff of the death consumption industries far outweigh the value of the individual's whole life presence. It seems that the opportunity to become a member of a privileged class and the opportunity to acquire things and stuff is far more important than one's wholesome mental, physical and spiritual health and well-being.

Therefore, the struggle continues. The lost and astray mind continues to seek ways and means by any means necessary to acquire fortune and fame within the death consumption culture. As a result, individuals decide to never reproduce another life in order to gain the opportunity of enjoying a self-centered life focused on things and stuff. Within the death consumption culture, Man, He and She, engage in vasectomies, hysterectomies and indulge in birth control pills and other contraceptives to prevent any additional responsibilities beyond the I-me-my syndrome.

Attitudes and behaviors regarding reproduction have been influenced by thoughts and reasoning concerning contraceptives and birth control. An individual may feel that he or she is making a personal and private decision that is based on free choice and free will. However, every influence of thought and reasoning within the death consumption culture is actually dictated by the energy that is opposite of Supreme Love. Consequently, the rationalizations and justifications for one's personal attitudes and behaviors have already been established by the routines and practices of death consumption. As a matter of fact, a program is simply a routine practice of attitudes and behaviors that has been run so long that one assumes that the program is actually a personal creation. Therefore, while the lost and astray mind is busy performing like a puppet within the energy that is opposite of Supreme Love, it is actually thinking that it is a real live entity.

When the lost and astray mind begins to sense that there are actually larger orchestrations in motion than can be comprehended, then the lost and astray mind sinks into anxiety, depression and looks for signs of a conspiracy. The truth of the matter is that the energy that is opposite of Supreme Love can be identified by certain vibrations or patterns. These vibrations can be seen as toxic or harmful when examining the consequences that manifest. Whether the energy that is opposite of Supreme Love is consumed by a cell, an individual, a family, a community, a nation, or an entire planet, the consequences of disease, disorder, and dysfunction become clearly identified. Thus, population-control issues expose issues of the destabilized family, the degraded role of mother, conflict in male-female relationships, drug-based health care, permissive child-rearing practices, lack of parental responsibility and disparity in social economic conditions to name a few that are all adverse affects of the death consumption culture.

Every child born within the death consumption culture becomes a victim of abuse and neglect by the very nature of the toxic energy that is consumed by the mother and the father. The whole life presence is neglected and abused when one continues to consume of toxic, depleted, and devitalized energy, i.e. toxic, depleted and devitalized food substances, thoughts and reasoning, or spiritual/religious practices. When one continues to act out attitudes and behaviors of hostile aggression and toxic consumption, one is maintaining an abusive relationship with oneself and others. A child inherits the sum total of the parents' consumption. This inheritance crosses all lines be they mental, physical or spiritual/religious. Passing the same old toxic thinking, reasoning, and consumption patterns on to one's offspring is akin to offering that offspring's life as a sacrifice to the energy that is opposite of Supreme Love. Indeed, it is the parents, the relatives, the childcare providers, and the educational professionals who actually baptize the child into the vibrations and sensations of the death consumption culture. In this way, the vulnerable and innocent child is exposed to the toxic characteristics of lust, lies, illusions, confusion, death and deadly destruction at a very early age.

Neglect and abuse are rampant as the child is left unprotected from the disorders of sex and violence that lurk in every corner of the death consumption culture. Parents willfully expose their child to television programming, fairy tales, nursery rhymes and other media of sex and violence as ways to pacify, entertain and occupy the impressionable mind of the young child. The same parents who would be appalled at the thought of allowing their child to drink bleach, allow the very same child to consume junk food, violent cartoons, sexually explicit music videos, racial stereotypes, and other fond pastimes of the death consumption culture. Parents who consider themselves well-educated and progressive eagerly dress their child up in finery to attend religious practices that indoctrinate the child into holidays of death consumption and merchandising. The same vibrations of neglect and abuse can create a mother who will drown her own children in severe depression or a father who will break his child's arm in a violent rage. Unfortunately, the lost and astray mind tends to recognize only the most gross examples of the energy that is opposite of Supreme Love, comforted by the thought that the behavior of the other guy is deplorable. All the while the lost and astray mind sucks on the very same toxic vibrations and sensations of the ice-cold, deep-freeze mentality committing acts of neglect and abuse in private.

### *Examining the Mental Space of the Unholy Parallel*

Man, He and She, will have to decide whether to continue believing the lost and astray mind of the ice-cold, deep-freeze mentality or whether to submit to the holistic living truth about Supreme Love. It is clear that Man, He and She, is being led, manipulated, and orchestrated by the toxic and depleted energies of lust, lies, illusions, confusion, death and deadly destruction. Unless, there is an immediate, urgent, swift, quick, and fast change of direction, the fatal attraction to the death consumption culture will take its due course, with Man, He and She, colliding with the immovable object of a dead end.

It should now be clear that the ice-cold, deep-freeze mentality descends from a toxic space and place, an environment that perpetuates the energy that is opposite of Supreme Love. In fact, one can maintain the ice-cold, deep-freeze mentality while consuming raw and living fruits, vegetables, seeds and nuts—at least for awhile.

Consumption is more than just the food that you consume and put in your stomach. In fact, the only way to rid oneself of the ice-cold, deep-freeze mentality is to begin to function with thoughts that perpetuate the holistic living truth about Supreme Love. If one claims that one is truly seeking peace, love, and harmony, how can one continue to feed on the ice-cold, deep-freeze mentality? If one is truly seeking peace, where else can one go beyond the holistic living truth about Supreme Love? There is in fact no true mental peace, no true physical harmony or no true spirit tranquility beyond the holistic living truth regarding the divinity of the sacred garden culture.

Deep inside the lost and astray mind anguishes in emptiness, sadness and blueness. The adaptations and natural selection within the death consumption culture favor the addictive behaviors that perpetuate a drug culture of substance abuse, obesity, shopping orgies and mob frenzies, gossip, the thrill of the hunt, espionage dramas, and, of course, the major pastime—war and conflict. There is absolutely no question that the dominant vibration of the lost and astray mind has led the mass majority of Man, He and She, into the cycle of the unwholely (unholy) parallel. This dominant parallel of the ice-cold, deep-freeze mentality can produce nothing but fatality, suffering, misery, aches and pains for all disciples and followers of the energy that is opposite of Supreme Love.

The suffering of misery, aches and pains that were bred within the ice-cold, deep-freeze are so well-ingrained that they have become an addiction within the lost and astray mind. It is no surprise that inflicting death upon the innocent is a pleasure-seeking device within the ice-cold, deep-freeze mentality—a favorite sport and pastime of enthusiastic hunters of all stripes and shapes.

Within the hands of the ice-cold, deep-freeze mentality, technology provides simply another means to perpetuate lust, lies, illusion, confusion, death and deadly destruction. The computer, for example, which has been designed by the Most Supreme Seen and Unseen forces of the Universe of the Most High, has been sent to eradicate the mental and physical diseases of ignorance through a freed link of mass communication. However, within the mental space of the unholy parallel, technology is used to further the death consumption culture's ideology of seek, search and destroy. Current events regarding technological advancements and achievements continue to be a statement of the ice-cold, deep-freeze intellect:

> Ever since man picked up a rock to kill dinner, hunters have been technology pioneers. These days, they've got more gadgets than ever to choose from. Heat sensors will spot wounded game in dense brush, remote-controlled cameras can scout game trails. There are motorized duck and deer decoys, electronic duck and coyote calls and even holographic archery sights. But some of the latest in hunting tech pushes the ethical envelope, and some states are outlawing high-tech innovations that game managers feel give hunters an undue advantage. A San Antonio entrepreneur recently created an uproar with a Web site, www.live-shot.com, that aims to allow hunters to shoot exotic game animals or feral pigs on his private hunting ranch by remote control, with the click of a mouse, from anywhere in the world. [57]

The eugenics movements advocated by those who are supposed to be intellectually and financially elite never target the ice-cold, deep-freeze mentality as a degenerated and

[57] *New Gadgets Push the Envelope in Hunting.* Jeff Barnard. Associated Press. March 04, 2005. Online Source: http://www.msnbc.msn.com/id/7084990/.

defective mental condition. The I in I would presume it is because they are the very same individuals who wallow in the ice-cold, deep-freeze mentality or they are the offspring of the fathers and grandfathers who were overt and blatant in their fear, greed, hatred, and violence. The I in I have brought forward messages regarding the lost and astray mind and the ice-cold, deep-freeze mentality for well over a generation, having observed many disguises of the toxic vibrations during the last several decades.

### *Desperate Need for a Change in Direction*

What happens when the lost and astray mind goes on a rampage and calls forth the cultural war cries of the ice-cold, deep-freeze mentality? Even those in the seat of power are not safe when the runaway child of the ice-cold, deep-freeze mentality is running wild. One wonders if there is anyone who is safe from this cold-blooded mentality of seeking to search and destroy as the frenzied hunter howls at the sight of blood. In truth and reality, there is absolutely no safety valve against the lost and astray mind. It is quite clear that anyone can be targeted as the prey as the vicious killing vibrations of the cold-blooded warrior are activated by the energy that is opposite of Supreme Love.

How easily the killer instinct can be unleashed in the lost and astray mind as it mirrors the war god of envy, jealousy, vengeance, greed and spite. The collective consciousness of the ice-cold, deep-freeze mentality is a toxic memory bank filled with anger and hate that inflames the behaviors of lust, lies, illusions, confusion, death and deadly destruction. The defective reasoning and disabling attitudes and behaviors of the ice-cold, deep-freeze mentality are considered as unexplainable aberrations by the lost and astray mind when, in fact, the acts of violence, cruelty, brutality and destruction are the heritage, the birthright, of the energy that is opposite of Supreme Love.

It is unquestionable that there are souls that have been put on ice or, should we say, souls that are locked tight within the ice-cold, deep-freeze mentality. The Children of the Sun who lost their tan constantly rant and rage about technological advancements and the ability to go to the moon or elsewhere. These technological advancements have created a powerful and mighty machinery that quickly provides the ability to kill, destroy and maim, i.e. the nuclear bombs, the atomic bombs, and all of the other so-called great achievements and accomplishments of modern technology. For example, a highly acclaimed Nobel prize-winning scientist who was rewarded for figuring out how the sun and other stars generate energy became a key figure in building the first atomic bomb. It is unquestionable that the ice-cold, deep-freeze mentality perpetuates a technology of gross insanity that disrespects and disregards the whole life presence of Man, He and She and every other living thing It is absolutely amazing that the technological advancements have all been inspired by a driving desire to accelerate in war and excel in the swift ability to kill.

The superiority of the ice-cold, deep-freeze mentality has nothing to do with divine spirit consciousness or the spirit elevation of Man, He and She. Rather, the claims of superiority are based on superficial, artificial, materialistic gains and paper money, fronted by a dialect of intellect and the swift ability to kill. It is truly acknowledged that intelligence is not the priority; the priority is how one packages oneself in expressions that are shallow, empty and vague. As a result, there are many children running around who act and talk like a photo static copy of the television programs that they consume. These children can mimic and imitate the television characters that they watch, but they have not the sense to reason with the slightest degree of divine spirit consciousness.

There is indeed a raging and rampaging child running buck wild upon the planet Earth who is seeking to search and destroy by any means necessary in a bloodthirsty lust for dominance. The thrill of the kill and the excitement of the hunt are simply the way of life within the hunting, scavenging and herding culture. Suicide, homicide and genocide go hand in hand within the ice-cold, deep-freeze mentality as a response that reflects a soulless and spiritless state of being. A state of being that has been passed on like a plague and has been well assimilated by the suntanned disciples and followers.

What would cause an individual to go berserk and plot the death of someone else? Research indicates that a convicted "white" supremacist solicited an undercover FBI informant to assassinate a federal judge; the informant is said to have been wired and taped the conversation. Let's take a look this "white" supremacist's ideology:

> Matt Hale is quoted as saying: "Does the Church still support the idea of shipping the mud races back to their native lands? Of course, we have never deviated from that position. We never will and that's only the first step. We will withdraw all aid to them and they will wither on the vine. And one day white people will be basking in the sun of Africa in their own countries. I like that thought, Africa is a beautiful continent let's colonize the place as it should have been done, it was done at one time but it wasn't done right. It's time to do it right and drive the non-whites off the face of the earth."[58]
>
> The Creativity movement was founded by Ben Klassen…The current leader is Matt Hale. According to Klassen, his religion—Creativity—is the recognition that the natural destiny of the White

---

[58] One People's Project. Online Source: http://www.onepeoplesproject.com/index.php?option=content&task=view&id=89&Itemid=29

> Race is to rule the world and thus fulfill the purpose of the universe. To attain this destiny, it is necessary to destroy the enemies and race traitors who prevent this from happening. The primary enemies are Jews, Blacks and other "mud people," and White race traitors, including most Christians...In *White Man's Bible,* Klassen writes: "The niggers is [sic] the vital means of bastardizing the White Race...The Jews are therefore madly pushing a program of upgrading the niggers and pulling down the White." The suggested solution is to ship Blacks back to Africa, "drive the Jews from power and render them harmless," and "hang the traitors of our own race."[59]

It is noted that Klassen committed suicide. We present a quote from Rev. Matt Hale of the Creativity Church on the subject of consumption:

> There are no dietary requirements; however, our church does promote the concept of salubrious living. What salubrious living is, is a return to nature's laws in the field of nutrition as much as we have returned to nature's laws in the field of society, of government, of religion. White creatures, and all creatures that can speak and walk on two legs for that matter, eat the most hideous substances that their bodies have no use for or are completely harmful to their bodies. We need to reverse this situation; it is not a requirement of the church but we do promote the raw food, salubrious diet. We promote our members' eating foods only

---

[59] *White Supremacist, Antisemitic, and Race Hate Groups in the U.S.* Article by Chip Berlet. PublicEye.org, the Website of Political Research Associates. Online Source: http://www.publiceye.org/racism/white-supremacy.html

> in their raw, natural state. This is what nature intended.[60]

Clearly, one can declare a doctrine of raw and living foods yet remain in the unholy parallel. It is not possible to maintain the vibrations of racist ideologies and exist within the divine parallel. It is absolutely necessary to de-tox the racist and sexist ideologies that dictate control by force through the triple-six energies of lust, lies, illusions, confusion, death and deadly destruction.

The I in I have perpetuated the principles and practices of divine consumption, i.e. a holistic living way of life, for nearly two generations. Divine consumption includes the consuming of raw and living fruits, vegetables, seeds and nuts. However, divine consumption includes far more than the food that you put in your stomach. The top priority of divine consumption is divine humility to the holistic living truth about Supreme Love. A prerequisite of divine humility is divine spirit consciousness which encompasses the thoughts that one thinks and the acts that one commits. Divine spirit consciousness requires one to honor the most supreme sacred and original presence of the Divine Children of the Sun and the sacred garden culture.

With all of this mind, one wonders if it is possible for anyone of the lost and astray mind to begin to exit the ice-cold, deep-freeze mentality. Let us examine this point in our search for solutions to de-tox this cold blooded mentality:

> During the 1990's a single hate-rock band built a larger audience of white supremacists than any other, mostly through the distribution of their underground recordings. That band was RaHoWa (short for "Racial Holy War") and George Eric Hawthorne, also known as George Burdi, was its

[60] Weekly news from World Church of the Creator. July 7, 1999. Online Source: http://www.salon.com/news/feature/1999/07/07/hale/print.html

front man. In addition to leading RaHoWa, he also founded a very well known white supremacy music label called Resistance Records. Additionally, George was one of the largest promoters of white supremacy material in the United States, Canada, and throughout Europe, and has been interviewed on such public media venues as CNN and MTV.[61]

In an interview, George Burdi stated:

> In an unpublished essay titled *The Eternal Winter of the White Man's Soul*, I discuss a theory that the evolutionary effect of the harsh northern winters produced in the white man a human creature well adapted to cooperation and hard work, but easily enamored with the material dimension (note the preponderance of efficiently organized white neighborhoods that amount to a cultural zero) when the primordial tension has been removed. In the modern world we have the glorification of technological science, the result of which is the reduction of human potential and the degradation of human culture. And the bastard son of this materialization of the mind is the racist doctrine that places biological heredity above the strength of the soul and quality of the personality.[62]

Research indicates that after his release from jail, George Burdi stepped away from the white supremacist movement,

---

[61] *Hate Rock to Spiritual Revelation - The Transformation of George Burdi.* An Interview by Brian W. Blueskye. The Engaged Zen Foundation. Online Source: http://www.engaged-zen.org/articles/Brian_W_Blueskye-Hate_Rock_Spiritual_Revelation.html

[62] *Interview: George Burdi.* Vanguard News Network. April 27, 2004. Online Source: http://www.vanguardnewsnetwork.com/v1/2004b/42704burdiinterview.htm

formed a multicultural band, and pursued spiritual teachings. In an interview addressed to his former white supremacist comrades, George Burdi is quoting as saying:

> Judge a tree by the fruit it bears, brothers. The white power movement has borne bitter fruit. Don't treat me like I'm insane when I point it out. I could tell you some stories, as I'm sure you all could, about some of the lowlifes that populate the movement. But let's take that as read. I raise the issue only to ask a more meaningful question: what does it tell us about the errors of the ideology itself? Doesn't the dearth of quality membership (and leadership) suggest that race, although a scientific truth in the world of matter, is only a small piece of a much bigger picture?
>
> Want to save the white race? I'll tell you how. Reconnect to the divine element that has been lost. Then, the vital fluid will be present again, and the energy of the folk will return. This reconnection cannot be performed collectively, nor can political action evoke it. The journey must start with the individual who sets out, on his own accord, to discover what has been lost, to purify both body and mind, to make themselves worthy, and then to express, through every thought, word, and deed, the integrity of their being. Striking out with obscene attacks on others will not change your inner constitution for the better, it will hurt you first, before it hurts the other. It will puff you up with vain self-satisfaction, and in this state of mind you will wither and fail to reach your true potential.[63]

---

[63] See footnote 62.

George Burdi was quoted as saying, "I eat raw, organic food for the health of my body."[64] When one comes down to the nitty gritty, what is life itself except an experience to be lived and to be enjoyed and to be appreciated in honoring the sacred glory of the earth, wind, rain and sun? Why is it then that one would have such vicious, cruel, cold-blooded and callous programs installed to rape, murder, steal and take, except that the ice-cold, deep-freeze mentality is so well-ingrained in so many?

If one takes a looks at the prisons and incarceration circumstances, if one takes a look at the shortening of life expectancy, if one takes a look at the depletion in birth rates, one can see clearly and beyond a shadow of a doubt that there are social economic states that perpetuate adverse effects against target groups. Clearly and beyond a shadow of a doubt, when one takes a look at the historical patterns of rape, murder and destroy, if one takes a look at the racist ideologies and the perpetuation of hurt and harm against others, it is quite clear that the Children of the Sun who lost their tan sit in the driver's seat of the death consumption culture.

Why spend one's time running around in conflict, confusion, lust, lies, illusions, death and deadly destruction perpetuating the energy that is opposite of Supreme Love? How does it calculate in real terms when one begins to evaluate one's existence upon the planet? It is clear that there is more than ample space for all of Man, He and She, upon this glorious planet. It is quite clear that the divine order of a holistic living way of life will, in fact, cause a re-emergence forward into divine oneness for Man, He and She. It is quite clear that the dominant genetic expression upon the planet is the genetic expression of the origin of Man, He and She, i.e. the Divine Children of the Sun with the golden tan.

How then can Man, He and She, continue to survive upon the planet without the urgent and immediate implementation of

---

[64] See footnote 61.

divine spirit consciousness within the divine parallel of the Supreme Love vibration? What else is there other than to move into a state of divine spirit consciousness where one perpetuates the ideology of live and let live and life is for the living? It is the divine duty, obligation and responsibility of a sacred few to harmonize in divine oneness as the sacred and blessed example that life is for the living. As the I in I have said, no toxic condition is permanent. We, the sacred sons and daughters of Man, He and She, the Divine Children of the Sun, have the ability to resolve this insanity.

# Chapter Seven:
# The Social and Sexual Agenda of the Ice-Cold, Deep-Freeze Mentality

# Chapter Seven: The Social and Sexual Agenda of the Ice-Cold, Deep-Freeze Mentality

***Reviewing the Social Economic Struggles to Concede Nothing***

Regardless of one's level of intelligence, regardless of one's social or political agenda, regardless of one being blonde or bald or natty, natty dread, one's attitudes and behaviors will tell the true story of the energy of one's consumption patterns. A case in point reflects the utter disregard for the whole life presence that is the base and foundation of death consumption. Eliminating, enslaving or consuming others for one's personal gain is the name of the game within the energy that is opposite of Supreme Love. For example, top-secret files recently declassified from the National Archives of Australia indicate that one of the so-called fathers of modern biotechnology and genetic engineering advocated germ warfare as a means of reducing a population of dark-skinned peoples.

Nobel prize-winning microbiologist, Sir Macfarlane Burnet, reportedly advocated the use of biological weapons against Indonesia and other "overpopulated" countries of Southeast Asia in a secret report from 1947 that recommended targeting food crops and spreading infectious diseases. Burnet advised a government committee, "In a country of low sanitation the introduction of an exotic intestinal pathogen, e.g. by water contamination, might initiate widespread dissemination." He further advised that the "introduction of yellow fever into a country with appropriate mosquito vectors might build up into a disabling epidemic before control measures were established." Research indicates that while outlining the benefits of the population elimination program, Burnet pointed out that using germ warfare "has the tremendous advantage of not destroying the enemy's industrial potential, which can then be taken over intact."

The same cold-blooded mentality that emerged in the ice-cold, deep-freeze continues to surface again and again in the modern and sophisticated death consumption culture. The attitudes and behaviors of mutation and degeneration continue to expose the adverse effects of toxic consumption. And the mutation and degeneration continues to intensify.

The death consumption culture has been the breeding ground for an entire family branch of mutation and degeneration that produced violent, brutal and cold-blooded invaders, generation after generation. Now it becomes an official statement since the brilliance of modern scientific research has recently identified specific genes that are responsible for violent behavior. Research subjects would most likely include inner city youth of the darker hue who fit the criminal profile designed by the blue bloods and other disciples and followers of the ice-cold, deep-freeze mentality. The educated elite will quickly project the appearance that the driving force of research and study serves to advance the nobility of mankind. Targeted and well-funded research projects totally ignore the fact that the social ills of the death consumption culture were created by the adverse effects of a social economic hierarchy rooted in the ice-cold, deep-freeze mentality. It seems to be conveniently forgotten that the social economic hierarchy of the death consumption culture is based on conquest, murder, rape, steal, take and enslavement. It seems to be conveniently forgotten that the philosophy of this hierarchy is to seek, search and destroy or reduce one's adversaries or one's victims to their lowest terms and conditions.

A case in point is a social economic system where the privileged elite orchestrate and instigate impoverished conditions by maintaining a slave labor mentality long after the overt structure has been dismantled. The process of degrading

Man, He and She, to the status of property requires a systematic elimination of access to education, land, family stability, and business opportunities. After manufacturing these impoverished conditions and breeding the impoverished state of mind of the enslaved for economic gain, the privileged elite sit back in leisurely comfort, pointing the finger at the wretched and despicable conditions of the so-called lower class. The blue bloods, having already carved out their position of dominance in industry, land ownership, and education, justify and rationalize the critical need to rid society of the unfit breed that has been used like beasts of burden. Domestic and international programs of social welfare follow a genocidal-like pattern of targeting populations of a darker hue. Population control and family planning systems that plan families completely out of existence are a way to control populations that could become a threat to the blue blood wealth base if they awakened and rose up against the interests of the privileged elite.

### *Breeding the Deceptions of the Social Economic System*

The social economic system of the ice-cold, deep-freeze mentality closely relates to the patterns and behaviors of the chattel slavery system of old. The major difference between the two reflects the difference of overt and covert attitudes and behaviors. Even though the slave codes are no longer written in the law books, the thoughts and reasoning of so many still reflect the slavery mentality. The impoverished populations function as wage slaves on the hustle living from paycheck to paycheck. The middle class functions as a buffer to keep the impoverished population under control. Like overseers, they keep themselves in check with dreams of one day becoming the master. The social economic system is a replacement of the indentured servant system with a revised edition of the chattel slavery system. What else could the social economic system of the ice-cold, deep-freeze mentality be other than the root and foundation of it social economic origin? Some members of the impoverished population would enlist in the military to fill the rank and files of the war machine to protect and to serve the status quo.

A small percentage, 10 percent or less as a younger W.E.B. Dubois stated, would be spring boarded into the "Black Bourgeois" as a middle class with access to educational achievements, status, careers, aspirations of integration and assimilation, an accumulation of things and stuff, and a dream of going beyond the above. Their bank roll would be credit cards and their inheritance would be credit and debt which was a statement that they didn't really own nothing yet except a dream deferred. Through time, many of the privileged suntanned Children drew favor, because they were "light bright and damn near white." The mulatto concept represents the illegitimate offspring of the "master" race.

Often the hunter, scavenging, and herding culture defined the relationships of Man, He and She, with terms used for stable animals. The term mulatto comes from the Spanish word for a young mule. It is noted that a mule is the offspring of a male donkey and a female horse. The breeding and cross-breeding of domesticated animals is a practice that is familiar in animal husbandry. Findings show that mules are usually sterile, because of the mixture of genes. It is noted that one of the mottoes used by the American Birth Control League was "breeding a race of thoroughbreds," using the language of stables and barnyards while referring to Man, He and She.

The issues of identity facing many mulatto offspring echoes the same historic patterns that plagued the mixed breed offspring who were born from the cold-blooded and vicious invasions launched against the ancient garden culture. The mixed breeds, otherwise classified as Semitic tribes, grew to honor their invader father who descended from the Caucasus Mountain and steppe region while scorning the darkness of skin from the mother and her father's tribe. In each instance, up until today, many mulatto offspring forget the cold-blooded vibrations of rape, hostile aggression and terrorizing circumstances that originated the mixed-breed mentality.

Many of the mulatto genealogy charts dipped into the blue-blood family lines of slave master fathers. What the wealthy elite discovered is that the "talented tenth" of the darker hue served well as a buffer class. The fortunate few who rose in social economic status would uphold the death consumption culture more tenaciously and with a greater focus to keep the lower classes in check, i.e. in their place, thus securing the thoughts of being privileged by one's color. In fact, these near-white suntanned Children would have a vested interest in maintaining the whiteness concepts and theories of the status quo. This would cause this mixed breed of children to have extreme difficulty in having humility towards their darker ancestors while holding great pride in their "whiteness," regardless of the circumstances that caused that whiteness to come to be. This striving class of the darker hue would also serve to mobilize the majority population in a competitive race for the vacant positions on the ladder of social economic status.

The suntanned elite although far removed from their blue-blood counterparts would establish the same attitudes and behaviors regarding the paleness of skin and the superiority of breeding. The thought and reasoning of integration and assimilation maintained that the more closely one resembled the model of mutation and degeneration, the more accepted one becomes and the greater one's chances of gaining entry into the hallowed halls of the upper class. The females of the darker hue would resort to straightening and perming their hair in order to imitate the beauty standards of the death consumption culture.

With the stronghold that the talented tenth had on a dream to get a piece of the pie, so many would be willing to hustle votes to legislate systems to eliminate the burden of populations from which they themselves had emerged. In this way, so many become enticed to work on jobs looking forward to retirement one day. The plan is to retire, forgetting that the programs totally control their wants, their needs and their desires. Furthermore, by retirement age, the individual has become so entrenched that they have no recollection of an identity beyond the one given to them by the status quo.

The time-tested strategy of the vicious invader clans relies on the old philosophy that whoever controls the hands that rock the crib controls the nation and every generation of that nation. The first step in population control is to destabilize the family structure so that any offspring produced suffer from a weakened base of nurturing and fail to thrive. Issues of basic survival become the overriding concern in any impoverished condition, and a population struggles to exist from generation to generation. This is how the mutated and degenerated breed of the ice-cold, deep-freeze mentality infects other populations with the toxic vibrations and sensations of their origin from the Caucasus Mountains and steppe region. Inflicting the vibrations and sensations of deprivation, depletion and hardship on the suntanned populations of the planet through murder, rape, steal and take is the way that the mutated and degenerated breed has spread the energy that is opposite of Supreme Love like a plague all over the planet.

In any enslavement system, the female is placed in a position of dependence and submission to the dominant power structure so that the male authority figure of guidance and protection becomes the image of the vicious invader rather than a male of her own kind. In such a social welfare system, the female is given financial aid based on the number of children she breeds with the restriction that no male can be present as the head of the household. The more children that she breeds, the more aid she receives. The system functions to keep the female in her enslavement role of breeder while the male is reduced to stud status. The generations of children who grow up in such a system with the father presence severely weakened or absent have received minimal guidance and protection from a responsible male role model. The aid that is received on social welfare provides just enough income to live in a low-rent neighborhood where crime and drug abuse are common responses to impoverished circumstances. The quality of food and education in the impoverished environment is deficient in many ways. The female struggles to raise her children in the lower end of the death consumption culture, and mutation and degeneration intensify.

An unforeseen problem arises within the case scenario just outlined. The vibrations and sensations of the ice-cold, deep-freeze emerged out of a harsh, cold and barren environment. The privileged elite have orchestrated an entire death consumption culture that serves to multiply the toxic vibrations and sensations of their origin. In this way, the hostile aggression, genetic deterioration and sex and violence that fester in the inner cities of urban landscapes is the mirror image of the same harsh, cold and barren vibrations of the ice-cold, deep-freeze mentality. Even the sun has difficulty shining through the smog and toxic waste of what has been identified as the concrete jungles of urban blight.

The conquered and enslaved masses of suntanned populations serve as a breeding ground for the mutation and degeneration inherent in the death consumption culture. It is no wonder that young males in the harsh, cold and barren ghettos and slums of the inner cities of the death consumption culture would act out the same vicious and cold-blooded attitudes and behaviors that descendants from the Caucasus Mountain and steppe region inflicted upon the sacred garden culture. When considering the fact that many of the wealthiest and most elite blue-blood families secured their wealth in the lucrative opium trade of the 1800's after many before them made massive fortunes in the slave trade, it is no surprise to see young hustlers selling drugs on street corners of the death consumption culture. It is also no surprise to see young females prostituting and whoring themselves on the streets as a reflection of familiar patterns of the good-old-slavery days where the female was available for service to the master, the overseer or another stud. It is also no wonder that the scientific researchers of the death consumption culture have identified specific genes that are said to be responsible for violent behaviors. Sex and violence are the DNA profile of the mutation and degeneration breed.

Toxic thoughts, attitudes, and behaviors have the uncanny ability to become self-fulfilling prophecies, because the more toxic vibrations and sensations one consumes, the more toxic experiences one manifests. It is not unlikely that genetic testing and genetic counseling could be used to target those who maintain an ethnic profile and stigma that is projected as having a threatening potential. The real fear involves the possibility that those who have been historically violated and abused will rise up one day with enough vigor and vitality to inflict the big pay back upon those who have instigated and perpetuate the violations and abuse. As a result, the vibrations and sensations of eugenics remain very active in the lost and astray mind. Someone who can kill without a conscience may be labeled as a psychopath. However, in the death consumption culture war is glorified, and killers are considered heroes, especially when a young personality like an Emmett Till is identified as whistling in admiration of the glamorized beauty standard of the death consumption culture. What is the divine parallel that will allow one to escape all of this death consumption madness?

Revised systems of the same old systems are developed to maintain breeding control, imprisonment, and social economic limitations that function in ways very similar to the slave labor system. When one looks in truth and reality, the means begin to meet its end as a population of people indulge in inferior consumption and become inferior in attitudes, inferior in behavior, and breed that inferiority into any offspring who are produced. The tragic irony is that inferiority is indeed bred. Inferiority is bred through the errors in the DNA that manifest from inferior consumption. Thus, those who proclaim to be of a middle class or of an upper class even among the suntanned Children begin to look around at the massive chaos and disorder surrounding them. From their positions of relative material comfort, they quickly point the finger at the adverse conditions of impoverished populations of the have-not's. From their clone-like zone, those races and classes who feel like they have made it over the hurdle and are moving on up begin to reason with the concepts of population control as the solution to societal ills. Seldom do these individuals reason that the impoverished populations are the present scapegoats, and if the impoverished were eliminated, then the next class up the ladder would become the next scapegoats.

Within the death consumption culture, principles and practices of eugenics find unconscious supporters who are so entrenched in the self-centered syndrome of the I-me-my fixation that they can not read the writing on the wall. Quickly these individuals who hide behind the blindfolds of acquiring things and stuff start to assess that there are truly populations that no longer need to reproduce because of the inferior state of being of their social economic status. It is ignored that this economic status is being programmed, controlled, manipulated, instigated, and maintained in order to allow a privileged few to be able to acquire a wealth base far beyond their ability to spend.

The wealth base of the death consumption culture is orchestrated to be passed on through genetic lines so that the offspring born from this mutated and degenerated breed can continue to maintain the upper hand. In this way, families of the wealthy elite continue to be the controlling hand of the status quo. There would even be individuals from the cold-blooded and selfish vibrations of the ice-cold, deep-freeze mentality who establish trust funds to lock up a bulk of wealth in the hope that they will be able to return from a deep freeze called cryonics. The strategy is to thaw out and return later to continue their feast of financial control. And as for individuals born within the elite status of the death consumption culture, they would have every reason to dig deeper and deeper to maintain their privileges and status.

The privileged offspring would function with the same free-range frame of reference with the earth and its global suntanned populations as their playing ground. These offspring would have no worry or fear about any economic issues as they roam freely around the Earth, seeking to search and control or destroy the will of others. Anyone who thinks that this habitual circle of control will be relinquished without the most violent and vicious struggle is underestimating the tricks and deceptions used by the powerbrokers to maintain themselves. Let us not forget, we are talking about the powerbrokers of the death consumption culture who feast on an energy that is opposite of Supreme Love.

And so, insensitive and non-compassionate plots and schemes would be orchestrated under the guise of scientific research. Callous ventures like the Tuskegee Syphilis Study would be conducted with the justification that the research was designed to benefit mankind. It is amazing that a breed of mankind born of an ice-cold, deep-freeze mentality would indeed glorify the cold-blooded birthmark of mutation and degeneration. It is amazing that the birthmarks of mutation and degeneration have become the standard norm.

The mutated and degenerated breed is genetically linked in a triple-six alliance with the vibrations of lust, lies, illusions, confusion, death and deadly destruction. It is amazing that there are so many disciples and followers aligned with this energy that is opposite of Supreme Love, regardless of them being blonde or bald or natty, natty dread. However, the fact remains that a privileged few have accelerated the disorder of mutation and degeneration through their breeding patterns and have established the social economic and religious structures to maintain that control. As it is, the death consumption culture has quickly become a norm among Man, He and She. Many would think that anything beyond the death consumption culture is an inferior lifestyle and a step backwards for humanity. The underlying thoughts and reasoning are, "I'm going to get mine, you'd better get yours." By any means necessary.

Thus, if the general population of Man, He and She, has to suffer degradation and humiliation so that a few are able to live a privileged life, then so be it, says those who benefit. If the wealthy and privileged elite consume the mass majority of the wealth base and natural resources of the planet Earth to enrich themselves, while others in that social environment receive the leftovers, then so be it, says those who benefit. If so many of those within the class structures of the social environment are devoted to the trickle-down theory of economics where something is better than nothing, or it is better to have than to have not, then so be it says those who benefit. As for the massive populations of the have-nots, it is reasoned that they were unfortunately born as an inferior outcast cursed by the great white father in the sky.

On the other hand, there are those who reason that the have-nots just don't have the smarts or the military might to be able to dictate favorable terms in the negotiations for their natural resources. It is reasoned that the control of global natural resources is determined by the survival-of-the-fittest mentality, and the fittest are determined by the intellect to instigate massive terror, fright, fear and the ability to swiftly kill, destabilize and destroy. Terror can be orchestrated by nuclear weapons, or terror can be orchestrated by a rope and tree or by a group of police shooting a single unarmed man nineteen times or more. It is clear that this reasoning of survival of the fittest originates in the ice-cold, deep-freeze mentality and perpetuates the vibrations of lust, lies, illusions, confusion, death and deadly destruction.

It is also clear that the disciples and followers of the death consumption culture automatically breed rivalries and rivals who seek to claim the top dog position. These rivalries may appear as Aryan/Semitic conflicts or as east/west conflicts or even the north/south conflict of the good-old-slavery days, but the real deal is all of the rivalries are born and bred out of the ice-cold, deep-freeze mentality. The primary rivalry focuses on 1) controlling the natural resources of those of color, 2) concepts of superiority based on color, and 3) the purity of specific racial characteristics that reflect the original invader culture of hunters and herders. This frame of thought would occur within and among those classified as Euro-centric, within and among those classified as Semitic, i.e. Arabs, Jews, etc., within and among those classified as Asians, and even within and among those classified as Afro-centric.

The modern philosophy would be that the natural resources of the planet belong to everyone, especially since the "modern" discovery that Man, He and She, originally descended from an Afro-centric mother and father. The aggressor and invader culture would say, "Your land is my land, but my land is not your land. Your wealth is my wealth, and my wealth is my wealth. Your woman is for my use, but my woman is for my use and off limits to you. Your children are to build my empire, and my children are to inherit my empire." And as the old British saying goes, "That is the bloody truth, so take it on the chin, old boy." In fact, it is the bloody truth that comes from the blood-spilling vibrations of the ice-cold, deep-freeze mentality.

When it comes down to the real nitty, gritty, the natural resources are horded to over inflate the wealth base of the privileged elite and their offspring. The wholesome and healthy well-being of the planet, the water, the soil, the air, and the population become irrelevant so long as the cash keeps flowing and the personal accounts keep growing. If one takes a look at the conflict-resolution tactics within the global struggle for dominance, one can see that the Armageddon mentality is the self-fulfilling prophecy for all the masters, grand masters, disciples and followers of the death consumption culture.

### *The Public Face of Domination and Control*

What is the nature of the defects and the hazards of the sexual and reproductive organs related to the political social economic order that has manifested a culture of death consumption? The death consumption culture breeds slave labor principles, morals and practices of the hunting and herding mentality. The enslavement mentality produces worker drones to provide a docile labor force and a ready consumer base that has no spiritual, mental or physical connection to the whole life presence. Within the culture of death consumption, social religious orders function to pacify Man, He and She, into believing that their greater life will come after death.

The modern day beliefs and attitudes were actually shaped by kings and rulers of the death consumption culture who secured economic and political power by promoting favorable religious texts and teachings. For instance, the translations and version of the religious text instigated by King James of England actually replaced another popular version of the same text. In an effort to secure his political power based on the "divine right of the kings," King James created a new version of the religious text. The divine right of kings was a belief that the king was granted his authority by god and was above questioning. King James expressed this belief in the following statement which equates the king with god:

> The state of monarchy is the supremest thing upon earth ... Kings are justly called Gods, for that they exercise a manner or resemblance of divine power upon earth. For if you will consider the attributes to God, you shall see how they agree in the person of a king. God has power to create, or destroy, make, or unmake at his pleasure, to give life, or send death, to judge all, and to be judged

> nor accountable to none: to raise low things, and to make high things low at his pleasure…[65]

It is noted that King James outlawed the old version of the religious text, and persecuted the disciples and followers of the old version, forcing many to flee England. Findings show that King James imprisoned those who held different religious beliefs and were labeled as heretics. According to the British law of the time, heretics were to be burned at the stake. The King James version became the authorized version of a religious text that has affected the minds of many. King James and others in a similar pattern had a very serious political and economic agenda to ensure that the mass population would give allegiance to his rule and leadership.

Research indicates that throughout the reign of King James, his personal relationships with males caused much debate regarding his homosexual affairs. Findings show that when James inherited the English Throne in 1603, it was openly joked in London that *Rex fuit Elizabeth: nunc est regina Jacobus* (Elizabeth was King: now James is Queen). Historical records state that in 1617 King James is noted to have addressed the Privy Council with an official statement defending his affairs: “Christ had John, and I have George.” Findings show that there a large number of “love letters” from King James to his various male companions, such as the Earl of Buckingham, who was later promoted to the post of "gentleman of the king's bed chamber." Many of King James’ personal letters that reference his affairs are noted to be archived in manuscript collections at the British Library, the National Library of Scotland, and the Bodleian Library at Oxford.

One should expect nothing more from a leader within the death consumption culture. The leader who indulges in the

---

[65] King James, excerpts his from speech to Parliament, March 21, 1609.

toxic vibrations of the death consumption culture by definition indulges in the same vibrations of conquest and enslavement that caused the vicious invasions and attacks against the sacred garden culture of old. The masters and grand masters of the death consumption culture can only manifest the same political maneuvers and control tactics that have been repeated throughout the brief history of mutation and degeneration. Either overtly or covertly, the ice-cold, deep-freeze mentality remains within the vibration of hunting and herding which seeks to amass ways and means to mentally and physically control populations in order to impose one's will upon them. The overall objective is to break the spirit of one's victim or convert the allegiance to one's own agenda.

### *Mutation Time Bomb*

The DNA encodes physical traits and behavior characteristics that allow for the survival of an organism in relationship to its natural habitat. Let it be clearly understood that the natural habitat of Man, He and She, was not the ice-cold, deep-freeze environment of the northern regions of the planet. Research in DNA tracking indicates ancient migration patterns of Man, He and She, that led out of the land now referred to as Afrika. The natural habitats of tropical and sub-tropical regions of the planet are in direct contrast to the icy northern tundra of the last Ice Age. All aspects of living, including adequate food and shelter, would be severely limited in such a cold and barren habitat. Within the death consumption culture, many of Man, He and She, consider sickness, disease and disorder to be natural and normal; they quickly point out the benefits of mutation and the way of life born and bred in death consumption. Unfortunately, the reasoning capacity of the lost and astray mind has depleted to the point where the direct connection between toxic consumption and adverse effects is a missing link.

As mutation and degeneration continue, a time bomb begins to tick off in the cell structure signaling error. The Most

Supreme Unseen does not maintain errors. Unless corrective action is immediately pursued, the consequence of error is self-destruction through system breakdown. Little do Man, He and She, seem to realize that the death consumption culture and the ice-cold, deep-freeze mentality have had many hosts over these past several thousand years. The only thing that has kept this ice-cold, deep-freeze mentality from implementing massive self-destruction has been the continued availability of hosts. The tragic irony is that each time a host is encountered and invaded, the host is transformed from a holistic living presence into a depleted and unwhole presence. The vicious invaders deposit toxic residue while stealing vital life energy in the form of treasures, stolen legacies, and knowledge. The invading force utilizes the female from the host to breed and multiply their toxic vibrations of control.

The death consumption culture has managed to find fresh hosts for rape, murder, steal and take all over the planet Earth. In every instance, the host has been used to divert an internal attack of self-destruction. There will come a time when the death consumption culture will have no hosts left to attack, and then the death consumption culture will begin to consume of another faction within itself until self-destruction occurs. This is the destiny of the death consumption culture; it is a dead-end proposition. It is unfortunate, however, that the sacred message of divine reasoning cannot penetrate the toxic and degenerated state of mind of the ice-cold, deep-freeze mentality.

At this point in time there are still a few hosts to prey upon, regardless of how meager their presence. The death consumption culture sucks on the cultural values, behaviors, and resources of the sacred garden culture while maintaining the values of the hunting, herding and scavenging culture at the same time. What this means is that the host, i.e. the suntanned Children of the sacred garden culture, have actually provided a mechanism of survival for the lost and astray Children who lost their tan. The toxic side effect of this relationship is that the suntanned Children of the sacred garden culture have been forced, coerced, terrorized, and deceived into integrating and assimilating the values and the behaviors that remain from the ice-cold, deep-freeze mentality.

### *Reproductive Issues: Abortion*

It is noted that while the federal government will not pay for abortion, it does allow Medicaid to pay for sterilization services. Research indicates that during the 1970's sterilization became the most rapidly growing form of birth control in the United States, rising from 200,000 cases in 1970 to over 700,000 in 1980. What is disturbing is not the prevalence of sterilization as a form of birth control, but the fact that many women were noted to have been sterilized without knowing. Findings show that many women on Medicaid have indicated that they were subjected to tubal ligations and hysterectomies while being operated on for other medical reasons or were coerced into consent when doctors refused to perform abortions or deliveries until they signed.

It has been pointed out that many are unaware that a major organization, such as Planned Parenthood, whose operations include nearly 850 health centers in 49 states and the District of Columbia, serving nearly five million women, men, and teenagers each year has its beginnings in alliance with the early eugenics movement. Planned Parenthood founder, Margaret Sanger, reportedly followed similar lines of reasoning regarding birth control and targeted populations that were expressed in eugenics. BlackGenocide.org states that "Planned Parenthood is the largest abortion provider in America. 78% of their clinics are in minority communities. Blacks make up 12% of the population, but 35% of the abortions in America. Are we being targeted?" It is noted that Margaret Sanger developed the "Negro Project" which had goals and objectives of restricting, thus reducing, the "Negroid" population. Reports indicate that Sanger created this program in 1939, after the organization changed its name from the American Birth Control League to the Birth Control Federation of America.

Sanger reportedly aligned herself with the thoughts and reasoning of the eugenics movement. These attitudes of preserving racial superiority through population control and restricted breeding practices were gaining popularity in the early 1900's under the banner of scientific theories about genetics. The eugenics concepts of "white" racial supremacy and "racial purity" reflect a strain of the ice-cold, deep-freeze mentality that has existed since the earliest vicious invasions by the lost and astray Children of the Sun who lost their tan. It is not coincidental that the I in I refer to the ice-cold, deep-freeze mentality as being the energy that is opposite of Supreme Love.

The values of a nomadic invader culture that honors war, bloodshed, hostile aggression and carnivorous consumption stand in absolute and total opposition to the peaceful and harmonious vibrations of the sacred garden culture. The conquering forces of the ice-cold, deep-freeze have established the standards, values, and accepted qualities of every social structure within the death consumption culture. Therefore, the conquering forces have defined superior based on the cunning, vicious, ruthless, and cold-blooded patterns of the hunter, scavenger, and herder way of life. The intelligence of a blood-thirsty hunter breed does not equate to the intelligence of the master gardener breed. As a result, the suntanned Children of the sacred garden culture have historically been viewed as vastly different, and that difference has been defined as inferior. One wonders about the intelligence of a hunter, scavenger, and herder breed of man that glorifies violence, war, slaughter and bloodshed and continues to wallow in disease and disorder that results from the indulgence in toxic consumption.

Taking this inferior-superior concept a little further, one wonders how the acts of sex and violence and the worship of a male war god that gives his blessings to the murder, slaughter, and enslavement of the other guy could ever be considered a truly civilized way of life. It is amazing that maintaining a Supreme Love vibration in one's consumption and cultivating a social environment that honors the divine union of Man, He and She, as the true essence of the supreme creator is not valued or honored by the hunting, scavenging, herding breed. It is amazing that protecting the integrity of the earth, wind, rain and sun and every other living thing; and honoring the melanination of the sacred suntanned presence of Man, He and She, as vital keys in harmonizing with the earth, wind, rain and sun are not valued or honored by the hunting, scavenging, and herding breed. It is indeed a fact that the death consumption culture is a superior way of life within the ice-cold, deep-freeze mentality. As has been witnessed throughout history, the nomadic invader tribes are not able to peacefully coexist by the very nature of their toxic consumption patterns. The I in I have every confidence that the divine wisdom, innate intelligence, and natural superiority of the sacred garden culture will be seen by all those who have the spirit to see.

It is noted that eugenicists hope to purify the bloodlines and "improve the race" by encouraging the "fit" to reproduce and the "unfit" to restrict their reproduction. The methods of controlling the so-called "inferior" races were noted to be through segregation, sterilization, birth control and abortion. Since the United States Supreme Court legalized abortion in 1973, it is noted that approximately 32 million abortions have been performed which includes over ten million abortions on "African-American" females. That is about one third of the "African-American" population in the United States. Research indicates that, in 2000, the average cost of a non-hospital abortion with local anesthesia was about $372. Using that average rate of cost multiplied by the number of "African-American" females who have had abortions since 1973, it is calculated that an estimated $3,720,000,000 has been received for aborting "African American" births.

***Population Control***

Research clearly indicates that the rate of world population growth is in rapid decline, and mortality rates throughout the developing world are at an all-time high. According to a report by the U.S. Census Bureau, "The slowdown in the growth of the world's population can be traced primarily to declines in fertility." If indeed HIV/AIDS was developed as a biological warfare method, then it is very effective. Findings show that the HIV/AIDS pandemic has contributed to the decline in the world's population growth. The Census Bureau reports:

> Since the beginning of the epidemic two decades ago, more than 20 million people have died of AIDS. Twice that many — 40 million — are now living with HIV. Barring some major breakthrough, most of these people are expected to die during the next 10 years or so. Over 90 percent of people infected with the Human Immunodeficiency Virus (HIV), which causes AIDS, live in the developing world. The Joint United Nations Programme on HIV/AIDS (UNAIDS) expects that this "proportion will continue to rise in countries where poverty, poor health systems, and limited resources for prevention and care fuel the spread of the virus"[66]
>
> Over 30 percent of all children born to HIV infected mothers in Sub-Saharan Africa will be HIV positive. High rates of mortality, combined with lower levels of fertility, will lower the average life expectancy at birth to around 30 years by 2010,

[66] *Global Population Profile, 2002. The AIDS Pandemic in the Twenty First Century.* U.S. Census Bureau. Online Source: http://www.census.gov/ipc/prod/wp02/wp-02006.pdf

> a level not seen since the beginning of the 20th century.[67]

With all of this being as it is, the United States Agency for International Development (USAID) continues to promote population reduction through family planning in third world countries that have already become at-risk populations. The issue of global population decline is addressed by accelerating programs for population reduction through the spread of birth control pills and condoms. Billions of dollars are spent to support programs on reproductive health issues that promote birth control, sterilization and abortion. Like many branches of the eugenics programs of the past, the modern day population control programs are well financed by an elite group of wealthy financiers.

The most profound means of population control within the death consumption culture is to target the female. If the female is put under physical, mental and spiritual constraints, conditioned by contradicting values, then she will spend her entire life perpetuating the errors in thought and reasoning that nurture the death consumption culture. The female will multiply the errors in thought and reasoning into her offspring, and she will be a loyal supporter of the death consumption culture values, attitudes and behaviors as she nurtures her offspring.

What better way of controlling a population than to bombard the thoughts and reasoning of that population with images of the female as "the weaker sex," lesser creation, or sinful temptress based on mainstream religious concepts or standards of hostile aggression and brute strength? The cosmetics industry, fashion industry, and feminine-hygiene industry can then make billions of dollars on products designed to capitalize on the female's lack of self-esteem. Makeup,

---

[67] *USAID Unleashes More Population Control*, April 7, 2004. Online Source: http://www.pop.org/20040408606/usaid-unleashes-more-population-control

deodorized douches, perms, hair and skin bleaches and dyes, diet pills, high-heeled shoes and other merchandise are promoted to keep the female from connecting with and appreciating the natural appeal of her whole life presence in divine order. As a result, within the death consumption culture, the female is under a great deal of pressure to maintain an artificial, superficial, and false appearance that robs her of self-esteem and causes deep insecurities.

Boys born from esteemless females turn into adult males who have already been nurtured in esteemlessness and are unable to provide the divine guidance and protection that is required of them in mature male-female relationships. The first parental relationships set a vicious pattern within the death consumption culture that keep the offspring in a downward spiral of mutation and degeneration within the toxic vibrations and sensations of conflict, confusion, lust, lies, illusions, death and deadly destruction.

Add a massive dose of materialistic obsession with stuff and things and the powerful lure of mass media campaigns, and one has formulated a well-trained consumer base that is programmed to purchase based on jingles, hot new items, popular trends and the thrill of shopping. Add to this mix a little reverse color psychology and one has created a consumer monster on the prowl who seems to live just to purchase that new stuff or that latest thing. The death consumption culture capitalizes on the lost and astray mind with schemes that thrive on manufacturing another product to purchase for every problem that is amassed.

It should become clear that if one has a capitalizing scheme that profits on almost every problem, then one is sure to have a mechanism within that organized structure to instigate and to maintain the problems, such as esteem deficit disorders, anxiety and insecurity, male-female relationship issues, vanity and arrogance. As a matter of fact, sex and violence would simply be a mass media campaign within that social structure so that one could capitalize on pornographic images. The entertainment industry would then appeal to the toxic vibrations and sensations of lust and make huge profits on projects that follow a formula of sex and violence.

Those who feed off of these toxic vibrations, be they blonde or bald or natty, natty dread will come to see that the way to succeed within the death consumption culture is to cater to the lust, lies, illusions, confusion, death and deadly destruction of the energy that is opposite of Supreme Love. Within the death consumption culture, the ticket to escape the poor and wretched state of the inner city ghettos, crime-ridden slums, and so-called lower class neighborhoods and make it into the ranks of an upper class is to capitalize on the ignorance of the mass populations. Therefore, one calculates one's escape by first making sure that those loyal consumers who are ignorant, oblivious and confused remain ignorant, oblivious and confused. Those consumers who are in a problematic circumstance remain entrenched in the problems or at least remain within a controlled environment where the problem still requires the products and services of the death consumption culture. However, if the problem gets out of control, then that particular problem can amass a tidal wave of greater problems.

Thus, one comes to see that population control is established by controlling the reproductive system and the sexual organs of Man, He and She, as vital instruments in assuring that the lost and astray mind is all that will be reproduced. Masters and grand masters within the death consumption culture have masterminded patterns of selective breeding that began with the hunting and herding mentality of breeding livestock and then slaves. The selective breeding continued as the forefathers and grandfathers who acquired land, trading goods, and wealth through murder, rape, steal and take, invasion and enslavement enforced social economic and religious programs to secure their position. These forefathers established wealth through different systems and schemes based on the vibrations and sensations of lust, lies, illusions, confusion, death and deadly destruction. The overwhelming majority of moguls, magnates, tycoons, and capitalists of the United States of America and elsewhere were established through the slaughter of indigenous and native people, the transporting and selling of opium, the transporting and selling of cocaine, sugar and liquor, and the trafficking of slaves via the Trans-Saharan slave trade, Trans-Atlantic slave trade, etc. The railroad, shipping, and oil fortunes all supported the trade routes of commerce backed by the slave-labor system.

The vibrations of social economic slavery were born and bred off of the same system created by the vicious invasion culture that descended from the Caucasus mountain region with the ice-cold, deep-freeze mentality. The elite social economic class within the death consumption culture has maintained a lust for power that remains from the vibrations and sensations of cold-blooded warlords of the nomadic tribes that invaded the sacred garden culture across the planet. The concepts of an aristocratic or privileged upper class position based on social economic status and held by hereditary title began in the ice-cold caves and clan rivalries of the deep-freeze mentality, where those who had the biggest club, and the fiercest and swiftest ability to kill were the elite class of the death consumption culture. The upper class or highest position within the social hierarchy corresponds to those who have the dominating control of wealth, influence and political power within the death consumption culture. The birth right of such families is that the offspring are entitled to their status and position because of heredity.

The weapons changed and the tactics varied, but the hierarchy of power and control remains the same. The position of superior status and privilege within the death consumption culture automatically meant that someone else was designated as inferior, subservient and valued only in terms of serving the master's will. Toxic consumption and the cold-blooded way of life caused severe mutation and degeneration of the lost and astray mind and led to even more vicious attitudes and behaviors, both overt and covert.

One can very quickly begin to understand the various kinds of genocidal programs that have amassed, programs that, in fact, created the mentality of an Indra, Ghengis Khan, Ivan the Terrible, Attila the Hun, Arab Muslims and the jihads, Christopher Columbus and the "New World" invaders of America, Stalin, Mussolini, Adolf Hitler, the German Nazi party, and those who dropped that bomb on Hiroshima that devastated innocent populations and the environment all to showcase a new instrument of mass destruction. Keep in mind, this is but a very brief list. The rampage of massacre, slaughter, extermination, and enslavement of the indigenous and aboriginal suntanned populations was globally inflicted by the population of the ice-cold, deep-freeze mentality and their disciples and followers.

### *Mutation and Degeneration through Toxic Consumption: Evolution and the Superior Breed Concept*

Even the theory of evolution as proposed by Charles Darwin was used to justify a position of mutation and degeneration. Beyond a shadow of a doubt, the warring nomadic tribes who descended from the Caucasus Mountains and steppe region did not reflect the original and divine blueprint of Man, He and She. Darwin's book, *The Descent of Man*, explains the process of natural selection and survival of the fittest in the death consumption culture,

> Of the high importance of the intellectual faculties there can be no doubt, for man mainly owes to them his predominant position in the world. We can see, that in the rudest state of society, the individuals who were the most sagacious, who invented and used the best weapons or traps, and who were best able to defend themselves, would rear the greatest number of offspring. The tribes, which included the largest

> number of men thus endowed, would increase in number and supplant other tribes.[68]

In speaking of natural selection, Darwin is quick to make a distinction between savages and civilized man; his comprehension of civilized is based on the thoughts and reasoning of the death consumption culture born in the ice-cold, deep-freeze environment. His designation of the weak and the strong echoes the cave-clan hierarchy where brute strength, domination and superior ability to kill were glorified, honored and upheld as the highest qualities of Man He.

The racist and cold-blooded thoughts and reasoning that would later appear in the United States of America as the eugenics movement began in theories that were praised as the intellectual genius of civilized men. Darwin reasoned that even though the strong survived they were burdened by the weak, "We must therefore bear the undoubtedly bad effects of the weak surviving and propagating their kind; but there appears to be at least one check in steady action, namely that the weaker and inferior members of society do not marry so freely as the sound; and this check might be indefinitely increased by the weak in body or mind refraining from marriage, though this is more to be hoped for than expected." Such obnoxious vibrations of thought and reasoning are rampant within the death consumption culture and have formulated the educational, religious, political and social economic programs that control mass populations of Man, He and She.

There are many who readily accept such statements of survival of the fittest, natural selection and the superior evolution of mutation and degeneration. In every case where an individual accepts these concepts and values, he or she is

---

[68] *The Descent of Man.* Charles Darwin. Chapter Five: On the Development of the Intellectual and Moral Faculties During Primeval and Civilised Times. 1871. Online Source: http://www.zoo.uib.no/classics/darwin/descent.chap5.html.

always pointing the finger at the other guy as the target group. The lost and astray mind takes a little bit of the holistic living truth and spreads it through massive deception, and then starts to talk about superiority.

In truth, weakness is relative to one's analysis of strength. Strength to kill is the glory of the death consumption culture, whereas, the strength to cultivate life is the glory of the sacred garden culture. Within the death consumption culture, there are those who suffer the adverse effects of toxic consumption to a greater or more visible degree, and they become the scapegoats of the social order. Those who are certified as mentally ill get stigmatized and labeled as unfit. These individuals are given prescription mind-bending drugs and told that they will have to take these medications for the rest of their lives. This is their solution within the death consumption culture…Healing is not an option. On the other hand, so many among Man, He and She, walk the streets in severe mental disorder, manifesting the most insane and confused attitudes and behaviors while being declared normal. To address their stress, depression, and anxiety; their solution is to eat, drink, and be merry and enjoy a good movie or television program. Within the death consumption culture, good entertainment features sex and violence, even if it is a cartoon. The insanity of the ice-cold, deep-freeze mentality is declared normal within the death consumption culture.

Those who are labeled as mentally retarded are stigmatized and labeled as unfit while so many among Man, He and She, are stuck in the thinking and reasoning of a violent cave-man mentality. The visible damage of toxic consumption and the visible eruptions of toxic reaction are a severe indictment of the death consumption culture, yet those of the ice-cold, deep-freeze mentality praise themselves on a superior civilized way of life. Unfortunately, individuals locked in the ice-cold, deep-freeze mentality are unable to reason with the holistic living truth that any social order is the sum total of the energy that is consumed by its population. Toxic consumption breeds disorder and disease. Whereas, the eugenics advocate or "white" racist identifies the problem as a breeding problem or "race" problem, the comprehension that degeneration and mutation is the result of toxic consumption completely escapes the mental capacity of the ice-cold, deep-freeze mentality. For this reason, those who espouse "white" racism are completely unable to see and reason with the adverse effects caused by the ice-cold, deep-freeze mutation and degeneration.

The emergence of the Caucasian breed is noted as a later occurrence in the timeline development of Man, He and She. The lost and astray mind dwells on intellectual debates to justify its mutated and degenerated state, completely wiping out the memory of a truly divine origin. Nevertheless, as Darwin readily admits about his own kind, "But there can hardly be a doubt that we are descended from barbarians." Darwin, however, overlooked the fact that his mutated and degenerated frame of thought was the epitome of barbaric reasoning. You see, a little bit of the truth can go a long way to create a whole lot of conflict and confusion.

In disorder, the brain produces the lost and astray mind of thought that feasts on toxic thought and reasoning. The lost and astray mind consumes energies, vibrations, and sensations that cause degeneration and mutation to the wholly temple of Man, He and She, until a weak and feeble spirit is all that remains of the sacred presence. The superiority of the lost and astray mind is actually reducing Man, He and She, to a life presence of depletion, disorder, and disease. The concepts of cloning truly represent the reproduction of mutation and degeneration in the attitudes and behaviors that reflect a depleted spirit presence. Cloning can be defined as a process of reproducing multiple identical copies. The mass majority of Man, He and She, is in a clone-like state of toxic consumption within the death consumption culture, reproducing the mental, physical and spiritual mutation and degeneration of the lost and astray mind. This is truly and sincerely the cloning process of

Man, He and She. This is in fact the outer limits of the death consumption culture.

# Chapter Eight: The Meltdown of the Deep-Freeze Mentality

# Chapter Eight: The Meltdown of the Deep-Freeze Mentality

It is very important for every Man, He and She, to comprehend that until you have researched a problem, you have not a right to speak about the problem. Unless one has fully comprehended the problem, it is virtually impossible to comprehend a divine solution.

The difference between the sacred garden culture and the death consumption culture is worlds apart. And the primary difference is immediately evident in the respect that Man, He and She, hold for themselves, each other, and those born of them. This most sacred respect is played out in divine union, divine consumption and going forward to multiply divinity in the offspring. The mother spirit is honored and respected within the sacred garden culture as the vital link to nurturing the whole life presence of Man, He and She.

It was comprehended within the sacred garden culture that each part works in harmony to manifest the whole life presence in going forward to multiply divinity. The harmony of divine union is actually experienced as a deep and profound pleasurable sensation within the vibrations of Supreme Love. Supreme Love is not to be found anywhere or anytime within the energy that is opposite of Supreme Love. Lust is what one finds within the energy that is opposite of Supreme Love. Lust is the nagging and insatiable urge to satisfy a physical appetite and the gnawing ravenous hunger is never truly satisfied. One becomes an addict on the hunt for one more hit. For this reason, Man He and Man She relate to each other in calculating terms to satisfy their addictions, whether the addiction is for sex, ego gratification, or things and stuff.

### *Enslaved to Sexual Stereotypes*

Within the death consumption culture, there exist many stigmas and stereotypes that degrade the image of the suntanned female. The mammy stereotype characterizes the melaninated female who is fat and obese. Mammy is presented as a female who dominates in the kitchen cooking soul food. The mammy has greasy fried hair and lots of children. Within the ice-cold, deep-freeze mentality, Mammy is identified as the mother image of the suntanned female in the acceptable role of domestic servant and caretaker. The feminine presence is free to become obese and gluttonous and have no shame, because she fits into a stereotype that has been perpetuated for generations and generations.

There is absolutely no shame when a female from the melaninated vibration struts around with permed hair. There is no thought about putting lye and chemical treatments on her scalp just inches away from her brain cells. There is absolutely no shame in the masculine spirit who walks around with her, so long as she has something to offer, especially when she is youthful, shapely and fashionable. There is no shame in taking the little girls and perming and frying their hair and calling it beautiful. There is no shame in looking like a freak of nature, totally opposite of one's holistic living presence as Man She, totally rejecting one's original presentation, totally rejecting one's natural and innate state as the mother spirit of the planet Earth.

The sexual stereotype of Jezebel is another common image that is projected on the suntanned female within the ice-cold, deep-freeze mentality. The Jezebel stereotype represents the suntanned female as sexually aggressive, seductive and manipulating. The portrayal of the suntanned female as being promiscuous with an insatiable sexual appetite stands as a pale reflection in the face of the historical occurrences of repeated patterns of vicious and brutal rape against the suntanned feminine presence. Another stereotype characterizes the suntanned female as bossy, domineering and spiteful in her relationships with the suntanned male. This Sapphire stereotype emphasizes the suntanned female's contempt for the suntanned male, and portrays her as an instrument of his further decline.

We have talked about some of the stereotypes that have been adopted. Now here is the real deal that has always been the primary ace in the hold of the ice-cold, deep-freeze mentality. Let us not forget the well-educated, uppity, sophisticated socialite of the suntanned feminine presence who is portrayed as being the high achiever among her kind. It is clear that she is usually light bright and almost white with a pure focus on the I-me-my syndrome, or she may be the "exceptional" one of a darker hue. At all points in time, she tends to feel more comfortable rubbing shoulders and socializing with those of the dominant culture. Just as so many in the past, she owes no honor and allegiance to anything darker than her.

Her fantasy is to fully assimilate into the ice-cold, deep-freeze mentality. If and when she should have children, it is her desire that they should go the same route and even a little farther, regardless of the social and personal pressures that cause blatant esteemlessness. She aspires to rise in the social order by achieving through education and in her career, and she seeks to find a mate who meets her expectations of success. She passes the same attitudes and behaviors of achievement on to her offspring. If she has a son, he will grow to identify with the dominant male image that represents the ice-cold, deep-freeze mentality. The only thing that the I in I can say about this particular feminine presence is that she is armed and dangerous. This feminine presence has always been the first line of defense and the watchdog to protect and to serve the status quo. She is indeed very patriotic to the death consumption culture and the ice-cold, deep-freeze mentality and stands ever ready to pledge allegiance to the dominant male even while she is snuggled in bed with a suntanned brother man.

The thought and reasoning of devitalized and depleted consumption and the vibrations of enslavement have become more refined and covert. The difficulty with the lost and astray mind is that it quickly gets stuck on specific details of isolated events without being able to recognize an overall pattern of behavior and energy consumption. For example, a debate continues about whether or not Thomas Jefferson, drafter of the Declaration of Independence, U.S. President, and noted slave owner, was the father of children by his "Negro" slave, Sally Hemings. It is noted that Sally Hemings was the half-sister of Jefferson's wife. Much effort has been exerted to refute the claim and uphold the image of a glorious patriot and statesman.

The issue is not even about attributing guilt or pointing the finger at a guilty party. The issue is about identifying patterns in attitudes and behaviors that reflect the ice-cold, deep-freeze mentality. The issue is about identifying the adverse effects of toxic consumption on one's mental, physical, and spiritual health and well-being. We must understand that in the death consumption culture it is not about what a thing is, but what it looks like. It is about what a thing appears to be. It is all about appearance.

A historical pattern emerges that reveals the ice-cold, deep-freeze mentality of wealthy "white" plantation owners and slave owners who denounce race-mixing in public, while raping the "Negro" slave population and fathering slave children who could be, and oftentimes were, sold for profit. The question of rape against the "Negro" female was not an issue, because the laws of slavery considered the "Negro" female to be a piece of property. Therefore, the "Negro" slave female was legally placed in the position of having no right to refuse the sexual abuses inflicted by her "white" slave master. As the old saying goes, "Consent that can not be given, can not be denied." Therefore, the attitudes and behaviors of Thomas

Jefferson as revealed in his following statements were representative of the founding fathers' vibrations that were bred into the offspring within a nation established in slavery. These statements are perhaps a little less well known than the eloquent words of the Declaration of Independence:

> There must doubtless be an unhappy influence on the manners of our people produced by the existence of slavery among us. The whole commerce between master and slave is a perpetual exercise of the most boisterous passions, the most unremitting despotism on the one part, and degrading submissions on the other. Our children see this, and learn to imitate it; for man is an imitative animal…
>
> It will probably be asked, Why not retain and incorporate the blacks into the state, and thus save the expence of supplying, by importation of white settlers, the vacancies they will leave? Deep rooted prejudices entertained by the whites; ten thousand recollections, by the blacks, of the injuries they have sustained; new provocations; the real distinctions which nature has made; and many other circumstances, will divide us into parties, and produce convulsions which will probably never end but in the extermination of the one or the other race.—To these objections, which are political, may be added others, which are physical and moral. The first difference which strikes us is that of colour. Whether the black of the negro resides in the reticular membrane between the skin and scarf-skin, or in the scarf-skin itself; whether it proceeds from the colour of the blood, the colour of the bile, or from that of some other secretion, the difference is fixed in nature, and is as real as if its seat and cause were better known to us. And is this

difference of no importance? Is it not the foundation of a greater or less share of beauty in the two races? Are not the fine mixtures of red and white, the expressions of every passion by greater or less suffusions of colour in the one, preferable to that eternal monotony, which reigns in the countenances, that immoveable veil of black which covers all the emotions of the other race? Add to these, flowing hair, a more elegant symmetry of form, their own judgment in favour of the whites, declared by their preference of them, as uniformly as is the preference of the Oranootan [sic]for the black women over those of his own species. The circumstance of superior beauty, is thought worthy attention in the propagation of our horses, dogs, and other domestic animals; why not in that of man?

The improvement of the blacks in body and mind, in the first instance of their mixture with the whites, has been observed by every one, and proves that their inferiority is not the effect merely of their condition of life. We know that among the Romans, about the Augustan age especially, the condition of their slaves was much more deplorable than that of the blacks on the continent of America. The two sexes were confined in separate apartments, because to raise a child cost the master more than to buy one. Cato, for a very restricted indulgence to his slaves in this particular, took from them a certain price. But in this country the slaves multiply as fast as the free inhabitants. Their situation and manners place the commerce between the two sexes almost without restraint.—The same Cato, on a principle of economy, always sold his sick and superannuated slaves. He gives it as a standing precept to a master visiting his farm, to sell his old on, old waggons, old tools, old and diseased servants, and every thing else become useless…

That disposition to theft with which they have been branded, must be ascribed to their situation, and not to any depravity of the moral sense. The man, in whose favour no laws of property exist, probably feels himself less bound to respect those made in favour of others. When arguing for ourselves, we lay it down as a fundamental, that laws, to be just, must give a reciprocation of right: that, without this, they are mere arbitrary rules of conduct, founded in force, and not in conscience: and it is a problem which give to the master to solve, whether the religious precepts against the violation of property were not framed for him as well as his slave? And whether the slave may not as justifiably take a little from one, who has taken all from him, as he may slay one who would slay him?

To our reproach it must be said, that though for a century and a half we have had under our eyes the races of black and of red men, they have never yet been viewed by us as subjects of natural history. Advance it therefore as a suspicion only, that the blacks, whether originally a distinct race, or made distinct by time and circumstances, are inferior to the whites in the endowments both of body and mind. It is not against experience to suppose, that different species of the same genus, or varieties of the same species, may possess different qualifications. Will not a lover of natural history then, one who views the gradations in all the races of animals with the eye of philosophy, excuse an effort to keep those in the department of

> man as distinct as nature has formed them? This unfortunate difference of colour, and perhaps of faculty, is a powerful obstacle to the emancipation of these people. Many of their advocates, while they wish to vindicate the liberty of human nature, are anxious also to preserve its dignity and beauty. Some of these, embarrassed by the question `What further is to be done with them?' join themselves in opposition with those who are actuated by sordid avarice only…Among the Romans emancipation required but one effort. The slave, when made free, might mix with, without staining the blood of his master. But with us a second is necessary, unknown to history. When freed, he is to be removed beyond the reach of mixture.[69]

Research findings indicate that DNA testing conducted in 1998 indicated a genetic link between the Jefferson and Hemings descendants. The results of the study established that an individual carrying the male Jefferson Y chromosome fathered Eston Hemings, the last known child born to Sally Hemings. Findings show that the Thomas Jefferson Memorial Foundation issued a report in January 2000 concluding that Thomas Jefferson was the father of at least one and perhaps all the children of Sally Hemings.

The practice of slave owners sexually abusing their slaves is not a new story within the death consumption culture. Many of the slave plantations were producing very light slaves and some that even appeared to be white although the studs and other male's in the plantation outside of the male's in the master's family were melaninated. Oftentimes the resemblance of master and slave was so similar that if not for the melanination and afro-centric characteristics one would think that it was the master's younger sister or family member. Yet

[69] See footnote 41.

and still, acts of violation and the use and abuse of Man, He and She, for one's personal gain are daily occurrences within the death consumption culture. The point is to acknowledge the thoughts and reasoning that continue to fester in one's own mind as a result of a deep indulgence in the ice-cold, deep-freeze mentality.

More recent news stories continue to highlight a common pattern of thought and reasoning regarding "African Americans" within the structures of American society. The sexual and reproductive position of the "African American" female remains a political and social economic issue, as the dominant males of the social order hold sway on the thoughts and reasoning of massive populations. Strom Thurmond, the longest-serving senator in U.S. history, ran for U.S. president as a racial segregationist and opponent to the civil rights movement. Numerous news articles quote Thurmond as declaring that "all the laws of Washington, and all the bayonets of the Army, cannot force the "Negro" into our homes, our schools, our churches and our places of recreation." It is noted that after Thurmond's death in 2003 at the age of 100, the Thurmond family attorney confirmed that former U.S. Senator Strom Thurmond had fathered a child with a "black" teenage maid who worked in his family home in 1925. It is clear that although "all the bayonets of the Army" could not force the "Negroes" into "white" homes, schools, churches and so on, Mr. Thurmond could force himself between the thighs of a young "Negro" female. Miss Essie Mae Williams came forward as Strom Thurmond's daughter. The Thurmond family reportedly desired Thurmond's suntanned daughter to claim her heritage.

Realizing that one's opinions, preferences, values, attitudes and behaviors are conditioned by the social environment that one is nurtured within, the adverse effects on the female within America's earliest formation are profoundly damaging. Research indicates that during slavery, "white" males' rape of female slaves was explicitly legal. It is also been noted that during the early American days, "white" males' rape of "American Indian" women was rampant, and went unpunished by "white" law. During the Reconstruction period in America, it is noted that the Ku Klux Klan, a violent white supremacist group, used the rape of "African American" females as a weapon of terror. At the same time, "African American" males were falsely accused of raping white women by sight, imagination or dream, and the accusation was used as an excuse for lynching.

Research indicates that Harriet Jacobs is recognized as the first "African American" female to write a slave narrative. Her first hand account provides a personal memoir of the vibrations and sensations of violation and abuse that are a daily encounter within the death consumption culture. Her slave narrative entitled, *Incidents in the Life of a Slave Girl*, exposes the sexual and reproductive exploitation of the female slave,

> "The secrets of slavery are concealed like those of the Inquisition. My master was, to my knowledge, the father of eleven slaves. But did the mothers dare to tell who was the father of their children? Did the other slaves dare to allude to it, except in whispers among themselves? No, indeed! They knew too well the terrible consequences." The author writes in her preface, "Reader, be assured this narrative is no fiction....I have not exaggerated the wrongs inflicted by Slavery; on the contrary, my descriptions fall far short of the facts.[70]

One must acknowledge the level and degree of damage that has been done within the thoughts and reasoning of those

[70] *Incidents in the Life of a Slave Girl. Written by Herself.* Harriet A. Jacobs, c1860. Online Source: http://docsouth.unc.edu/fpn/jacobs/jacobs.html.

who have consumed of the toxic vibrations of lust, lies, illusions, confusion, death and deadly destruction. Within the death consumption culture, one's personal experiences are indulged in the same toxic vibrations and sensations that manifested every act of rape, murder, steal and take against the sacred garden culture. One's sexual expressions have been corrupted by the same ice-cold, deep-freeze mentality that formulates the attitudes and behaviors of enslavement and death consumption. Either one has become numb and oblivious or one is heavily addicted to some form of distraction, amusement, ego gratification or substance abuse, including toxic food substances, or… one is simply in denial. How else can one not be affected by the acts of vicious and cold-blooded invasion that were waged against the sacred presence of Man, He and She? Jacob's slave narrative expresses the depth of violation and the atrocities that have occurred and continue in varying forms to this day:

> No matter whether the slave girl be as black as ebony or as fair as her mistress. In either case, there is no shadow of law to protect her from insult, from violence, or even from death; all these are inflicted by fiends who bear the shape of men. The mistress, who ought to protect the helpless victim, has no other feelings towards her but those of jealousy and rage. The degradation, the wrongs, the vices, that grow out of slavery, are more than I can describe. They are greater than you would willingly believe.[71]

The brutal and vicious violation of "African American" girls and women by "white" slave-masters was a way of life within the slavery culture. The "white" slave-masters justified their degrading and cold-blooded treatment by projecting the

[71] Same as footnote 70.

slaves as "sexual savages." Female slaves were stripped, beaten, raped and forced to breed more slaves. What damage is done to the thought and reasoning of the predator and the prey in such an environment of toxic consumption? The slave narrative goes on to describe the corruption and pollution that was inflicted by the ice-cold, deep-freeze mentality:

> For years my master had done his utmost to pollute my mind with foul images and to destroy the pure images inculcated by my grandmother.... He tried his utmost to corrupt the pure principles my grandmother had instilled. He peopled my young mind with unclean images, such as only a vile monster could think of. I turned from him with disgust and hatred. But he was my master. I was compelled to live under the same roof with him—where I saw a man forty years my senior daily violating the most sacred commandments of nature.[72]

Sexual promiscuity, rape and forced breeding of female slaves showed a profit margin in the death consumption culture. With no restraints and no measure of self-control…lust, lies, illusions, confusion, death and deadly destruction became the means to the ways of today. The I in I would like to offer a brief notation by W.E.B. Dubois noted as the "Father of Modern Social Science," as stated in his classic work *The Souls of Black Folk:*

> The red stain of bastardy, which two centuries of systemic legal defilement of Negro women had stamped upon [this] race, meant not only the loss of ancient African chastity, but also the hereditary weight of a mass of corruption from white

[72] Same as footnote 70.

> adulterers, threatening almost the obliteration of the Negro home.[73]

### *Breeding Grounds: The Family Unit*

Within this country there have been many plots of deteriorating thoughts and reasoning that have manifested. These toxic thoughts and reasoning have been the backbone and foundation of a social disorder that created slavery. The institution of slavery is unquestionably the foundation of the social economic presence of the United States of America. These founding toxic thoughts and reasoning have produced laws and codes that were established to perpetuate the mentality of slavery. The long-standing adverse effects remain today. The relationship of the enslaved male and female was intended to produce generations of slaves. A committed bonding of male and female was not a part of the slavery plan as noted in an excerpt from the document, "The American Slave Code in Theory and Practice," published in 1853:

> The obligations of marriage are evidently inconsistent with the conditions of slavery, and cannot be performed by a slave. The husband promises to protect his wife and provide for her. The wife promises to be the help-meet of her husband. They mutually promise to live with and cherish each other, till parted by death. But what can such promises by slaves mean? The "legal relation of master and slave" renders them void! It forbids the slave to protect even himself. It clothes his master with authority to bid him inflict deadly blows on the woman he has sworn to protect. It prohibits his possession of any property wherewith to sustain her. His labor and his hands it takes

[73] *Souls of Black Folk.* W.E.B. Dubois. Chicago, 1903. Online Source: http://www.bartleby.com/114/.

> from him. It bids the woman assist, not her husband, but her owner! Nay! it gives him unlimited control and full possession of her own person, and forbids her, on pain of death, (as will be shown,) to resist him, if he drags her to his bed! It severs the plighted pair, at the will of their masters, occasionally, or for ever! The innocent "legal relation" of slave-ownership does or permits all this, and without forfeiting clerical favor, or a high seat in the Church, or in the Senate, or Presidential chair. What, then, can the marriage vows of slaves mean? [74]

There were laws that stated that if one had one tenth of a percent of "Negro" blood then one was declared as colored. Being declared as colored was not a sin, however if one was declared as colored then one could be considered 3/5 of a human being and therefore, not entitled to the fullness of the rights and privileges under the Constitution of the United States of America. Whether one had the wit and intelligence to reason that the Constitution said all men are created equal, the various clauses that were created by the lawmakers were in place to make sure that one understood that the suntanned male and his Afro-centric characteristics were not included. In truth and reality, the thoughts and reasoning of this vibration continue into today. The more that one learns to reject and move away from one's innate characteristics and Afro-centric origins, the more one tends to become accepted within the ice-cold, deep-freeze mentality.

It stands to reason that the same reasoning that has been perpetuated generation after generation has perpetuated the

---

[74] *The American Slave Code in Theory and Practice: Its Distinctive Features Shown by Its Statutes, Judicial Decisions, and Illustrative Facts.* Chapter VII: Slaves Cannot Marry. William Goodell, New York: American and Foreign Anti-Slavery Society, 1853.

same results. Why would it be different today? These are some of the reasons why the individuals began to develop social programs that were aimed at correcting adverse effects. What wasn't fully comprehended was that one can write regulations, but one cannot legislate one's thought and reasoning. Therefore, that thought and reasoning is continuing to be ejaculated into the mother spirit, regardless of her being blonde or bald or natty, natty dread. The same thing is being reproduced over and over again, although many are expecting different results. A true parallel is that degeneration and mutation are continuing to deteriorate one's presence.

There is little or no concern, thought, reasoning, sensitivity, or compassion in the expressions of the youth toward each other as He and She, because of the level and degree of mutated and degenerated thoughts that have been continuously passed on into their gene pool from the first invasions out of the Caucasus mountain and steppe region. Deprivation formed the frame of thought. The consequences were rape, murder, steal and take which provided momentary satisfaction and relief from the feelings of deprivation. War as way of achieving one's social economic desires became a way of life. From that point until today, the characteristics are continuing to be passed on into the gene pool. The suntanned daughter would be the primary target of every movie plot and marketing scheme, and she would be manipulated, forced or coerced into an awkward, promiscuous lifestyle.

**There is Much Owed to the Suntanned Daughter**

The masters and grand masters of deceit
would play her like a puppet on a string
while she dances and sings
as she faces the lonely teardrops
of her deferred American dream.
Every male or female child that she would born
would be engulfed in the bitterness and the scorn

of a glorious color divine
re-defined by a lost and astray mind.
And so it was, and so it is, and so it continues to be.
So every suntanned Man, He and She
would be deaf, dumb and blind to divinity.
The suntanned Children would know no happy home
because from birth the suntanned female would be all alone,
because her man would live in fright and fear
whether he is at home or whether he would roam.
So who would protect this once sacred daughter of the golden tan
from the vicious and cruel raping vibration
of the ice-cold, deep-freeze mentality clan?

***The Necessity for Divine Spirit Consciousness***

It is a time upon the planet when a more profound comprehension of divine solutions is required. It is a time upon the planet when massive mental, physical and spiritual disorder and disease afflict Man, He and She, to the point where survival is critically threatened. The level and degree of sickness, disease, and disorder is at an alarming state in many of Man, He and She. The best way to determine the level and degree of disorder is to examine the conflict between Man He and Man She, and the conflict between groups based on concepts of race, creed, color, religion, politics and social economic stratification. The level and degree of violent, abusive, and toxic relationships is at an alarming state in many of Man, He and She, both as individuals and as groups.

The best way to determine the level and degree of toxic relationships is to examine the effects on the offspring. The level and degree of degeneration and chaos in the offspring is at an alarming rate in many of Man, He and She. The health of the planet suffers in conditions of pollution, waste and neglect. As the overall conditions of health deteriorate in sick societies of sick mentalities, vibrations of destruction and self-destruction manifest on a global scale.

In the culture of disorder, the female is particularly vulnerable as she nurtures whatever disorder is brought to her by the social environment, in general, or by the male, specifically. When the male acts out the vibrations of hostile aggression that were born and bred in the ice-cold, deep-freeze mentality and brings that to the female in intimate relationships, then severe damage occurs within that union of Man, He and She. When the female nurtures the vibrations of the ice-cold, deep-freeze mentality that are brought to her, then every child born from her becomes a victim of a toxic inheritance. When Man, He and She, is born and bred on the toxic vibrations of the ice-cold, deep-freeze mentality, then further mutation and degeneration of brain, body and spirit is multiplied as disease, disorder, dysfunction and deadly destruction. As a result, mental illness, physical disease, and spiritual depletion are the signs of the times of the lost and astray mind entrenched in the ice-cold, deep-freeze mentality.

### *Repairing the Damage of Degeneration and Mutation*

It is crystal clear that Man, He and She, has to stop this ludicrous behavior, but what is not crystal clear is how this vicious and cruel state of being has been allowed to continue in the first place? With all of the military might and all of the control factors that those possessing military might hold over the natural resources of the planet, it is self-evident that the focus is on terror, fright, fear and the ability to swiftly kill. The objective of the elite powerbrokers is to destabilize and destroy anything or anyone who poses a threat, real or imagined. As a result, natural resources are invested in the hands of a few greedy and possessive individuals who definitely perpetuate the ice-cold, deep-freeze mentality. Any opposition to this mentality is viewed as a threat.

Can the holistic living truth about Supreme Love deliver Man, He and She, from this state of toxic ignorance and deception? Or will this "elite" breed of Man, He and She, continue to squander the natural resources of the planet, continue to set off explosive reactions, continue to manifest toxic disorder, and continue to pollute and dilute the environment? Will this group continue to squander scarce natural resource energy while inflicting genocidal programs of dominance and control over indigenous populations?

What are the options if the planet has been drained and depleted of the spiritual essence of life? What are the options if Man, He and She, has become so weak and feeble that there is no true relationship with divine spirit consciousness of the essence of life? What are the options if Man, He and She, has been so diseased and so afflicted with mutative and degenerative disorders that the body temple is unable to sustain the divine order of the whole life presence? What will those disciples and followers of the ice-cold, deep-freeze mentality do when there are no more hosts to host their degenerative attitudes and behaviors other than self-destruct? If the option is a space program and/or creating clone-like slaves to serve the blue-blood lines of the privileged elite, then it is a true sign that the ice-cold, deep-freeze mentality is a self-destructive parasite that threatens the entire universe. Man, He and She, can not afford to sit idly by and wait for any one of these options to come to be.

Man, He and She, is, in fact, at that point at the fork in the road that will determine his or her destiny. This is that time at the fork in the road where it will be all the way or not at all. Either one will follow the ice-cold, deep-freeze mentality to the point of busting hell wide open or one will disengage from the ice-cold, deep-freeze mentality, not dealing with it at all. The choice is either one of self-destruction or one of divine emergence into the holistic living way of life of the sacred garden culture. In truth and reality, a divine and sacred few will continue to emerge to set a divine example of the holistic living way of life, a divine example of the sacred garden culture and the principles, morals and values born of divine spirit consciousness. It must become clearly understood that Man, He and She, cannot wage a physical war against the lost and astray mind of thought and reasoning that creates from an energy that is opposite of Supreme Love. It must be clearly understood that Man, He and She, cannot wage a mental war against the lost and astray mind of Man, He and She, dedicated to the ice-cold, deep-freeze mentality. This has nothing to do with wars or battles or fighting or conflict.

It must be clearly understood that the true salvation of this planet and its inhabitants requires a holistic living relationship with divine spirit consciousness. This is an encounter that is totally and absolutely beyond the lost and astray mind; this is an encounter that is totally and absolutely beyond the death consumption culture; this is an encounter that is totally and absolutely beyond the energy that is opposite of Supreme Love. This encounter is nothing short of a divine innercourse, unifying brain, body and spirit. This is about a relationship with the sacred origin of Man, He and She, and the perpetuation of the holistic living truth about Supreme Love. The glory and magnificence of the holistic living relationship of the sacred garden culture must re-emerge upon the planet.

The pure nature of this re-emergence begins within. The primary duty, obligation and responsibility of every Man, He or She, is to re-connect with the supreme spiritual essence of life. In this way Man, He and She, initiates the basic phase of correcting errors that are being transmitted within the sexual organs and the reproductive systems. Let us be reminded here that the primary sexual organ is the brain. The gross errors produced by toxic consumption adversely affect the reproductive system and serve as the breeding ground for the ice-cold, deep-freeze mentality. The essence of life and the vibrations and sensations of supreme self-love are what we are talking about here. That is totally and absolutely beyond the philosophies of eugenics and the privileged-class solutions that are merely an extension of the toxic, dead, devitalized and depleted problem that originated within the ice-cold, deep-freeze mentality in the first place.

Man, He and She, must begin to address the errors within the DNA. Man, He and She, must begin to address the mutation and degeneration that is the consequence of toxic consumption. Man, He and She must cease and desist from feeding the vibrations and sensations of the plagues of the ice-cold, deep-freeze mentality. Man, He and She, must come to realize that this glorious planet houses enough space and natural resources for all of us when living in divine order. With divine consumption for the brain, the body and spirit as the top priority, Man, He and She, will again move into the most glorious state of divine oneness.

Many will claim that this is an ideology of utopia or something to achieve in the hereafter, i.e. in paradise or in heaven. In fact, there are only religious doctrines, jargon, fantasies and delusions of an afterlife within the death consumption culture. Within an ice-cold, deep-freeze mentality, this is all that one will be able to reason or imagine, for there is no divine spirit consciousness within an ice-cold, deep-freeze mentality.

It was a horrifying lesson to learn that the smiling faces of the lineages of vicious invader tribes did not represent peaceful intentions. The grand deception of the death consumption culture is that those of the ice-cold, deep-freeze mentality are actually capable of establishing and maintaining peace, love and harmony. The historical facts speak loud and clear: the attitudes and behaviors of the ice-cold, deep-freeze mentality have established an undeniable pattern of selfish greed, hostile and deadly aggression and schemes of conquest. It is not possible for one to be of a Supreme Love vibration while maintaining the ice-cold, deep-freeze mentality. It is not possible to be of a Supreme Love vibration while entrenched in the death consumption culture. It is not possible to be of the Supreme Love vibration while indulging in the energy that is opposite of Supreme Love. The divine lesson is that when one is dealing with a cold-blooded predator, one had better learn to comprehend the cold-blooded, predator mentality.

Clearly, the plots and schemes of eugenics, "white"-racist ideology, and the religious, social economic, and political orders of the ice-cold, deep-freeze mentality are an indictment of the cold-blooded and vicious predator mentality that descended from the ice-cold, deep-freeze. The solutions of violence, destruction and annihilation that are proposed and enacted within the ice-cold, deep-freeze mentality are simply the manifestations of the energy that is opposite of Supreme Love. Killing and deadly destruction have never been life-affirming propositions. Anyone who comes with that corrupt bag of tricks has already exposed his or her allegiance to the toxic vibrations of opposing the whole life presence.

It is a certainty that the crime and the punishment of the ice-cold, deep-freeze mentality will come to bow to the justice of divine order. Every step that has been taken in error must be addressed and corrected so that one may emerge into one's original and sacred spirit presence. The justice of the sacred garden culture is well-comprehended within the cycles of planting and harvesting. One must reap from what one sows. When one comprehends the full accountability that one has for one's attitudes and behaviors, one will comprehend the consequences of one's toxic consumption. These consequences serve as the keys to increased self-awareness so that the errors are never repeated. The greatest justice is regaining the sense of divine humility that will allow one to be obedient to the divine order of the Supreme Love vibration. There is no hierarchy or top dog in the sacred garden culture; there is, however, a circle of responsibility, obligation and duty that radiates from the innermost core of the Most Supreme Seen and Unseen Essence of Life.

One suffers from the total recall of one's past toxic consumption. The de-tox process causes every vibration and sensation of lust, lies, illusions, confusion, death and deadly destruction that one has consumed to surface for release. It becomes clear why the "white" man lives in such a terrorizing state of paranoia regarding the resurrection and the big payback. The ice-cold, deep-freeze mentality creates a cold and intensely suffocating blanket of guilt that festers within the lost and astray mind. Yet the lost and astray Children who lost their tan continue to perpetuate the selfish and greedy ideology that the suntanned populations of the planet owe servitude to them.

When one is not prepared to render oneself a slave to the "white" racist ideologies, the lost and astray Children who lost their tan seek vengeance through death and deadly destruction. It does not help that there are so many suntanned Children who are guilty of pledging allegiance to the vibrations and sensations of the ice-cold, deep-freeze mentality. This pledge of allegiance to the ice-cold, deep-freeze mentality is nothing short of worshipping the death consumption culture. Any set of statistics that highlight physical disease and disorder, social disease and disorder, or economic disease and disorder is a clear statement that the ice-cold, deep-freeze mentality is a total and absolute conflict of interest to the whole life presence. Clearly, these lost and astray Children with a golden tan continue to reap and weep from the toxic, dead and devitalized seeds that they have sown. The lost and astray Children who lost their tan are riding high and mighty on the backs of these suntanned Children as they gallop off into the stale and pale reflections of a dead end.

The lost and astray Children who lost their tan and their suntanned disciples and followers are intoxicated with the addictions of the death consumption culture. And so it would come to pass that all of the disciples and followers of the ice-cold, deep-freeze mentality would become deeply immersed into the delusions and fantasies of a great beyond. Within the concept of the great beyond, it is fantasized that all of one's earthly sins, defilements, abuses and atrocities will be forgiven.

## CHAPTER EIGHT: THE MELTDOWN OF THE DEEP-FREEZE MENTALITY

Within the ice-cold, deep-freeze mentality, to be forgiven implies that one will be free from the consequences of one's actions. Therefore, it is often reasoned that one can murder, rape, steal and take in order to acquire wealth and domination by any means necessary. The art would be to take no prisoners and leave no evidence. This would explain the ideology of murder, rape, pillage and burn.

This vibration would be spearheaded by the cold-blooded male-war-god complex that descended from the vicious nomadic invading warlords. The motto of the pale breed of Man, He and She: murder, rape, pillage, and burn would leave blistering sores and scars throughout the planet. There would be no place that this pale breed roamed that could ever be looked at again as a heavenly home. Therefore, the social economic, political and religious agenda would begin to focus on a world beyond the devastated sphere of the planet Earth. The pale breed had violated, infested and contaminated the planet with sex and violence, and other mental, physical, and spiritual disease. When seeking to identify the cause of the damage and disorder upon the planet, the mutated and degenerated breed has been unable and unwilling to acknowledge their own mutation and degeneration as the genesis of disorder.

The social order has been established and maintained to serve the privileged and wealthy elite of the death consumption culture. These privileged classes actually rode the backs of enslaved populations into a galaxy of wealth, advantage and achievements. Laws would be created to mastermind thefts of inventions through patent prohibitions against inventors of color. Great promises to share the wealth as well as promises to provide equal opportunity and access to profit-sharing would become empty words spoken by forked tongues. Even worse, promises to the enslaved suntanned concubines to set free the offspring born of miscegenation would manifest into yet another deception.

Promises of great rewards of freedom to the suntanned soldiers and the families of those soldiers during the many battles of war went unfulfilled. Reparations for the crimes of enslavement, the Black codes, and the Jim Crow laws would simply become justice denied as COINTELPRO plots and schemes would be actualized. Inclusively, massive genocidal drug programs would be established, implemented and maintained as hallucinogenic drugs and eventually crack would be put on the attack to flood the Afro-centric communities along with Big Mack. In the midst of this orchestrated decadence and decay, the response is alarm, bewilderment, and dismay when the social order is exposed as rampant disorder gone astray. To justify the infestation and contamination of the planet, eugenicists and others who perpetuate a "white" racist ideology conveniently target a common scapegoat.

The traditional target population from the suntanned family tree would become the automatic profile of a target, conveniently. Let us be reminded that during the earlier settlement times in North America the primary settlers would attempt to enslave other "white" populations through indentured servitude. Those who were placed in indentured servitude could run away and could not be easily singled out or identified in an all "white" population. Therefore, the founding fathers of America turned to a profile target group that was easily identified by physical traits. Chattel slavery in America had found a convenient host in the Afro-centric population. From that time forward in the Americas, for every social economic problem that would emerge, the Afro-centric population would become the convenient scapegoat. The Afro-centric population would indeed be a scapegoat that was approved by popular demand. As the accepted scapegoat, the suntanned populations would be penalized for merely being a member of the target population, and their reactions to the disorder of the death consumption culture would be viewed through the double standard of presumed guilt.

The penalties are upheld in the penal institutions. The justifications and deceptions of the ice-cold, deep-freeze mentality are upheld and promoted in the educational institutions. The violent and cold-blooded hierarchy of the male-war-god syndrome are upheld and worshipped in the religious institutions. The steal-and-take vibrations of selfish greed and the hunting, scavenging and herding way of life are upheld in the social economic and political institutions. These toxic attitudes and behaviors are reflected back to the mutated and degenerated breed through those who were conquered and enslaved by the ice-cold, deep-freeze mentality. The dark mirror of the suntanned populations is the looking glass that the mutated and degenerated breed gazes upon with nagging guilt, raging denial and gnawing self-loathing.

The very presence of the suntanned population unleashes the toxic impulses to seek, search and destroy from deep within the ice-cold, deep-freeze mentality. And so life on the planet would become a glorified version of hell covered with artificial flavors, colors and smells. The ice-cold, deep-freeze mentality can only reference its origins of savage and brutal survival in the caves; the memory of a glorious and radiant presence is projected as a faraway paradise in another life. The image of the Divine Children of the Sun with the golden tan is rejected and projected in reverse images as the dark and fearful shadows, the hidden and mysterious blackness, and the color code that needs to be exterminated in order to justify one's own paleness.

### *The Garden Paradise of the Divine Children of the Sun*

The Divine Children of the Sun with the golden tan were not imagining a garden paradise or utopia or a heaven somewhere beyond the Earth. As a matter of fact, before the suntanned Children encountered the ice-cold, deep-freeze mentality, they were experiencing paradise right here on Earth. Paradise was the harmonious blends of the sacred garden culture. The suntanned Children signaled this glorification of paradise by honoring every living thing and praising every ancestor, He and She, as well as the most supreme ancestor, He and She. These Divine Children of the Sun with the golden tan comprehended well that it was their duty, obligation and responsibility to honor the whole life presence of Man, He and She, through the acts of divine humility and Supreme Love. Unfortunately, for the Divine Children of the Sun with the golden tan across the planet, the lost and astray Children who lost their tan appeared on the scene from the ice cold and turned the glorious paradise into an ice-cold hell.

Therefore, that which is normal for Man, He and She, to acquire upon the planet when living in divine order is impossible to acquire within the death consumption culture. For this reason, the majority of Man, He and She, continue to reside within the illusions and delusions of the after-death syndrome or the utopia frame of reference until death do its part. So the book revised by King James and others along the trail was handed down as diluted and polluted stolen legacies from the sacred garden culture. Amazingly, these stolen legacies that were distorted and re-told by traders and merchants of the Semitic tribes continue to be the foundation of religious doctrines and orientation of Man, He and She, to this day.

These religious doctrines serve to provide the ways and means to acquire social economic privileges and control over others by those who claim a divine right to rule. It has never been reasoned that one cannot possibly have divinity without divine spirit consciousness. Needless to say, divine spirit consciousness cannot possibly exist within the thoughts and reasoning of the ice-cold, deep-freeze mentality. Man, He and She will continue to look at these doctrines of indoctrination as the pathway to gaining the greater riches in the hereafter, for dying is the kingdom, the power, and the glory. The fact that life is for the living is ignored. Instead, the principles, morals, and values of death and the life-after-death syndrome are upheld.

Within the concept of democratic rule, it is clear that a privileged elite class is financially positioned and does, in fact, strongly influence rulership choices for the mass majority. The principles, morals and values of the status quo are invested within the social economic industries of the death consumption culture. The social economic industries of the death consumption culture perpetuate the enslavement and slaughter of man and animals, the use of drugs as the primary choice of medical treatment, toxic consumption, promiscuous and out-of-order relationships, and sex and violence through mass media to name a few.

The adverse effects of the death consumption culture are multiplied over and over again in the offspring as a result of toxic consumption that those before them practiced. It becomes clear that this vicious cycle, this massive maze of confusion can only consume of itself. So for these reasons, the divine and sacred few must have a tenacious focus on following the divine guidance that will lead them out of this massive maze of confusion. It must be realized that the sacred garden culture is a divine parallel to the death consumption culture. Within the sacred garden culture, divine spiritual leadership is based on the principles and practices of a holistic living way of life. The basic acts and requirements of a holistic living way of life are divine consumption, inclusive of the physical consumption of raw and living fruits, vegetables, seeds and nuts. Additionally, the base requirement is having divine humility to the whole life presence of every living thing.

The vibrations of lust, lies, illusions, confusion, death and deadly destruction are the stimuli and the response of the ice-cold, deep-freeze mentality. One must step outside of the vibrations and sensations that breed lust, lies, illusions, confusion, death and deadly destruction. The only way that one can step outside of this ice-cold, deep-freeze mentality is to step inside of a holistic living way of life through divine spirit consciousness. It must be noted that everything that is outside of divine consumption is the death consumption culture. Everything that is outside of divine spirit consciousness is the ice-cold, deep-freeze mentality. Everything that is outside of the Supreme Love vibration of a holistic living way of life is the energy that is opposite of Supreme Love.

Man, He and She, has a tremendous task upon the Earth if they wish to survive as a species reflecting their divine origin. It is a choice: either become a weak and feeble clone-like being perpetuating the death consumption culture to the end of one's short and painful presence, or emerge into a holistic living way of life where divine spirit consciousness is your guide into your whole life presence. Divine spirit consciousness is your guide into the holistic living truth about Supreme Love. Divine spirit consciousness is your guide into the sacred garden culture of the Divine Children of the Sun. If Man, He and She, determine that they will take one step forward in advancing the Supreme Love vibration, in advancing divinity, the first divine act and requirement still remains—divine consumption for the brain, the body and the spirit.

In order to begin to correct an error within the body, one thing is very clear, the most wholesome and complete kind of raw and living energy available must be consumed by Man, He and She. It is quite clear that the most wholesome food consumable by Man, He and She, is raw and living fruits, vegetables, seeds and nuts, i.e. the fruits of the tree of life. It is very clear that the photosynthesis relationship of the sun in its innercourse with Man, He and She, and the fruits of the trees of life provide the whole life energy necessary for the resurrection of the divine mental, physical and spiritual presence of Man, He and She.

Man, He and She, must recognize that divine things start within. The first place of correction that is necessary in order to go forward and multiply divinity is regeneration of the organs within the body, especially the brain. Once this sacred order of regeneration has begun to pay dividends, it becomes necessary that those dividends be focused on divine union. If one does not focus from a divine spirit consciousness, then divine union can not possibly take place. In order for divine union to take place, Man, He and She must rekindle the sacred vibrations of divine guidance, divine protection and divine nurturing.

Without divine union, there can not be any possibility of harmony in reproduction. Even with divine spirit consciousness as your guide, divine union will be a tough ordeal because of the damage that has been done, internally and externally. It should then be very clear that the only option available to Man, He and She, is holistic living healing through divine lifestyle change. Without this total and absolute commitment, one will continue to breed the ice-cold, deep-freeze mentality until death do its part.

It is clear that the relationship between Man, He and She, has been one of misuse, misrepresentation, misdirection, degeneration and mutation into utter chaos and disorder. The only thing that can be reproduced by the reproductive system in disorder and chaos is the energy that has amassed within these systems and organs. This is compiled by the fact that the cells must be in error in order for one to think and reason in manners and ways to misuse and abuse the sexual organs and the reproductive system. It should be very clear that Man, He and She, is living in gross error in order for Man, He and She, to amass such toxic disorder between and among themselves. In order for Man, He and She, to misuse and abuse the divine and original presence of Man, He and She, i.e. the Afrikoid mother and father spirit, one's mental state must be of gross error. By the same token, in order to misuse and abuse the sexual reproductive organs that are responsible for reproducing one's presence, one's mental state must be one of gross error.

Man, He and She, has a tremendous task in activating the divine duties, obligations and responsibilities to the Supreme Love spirit. And as it was in the beginning, so it has begun again with the divine and sacred few devoted to the vibration of going forward to multiply the divinity of the sacred garden culture.

### *The Urgent Need for the Divine Union of Man, He and She*

It is quite clear that the masculine spirit and the feminine spirit have become victims of prey and the predators at the same time. By the same token, it is very clear that the masculine spirit must move into a divine alignment with the practices and principles of the sacred garden culture. The masculine spirit has the duty, obligation and responsibility to provide divine guidance and protection for the feminine presence. It is an absolute necessity that the feminine presence be of a mental, physical and spiritual state of mind that rejects the principles and the practices of the death consumption culture in order to receive divine guidance and protection. It would be a cold-blooded shame to continue to watch the most precious jewel of the planet, i.e. the mother spirit and the feminine presence of Man, He and She, continue to face degradation, humiliation, utter disrespect, scorn and ridicule. It would be of the utmost shame for the masculine presence to witness and watch the mother spirit go out without raising an arm of giving every inch of his whole life presence to provide divine guidance and divine protection for her. It would be more shameful for the masculine spirit to continue to bathe in his ego-mania and the macho syndromes of deception while playing a hand in the misuse and abuse of the mother spirit to satisfy his vibrations of lust, lies, illusions, confusion, death and deadly destruction.

What the I in I am saying is that the holistic living truth about Supreme Love must become the way of life for Man, He and She, or the consequences will remain death and deadly destruction within the vibrations and sensations of misery, aches, and pains all the days of one's life. The only remedy to numb these sensations and vibrations of misery, aches, and pains will be toxic substance abuse, via drugs, dead, devitalized, and depleted food substances, media, sex and violence, and the associated delusions and fantasies. When the deal goes down, one has to face oneself. All that one will see is the frustration and the aggravation of an empty and depleted life staring back from the mirror, hoping to disguise what one truly and sincerely feels inside, hoping to disguise the low self-esteem with a falsified appearance and glorified perceptions.

The present state of strained relationships between Man, He and She, is a tragic reflection of the absence of Man He as the divine guiding and protecting presence for Man She. The imbalance in the numbers of Man He to Man She, most especially among the suntanned males, is creating a desperate and despairing circumstance where Man She is unable to have her basic needs met. A situation of desperation in the mother spirit of Man, He and She, serves as a critical warning. It is clear that the predatory system that evolved from deep freeze experience is a mutated and degenerated system of disorder.

As one takes a look at the system of disorder and the statistics that relate to that system of disorder, one thing is very apparent. It is very apparent that the male-female relationships and the pattern of family structure bred within the system of the ice-cold, deep-freeze mentality do not work for Man, He and She, most especially the suntanned populations. In fact, this system of disorder cannot possibly work for anyone who is focused on the divine order of a holistic living way of life. Another thing that is very apparent is that the suntanned male is on the brink of destruction while breeding self-destruction as a result of assimilating and maintaining the values of the death consumption culture.

In real terms, the suntanned male, most especially the Afrikoid male, has become an endangered species. And if that is the tragic case, what is to happen to the suntanned female, most especially the Afrikoid female? Is she to sit and wait and hope that a vicious system of disorder will suddenly change and that a male savior will appear to rescue her from despair and loneliness? Is she expected to make divine and holistic living change without the divine guidance and protection provided by Man He? Or is Man She of the suntanned or Afrikoid stock to focus on establishing a She/She relationship to substitute for the divine order of Man, He and She? These are very serious questions that Man, He and She, must begin to divinely reason with as they are called by the universe of the Most High Essence of Life and Supreme Love. Man He is called to play a greater role in masterminding a sense of divine order, a sense of divine corrective action. The masculine presence is called upon to deliver a greater sense of divine guidance and protection. He is called upon to come up with a divine solution to a very critical and serious problem for Man, He and She, in general, and most especially for the Afrikoid Man, He and She, and their offspring.

**Comprehending Divine Sexuality**

The exploration of divine sexuality begins within the vibrations and sensations of the sacred garden culture and remains within the sacred sphere of divine consumption. Divine sexuality actually refers to divine stimulation of the whole life presence, mentally, physically, and spiritually. The honoring of the whole life presence requires acts that express the Supreme Love vibration, i.e. the utmost respect and care for oneself and every living being/creature. The whole life presence can only be honored within the divine order of Man, He and She, in the full realization of their divine duties, obligations and responsibilities.

The expression of mutual respect and abiding adoration between Man He and Man She is not possible within the ice-cold, deep-freeze mentality. The overload intensity of violence, rage, terror, and ice-cold temperatures within the deep-freeze environment damaged the warm and loving connection between the masculine and feminine presence. The damage became an inherited trait passed from parental attitudes and behaviors to the offspring. The union of Man, He and She, suffered a breaking point in the freezing environment, and the internal conflict, stress and strain that the individual felt within was then projected outward upon others. The hostilities and conflicts between the male and female cave-dwellers were simply a manifestation of a separated, isolated, and diminished sense of self in opposition to everything that was outside of self.

The lost and astray mind would view every external presence as either a threat, an obstacle, a burden or as an object to be used for one's benefit. Offspring would serve the useful purpose of increasing one's stock, or they could be considered as an undue burden, depending on the circumstances. Likewise, the male would come to view the female as either a threat to his freedom, a nagging burden, an obstacle to his movement, or as an object to satisfy his physical desires. The female would come to view the male as a physical threat, an oppressive burden, an obstacle to her personal goals, or as an object to satisfy her needs. The relationship dynamics that cause one to view others as objects is a direct consequence of being disconnected from the Most Supreme Unseen Essence of Life. In a state of disconnection, one is left to wrestle with the seen presence without a way to tap into the unseen presence. As a result, the intelligence of the ice-cold, deep-freeze mentality is a severely retarded ability that can barely scratch the surface of comprehension regarding the whole life presence.

The deep-freeze environment would be experienced as a forbidding, harsh and cruel adversary which was a complete reversal of the welcoming and bountiful atmosphere of the sunny garden environment. The relationship of self was shattered and reversed as the spirit presence became dominated by the physical signals of hunger, fear, cold, pain, and helplessness. As the spirit presence became further weakened by the toxic consumption of depleted and devitalized energy in the form of food substances, the reversal of presence would intensify. The suntanned presence of the Children of the Sun would become pale due to a reversal in environmental conditions. The regenerating and refining effects of whole life consumption within divine order would be reversed into the mutating and degenerating effects of toxic consumption within disorder.

The reversal resulted in the sacred spirit presence of Man, He and She, being reduced to a mere physical presence that had to rely on the limited perceptions and comprehension of a superficial intellect informed by the physical senses. Therefore, within the thoughts and reasoning of the ice-cold, deep-freeze mentality, the appearance of things became more important than the life essence. The reversal of presence would mean that the male would become completely opposite in his role of providing divine guidance and divine protection. As a result, the male would reverse into a brutal abuser. The female would reverse her role in nurturing divinity. The female would reverse into one who nurtures abusive attitudes and behaviors and then begins to inflict the abuse upon the offspring. The reversal resulted in sexual acts that became mere physical and mental feats that had absolutely no connection to the Supreme Love vibration.

There is no possibility of a divine solution without correcting the toxic attitudes and behaviors by moving forward into divine spirit consciousness of a holistic living way of life. The reversal of divine order into disorder is what has been addressed within this text. The consequences of the reversal from divine consumption to toxic consumption are plain to see on a daily basis in one's personal relationships, on the national scene, and on a global scale. For this reason, one must begin at the personal and intimate level in order to correct the damage that has been done. The correction can multiply in one's own existence in a widening circle of influence. The unit of the family is the nucleus of every organization within the social order just as the cell is the basic structural and functional unit of every living thing. The offspring are the future direction of one's life presence. As the basis of the divine social economic family community, strong and harmonious relationships between Man, He and She, are vital.

The first step is to develop a strong base of the Supreme Love vibrations within self by implementing the practices and procedures of divine consumption, mentally, physically and spiritually. One will think twice about indulging in toxic consumption when one begins to gain a sense of dignity and self-esteem. As a matter of fact, willful indulgence in toxic consumption is a sure sign of esteemlessness regardless of the arrogant, vain and cocky postures that usually accompany a vague and empty self-image. Oftentimes, the insecure individual who is struggling with low self-esteem will use sexual activities to gain a sense of gratification that can mask the lonely and numb sensations of the ice-cold, deep-freeze mentality. Therefore, toxic sexual encounters are the quickest way to spread the energy that is opposite of Supreme Love to others. The vicious nomadic invading warlords ejaculated a breed of contemptuous, conniving, and manipulative offspring that reflected the toxic residue of lust, lies, illusions, confusion, death and deadly destruction.

In order to correct the pattern of toxic sexuality, one must begin to comprehend the difference between the sexuality of the ice-cold, deep-freeze mentality and the divine sexuality as experienced within divine spirit consciousness. When one usually refers to sexuality, there is tendency to focus on the sexual organs of Man, He and She, and the act of sexual intercourse. Sex within the death consumption culture becomes limited to the physical acts of the physical parts. There is no doubt that the physical presence has an impressive role to play in divine sexuality. However, the focus of expression within divine spirit consciousness remains within the sensations and vibrations of divine oneness, the utmost care, tenderness and devotion to the whole life presence in connection with the Most Supreme Unseen Essence of Life.

EXPOSING THE ICE-COLD, DEEP-FREEZE MENTALITY AND WHOLE LIFE HEALING OF SEXUAL ENERGY WITHIN THE DIVINE PARALLEL

The entire body temple of Man, He and She, can be aroused to receive pleasurable sensations of whole life energy.

It is sorrowful plight that Man She has found herself succumbing to Man He who holds a predator-like appetite for her rather than upholding a whole-life appreciation for her mental, physical and spiritual presence. As the male became stimulated by acts of violence, the female became stimulated by acts of violation, for that was all the cave-dwelling male could bring to her based on his toxic consumption. The vibrations and sensations of toxic consumption are passed through sexual encounters. The vibrations and sensations of toxic consumption are bred into the offspring.

The largest sensory organ for both males and females is the skin itself. The skin is filled with sensory nerve endings, and stroking, caressing, and gently massaging any part of the body can produce soothing and sensual pleasure. Some areas are more sensitive, especially the inner thigh area, the neck, the belly button, the breasts and nipples, the eyelids, the ears, and the shoulders. Many people also find that having their feet stroked is arousing. The sexual organs of Man, He and She, are highly concentrated with sensory nerve endings. The mouth, including the lips and tongue, for most people, is an area of high sensitivity. Oral expression is one act that uses the sensitivity of this area in a stimulating way. The skin is a glorious receptor of whole life sensations and vibrations when one resides within the sphere of the sacred garden culture. The pleasures and delights of Man, He and She, in divine union are immense. However, the very same physical acts performed within the ice-cold, deep-freeze mentality carry the contamination and depleting effect of the energy that is opposite of Supreme Love.

In frigid climates, the skin and body parts are adversely affected by the cold, and frostbite can occur. Frostbite is literally frozen body tissue. Frostbite is characterized by white, waxy skin that feels numb and hard. The skin and underlying tissues are damaged by extreme cold, and the sensitivity of the skin is lost. The simple and natural pleasures of touching, caressing and gentle affection are lost in the numbing ice cold vibrations. Touch becomes a painful or numbed experience in such a cold situation. One can imagine being caught out in a blinding snowstorm. The severe trauma of freezing to the point of hypothermia means the body is unable to maintain a core temperature necessary for the brain and muscles to function properly. The ice-cold, deep-freeze was a period of isolation when the lost and astray Children had to survive in the midst of ice, glaciers, snow and extreme and bitter cold. The reported effects of hypothermia must have been a daily and wretched danger in such a harsh and icy environment.

The effects of hypothermia are stated to include dazed consciousness, loss of fine motor coordination—particularly in hands—due to decreased blood flow, slurred speech, violent shivering, irrational behavior, and an "I-don't-care attitude." Further studies indicate that severe hypothermia occurs when the core body temperature is between 92 and 86 degrees, and shivering occurs in violent waves and finally stops because the heat output of the muscles is insufficient. In such a state, the body reportedly shuts down to conserve energy; an individual can't walk and curls up into a fetal position to conserve heat; muscle rigidity develops; skin is pale; pupils dilate; pulse rate decreases; at 90 degrees the body tries to move into hibernation, shutting down all peripheral blood flow and reducing the breathing rate and heart rate; at 86 degrees the body is in a state of "metabolic icebox." According to reports, the person looks dead but is still alive.

The vibrations and sensations of the ice-cold, deep-freeze were inbred through genetic codes and energy codes within the lost and astray Children who lost their tan. The day-to-day reality of those who reside within the culture of disorder thus reflects sexuality that is marked by cold, harsh and cruel relationships, a lack of feeling and tenderness, and senses that are numbed, insensitive and unresponsive to anything but gross mental and physical stimulation.

The ancient women's societies of the sacred garden culture maintained the divine knowledge, wisdom and understanding of the feminine presence. In the beginning, the Most Supreme Unseen created Man, He and She, in divine oneness. This sacred and blessed union of divine oneness was given the fruits of the trees of life to consume for holistic living health. Within the sacred and blessed union of divine oneness and the consumption of the sacred fruits of the trees of life, Man, He and She, was ordained to go forward and multiply divinity. Therefore, the divine order of sexuality is the holistic living expression of divine oneness of brain, body and spirit between Man, He and She.

The basic characteristic of divine union is that Man He, the father spirit, is to provide divine guidance and protection over Man She and their offspring; and that Man She is to nurture the divine guidance and protection that is brought forward to her, the mother spirit. The sacred garden culture which was maintained by these sacred principles of divine union has been under siege and attack for so long that Man, He and She, has forgotten their divine position.

# Chapter Nine:
# The Key of Life–Whole Life Healing of Sexual Energy within the Divine Parallel

# Chapter Nine: The Key of Life–Whole Life Healing of Sexual Energy within the Divine Parallel

## Theories, Facts and the Holistic Living Truth

Time and time again the various theories proposed by the lost and astray Children who lost their tan have been presented to provide solutions to the personal and social ills within the death consumption culture. Social welfare programs, mental health initiatives, education reform, religious evangelism, theories of eugenics, trickle-down economics, global strategies to spread democracy, and homeland security to prevent terrorist attacks provide layers and layers of bandages to cover the oozing, festering, gangrenous sores upon the social body. What is the cause of the pustules and blistering sores that erupt in violence, chaos, massive outbreaks of fatal diseases, mental illness, and war? Is it the nature or essential state of being for Man, He and She, to exist in disorder? Can Man, He and She, simply eliminate the degenerate elements of society, the "unfit," "defects," and the so-called "inferior" breeds and then proceed in peace?

There are numerous theories within the death consumption culture that attempt to answer these questions. The theories cover a range of social economic, scientific, political, and technological solutions to address the deteriorating condition of Man, He and She, in a world teetering at the brink of mass destruction. The religious/spiritual theorists aspire to transform their minds and the minds of others into a more peaceful, loving model. All of these theorists puff up in great pride and arrogance as they wave their huge intellects around and offer the "final solutions," the way, the truth and the light for the salvation of humanity or at least for their special interest group. How does one go about implementing one's theories, and how long does it take to realize that the theories are continuing to produce grave errors?

When religious groups bomb and kill each other in the name of their god, and then other religious groups downplay their history of bloody crusades and burning people to death, one has to look at the collective religious theories of the death consumption culture and begin to notice glaring contradictions. When the spiritual/religious groups that splinter from these main branches attempt to institute new-age practices while still maintaining the same old practices and behaviors of the death consumption culture, one begins to wonder how long the lost and astray mind can pretend that it has any sense of direction. The nature of religious/spiritual theories within the death consumption culture is that they are devised within a frame of reference that can only reproduce some aspect of the death consumption culture in greater or lesser degrees, but always maintaining the energy that is opposite of Supreme Love. As a matter of fact, any theory proposed within the death consumption culture becomes a blueprint for the further reproduction of lust, lies, illusions, confusion, death and deadly destruction.

A major function of theories is to provide so many different perspectives within the ice-cold, deep-freeze mentality that one becomes further dazed in the haze of illusions and confusion of the lost and astray mind. Passionate theorists can spend their time and energy disproving theories, debating theories, and promoting theories without making any fundamental changes in their way of life within the death consumption culture.

Theories come and theories go, because theories are little more than guessing games that cannot be disproved until more information on the topic is made available. Although a theory can immediately change based on new evidence that provides greater comprehension, many individuals display outright hostility when their personalized theories are disproved. The way to handle new information then is to destroy, dismiss, discredit, or downplay any source that will in fact dismantle the popular theory, i.e. the theory in which one is well-invested. Theories offer explanations and interpretations based on the thoughts and reasoning that are formulated within the cultural context of the theorizing individual.

One's cultural context either serves to distort the facts or to provide clarity to the point where divine reasoning can emerge. The cultural context of the ice-cold, deep-freeze mentality is first and foremost a culture of distortion in and of itself. It is a culture where the root and foundation of that culture is fueled by the energy that is opposite of Supreme Love. In fact, the culture of the lost and astray Children who lost their tan has proven time and time again to be a culture that provides adverse effects to the suntanned populations. In theory, the culture of the lost and astray Children who lost their tan is established for the good of all humanity. As any conscious personality has come to witness, the culture of the lost and astray Children who lost their tan perpetuates theories that serve to further the vibrations of lust, lies, illusions, confusion, death and deadly destruction. All one has to do is examine the outcomes or the state of affairs within the death consumption culture on a global scale, and one can begin to connect the dots of massive disease, dysfunction and disorder that are the greatest achievement of the lost and astray Children who lost their tan.

Within the divine parallel, divine spirit consciousness allows one to reason with whole life energy so that whole life patterns are revealed. When whole life patterns are revealed, one is able to detect the errors that cause disorder. When one is able to detect errors, the missing links are seen as the steps to corrective actions. It is not any wonder that divine solutions create a greater degree of peace, harmony and Supreme Love vibrations within the highest interests of all concerned.

Outside of the divine parallel, theories are systematically devised to justify and rationalize the ways and means of the death consumption culture, or theories are devised to validate conclusions that have already been reached, or theories are devised to speculate about issues that have no relationship to one's whole life presence. The shattering and scattering effect of superficial reasoning and shallow thinking serves to create division, strife, and superiority-inferiority complexes that are the inheritance of the mutated and degenerated breed and all the disciples and followers of the ice-cold, deep-freeze mentality. Any sense of wholeness is shattered within the lost and astray mind, and the fragmented pieces are scattered to and fro so that the theories reflect the inner state of disconnection that characterizes the lost and astray Children who lost their tan.

It is imperative, essential and of absolute necessity that Man, He provides the holistic living truth about Supreme Love to the feminine presence and the offspring. The truth of the matter is that the masculine presence has the divine obligation, duty and responsibility to provide divine guidance and divine protection to that most glorious gift of life, the feminine presence. It is indeed a fact that the feminine presence will nurture whatever the masculine presence of that social environment brings forward to her. It is also a fact that whoever gives guidance to the hands that rock the crib gives guidance to that nation and every generation of that nation. It is also a fact that the Children of the Sun learn by example and not by words. It is a fact that only words that are expressed through the actions of life examples have meaning, and the actions speak louder than the words.

The contradiction between sweet words and bitter actions is a major deception that is an inherited trait of the ice-cold, deep-freeze mentality. To speak of the glory and victory of the carnage and atrocities of war is a contradiction to the whole life presence. To speak of the good and satisfying meal of a slaughtered animal with burned vegetables is a contradiction to the whole life presence. To speak of liberty and democracy while enslaving one's fellow man is a contradiction to the whole life presence. To speak of intelligence and superiority while engaging in genocidal acts is a contradiction to the whole life presence. As even the smallest child within the sacred garden culture comprehends, what goes around comes around, and there is no escape from the universal law: one must reap from what one sows. Unfortunately, as the consequences begin to mount, the ice-cold, deep-freeze mentality begins to target a scapegoat.

Words are meaningful when they express the whole-life presence of brain, body and spirit in a unified focus of purpose. Words spoken from the ice-cold, deep-freeze mentality ring hollow and false, because the life presence, i.e. the spirit, can not be integrated into the definitions of lust, lies, illusions, confusion, death and deadly destruction. One's existence is self-defining. The nature of one's consumption is self-defining. Regardless of the words that are used to construct theories about greatness and brilliance, the attitudes and behaviors of one's existence speaks volumes. Therefore, when the lost and astray Children who lost their tan boast of being great builders of great civilizations, it is possible to examine their long and winding history of murder, rape, steal and take, i.e. murder, rape, pillage and burn. The acts of death and deadly destruction speak louder than any words that may serve to whitewash the mutated and degenerated breed. However, as one begins to divinely reason with the origin of Man, He and She, one will comprehend that the mutated and degenerated breed is the result of the massive deterioration of the Children of the Sun with the golden tan in the first place.

The blame game is a convenient pastime within the ice-cold, deep-freeze mentality that keeps one distracted from the nature of one's own consumption. While eugenicists identify the degenerates of the social order, they are unable or unwilling to recognize and acknowledge their own original degeneration and mutation into the selfish, greedy, cold-blooded predatory vibrations of the ice-cold, deep-freeze mentality. There is absolutely no comprehension that the social order that the mutated and degenerated breed created is a direct reflection of the depleted and deprived conditions of the ice-cold, deep-freeze mentality. There is absolutely no comprehension that the lost and astray Children who lost their tan are incapable of leadership, except the leadership of reproducing the mentality of the ice-cold caves. As the suntanned populations suffer further mutation and degeneration in the sunshine, they identify the hurt and harm that has been inflicted by the lost and astray Children who lost their tan. However, the suntanned populations are unable or unwilling to comprehend how they serve as the instruments of their own destruction as they continue to integrate and assimilate the ice-cold, deep-freeze mentality.

As long as one is unable to identify the nature of the ice-cold, deep-freeze mentality, one will be lost and astray in theories that have no relationship to the holistic living truth about Supreme Love. What the I in I am saying here is there are very many reasons why the Children of the Sun are existing in the chaos of lust, lies, illusions, confusion, death and deadly destruction. The fact is that the base, root and foundation of a way of life determine the outcome of the social order, which is then reflected in the offspring. If the fathering presence of Man, He and She, perpetuates the conflicts of lust, lies, illusions, confusion, death and deadly destruction, i.e. the way of life of the ice-cold, deep-freeze mentality, one can only expect that the mothers, sons and daughters will be a sum total of the energy consumed. Regardless of how deeply devoted the masculine presence is to the deceptions and the erroneous theories; regardless of his level and degree of ignorance, innocence, or intellectual claims, the results remain the same. Therefore, it becomes an absolute necessity that Man He and Man She focus from the perspective of divine spirit consciousness and seek to acquire the holistic living truth about Supreme Love by every divine means necessary.

**Beginning at the Beginning**

In order for one to reclaim divine spirit consciousness, one must begin to reclaim one's sacred origin as a Divine Child of the Sun. Thus, a tremendous dismantling of the ice-cold, deep-freeze mentality must occur, beginning with one's basic patterns of consumption. So long as one claims the ice-cold caves as one's original presence, one will continue to reproduce ice-cold, cave attitudes and behaviors that are the pale reflection of the energy that is opposite of Supreme Love. One will continue to function in the greedy self-interest of lust, lies, illusions, confusion, death and deadly destruction. One will continue to function with a complete lack of self-awareness while claiming intelligence and pointing the finger at every thing outside of self as the cause of one's problems. One will spend vital energy in debating theories that are completely useless, meaningless, and irrelevant to the whole life development of Man, He and She, while feeling arrogant and cocky about one's brilliant ideas.

Divine spirit consciousness originates with the Divine Children of the Sun with the golden tan within the sacred garden culture. Divine spirit consciousness is fueled by divine consumption for the brain, the body and the spirit. There is no other origin of the sacred spirit presence of Man, He and She, except the cultural context of a holistic living way of life within the sacred garden culture. The fact is that the environment that manifests the sacred garden culture is the same environment that manifests the Divine Children of the Sun. It is a fact that life did not begin in the ice, although the emergence of the mutated and degenerated breed occurred in the ice-cold, deep-freeze environment.

As a matter of fact, the garden symbolizes the warm fertile birthplace of life, whereas the ice cold cave symbolizes death and sterility. It is a fact that death is not a part of life, because life is a continuation of life; death is outside of the cycle of life and represents an energy that is opposite of Supreme Love. Therefore, the theories regarding the origin of man that have been presented within the death consumption culture are simply theories that are addressing the emergence of the ice-cold, deep-freeze mentality and justifying the presence of the mutated and degenerated breed.

Starting from the ice-cold caves, one is at a disadvantage; one has become disconnected from the Most Supreme Unseen Essence of Life and Supreme Love, and one begins to show physical signs of degeneration and mutation. One can only reason from the references of one's impoverished conditions. The debates that rage about conflicting theories within the death consumption culture are a reflection of the ice-cold, deep-freeze mentality at work. For example, theories regarding "nature" versus "nurture" seek to explain the roles of heredity and environment in human development with each theory vying for the top position of being "right." However, within divine spirit consciousness, it becomes clear that those who have perpetuated the ice-cold, deep-freeze mentality have upheld attitudes and behaviors that emerged in the ice-cold, deep-freeze environment. These attitudes and behaviors are socially reinforced within the death consumption culture. These attitudes and behaviors are genetically reinforced through toxic consumption.

Somehow in the midst of the chaos and confusion of the ice-cold, deep-freeze mentality, the life presence struggles for expression; however, every expression that surfaces is immediately absorbed into the death consumption culture. Therefore, while one speaks of genius or gifted talent or artistic mastery within the death consumption culture, one is still speaking of nurturing the nature of the ice-cold, deep-freeze mentality. As occurred in the ice-cold caves, the depleted environment perpetuated toxic and depleted consumption, which manifested mutation and degeneration. The inherited mutation and degeneration of toxic consumption then, in turn, promotes the attitudes and behaviors of the ice-cold, deep-freeze mentality. The attitudes and behaviors of the ice-cold, deep-freeze mentality serve to maintain the toxic consumption patterns that reproduce the conditions necessary to breed further mutation and degeneration. As a result, within the death consumption culture, one is born and bred into the vibrations of lust, lies, illusions, confusion, death and deadly destruction. One then perpetuates those toxic vibrations through the consumption of dead, devitalized and depleted energy for the brain, the body and the spirit.

In the truest sense, the concepts of art, intelligence, superiority, genius, mastery, brilliance, advancement and such other accolades that are brandished by the lost and astray mind are meaningless within the death consumption culture. These marks of achievement are meaningless within a context of toxic consumption where the life presence of Man, He and She, continues to deteriorate to the point of death and deadly destruction. These marks of achievement are meaningless as the rubble and remnants of buried artifacts of peoples and societies that have vanished from the face of the earth in extinction. The ultimate lessons of life went unheeded by the high-achieving lost and astray mind. If the purpose is to reason with a better way of life, then one must begin to reason beyond the ice-cold, deep-freeze mentality.

Another example of an ongoing debate within the death consumption culture that keeps the lost and astray mind embroiled in controversy is the debate of theories regarding evolution versus creationism. It is difficult for the fragmented and limited perspective of the lost and astray mind to perceive that two opposing issues within the ice-cold, deep-freeze mentality are simply the back and the front of the same deception. It is a fact that Charles Darwin was not the first theorist to propose a hierarchy of origin for Man, He and She. The earlier theory of the "Great Chain of Being" held that a god created an infinite and continuous series of life forms, each one grading into the next, from simplest to most complex, and that all organisms, including humans, were created in their present form relatively recently and that they have remained unchanged since then.

Research indicates that in the early 18th century, a biological scientist named Linnaeus developed a classification system to name *Homo sapiens,* i.e. Man, He and She, and placed man in the order of Primates along with all of the apes, monkeys, and positions. It is noted that this classification was very controversial at the time since it implied that people were part of nature, along with other animals and plants. In addition, his theory implied that man was biologically closer to the other primates than to all other animals. It is also noted that, late in the 18th century, a small number of European scientists began to suggest that life forms are not fixed, but, in fact, change over time. Findings show that Charles Darwin's grandfather wrote about the changes that occur in living things, including humans. As a matter of fact, the various theories regarding an evolutionary process continued as the lost and astray Children who lost their tan grappled with their origin and their position in the scheme of life.

Findings show that Darwin was a product of his environment, i.e. the environment of the ice-cold, deep-freeze mentality, and that during 19th-century, England, that environment, reflected strong racist attitudes regarding "Negroes." The basic assumption of the ice-cold, deep-freeze mentality is that the suntanned populations are culturally and intellectually inferior. These assumptions were part and parcel of the theories that were developed within the death consumption culture. It is a fact that one can not function outside of one's cultural context; one merely reflects one's cultural context to various degrees. One may have a public and a private face; however, the context of all of one's definitions, interpretations, perceptions and theories will be infused with the energy of one's consumption and the cultural context of one's attitudes and behaviors. Therefore, it becomes easy to see within divine spirit consciousness how Darwin's theories, such as those expressed in "The Descent of Man," can only serve to preserve and perpetuate the ice-cold, deep-freeze mentality.

> Extinction follows chiefly from the competition of tribe with tribe, and race with race. Various checks are always in action, serving to keep down the numbers of each savage tribe,- such as periodical famines, nomadic habits and the consequent deaths of infants, prolonged suckling, wars, accidents, sickness, licentiousness, the stealing of women, infanticide, and especially lessened fertility.
>
> The decrease of the native population of the Sandwich Islands is as notorious as that of New Zealand. It has been roughly estimated by those best capable of judging, that when Cook discovered the islands in 1779, the population amounted to about 300,000. According to a loose census in 1823, the numbers then were 142,050… We here see that in the interval of forty years, between 1832 and 1872, [1832: 130,313 to 1872: 51,531] the population has decreased no less than sixty-eight per cent! This has been attributed by most writers to the profligacy of the women, to former bloody wars, and to the severe labor imposed on conquered tribes and to newly introduced diseases, which have been on several occasions extremely destructive.
>
> When Tasmania was first colonised the natives were roughly estimated by some at 7000 and by others at 20,000. Their number was soon greatly reduced, chiefly by fighting with the English and with each other. After the famous hunt by all the colonists, when the remaining natives delivered themselves up to the government, they consisted

only of 120 individuals, who were in 1832 transported to Flinders Island. As they continued rapidly to decrease, and as they themselves thought that they should not perish so quickly elsewhere, they were removed in 1847 to Oyster Cove in the southern part of Tasmania. They then consisted (Dec. 20th, 1847) of fourteen men, twenty-two women and ten children. But the change of site did no good. Disease and death still pursued them, and in 1864 one man (who died in 1869), and three elderly women alone survived. The infertility of the women is even a more remarkable fact than the liability of all to ill-health and death...

We thus see that many of the wilder races of man are apt to suffer much in health when subjected to changed conditions or habits of life, and not exclusively from being transported to a new climate. Mere alterations in habits, which do not appear injurious in themselves, seem to have this same effect; and in several cases the children are particularly liable to suffer. It has often been said, as Mr. McNamara remarks, that man can resist with impunity the greatest diversities of climate and other changes; but this is true only of the civilised races. Man in his wild condition seems to be in this respect almost as susceptible as his nearest allies, the anthropoid apes, which have never yet survived long, when removed from their native country.... Civilised races can certainly resist changes of all kinds far better than savages; and in this respect they resemble domesticated animals, for though the latter sometimes suffer in health (for instance European dogs in India), yet they are rarely rendered sterile, though a few such instances have been recorded. The immunity of

> civilised races and domesticated animals is probably due to their having been subjected to a greater extent, and therefore having grown somewhat more accustomed, to diversified or varying conditions… But sterility and ill-health would probably follow, if savages were compelled by any cause, such as the inroad of a conquering tribe, to desert their homes and to change their habits.[75]

These are just a few of the theories projected by the invader population as they inflict their brutal violence and raging madness of intellect and their toxic habits on the target groups among the suntanned Children. In every instance, when examining any of the theories as to why the "white" man has been the instrument of fatality, destruction, annihilation, and the extinction of so many populations of suntanned Children, it is never reasoned that the basic instrument of destruction is the breaking of one's spirit presence. The theories are formulated from an ice-cold, deep-freeze mentality that has become disconnected from the divine spirit presence, therefore excuses, rationales and justifications will always manifest speculative theories as to why these "uncivilized" populations simply died out. The holistic living truth about Supreme Love is also a missing link within the lost and astray mind of the ice-cold, deep-freeze mentality. Thus, the lack of ability to see one's own deadly and destructive role is simply denied and transferred over to a scapegoat, i.e. the targeted population.

It is amazing how the scientific "genius" of the lost and astray mentality is sent in to analyze the situation after the warlords have completed their slaughter. Occasionally, there will even be prayer vigils given out by the religious benefactors of the slaughter as they beg for forgiveness for the sins and

---

[75] *Descent of Man*. Chapter Seven: On the Races of Man. Charles Darwin. 1871. Online Source: http://www.zoo.uib.no/classics/darwin/descent.chap7.html.

atrocities against the young and the innocent. It is noteworthy that in no instance does the lost and astray mind change from the practices and principles of the status quo. Reparations may even be given to the remaining survivors in honor of them adopting the assimilated cultural patterns and religious order of the ice-cold, deep-freeze mentality. There is always this missionary syndrome of transitioning the "heathens" into god-fearing individuals. To inflict this fear, the most bloodthirsty kind of terrorism is implemented. These are the matters of fact time and time again.

**Deep-Freeze Family Affair**

It is imperative that the sons of Man, He and She, come into the phases of divine spirit consciousness so as to be able to identify and personally rectify the damage caused by the ice-cold, deep-freeze mentality. If not, the masculine presence will be in denial of his divine duties, obligations and responsibilities to provide divine guidance and protection to the mother spirit and the offspring. To deny the mother spirit is to deny oneself. There are absolutely no and's, if's or maybe's about it, the whole life presence of Man, He and She, is nurtured within the womb of the mother spirit and is born out of the mother spirit. If the sacred feminine presence is not given the utmost of divine guidance and divine protection, Man, He and She, is being set up for self-destruction and extinction. Being trapped in the cesspool of the toxic reasoning perpetuated by the ice-cold, deep-freeze mentality has definitely caused Man, He and She, to reside in a state of delusions and fantasies regarding their sacred origin.

As has been pointed out through archaeological findings and ruins, the sacred sons and daughters of Man, i.e. the Divine Children of the Sun with the golden tan, have inhabited the planet Earth for millions of years prior to the emergence of the degeneration and mutation of the ice-cold, deep-freeze. These sacred suntanned sons and daughters of Man had maintained a magnificent history of honoring the Most Supreme Seen and Unseen Essence of Life and Supreme Love. Time and time again, example after example, ruins, artifacts, and findings show that Man, He and She, had a complete comprehension of the fact that the mother spirit must be exalted, for she is the womb or the keeper, the nurturing energy of the whole life presence of Man, He and She.

The masculine presence is historically identified as taking his sacred leadership role of providing divine guidance and protection for the mother spirit, i.e. the feminine presence of Man, He and She. In ruin after ruin and through tons of artifacts and archaeological findings, there is a clear statement of a divine order far beyond the imagination of the lost and astray mind of the ice-cold, deep-freeze mentality.

The lost and astray Children who lost their tan were well-aware of this divine presence prior to their encounter with the errors that befell them in the ice-cold, deep-freeze. However, the massive deprivation, deterioration and mental, physical and spiritual mutation and degeneration struck a devastating blow against the divine reasoning of the lost and astray Children. The true tragedy occurred as these lost and astray Children projected a male war god as the symbol of the most supreme creator when, in fact, this male war god is the symbol of horrifying levels and degrees of death and deadly destruction. Beyond a shadow of a doubt, the lost and astray Children who lost their tan consumed of an energy that is opposite of Supreme Love. The toxic consequences are mutation and degeneration, which resulted in the depletion of their divine mental, physical and spiritual presence. In other words, these Children would manifest an unwhole or incomplete presentation of Man, He and She.

Every thought and every reason of these lost and astray Children would be a reflection of the ice-cold, deep-freeze mentality. Every cultural pattern and habit would be a reflection of the death consumption culture bred within the ice-cold, deep-freeze mentality. The fact is this would be the baggage that formulates the reasoning of every social economic and religious declaration formulated from these lost and astray minds. The root and foundation of every creation would aid and abet the swift ability to kill, maim and destroy the whole life presence of others. The ice-cold, deep-freeze mentality would be taken from the practices of murder, rape, steal and take and translated into the theories of "civilized" and "intelligent" reasoning of the lost and astray mind. Thus would formulate a way of life rooted in lust, lies, illusions, confusion, death and deadly destruction. The basic principals of this way of life would be the survival of the fittest, and fitness would be based on having the swiftest ability to kill. The greatest master killers and conquerors would be deified to join the ranks of the one true god as defined by the ice-cold, deep-freeze mentality.

These toxic and depleted ways of life would be formulated into religious orders. These religious orders would be based upon slaughter, sacrifice, bloodshed, and conquest. As time would pass and as these Children would encounter the sacred suntanned Children, these religious orders that would later be referred to as paganism would eventually be formulated into four basic religious branches stemming from one father. That is to say that the father energy that would breed each of these religious orders would be an expression of the hunting, scavenging, herding/pastoralist culture born of the ice-cold, deep-freeze mentality.

The fact is that the basic characteristics of these new religious orders would continue to uphold the hunting, scavenging, herding/pastoralist culture. In other words, these religious orders would continue to maintain and forward the vibrations of murder, rape, steal and take. These religious orders would seed this mentality into the suntanned Children through slaughter, enslavement, rape, and domination via colonialism, the Trans-Saharan slave trade, the Trans-Atlantic slave trade, the chattel slave system and genocidal plots, schemes and practices. Holy wars, jihads, out-caste abuse and religious purgings would continue to be the orders of the all mighty gods of those descendants, disciples and followers of the ice-cold, deep-freeze mentality.

Equally, the slaughter, enslavement and experimentation would continue to be the plight of the guinea pig, be they animal or Man, He and She. The war culture of the ice-cold, deep-freeze mentality would, in fact, be declared as the superior culture of the superior breed bred in the ice-cold, deep-freeze mentality. The lost and astray Children with the golden tan who were born and bred within the vibrations and sensations of the ice-cold, deep-freeze mentality would continue to integrate, assimilate and adopt the self-destructive patterns of the ice-cold, deep-freeze mentality.

The masculine presence of the suntanned Children would become a weak, feeble and depleted presence exalting one or the other of the religious orders bred within the ice-cold, deep-freeze mentality. The mother spirit of Man, He and She, would be reduced to the wretched state of whoring and prostituting the ways and means of the ice-cold, deep-freeze mentality. In other words, the sacred mother spirit/feminine presence of Man, He and She would be reduced to an inferior state within the ice-cold, deep-freeze mentality. This would simply be a part of the self-fulfilling prophecy as the suntanned populations were relegated to inferior status within the hierarchy of the ice-cold, deep-freeze mentality. Thus, under the guidance and leadership of the lost and astray Children who lost their tan, the Children of the Sun with the golden tan would become a mutated and degenerated copy of their original selves. The mark of the beast would be reflected in permed hair, colored and dyed hair and skin, body alterations, homosexuality, mental and physical sickness, disease and disorder, and massive conflicts between Man, He and She.

Yes, it is a fact that the most sacred and divine family order of Man, He and She, would be conquered, divided, tricked and undecided as they continue to indulge in one or the other of the religious orders of the death consumption culture that are in truth the same game with another name. As the toxic attitudes, behaviors and addictions of the death consumption culture would take their toll, the masters and grand masters of deceit would plagiarize suntanned mythologies to create religious orders and then use these religious orders to orchestrate division.

The lost and astray Children who lost their tan would take bits and pieces of the holistic living truth and sprinkle it through their social economic, political and religious agendas. These lost and astray Children would formulate theories to justify the outcome. It is quite obvious that the primary goal and objective is to reverse the holistic living truth about Supreme Love so that it will reflect the opposite, i.e. projecting the theory to be a fact and the facts to be a theory. This is most especially true when one perceives all evidence to have been pillaged and burned. What is certain is that the sacred garden presence flourished in and throughout the rest of the world during the time when the mutated and degenerated breed was still trying to find their way out of the ice-cold, deep-freeze environment.

Yet and still with all of this being the case, the lost and astray Children who lost their tan would fabricate massive deceptive agendas to declare themselves as righteous and godly. These lost and astray Children would declare themselves as chosen, superior and endowed to inherit the earth as ordained by their war god of envy, jealousy, greed and spite. These brilliant intellectual minds would declare themselves as being anointed by god and able to discern all issues related to the worldly affairs of Man, He and She. These brilliant minds would become masters and grand masters of deceit while claiming to have full knowledge of creation down to the year, month and time. Let us take a look at the religious reasoning and thoughts of brilliant minds of the invader offspring who descended from the ice-cold, deep-freeze mentality.

Research indicates that Bishop James Ussher was able to use the ages of famous pre-flood personages in the Bible to estimate the number of years between creation and the flood. It is noted that in 1650 C.E., he published his book "Annals of the Old Testament, Deduced from the First Origins of the World." Ussher calculated that god had created the Earth in 4004 B.C.E. Studies show that a decade earlier, Dr. John Lightfoot, Vice-Chancellor of the University of Cambridge had already arrived at an estimate of October 23, 4004 B.C.E., at 9 a.m. Research indicates that most conservative groups within Christianity still follow Ussher's date. It is noted that some believe that since the world was created in six days, that it will last exactly six thousand years. According to these calculations, the present age should have come to an end circa 1996 CE.

Let us note when the Books of Moses were written. According to research, the Book of Genesis was written by Moses between 1450 and 1410 B.C.E. According to the biblical analysis, Moses went to the mountain and wrote on some clay tablets similar to the ones that we shall identify in this text. Among the Kushite people, writings and inscriptions upon clay tablets and papyrus were commonly used thousands of years prior to the invasions of the nomadic war cultures. These tablets were kept and maintained as the sacred texts of these Kushite populations. The keepers of these tablets were the priests and priestesses of each social order. The tablet served to teach the many lessons of life from the Most Supreme Unseen to the supreme presence of the seen. In other words, these tablets simply explained the essence of the lessons of life, and the Supreme Love vibrations required by every Man, He and She in order to establish and maintain a divine union. The priests and priestesses were the keepers of the sacred laws of divine order, and each individual within the family community setting was totally and absolutely responsible for his or her actions and consequences derived.

EXPOSING THE ICE-COLD, DEEP-FREEZE MENTALITY AND WHOLE LIFE HEALING OF SEXUAL ENERGY WITHIN THE DIVINE PARALLEL

Lust, lies, illusions, confusion, death and deadly destruction were, and remain as acts totally against the sacred laws of life. The holistic living truth about Supreme Love and the fact that life is for the living is, and remains, the supreme order of the Divine Children of the Sun with the golden tan. In the text that describes the life of Moses and the religions that descended from the Books of Moses, it had been spoken that Moses was married to the daughter of a priest. It was also mentioned that prior to his magnificent episode with his god, Moses had an historic encounter with his father-in-law who is said to have advised Moses.

It should be noted that Moses proceeded on to deal with some mysterious tablets that would emerge into the ten commandments, i.e. the laws of the religions that later descended from the Books of Moses. Let us keep in mind the commandments which covered thou shalt not kill, thou shalt not commit adultery, thou shalt not steal, thou shalt not bear false witness against thy neighbour, thou shalt not covet thy neighbour's house, thou shalt not covet thy neighbour's wife…It should be very clear that these commandments did not emerge from and have never applied to individuals who perpetuated a hunting, scavenging, and herding culture through acts of murder, rape, steal and take. These laws had no true relevance at that time and have no true relevance today, because these laws exemplify the way of life that ascends from the sacred garden culture of the Divine Children of the Sun. Let us witness the energy of the founding vibration of these religious traditions as the Semitic god speaks as told by the Books of Moses. Let us be reminded here that these are the "Books of Moses" and that Moses is desperately trying to gain control over his lost and astray followers.

> Behold, I send an Angel before thee, to keep thee in the way, and to bring thee into the place which I have prepared. Beware of him, and obey

his voice, provoke him not; for he will not pardon your transgressions: for my name is in him. But if thou shalt indeed obey his voice, and do all that I speak; then I will be an enemy unto thine enemies, and an adversary unto thine adversaries. For mine Angel shall go before thee, and bring thee in unto the Amorites, the Hittites and the Perizzites, and the Canaanites, and the Hivites, and the Jebusites: and I will cut them off….I will send my fear before thee, and will destroy all the people to whom thou shalt come, and I will make all thine enemies turn their backs unto thee. And I will send hornets before thee, which shall drive out the Hivite, the Canaanite, and the Hittite, from before thee. I will not drive them out from before thee in one year; lest the land become desolate, and the beast of the field multily against thee. By little and little I will drive them out from before thee, until thou be increased, and inherit the land. And I will set thy bound from the Red sea even unto the sea of the Philistines, and from the desert unto the river: for I will deliver the inhabitants of the land into your hand; and thou shalt drive them out before thee. Thou shalt make no covenant with them or their gods. Exodus 23:20 - 23, 27 - 32.

And Moses wrote all the words of the Lord, and rose up early in the morning, and builded an altar under the hill, and twelve pillars, according to the twelve tribes of Israel. And he sent young men of the children of Israel, which offered burnt offerings, and sacrificed peace offerings of oxen unto the Lord. And Moses took half of the blood, and put it in bason; and half of the blood he sprinkled on the altar. And he took the book of the covenant, and read in the audience of the people: and they said, All that the Lord hath said will we

> do, and be obedient. And Moses took the blood, and sprinkled it on the people, and said, Behold the blood of the covenant, which the Lord hath made with you concerning all these words. Exodus 24: 4 - 8.

Thus was the covenant of the god of the Children who descended from the ice-cold, deep-freeze mentality. Thus, was the covenant of the disciples and the followers of murder, rape, pillage and destroy. Thus, was the covenant of the hunters and herders of the death consumption culture. Thus, was the covenant of those who consumed of the energy that is opposite of Supreme Love. This would be a covenant that remained very familiar where bloodstained trails continued to signal slaughter and blood spill by the acts of murder, rape, steal and take.

And so it was, and so it came to be as this war god of jealousy, greed, vengeance and spite expressed vibrations and sensations that were all too familiar for Children with a blood lineage and alignment with the ice-cold, deep-freeze mentality. Yes, the spoken vibrations of this god would be all too familiar to the lost and astray Children who lost their tan, and their offspring who instituted the practices of lust, lies, illusions, confusion, death and deadly destruction as a way of life. Thus, the root and foundation of religious rationalizations, justifications, and excuses to maintain the mentality of murder, rape, steal and take was born. And so would it continue as this god of the children of the ice-cold, deep-freeze mentality would father a son through immaculate conception. And the covenant would continue as a holy communion which would serve as a sacrifice and a meal.

> Then Jesus said unto them, Verily, verily, I say unto you, Except ye eat the flesh of the Son of man, and drink his blood, ye have no life in you.

> Whoso eateth my flesh, and drinketh my blood, hath eternal life; and I will raise him up at the last day. For my flesh is meat indeed, and my blood is drink indeed. He that eateth my flesh, and drinketh my blood, dwelleth in me, and I in him. As the living Father hath sent me, and I live by the Father: so he that eateth me, even he shall live by me. This is that bread which came down from heaven: not as your fathers did eat manna, and are dead: he that eateth of this bread shall live forever. John 6: 53 - 58.

The I in I recall a passage in the Adam and Eve story of *Genesis* where the serpent told Eve that if she eats forbidden fruit that she would live forever, i.e. that she would surely not die. The "Aryans" and "Semites" would come together to settle a matter of common concern. It is then no wonder that after his crucifixion at the hands of the Roman authorities and the Jewish religious leaders, neither his body nor his blood would be seen. It makes one wonder if his last supper was indeed the last supper of his disciples and followers. The story includes the suggestion that his disciples came by night and stole him away…

Now that we have understood the father of this vibration and the son of this vibration, the I in I would be remiss not to mention the ghost of this vibration as brought forward by one who declared himself as the last prophet. The holy wars, i.e. jihads, would leave bloodstained trails throughout the ancestral motherland of Man, He and She. The cries would be to submit to this prophet's god or die. This prophet would see himself and his religion as the law enforcers, or those who carry forth the judgments against any Man, He or She, who refuses to submit to the omnipotent power of their version of the Semitic god.

Now these are the judgments that were brought forward by Moses in the earlier version of the Semitic god…."And if any mischief follow, then thou shalt give life for life, eye for eye, tooth for tooth, hand for hand, foot for foot, burning for burning, wound for wound, stripe for stripe." (Exodus 21: 23 - 25). Although the Muslim law would acknowledge the religions of "the book," i.e. the religions of Christianity and Judaism, anyone who does not submit to the teachings of Islam is considered an infidel. What this would declare is that everyone who is outside of Koranic law is an infidel. According to religious law, infidels should be dealt with severely. Muhammad left his followers these words to live by:

> Qur'an 8:65 "O Prophet, urge the faithful to fight. If there are twenty among you with determination they will vanquish two hundred; if there are a hundred then they will slaughter a thousand unbelievers, for the infidels [all non-Muslims] are a people devoid of understanding." Qur'an 47:4 "Thus are you commanded by Allah to continue carrying out Jihad against the unbelieving infidels until they submit to Islam." Qur'an 4:102 "For the Unbelieving Infidels Allah hath prepared a humiliating punishment." Qur'an 8:12 "I shall terrorize the infidels. So wound their bodies and incapacitate them because they oppose Allah and His Apostle." Qur'an 8:7 "Allah wished to confirm the truth by His words: 'Wipe the infidels out to the last.'" Qur'an 8:58 "The unbelieving infidels should not think that they can bypass Islam; surely they cannot escape." Ishaq:601 "The best men launch spears as if they were swords. They peer forward unweariedly. They devote their lives to their Prophet. ... (T)hey purify themselves with the blood of the infidels. They consider that an act of piety."

Indeed, the I in I would be out of order if there was no mention of the ill-willed hordes of deadly and merciless invaders who today identify themselves as "Aryan" Hindus. Divine reasoning makes it crystal clear that the original Sanskrit derives from the ancient Dravidian language that was both written and oral. However, the swift ability to kill, maim, and destroy creates dominance, and dominance is power. With the weapons of war one has the power to force personal deceptions upon the minds of so many. Research shows that the Hindu Brahmins redeveloped and restructured Sanskrit as it would become another one of the official stolen legacies. In later times, the Hindu Brahmins would alter the language in order to standardize Brahmanic scriptures, as well as to establish racist delusions of intellect among themselves. The art would be to set up the language and to set up educational institutes that would exclude all who are not declared as the privileged elite.

It is indeed irrefutable that the Dravidians were a Kushite people. In case one is not aware, the Kushites were indeed a "Negroid" population, and the Dravidians and the Sumerians were a Kushite people just as the Olmeks and Nubians were, among others.

The Brahmins, or "Aryans" as they now call themselves, are indeed a paler breed of Man, He and She. The various castes within India are various combinations that sprung off of the invasion culture from the deep-freeze environment. These cold-blooded "Aryan" populations of the ice-cold, deep-freeze mentality inflicted murder, rape, steal and take upon the "Negroid" populations who initially occupied the area called Asia Minor. As the pale breed inflicted their traditional pattern of murder, rape, pillage and burn, these "Aryan" warlords began to realize that the offspring born from the rapes lost the pale identity of the invading father. At the same time, these invading hordes needed able-bodied reinforcements to continue their vicious movements of murder, rape, pillage and burn.

The pale invading breed instituted a system to ensure that those of the pale breed would inherit the status of a privileged class who should have the first rights of refusal of the spoils from every victory. In truth and reality, the invading populations of the "Aryans" would have a similar kind of experience as the invader clans who would become identified as Semites, i.e. they would learn to speak an "Afro-Asiatic" language and adopt partial patterns of the Afro-Asian culture, i.e. the Afro-language which was, in fact, a "Negroid" language and the Asian language which was, in fact, a "Negroid" language. The dominant gene pool of the "Afrikoid" would begin to transform many of these pale breeds into a more colorful vibration of Man, He and She. However, they would maintain the ideology of being as pale or "white" as possible in order to be privy to social benefits. The proud mulatto breeds idolized and worshipped the ice-cold, deep-freeze mentality instead of their sacred garden culture. These lost and astray Children would continue to join forces with the ice-cold mentality of the pale ones in inflicting death raids against the sacred sons and daughters of Man, He and She, i.e. those who are today called the "Black Untouchables" and others of kin and skin.

Under the leadership of their warlord Indra, these unified forces would eventually murder, rape, pillage and burn their way into a position of power in India. It should be noted that upon Indra's death, he would be deified, becoming a god created in his own image. Indra, "the slayer of Vrittra, the destroyer of cities, who had scattered the Dasyu that sprung from a black womb," i.e. Indra, the warlord of the ice-cold, deep-freeze mentality who had murdered, raped, pillaged and burned would become Indra, the war god, the hater of "black" skin whom he swept out of heaven. What the I in I am stating here is that the warlord males of the ice-cold, deep-freeze mentality have consistently created gods in their own image.

The trick of deception is to then project the reasoning that god created man in his own image.

As time moved on, a new breed of "Aryan" would descend upon India. This new breed of "Aryans" would come to make up the Brahmin caste. The Brahmins would represent an entirely different invasion of the Aryan populations that descend from the ice-cold, deep-freeze mentality. The pale ones who had previously invaded the area would seek to reinforce themselves and they would be attracted to the idea of more "Aryans" coming into the area. As these pale ones came in there would be new sets of laws to make a stronger delineation of caste which identified the top caste of the Brahmin as the absolute rulers. India would be seen as the new "white" empire that had at its disposal a massive population to serve as an enslaved caste population to protect and to serve the Brahmins. Yes, these new breeds of "Aryans" identified as the Brahmin represent a breed of the pale children who had not experienced the consequence of breeding with the suntanned Children.

The Brahmins brought with them the toxic bags of tricks of the predator-like attitudes and behaviors that manifested in the ice-cold, deep-freeze mentality. They devised a unique system of "white" racist ideology that cast various other groups by various color categories where the paler, the more socially endowed. India's caste system would be very similar to the Apartheid system of South Africa, Australia, and the chattel slavery and the segregation era systems of the Americas. As a matter of fact, the system in India actually served as an example in the creation of the other systems. The Brahmin system would be well-supported by the colonial and neo-colonial systems that aligned with India.

The "Aryan" Brahmin would in fact be overt in establishing the religious ideology that the "Aryan" Brahmin should be the elite ruling class of the Hindu religion. The major difference between the "Aryan" Brahmins and the Semitic-bred religions of Judaism, Christianity and Islam is that these groups would be more covert in expressing the very same ideology, and as a result of association, would have grown to be more tolerant. Whereas the other systems have, at least, made cosmetic changes over suntanned populations among them, India remains locked and steadfast in maintaining the caste system and outcast system that dehumanizes the lives of over 300 million suntanned Dalits. It is the declaration of the Brahmin that this "white"-racist system shall be instituted forever as a manmade reflection of karma.

Imagine a population of over 300 million people so locked in religious deception, dogma and terrorism that they cannot see their way out of a maze that only offers one of the other trap doors of religious deception as the way out. It must be horrifying indeed to be so tricked and divided, conquered and undecided that one remains in an outcast of a status so low that those in that caste are considered untouchable. It is absolutely chilling to feel the cold-blooded vibration of an ice-cold, deep-freeze mentality that would commit such atrocities against the sons and daughters who descend from the majestic suntanned population who gave the pale breed so much for so little in return. In fact, it brings tears to my eyes to think of the masterful con games of lies and the international cries that are calls that only bring back a response of more alibis. How wicked can the ice-cold, deep-freeze mentality be to threaten the use of weapons of mass destruction to keep these suntanned Children from ever being free?

And so, the "Aryan" Brahmin would indeed create their supreme being in their own image and that being would be called Brahma. Research indicates that this word, "brahman," is common throughout Hinduism: Brahman, the one god of the universe, Brahma, the creator god, and brahmin, the priest caste. The various populations would be caste from the very darkest to the palest. From the bottom to the top, each one of the populations of castes would consider themselves a step above those who are darker than them in complexion.

Different levels and degrees of discrimination would be administered based on color and caste. As for those who feel that they are a step or two above the "Black Untouchables," they would suffer similar kinds of color discrimination although being described as steps above.

This creator god would ordain a vicious, cruel and cold-blooded caste system that inflicts different levels and degrees of mental cruelty, fatality, inferior status, and poverty upon the various offspring of color among the suntanned Children. And even more vicious, more cruel, and more degrading would be the outcaste system enforced against the darker population of suntanned Children who most closely represent the original Man, He and She, i.e. the "Black Untouchables." The Dalit people, who are called the "Black Untouchables," are the descendants of the original inhabitants of the land. What manner of heartless and insensitive being would this be to violate the supreme laws of the universe by enforcing the kind of violence and threat against a once-glorious population of sacred garden keepers. This would be the fate of the Dravidian populations that had brought forward so much to "modern humanity." As for the Hindu Brahmins and all the religious orders and male war gods that descended from the ice-cold, deep-freeze mentality, such would be their godly rituals of deception born from their blood-stained trails of lust, lies, illusions, confusion, death and deadly destruction.

The level and degree of severe damage perpetuated by the religious and social economic doctrines of the ice-cold, deep-freeze mentality is yet to be fully comprehended. The stripping away of whole life energy from the masculine and feminine presence of Man, He and She, has been a horrifying ordeal. The deceptive doctrines of fright and fear perpetuated by social economic and religious rituals have virtually paralyzed the spirit consciousness of the once-sacred sons and daughters of Man, He and She.

The toxic consequences of indulging in the life-depleting vibrations of the ice-cold, deep-freeze mentality and its social and religious disorder have caused bitter conflict and confusion between the masculine and feminine presence. Equally, this toxic and cold-blooded mentality breeds its very nature of war, sex and violence among the sacred sons and daughters of Man, He and She. It must be comprehended that the base and foundation of this devastating mishap is the result of perpetuating a male-war-god syndrome where all is fair in love and war. It is not understood that the male-war-god syndrome perpetuates major and massive contradictions from start to finish.

First and foremost, this male war god is perceived as being one who does not require the divine union of the masculine and feminine presence. The idea is that this deity emerges out of immaculate conception or some other kind of peculiar ordeal. This syndrome contradicts the supreme laws of the universe by projecting an all-omnipotent god who functions outside of the supreme laws. The most supreme law of universal order does indeed require the union of the masculine and feminine energy in order to perpetuate the creation of life. In fact, the only kind of god who could function outside of the supreme and holistic laws of the Essence of Life and Supreme Love would be a god of unwholiness/unholiness, a god that exalts in holy wars, jihads, crusades, and tribal, sexist and racist ideologies. All of the disciples and followers of this deity would reflect the vibrations and sensations of lust, lies, illusions, confusion, death and deadly destruction while glorifying the ways and means of the death consumption culture.

Imagine a mind so lost and astray that it perpetuates a man god as the Most Supreme Creator without the feminine presence as the sacred birthplace of all living things. It is as though the lost and astray mind has total amnesia regarding the fact that birth is the creation energy that requires union of the masculine and feminine presence. The male-war-god syndrome is the reflection of the energy that is opposite of

Supreme Love, born and bred in the deep freeze and perpetuated by the deep-freeze mentality.

The feminine presence would be labeled as Eve or the temptress who lures man into sin. These ideologies would breed the reasoning that women are the root of all sin and would cause a cold-blooded depletion in the spirit life presence of every Man She. As a result, the feminine presence resides in a more or less dormant state of spirit consciousness within the ice-cold, deep-freeze mentality. As she nurtures a lesser image of herself, the feminine presence diminishes her own state of being.

Imagine the damage to the female's self-esteem as she faces the disrespect and disregard that is projected upon her by the masculine presence of the ice-cold, deep-freeze mentality. Either the feminine presence develops a sense of hostility, antagonism and challenge towards the masculine presence, or she develops a passive attitude which absorbs the demeaning values of the female as weak, inferior and subservient. In either case, any child born out of these toxic experiences will emerge as a weak and feeble presence of Man He or Man She. In no instance does the feminine presence of Man, He and She, ever reason with the fact that being the divine nurturer makes her the key to life.

Within the ice-cold, deep-freeze mentality, the mother spirit perceives that she has no Supreme Goddess representation of her Most High Feminine Presence in union with the Most High Masculine Presence. This perception keeps her struggling against her own nature as well as against divine spirit consciousness. The result is a massive disconnection from the whole life presence. The son born of the damaged mother spirit receives a depleted presence to nurture him, and he, in turn, becomes a more depleted masculine presence. The daughter born of the damaged mother spirit becomes a diluted version of the depleted nurturing role model who is set before her. The conflicting and contradicting religious and social economic values undermine the divine union of Man, He and She, and set the stage for further contempt, bitterness, and competition between the masculine and feminine presence.

It is spiritual suicide to degrade the mother spirit. To maintain religious doctrines and social economic ideologies that oppose the divine order of the masculine and feminine union is to set the stage for Man, He and She's, ultimate destruction. It is an abomination of the whole life presence to reason with such contradicting and conflict-oriented doctrines that, in fact, defy the most supreme law of the Most High Essence of Life and Supreme Love. The male-war-god syndrome is indeed the worship of the god of the dead. This male-war-god syndrome is in fact the energy that is opposite of Supreme Love that fuels the death consumption culture. Let us take a few moments to explore the historical background of the male-war-god syndrome that descended from the ice-cold deep freeze mentality.

> Wodan was an ancient Germanic sky god. Wodan was known as Woden or Wotan to the Saxons and later Odin to the Norse. Wodan was also the god of war. Wodan became an increasingly popular Germanic god, who replaced Tiwaz (Tyr), as the chief sky god and war god. Odin inherited many of Wodan's roles and attributes, as well as those of Tiwaz.
>
> ...Wodan was not only the god of war; he was the god of victory in battle. Victory was achieved in battle, when he pointed his spear in favour of one army over the other. Wodan was death and blood sacrifice. The Cimbri, the Heruli and the Goths carrying out sacrificial rite, by stabbing and burning their victims. This would account for later Norse myths, when Odin stabbed with his spear and burned the Vanir goddess Gullveig three times,

but each time, the goddess would be reborn. This attack upon the goddess, resulted in a war between the Aesir and the Vanir.

Like Odin, Wodan was the god of hanging. The Cimbri sometimes hanged their captives over the bronze cauldrons, while the priestess cut their throats. These sacrifices to Wodan would then later be thrown into sacred lakes. However, the Norse myths say that it was Odin who hanged himself, in order to learn the magic power of poetry and the magic of the runes.[76]

The religion of the Teutons was in the main a religion of fighters, and we do not hesitate to say that they, more than any other people on earth, developed the ethics of struggle…Their chief god was the god of war, and their noblest consummation of life was death on the battlefield…The idea of evil played an important part in the religion of the Teutons.

Loki, the god of fire, the cunning mischief-maker among the Asas, is believed to have brought sin and evil into the world. In the younger Edda, Loki takes part in the creation of man, whom he endows with the senses, passions, and evil desires. Loki's children are (1) the Fenris wolf, (2) the Jormungander, i.e., the Midgard serpent, and (3) Hel, the queen of Nifelheim, the world of the dead…The most remarkable feature of Teutonic mythology is the conception of doomsday or Ragnarok (the twilight of the gods), boding a final destruction of the world, including all the gods. At

---

[76] Teutonic Deities. Online Source: http://www.timelessmyths.com/norse/teutonic.html.

present the powers of evil are fettered and subdued, but the time will come when they will be set loose. Loki, the Fenris wolf, the Midgard serpent, and Hel, with their army of frost giants and other evil beings, will approach; Heimdall, the watchman of the gods, will blow his horn, and the Asas prepare for battle. The combat on the field Vigrid will be internecine, for the Asas are to die while killing the monsters of wickedness whom they encounter, and the flames of Muspil will devour the wrecks of the universe.

The world had a beginning, it therefore must come to an end; but when the world is destroyed a new heaven and a new earth will rise from the wreck of the old one, and the new world will be better than the old one. Leifthraser and his wife Lif (representing the desire for Life and potential Life) remained concealed during the catastrophe in Hodmimer's grove and were not harmed by the flames. They now become the parents of a new race that will inhabit the new abode, called *Gimel* (the German *Himmel*), and among them will be found Odhin with his sons, Thor, Baldur, Fro, and all the other Asas…The very name "hell" is a Teutonic word which originally signified a hollow space or a cave underground, and denotes the realm of Hel, Loki's daughter…In the last song of the Inferno, Dante describes the residence of the sovereign of hell, which is surrounded by a thick fog, so as to make it necessary for the poet to be led by the hand of his guide. There the ice-palace stands almost inaccessible through the cold blizzards that blow about it; and there the ruler of

> hell and his most cursed fellows stand with their bodies partly frozen in the transparent ice.[77]

Enough of these bloodbath tales, enough of these blood stained trails, enough of this misery, aches and pains, enough of these death consumption culture games which are, in fact, one in the same that differ and vary only by name. Not to mention those lost and astray Children of the Sun with the golden tan who have been so devastated by the triple-six marks of lust, lies, illusions, confusion, death and deadly destruction. These lost and astray Children with the golden tan actually implement, in part or in whole, the very same acts disguised as traditional indigenous religions.

It is a heck of a fix that Man, He and She, find themselves in as we witness cold-blooded predators in conflict with cold-blooded predators while they both use the suntanned Children as their scapegoat. Clearly and beyond a shadow of a doubt, these social economic religions are about as far as those of the ice-cold, deep-freeze mentality have reached in expressions of spirituality. One would wonder whether there was ever anything beyond the mutations and degenerations of the ice-cold, deep-freeze mentality.

## Remembering the Garden: The Ancient Earthly Paradise

The creative, artistic, spiritual expression of the Divine Children of the Sun with the golden tan calls forth the Most Supreme Essence of Life and Supreme Love into the embodiment of story, music, dance, and song. The creative expression of the masculine and feminine presence manifests in the order and design of the garden, the family household, and the community at large. The styles of natural hair, the designs of clothing, the pottery, the sculptures, the paintings as well as

---

[77] The Demonology of Northern Europe. Online Source: http://www.public-domain-content.com/books/history_devil/hod14.shtml

the delicious dishes of raw and living fruits, vegetables, seeds and nuts are all expressions of honoring the whole life presence within the sacred garden culture.

The signature and trademark of the Divine Children of the Sun with the golden tan are identified in the vibrations of divine consumption, divine union, multiplying divinity through the offspring, wholeness, peace, joy, harmony, patience, collective responsibility, and the honoring of the whole life presence of every living thing. The oral tradition of stories within the sacred garden culture serves to encompass spiritual lessons that communicate the seen and unseen reality of divine order. Patterns of vibrations are personified, described as gods and goddesses, and embodied within stories that address the reality of divine order. When divine order is broken, the "moral" of the story serves to reinforce corrective action.

Sacred stories are used to describe, define, and expose that which is hidden from physical sight. The primary focus of the sacred stories is to provide greater self-awareness and comprehension regarding the practices and principles of a holistic living way of life. The primary purpose of the sacred story is to establish greater spiritual maturity and increased responsibility within the divine social economic family community. It is comprehended within divine spirit consciousness that the physical manifestation is simply an outer expression of the sacred spirit presence. Therefore, the qualities and characteristics of the sacred spirit are translated into narratives and accounts of the Most Supreme Unseen in the seen. The spiritual growth and development of the Divine Children of the Sun is rooted in the divine knowledge, wisdom and understanding that emerges from the Most Supreme Unseen Essence of Life and Supreme Love.

Beyond the concepts of fiction, fantasy, make-believe and pretending that are created by the lost and astray mind, there is the underlying divine reality of the Most Supreme Unseen that is seen, comprehended and expressed within divine spirit consciousness. The earth is identified as Mother Earth and the innate qualities of the feminine presence become symbolic and defined within the sacred story. The images of the Goddess, Mother Earth, and Queen Mother symbolize the many manifestations of the feminine presence. The father spirit is symbolized as the Sun, the unifying, generating and penetrating vibration, the river of life, the life stream and the solar pulse that ejaculates the whole life energy into the fertile feminine presence.

Within the sacred garden culture, every living thing has a divine spirit presence. The disorder that has occurred divided the masculine and feminine presence into a lost and astray state of being. The lost and astray mind manifested a male war god who in turn created a son without the sacred union of divine oneness. These acts of creation are unquestionably deceptions, fantasies, illusions, and delusions of a lost and astray mind. Any telling of divine creation that does not represent the divine union of Man, He and She, is a contradiction to the whole life presence itself.

The holistic living truth about Supreme Love is a reflection of the divine union of the masculine and feminine spirit as the Most Supreme Creation of the Essence of Life. The Most Supreme Spiritual Essence of Life is both seen and unseen, and is often identified as the ancestral presence. When Man, He and She, is truly in divine union with the Most Supreme Spiritual Essence of Life, every living thing is honored.

There are unquestionably two creations. The first and original creation is the divine parallel where the Most Supreme Unseen Essence of Life as the masculine and feminine spiritual essence created Man, He and She, and all living things upon the planet Earth. The divine parallel is the most supreme honoring of the earth, the wind, the rain and the sun. The original creation is the most sacred creation of the whole life presence that is a holistic living reflection of those most sacred and supreme seen physical energies. Energies have a seen presence and an unseen presence.

The Most Supreme creative spirit essence of all that there is of Supreme Love is the Most Supreme Unseen. Therefore, the Most Supreme Unseen Essence of the masculine and feminine spirit has created all living things within the Most Supreme image of divine oneness of the masculine and feminine presence.

The second creation emerged in massive disorder. Disorder occurs when Man, He and She, function outside of the divine parallel. The sacred sons and daughters of Man, He and She, must go within to the divine parallel. The manifestation of divine spirit consciousness will indeed lead these sacred sons and daughters of Man, He and She, into their holistic living presence as the Divine Children of the Sun residing within the sacred garden culture. It is absolutely impossible for Man, He and She, to divinely connect with the most Supreme Unseen until Man, He and She, first and foremost divinely connect with the Most Supreme Seen Spiritual Presence of all that they are as Man, He and She.

There is indeed an absolute requirement that Man, He and She, move into a divine oneness position through the acts of divine consumption and then go forward and multiply divinity through the offspring. Only through divine consumption will there emerge that most precious connection with the Most Supreme Unseen Essence of Life. Life is for the living and the living is the Most Supreme Seen and Unseen divinely connected in a divine oneness position of supreme love.

The recycling of life energy is a continuation of one's patterns of consumption, i.e. what you put in is what will come out and that is what will come back to you again. The key that was comprehended within the sacred garden culture is the healing quality of corrective actions through divine consumption that cause a divine change in one's whole life presence.

One is never locked into an energy cycle of depletion unless one continues to consume toxic, depleted and devitalized energy, mentally, physically and spiritually. It is indeed a time for divine clarity. We must begin to comprehend the divine parallel of the Most Supreme Seen and Unseen Essence of Life and Supreme Love. We must begin to expose the unholy parallel of the energy that is opposite of Supreme Love. Yes, it is indeed just that simple: Life is for the living and the purpose of living is to honor the Most Supreme Seen and Unseen Essence of Life and Supreme Love.

Yes, the sacred sons and daughters of Man, He and She, must return to the glorious foundation of their whole life presence where they honor the Most Supreme Spirit of Love, Righteousness, and the Holistic Living Truth About Supreme Love. The most supreme and glorious presence of the Essence of Life is the divine presence of Man, He and She, synchronizing in harmony and divine oneness as the expressions of the Most Supreme Seen of the masculine and feminine being.

We will identify one of many Kushite communities among the Children of the Sun with the golden tan who inhabited the land referred to as Sumeria. Kushite families populated up and down the Nile, i.e. the Nile Valley, the region that is now called the Middle East, the Indus Valley, the Mediterranean lands and what has been identified in modern times as "Old Europe" We must note that the Kushite people actually encompassed a vast population of suntanned Children who originally occupied the areas now known as Asia inclusive of China and Japan, southeast Asia, Malaysia, India, Australia, across to the Americas, the ancestral homeland of the Olmeks

Research indicates that these suntanned Children used a writing instrument made out of reed to make markings on wet clay tablets. Research indicates that over thirty thousand clay tablets and fragments were uncovered by archaeologists in the cities of Lagash in 1877 and Nippur in 1887.[78] Findings show that the cuneiform writing was not invented by a Semitic people or an Indo-European people, but rather a more ancient people who pre-dated the Semites and Indo-Europeans, i.e. an indigenous suntanned population that predated the nomadic invasions inflicted by the lost and astray Children who lost their tan.

Noted literary researcher, Samuel Noah Kramer, spent years studying the "unpublished literary pieces in the Nippur collection of the University Museum" and working to decipher the cuneiform writing on the ancient clay tablets. As Kramer notes, a particular unpublished piece of clay tablet belonging to a Sumerian epic poem is an ancient writing that refers to "Man's Golden Age," describing "the blissful and unrivalled state of man in an era of universal peace before he had learned to know fear and before the 'confusion of tongues.'"[79] The notations of this quote are a clear indication of the sacred garden culture of the Divine Children of the Sun prior to the invasions that inflicted murder, rape, pillage and burn followed by pilgrimages of murder, rape, steal and take. As has been well-indicated and documented in this text, the invasion culture of the lost and astray Children who lost their tan has totally destabilized the holistic living way of life that was the norm within the sacred garden culture of the Divine Children of the Sun with the golden tan.

The golden era of the golden suntanned Children who resided in the sacred garden culture must no longer be a dream deferred. This deferment of divine reality has occurred because the holistic living truth has been masked with racist deceptions and macho-male war god religious ideology. What the lost and astray mind has not comprehended is that the earth

---

[78] Online Source: http://www.cs.mun.ca/~david12/papers/sum_lit.html.

[79] *Sumerian Mythology. Man's Golden Age*. Samuel Noah Kramer. Philadelphia: University of Pennsylvania Press, 1941, revised 1961. Online Source: http://www.sacred-texts.com/ane/sum/sum00.htm

will continue to give birth to the holistic living truth as artifacts, ruins and fossils continue to be unveiled.

> Still almost entirely unknown to this very moment is Sumerian mythology, the sacred stories of the non-Semitic, non-Indo-European people…it was the Sumerians who represented the dominant cultural group of the entire Near East. It was the Sumerians who developed and probably invented the cuneiform system of writing; who developed a well integrated pantheon together with spiritual and religious concepts which influenced profoundly all the peoples of the Near East; who, finally, created and developed a literature rich in content and effective in form. Moreover, the following significant fact must be borne in mind. By the end of the third millennium B. C. Sumer had already ceased to exist as a political entity and Sumerian had already become a dead language, for by that time Sumer had been overrun and conquered by the Semites, and it is the Semitic Accadian [Akkadian] language which gradually became the living, spoken tongue of the land. Nevertheless Sumerian continued to be used as the literary and religious language of the Semitic conquerors for many centuries to come….Indeed for many centuries the study of the Sumerian language and literature remained the basic pursuit of the scribal schools and intellectual and spiritual centers not only of the Babylonians and Assyrians, but also of the many surrounding peoples such as the Elamites, Hurrians, Hittites, and Canaanites. Obviously, then, both because of their content as well as because of their age, the Sumerian mythological tales and

> concepts must have penetrated and permeated those of the entire Near East.[80]

First and foremost, the I in I would like to make the reader very clear that the population referred to as Sumerian is a name that has been tagged on the people to suit the occasion of individuals who were initially attempting to identify the language, the arts, and the culture with the Semitic people who later invaded and destroyed a precious social economic and spirit environment. The I in I would like to make it very clear that these ancient Children of the Sun, i.e. Kwasunic tribes, were identified as being Kushite people.

Clearly, many of the ruins were destroyed, by accident or through carelessness or other strange circumstances. The data and information that remain give us a clear indication that the various religious formats of Judaism, Christianity and Islam were formulated from the ancient Kushite communities. These sacred suntanned sons and daughters honored the divine presence of the earth, wind, rain and sun within the sacred garden. However, all that has been stolen by the lost and astray Children of the ice-cold, deep-freeze mentality has been tainted, distorted and reversed to suit the mentality of hunters, scavengers, herders and warlords.

After having a conqueror's relationship with the suntanned population, the invader tribes became very aware of the technology, advancements, and spirit wisdom of the Kushite people. It must not be forgotten that these invader tribes had begun to have a face change as a result of the dominant genes of the many suntanned mothers who were raped, enslaved and produced offspring from the experience. The fact is that the Semitic tribes continued to maintain devotion to their father's

---

[80] *Sumerian Mythology. Chapter One: The Scope and Significance of Sumerian Mythology*. Samuel Noah Kramer. Philadelphia: University of Pennsylvania Press, 1941, revised 1961. Online Source: http://www.sacred-texts.com/ane/sum/sum06.htm

lineage of the invader clans. The invading tribes had moved from a practice of murder, rape, pillage and burn to a practice of murder, rape, steal and take.

The I in I remind you that the priests and priestesses were the keepers of all written and oral records among the Kushites throughout the world, and the tellers of the sacred stories. The educational centers were considered to be temples. Therefore, the invading tribes would utilize tricks of deception and the claims of rulership to maintain the existing infrastructures while shifting the frame of reference to elevate themselves. Shepherd kings, for example, would assume the position of ruler and impose the ways and means of the ice-cold, deep-freeze mentality into the existing social structures. In that way, the sacred garden culture became contaminated with such vicious and cold-blooded acts as animal sacrifice, burnt offerings and other barbaric acts that were carried from the ice-cold, deep-freeze environment.

The lost and astray Children who lost their tan would place their own representatives into the existing systems and would eventually usurp power and control over the mental, physical, and spiritual/religious order of a people. The invading tribes utilized the stories, mythology, and folklore from the ancient Kushite populations to infuse their toxic vibrations into a spiritual/religious disguise that completely changed and distorted the holistic living truth about Supreme Love into a reverse presentation. Archaeological findings have categorized and labeled the movements of populations that inhabited the region that is referred to as Mesopotamia by making notations that the Sumerians were preceded by another population called the Ubaidians. The divine presence of the suntanned mothers and fathers of Man, He and She, is difficult for the ice-cold, deep-freeze mentality to acknowledge and comprehend. The I in I note that the Akkadians, known as the "black heads," are also noted to have given so much within the supreme love vibration while receiving so little in return from the invader cultures. Unfortunately, the Akkadian culture was completely destabilized through raids and invasions by the Semitic tribes. As a result, much of the Akkadian culture would later be claimed by the Semitic invaders. However, historical ruins, findings, and artifacts have begun to set the record straight. The names may change within the sacred garden culture communities of the Children of the Sun with the golden tan, but the whole life presence remains the same.

> The earliest settlement of the southern alluvial flood plain in the late 6th millenium was by a non-Semitic people called proto-Euphrateans.....This prehistoric Ubaid Culture had a long duration beginning before 5000 B.C. and lasting until the beginning of the Uruk Period. In the mid-5th millennium B.C. the Ubaid Culture spread into northern Mesopotamia and replaced the Halaf Culture. It is characterised by large village settlements and the appearance of the first temples in Mesopotamia.....The Ubaid Culture developed as a result of increasing sophistication in irrigation techniques. [81]

The presence of advanced irrigation systems within an ancient cultural context represents a major focus of the crop-growing populations of the sacred garden culture. It is noted that the irrigation systems of the suntanned Man, He and She, serve as a common identification of a community infrastructure among the suntanned Kwasunic tribes. The presence of pyramid temples or mound temples, also called ziggurats, is another common identification of a community infrastructure among the suntanned Kwasunic tribes. The presence of artistic representations that express honor to the feminine presence and the fertility of the mother spirit are another common

---

[81] *The History of the Ancient Near East*. Ancient Sumer History. Online Source: http://ancientneareast.tripod.com/Sumer.html

identification of the cultural context among the suntanned Kwasunic tribes. The handiwork techniques of using dried mud and clay to make tablets, pottery and statues represent another common identification of the Kwasunic communities of the sacred garden culture.

Excavations in the regions identified as Mesopotamia unearthed terrra-cotta clay figures and stone figures representing the feminine presence. Research indicates that collections held at the British Museum include representative artwork that reveals a clear pattern of ancient expression that characterizes the suntanned Kwasunic tribes. A stone female figurine was excavated from upper Tigris dated at around 7,000 years ago and a terra-cotta Halaf female figurine was excavated from Chagar Bazar also dated around 7,000 years ago.[82] Researchers note that the exaggerated female characteristics of enlarged breasts and buttocks suggest that the object served some religious purpose. Findings show that paint traces on the clay figurine suggest arm and leg jewelry or decoration and a loin cloth. Also exhibited at the Museum is a Ubaid terra-cotta female figurine from Ur dated around 6,500 years ago that shows a woman suckling a child. The figure has painted jewelry and an elongated head and protruding eyes that characterize the Ubaid figure style.[83]

Researchers have concluded that the Sumerians and Ubaidians were neither Semitic nor Indo-European. It is clear that these Kwasunic tribes of Kushite people were not descendants of the ice-cold, deep-freeze environment that existed in the Caucasus Mountain and steppe region. Rather, these Kwasunic tribes represent the true indigenous people of the suntanned land of the sacred garden culture. Their artistic patterns are not far-removed from the Nok culture of ancient suntanned Children, dated from about 37,000 B.C.E. or 39,000

---

[82] *Images from History:* Archaic Mesopotamia. Online Source: http://www.hp.uab.edu/image_archive/ue/uea.html

[83] *Images from History:* Archaic Mesopotamia. Online Source: http://www.hp.uab.edu/image_archive/ue/uea.html

years ago to 200 B.C.E. The mother spirit figurines are in fact consistent throughout all of the ancient finds of the Afrikoid or "Negroid" populations that make up the Kwasunic tribes.

It should not be a mystery that when the lost and astray Children who lost their tan mastermind their racist ideologies, the Machiavellian law becomes very clear and simple. Machiavelli expresses another one of the ice-cold, deep-freeze mentality codes in advising those in rule to secure their rulership through cunning, ruthless and vicious means, using deception at every turn while projecting honesty.

Even to this day Niccolo Machiavelli's *The Prince* remains a very popular instruction guide to social economic and political rule within the ice-cold, deep-freeze mentality. Machiavelli's observations regarding the toxic behaviors used as strategies within the death consumption culture are as accurate today as they were five hundred years ago when the book was written. Indeed, the toxic behaviors of seizing power, control and dominance based on greedy self-interest and deception are indicative of the schemes, plots and plans that have been repeated by the lost and astray mind of the ice-cold, deep-freeze mentality throughout its brief, but disruptive history.

Within the ice-cold, deep-freeze mentality, one uses any means necessary to project oneself as the prince of peace while one masterminds deceit, corruption and theft of stolen legacies under the auspices of science and intellect. The truth of the matter is that the dates to chart populations and cultural achievements have been twisted and mingled through time. Beyond all the twisting and mingling, the holistic living truth reveals that these ancient Kushite people far exceed 7,000 years ago. In fact, it has been shown that these Kushite populations far exceed even 10,000 years ago.

As it is now, we will rest our case with the fact that an ancient people of the suntanned Man, He and She, are the authors of the first ancient records and written script on this planet. It only stands to reason that the sacred garden culture would provide the stable and resource-rich environment to provide the root and foundation for the ancient civilizations. It only stands to reason that the nutritional base of raw and living fruits, vegetables, seeds and nuts would boost the brain capacity within a harmonious and cooperative environment.

It also stands to reason that the lost and astray Children who lost their tan were crouching in the ice-cold, deep-freeze caves deteriorating to scavengers and slaughtering to survive in the barren, harsh, bleak, and frigid caves. Let us move on to reviewing the text and enjoying the warmth and beauty of the expression of the ancient mothers and fathers of Man, He and She, in honor of the Divine Children of the Sun with the golden tan. Research indicates that there is a worldwide tradition of accounts that serve as a reminder of the ancestral garden paradise, i.e. the ancient presence of the Divine Children of the Sun with the golden tan within the sacred garden culture.

**Salvaging the Sacred Story of the Masculine and Feminine Presence**

Indeed, the sacred garden culture is the most supreme environment for Man, He and She, as it was in the beginning and as it shall forever be within the divine parallel of the Most Supreme Spirit of Love, Righteousness and the Holistic Living Truth about Supreme Love. Let us see what the ancient ones said about creation divine.

Let us make every effort to re-connect with the vibrations and sensations of this most ancient story that could have easily been told at least ten thousand years ago and more and more and more. Let us feel the vibrations of the ancient Nok culture which come through loud and clear through the honoring of the sacred mother spirit presence, the goddess of life. Let us feel the vibrations and sensations that created the fertility doll that has been found in so many ancient ruins that pre-date 50 to 60 thousand years ago and more and more and more.

EXPOSING THE ICE-COLD, DEEP-FREEZE MENTALITY AND WHOLE LIFE HEALING OF SEXUAL ENERGY WITHIN THE DIVINE PARALLEL

Let us look deep into the glorious tales that let you know clearly and beyond a shadow of a doubt that there is no feminine presence who can give birth to a child without the union of Man, He and She. There is no masculine presence who can become a god of divinity while holding the position of being a god of jealousy, envy, greed and spite. There is no god of divinity who would send soldiers, disciples, and followers on pillages of rape, murder, steal and take to enslave and to use the violent force of blood spill with declarations of "submit or die."

The Divine Children of the Sun reside within the divine parallel of the sacred garden culture. Let us now enjoy this ancient tale that, although translated and re-interpreted, still maintains the spiritual essence of the sacred garden culture. Below are excerpts from the ancient text translated from the clay tablets as the first English version of the Enki and Ninhursag myth which has been referred to as the Sumerian Creation Story.

> After time had come into being and the holy seasons for growth and rest were finally known, holy Dilmun, the pure clean and bright land of the living, the garden of the Great Gods and Earthly paradise, located eastward in Eden, was the place where Ninhursag, the Earth Mother, Most Exalted Lady and Supreme Queen, could be found.
>
> There she lived for a season during the Wheel of the Year, when the Earth lay deep in slumber and rest before the onset of Spring, in the land that knew neither sickness nor death or old age, where the raven uttered no cry, where lions and wolves killed not, and unknown were the sorrows of a widow or the wailing of the sick. And it was in Dilmun, at that time that Enki, the wise god

of…the Sweet Waters…met, fell in love and lied with the Lady of the Stony Earth, Ninhursag.

The Earth Mother's kiss did change the carefree and sexy Sweet Waters Lord: Ninhursag had wholly captivated him through the most profound of all bonds, the thread of enchantment, passion and daring called Love. So profound the feeling was that the God of all Sweet Waters…proposed to Ninhursag, with the enthusiasm of a young lover's heart.

…Ninshursag looked around the land, her stony body, and remembered the taste of the wondrous moisture of the Sweet Waters God within herself. She wondered whether the land should not feel the same loving touch without. She said then to Enki: 'I heard your heart speak, Enki dearest. But if I feel your wondrous moisture within me, I look at the earth of Dilmun, also my body, and feel it is the longing, the thirst for the gifts that you, dear heart, for sure can bring. Thus I ask you: what is a land, what is a city that has no river quay? A city that has no ponds of sweet water?'

Taken by surprise, Enki realized that indeed he had given his whole essence to the beloved, but forgotten to look after her Earthly body, the land. He then rose to the challenge of providing water for the land with aplomb.

He told then Ninhursag: 'For Dilmun, the land of my lady's heart, I will create long waterways, rivers and canals, whereby water will flow to quench the thirst of all beings and bring abundance to all that lives.'

Enki [the Sweet Waters God] then summoned Utu, the Sun God and Light of the Day. Together, they brought a mist from the depths of the earth and watered the whole face of the ground. Then Enki and Utu created waterways to surround the land with a never-ending source of fertile Sweet Waters, and Enki also devised basins and cisterns to store waters for further needs. From these fertile sweet waters flow the four Great Rivers of the Ancient World, including the Tigris and Euphrates. Thus, from that moment on, Dilmun was blessed by Enki with everlasting agricultural and trade superiority, for through its waterways and quays, fruits and grains were sold and exchanged by people of Dilmun and beyond.

Ninhursag rejoiced in Enki's mighty prowess and said to him: 'Beloved, the powerful touch of your sweet waters, the essence of Mother Nammu that lies deep within you, transformed the land, my stony body. I feel the power of life throbbing within to be revealed without my very depths as I give joyously birth and sustenance to the marshes and reed-beds, that from now on will shelter fish, plants, beasts and all that breathes. Thus I call myself Nintur, the lady who gives birth, the Womb of the Damp lands by the riverbanks.'

Enki replied: 'Ninhursag, dearest Nintur, beloved, how can anyone quite compare to you? I cannot resist your wild, sweet ways, so lie with me one more time and fill my body, heart, soul and mind with endless delights! For me you will forever be my fierce Damgalnunna, my Great Spouse, passionate and very much loved!

Ninhursag laughed and welcomed the eagerness of the Sweet Waters Lord. Nine days later, without the slightest labour or pain, the Great Mother Goddess gave birth to a lovely girl without the slightest travail or pain. The girl was called

Ninsar, Lady of Verdure, the Mistress of Vegetation, the green carpet of grass, leaves and flower beds that cover the surface of the earth.

Enki was overjoyed with the birth of his and Ninhursag's child: 'How perfect, how lovely is our Ninsar! I love already the woman in the girl-child, the young Anunnaki goddess and Mistress of Velvet Meadows and Green Fields. The ties that bind me to Ninsar are strong and tempered by an even greater love, for in her face I see also Ninhursag's…

It was the sacred duty of the Sweet Waters Lord to oversee the rise and fall of all fertilizing waters that flowed from Dilmun to feed the rivers, lakes and ponds of the Middle world to make the land ready to receive the Spring seeds. Thus, as much as he missed Ninhursag, Enki knew that he could not leave Dilmun before all waterways were filled to ensure that the people would have plenty of water to grow their crops. Enki's essence, the fertilizing power of the sweet waters, should reach every piece of land in the Middle world that had been worked and ploughed.

It was at the end of a day he had spent totally absorbed by the mighty task of controlling the water flow to the Middle world that Enki saw Ninsar walking on her own along the marshlands. Indeed, a lovely goddess she had become, and Enki's eyes fell on the Maiden's, the Sweet Waters Lord felt a longing he could not yet define. He only knew that after Ninhursag's departure, no other maiden had touched his heart the way this one did. Indeed, she who walked on her own along the marshlands was the closet version to Ninhursag his eyes had the luck to find. Enki did not lose time and immediately started wooing the young lady, encouraging her to love him wildly by the riverside.

Curious and eager as Ninsar was to experience the power of love in her body, mind, soul, and heart, she, the young goddess of Green Fields and Luscious Meadows, yielded to the Sweet Waters Lord, and together they made wild love.

...Enki stayed with Ninsar for a while, because he knew his seed would be her womb. So he stayed with her until the ninth day, when Ninsar gave birth to Ninkurra, another girl-child, the future goddess of Mountain Pastures.

...Another nine days passed by, and as Ninkurra played at a mountain top, curiosity led her to explore a well that surfaced out of the blue to water the greens and wild flower beds she had just made grow. To her sheer surprise and delight, the well took the shape of a handsome god, who introduced himself to her as Enki, the Sweet Waters Lord.

Again, Enki looked at Ninkurra's young and cheerful face, and desired to dive into the maiden's embrace, for she reminded him twice of Ninhursag, the one and only to Enki's wandering heart. The maiden at the mountain top although had attracted the Sweet Waters' Lord. Had he again fallen in love?

Ninkurra, who had lived a life so sheltered at the mountain heights, was fully bewitched by the easy charm of the older, more experienced god. Thus she joyously yielded to him and love they made for nine days and nine nights. But Enki soon realized that as lovely as Ninkurra was, she could not be compared to Ninhursag.

As before, the Sweet Waters Lord left Ninsar after nine days, when Ninkurra gave birth to another lovely girl-child called Uttu…

…Ninhursag, having kissed the earth to awaken for Spring to come, had returned to holy Dilmun. The Great Lady who saw and wisely judged all life forms, frowned at the sadness reflected in Ninsar's and Ninkurra's eyes, and frowned at Enki's unbridled lust. Ninhursag knew how charming Enki could be, but no matter what, young Uttu the Weaver should be advised to avoid the riverbanks, or the places where Enki and herself could be found alone or unchaperoned: 'Daughter Uttu, beware of the marshes and the riverbanks, where Enki, the Sweet Waters god, reigns as Sovereign. There he will see you, there he will desire you and want to make of you his own, only to leave you all alone later on!' was Ninhursag's stern advice to Uttu.

For a time young Uttu did follow the Great Lady's advice and kept her distance from Enki's lusty sight. But one day Enki's desire won the young goddess' heart, when he brought to her delicacies from the garden of delights: apples, cucumbers and grapes, all this and more Enki offered to the young goddess. Then Uttu, full of joy, opened herself to welcome Enki, the crafty god, and he embraced her with heartfelt glee, lying in her lap content and happy. Loving strokes, kisses and hugs they shared, until Enki's seed found its way to Uttu's young and yet untried womb.

Later, still lying on Enki's powerful arms, doubt entered Uttu's mind, body and heart: 'Tonight you loved me so dearly, tonight I was your spouse, the one and only, your dearest,' she thought. 'But will you love me in the morning, o lustiest of all gods? Will you stay in my arms and never let me go? And will you love for more than a holy night, and share with me happy and hard times?'

But when morning came and Uttu looked into Enki's eyes, she knew she still was not the one to hold captive the Sweet Waters Lord. With a tender kiss Enki took his leave, but did not say when he was going to come back, or ever returned to stay.

Uttu swallowed stubborn tears, but decided no to surrender to loss and sorrow, and more. 'I vow not to be bonded to Enki from this moment on,' she promised herself with a deep-rooted resolve. 'If he does not want me for myself, for what can we together be, I will not carry any of his seeds within or without my very being!'

Uttu immediately turned then to Ninhursag for help. The Great Mother goddess, beloved by all, would know what to do, would ensure the best course of action. 'Wipe out Enki's seed of your body, and bury within the depths of the Earth the promise of life you shared with him,' said the Great Lady and Womb of Creation. 'Let the Earth receive and transform yours and Enki's seed. And after you do this all, take your time so that your body, heart, mind and soul may heal. And I, who have known love, pain, sorrow and immense joy, give you, daughter, a very special blessing: may the wisdom of experience brought by such pain enter your being again and may you learn to ask as much as you give from your future lover for as long as you live. Reciprocation is the key for everlasting relationships!'

Where Ninhursag buried Enki's seeds, nine days later eight plants, luscious and strong, started to grow. Ninhursag laughed and declared happily to each of them: 'Out of the depths of the earth, out of my stony womb, eight plants came out to bring more blessings to the world. Eight they are, and from now on each of them will be both fathers and mothers, the very first Seed, of a new group of beings, whom I'll call Plants, creatures of green and colour, that will nourish, heal and grow in the glory of Dilmun and the Middle world.'

…'What sorts of beings are those, Isimud, my faithful servant and friend? What is in them so new and yet so old that fills my heart with desire and my mind with deep-rooted curiosity? I want to taste them, to know their hearts, I want to know their insides. What, pray, is this plant?' asked Enki to Isimud, pointing at the closest one. 'My king, this is a tree plant,' Isimud answered, and sworn as he was to serve the Sweet Waters Lord, Isimud then proceeded to cut down a piece of the tree-plant and passed it on to Enki, who immediatedly ate it with greed.

The taste of the tree-plant fuelled even more Enki's desire to know the nature of the other seven plants left. He asked Isimud about the nature of the seven plants, their essence and content. Isimud replied to all his master's questions, cutting down a sample of each and passing them on to Enki, who devoured them immediately with glee. This way Enki got to know the hearts of the Plants World.

Seeing that once again Enki had shown no respect of restraint, taking over to make his own not only young maiden goddesses, but also the Plants World angered Ninhursag beyond any measure. 'Enough is enough!' exclaimed the Great

Mother, Mistress and Supreme Queen of the Earth, outraged and furious at Enki's disdain for all beings, human or plants. 'Enki, you've gone too far by taking over the hearts' essence of not only young goddesses, but also by taking into yourself eight primeval samples of the Plants World. It is good to feel desire and experience the need to be one with the beloved. But there is profound responsibility implicit in falling in love and captivating someone's mind, body, heart and soul. You, Enki, came out of the blue into many maidens' lives, set yourself up like a squatter within their hearts only to leave afterwards, never to return. But even then you were not satisfied in your lust to know and experience everything, so you turned to the newly created Plants World. You, Enki, tasted each one of the eight sacred plants, devouring them next with greed. You never asked, but always took without giving anything back, a sign of acknowledgement, a simple caress.

To how many did you bring a little death to their spirit, to their hopes about a future with you? For all this, you deserve a mighty lesson, for it is high time that you, Enki, learn in sorrow what you did not learn in happiness: I will never look at you with a life-giving eye from this moment on. May the suffering you inflicted return to you threefold.'

With these words, Great Ninhursag disappeared, leaving Enki clearly divided between the joy of seeing the one and only to his heart and the growing concern for her parting words…Because indeed Enki's health began to fail. A strange illness this was: eight organs of his body fell progressively ill. Indeed, they started to die in Enki's living body. The Anunnaki, the Great

Gods, were disconsolate with Enki's suffering. Father An, the Sky Lord, Enlil, Lord Air and Enki's beloved older brother, all healer gods and goddesses of the land tried everything they could to no avail…

It was then that a fox, a sacred wild beast to Ninhursag who was passing by, came to console Lord Air. 'I've seen the suffering of the Sweet Waters Lord, I've witnessed the lament of the greatest of the Anunnaki for Enki, their beloved brother. Only Ninhursag can heal him, only the Mistress of All Creation can make him whole again. I'll do my best to go and find the Greatest Lady of Earth, holy Ninhursag I am sworn to worship and serve till the end of my days. I will find the Great Goddess and bring her here to accomplish the healing of the sick god.'

The fox disappeared, but kept her promise, for Ninhursag relented and came running to Enki's aid. She went straight to the chamber were Enki laid in agony, and, with a wave of her mighty hand, Ninhursag dismissed healers, nurses and well-wishers. Their work was done. Ninhursag's had just begun. With immense tenderness, the Mistress of All Creation made herself comfortable by on the bed, carefully placing Enki's head on her vagina. She then leaned forward and wrapped herself, arms, legs, breasts around the body of the Sweet Waters Lord. Enki was this way lovingly embraced by the Great Lady, kept safe and protected by her warmth, and arms that felt strong yet very sweet. Like a nurturing womb, the Great Lady wrapped herself around the Sweet Waters god.

Ninhursag whispered softly in Enki's ear. 'Dearest, what hurts you?' 'O, beloved, my whole

> body hurts me,' Enki managed to answer with visible effort. Ninhursag rocked gently back and forth with much care the sick god: 'I know your body hurts, dear heart, but soon you will be made whole again. Because I'll receive in my Womb of Abundance, the nest of creation, the seeds that you so greedily ate and that made you so ill. I'll take them all into my body so that they can bring healing, not harm to all beings. Let the Work begin"...[84]

Let us continue with the understanding that the Mother Earth goddess gave birth to many healing energies within the garden. These energies would transform into the seen. For every hurt, there was a healing energy that was birthed from Mother Earth and the fruits would be the foods and the green plants would house the healing energies of life. The divine healing process of the masculine and feminine presence is a pure reflection of the divine union of earth, wind rain and sun.

> Enki heard Ninhursag's voice resonate all over his being: 'The first seed you ate and made you ill, I take its power into myself and transform it into a newly born god, a younger brother and son to you, dearest. I therefore have given birth to the god Abu to set your body free.'
>
> The Great Lady continued her mighty healing ritual, asking Enki for the names of the organs that had been affected… 'Where do you still feel much pain, dearest? What hurts you?' 'My mouth hurts me.' Ninhursag kissed Enki on the mouth. 'To the goddess Ninkasi I have given birth for you to set your mouth free.'

[84] *Enki and Ninhursag.* Sumerian. Online Source: http://www.gatewaystobabylon.com/myths/texts/retellings/enkininhur.htm

> What hurts you most, dearest? 'My rib hurts me.' 'To the goddess Nin-ti, the Lady of the Rib and the One who makes Live, I have given birth for you to set your rib free.' As soon as Ninhursag uttered the last sentence, Enki felt no pain or ache, revitalized and stronger than ever. Indeed, as if he himself had been reborn in the close embrace of Ninhursag. Gone was the pain, the fever, the shivers. 'I am alive,' he said very simply, his voice full of wonder…
>
> He moved into Ninhursag's arms, for he wanted to see her face too. The Great Lady had closed her eyes, but there was a smile on her lips. She rested against the pillows of Enki's bed, still holding him in a loose embrace. Now it was his turn to act with immense tenderness, as he shifted positions to make her rest on his chest… [85]

It is a fact that the sacred garden culture was an ancient presence that flourished before the invasions of nomadic tribes of hunters, scavengers and herders. It is a fact that these vicious invaders were outsiders to a way of life that honored the fertility of the mother earth in divine union with the masculine presence and cultivated the soil to bring forward the fruits of the trees of life.

Research indicates that well over 7,000 years ago, major communities of the Children of the Sun with the golden tan resided in the garden culture environment around the lower Tigris and Euphrates rivers. The Kwasunic tribes throughout the region from the Sudan to Asia, called themselves Kushite. What is certain is that the sacred garden presence flourished in and throughout the regions during the time when the mutated and degenerated breed was still trying to find their way out of

---

[85] *Enki and Ninhursag.* Online Source: http://www.gatewaystobabylon.com/myths/texts/retellings/enkininhur.htm

the ice-cold, deep-freeze environment. It is noted that the ancient Kwasunic populations irrigated their crops by using a system of irrigation canals. By devising such an irrigation system that directed the river waters, the ancient suntanned populations were able to maintain stable garden communities with an abundant food supply of fruits, vegetables, seeds and nuts. Other Kwasunic populations that inhabited the Indus Valley regions and other fertile black lands also created massive irrigation systems that enabled them to become master cultivators of these garden communities. These were indeed people from the land of the Kush.

As has been noted, the Kushite people, i.e. suntanned populations of the garden culture communities were distinguished as pyramid builders. The Sumerian populations were builders of pyramid structures called ziggurats. The term ziggurat has been defined as "mountain of god" or "hill of heaven." These structures served as library temples, i.e. a sacred place for priests and priestesses. It must be understood that the Kushite populations not only left their mark in the middle world, i.e. the regions now known as Afrika and the Middle East, but in fact left these pyramid structures as a signature in every area in which they resided throughout the planet. The ancient pyramid is in fact the trademark of the Kwasunic Kushite people. Research indicates that a three-story pyramid dating 5,000 years ago was discovered in north China's Inner Mongolia:

> Seven tombs and one altar were also found on the top of the pyramid. Archaeologists also discovered a number of pottery pieces with the asterisk character inscribed on the inner wall. The asterisk character is believed to be related to the understanding of ancient people on astrology. Among the culture relics excavated from one of the seven tombs…a full-sized stone statue of Goddess

> unearthed from another tomb. What astonished the archaeologists is a palm-sized stone genital on the inner wall of a tomb with a small stone statue of Goddess below.[86]

When the holistic living truth about Supreme Love is revealed, the sacred sons and daughters must be well-aware of the reactionary behaviors of the dominant breed of the ice-cold, deep-freeze mentality. Examples of these destructive reactionary behaviors are easily identified by the fact that dominant rulers with racist ideologies have attempted to blow the head off of the Sphinx simply because of its unquestionable Afrikoid, "Negroid," Kwasunic features. The Sphinx represents a Kushite people of the ancient Nubian culture. Recently discovered geological evidence indicates that the deep erosion patterns on the flanks of the Sphinx were caused by 1,000 years of heavy rain. It is noted that such conditions last existed in Egypt at the end of the last ice age, about 10,000-9,000 B.C.E., meaning that the Sphinx may be more than 12,000 years old (not the generally accepted 4,500 years). Other noted geologists base their calculations on the difference between wind and rain weathering on the Sphinx and other structures 300 yards apart with totally different wear patterns.

It appears that the conspiracy to distort the holistic living truth that has been orchestrated by the science of Egyptology and the powers that be of the ice-cold, deep-freeze mentality is being burst at the seams. So much for the documentary, "They Came From Beyond," which is a hypothesis that the Divine Children of the Sun with the golden tan were aliens from beyond the Earth. How else could a lost and astray mind of the ice-cold, deep-freeze mentality reckon with such phenomenal creations from a people that these lost and astray minds have declared as inferior based on the color of their skin? It is then

---

[86] *People's Daily*. July 21, 2001. Online Source: http://www.2002china.net/china_columns/ancient_china/pyramidchina.shtml

no wonder that the lost and astray mind of the ice-cold, deep-freeze mentality projects deceptive excuses like maybe specific groups of suntanned Children came from beyond and they just happened to have "Negroid" features.

Let us take a look at a new piece of evidence that has emerged from the Most Supreme Seen and Unseen Presence of the sacred ancestry of Man, He and She.

> While excavating a cave near the southernmost tip of South Africa, U.S. and South African paleontologists discovered two pieces of ochre rock decorated with geometric patterns. The site, called Blombos Cave, is near the southern Cape shore of the Indian Ocean, nearly 200 miles south of Cape Town, South Africa. Sophisticated dating techniques led the researchers to conclude that the artifacts date back more than 70,000 years. That is more than 35,000 years older than any other 'stone age' art.... The artifacts discovered in Blombos cave were made of the iron ore stone ochre. Small pieces of ochre were first scraped and ground to create flat surfaces. The early artist decorated the stones with a complex geometric array of carved lines.[87]
>
> Pierced shells, with the strong implication of stringing for body ornamentation, are known from Porc-Epic Cave in Ethiopia at around 70,000 years ago....Blade tool industries, again formerly associated principally with the Cro-Magnons, are found at least sporadically at sites in Africa that date to as much as a quarter of a million years ago. Also in the economic/technological realm, such

[87] *Art Prehistory.* Sean Henahan. Stony Brook, NY 1/10/02. Access Excellence, the National Health Museum. Online Source URL: http://www.accessexcellence.org/WN/SU/caveart.html

> activities as flint-mining, pigment-processing and long-distance trade in useful materials are documented in Africa up to about 100,000 years ago.[88]

The nature of ancient Afrikan art history is a statement of a holistic living way of life that embodies the mental, the physical and the spiritual expressions. Research indicates that there are archaeological findings that uncovered thousands of paintings and engravings of human and animal figures, pertaining to the suntanned cultures of the fertile valley, i.e. that once massive garden area that is today the Sahara Desert, ranging from Mauritania to Sudan. Findings show that terra-cotta statues and figures of the Nok population represent a classic Afrikoid art style. On the site of Nok, stone adzes were discovered ranging in age from 37,000 B.C.E. or about 39,000 years ago until about 200 B.C.E. Archaeological evidence indicates that the suntanned Nok populations grew crops and were skilled in working iron. The Nok were Children of the Sun with the golden tan who are recognized for the abundance of terra-cotta figures that they created, ranging in size from a few inches to more than four feet in height.

The Nok drawings and clay figures reveal the honoring of the feminine presence. Findings show that the characteristics of many Nok sculptures include elaborate hair styles, intricate necklaces and waistbands crafted in smoothly finished surfaces with detailed designs. We remind you here that the Nok community shows evidence of holding the mother earth in highest esteem as represented in the artistic expressions. The feminine presence was honored as the fertility of life. The Nok population resided within a garden culture environment, and so

---

[88] Special Exhibition: *Genesis: Ideas of Origin in African Sculpture.* Nov. 19, 2002 to July 4, 2003. The Metropolitan Museum of Art, New York. Online Source: http://www.metmuseum.org/special/Genesis/tattersall_lecture.asp?page=4

the profound view of the feminine presence as expressed in the art showed an equal degree of thanks, praise and appreciation for the glory of earth, wind, rain and sun that sanctioned their crops and harvest. The work now is to amass divine spirit consciousness so as to gain divine clarity for the lost and astray mind of Man, He and She.

The mother spirit of the sacred garden culture is consistently represented in the mother earth/fertility/goddess figures that have been discovered around the world. The fact that remains constant is the ancient tradition of honoring the feminine presence through the statues and figurines within the sacred garden culture. The goddess figures represent a direct cultural contrast to the male war god culture that identifies the pale reflection of the ice-cold, deep-freeze mentality. Supreme thanks, praise and appreciation for the father spirit in upholding the social order of the sacred garden culture where the mother spirit is honored with such high esteem. Without the presence of this divine oneness relationship, the masters of deceit would create enough confusion to mask the holistic living truth about Supreme Love.

When looking at the ancient suntanned cultures, such as the ancient populations identified as the Nok who inhabited the glorious Sahara farmlands over 39,000 years ago, it is very clear that the sacred garden culture presence has been among the suntanned Children for a very, very long time. In fact, the sacred garden culture has been around since the sacred and blessed origin of Man, He and She.

### *Entering the Divine Parallel*

The lost and astray Children who lost their tan rationalize in their political science rhetoric that all is fair in love and war and to the victor goes the spoils. The victimized may look at these vicious invasions for what they are—vicious invasions. Many of the lost and astray Children who lost their tan can only see brilliant strategies and tactics, military genius, glorious invasions and the thrill of victory while looking upon the ruins, the raped, the dead and bloody remains, and dehumanized victims as simply the agony of defeat.

It seems that there is no place within the ice-cold, deep-freeze mentality for compassion beyond one's own selfish ideologies. Therefore, there is no comprehension of the ancient Nubian proverb, "Do unto others as you would have them do unto you," and what goes around comes back around. The lost and astray Children pass on the philosophy that some must die so that others may live. Unquestionably, the Children of the Sun with the golden tan have consistently been designated as those who must die or be enslaved, must be controlled, contained, or even exterminated, by any means necessary.

To make matters worse, the Children of the Sun with the golden tan have been enticed, coerced, persuaded, educated and bred into upholding the attitudes, behaviors and values of their ex-colonial and ex-slave masters. As a result, the Children of the Sun with the golden tan have become totally lost and astray in integration and assimilation of the social economic and religious ideologies of the ice-cold, deep-freeze mentality.

The goal is to bring divine clarity to Man, He and She. The objective is for the lost and astray Children who lost their tan and the lost and astray Children with the golden tan to realize that they must throw off the yoke of the ice-cold, deep-freeze mentality that breeds the death consumption culture. The merging point forward for Man, He and She, is the emergence into the divine oneness of the sacred garden culture as the Divine Children of the Sun. Divine oneness of thought and reasoning, divine oneness of body, and divine oneness of spirit.

Divine spirit consciousness must be the focal point of one's holistic living presence. In other words, it is not about the color of one's skin or texture of one's hair; it is about the complete release of the ice-cold, deep-freeze mentality and the death consumption culture that it breeds. It is about restoring a holistic living way of life…in divine order. The sacred garden culture of the Divine Children of the Sun has always been a culture of inclusiveness, i.e. open arms of welcome. In divine order, the open and welcoming vibration of the sacred garden culture is an asset; when encountering the toxic vibrations of the invading death consumption culture, it has been extremely detrimental. The cultural pattern that excludes, segregates, annihilates, and exterminates based on race, creed, color, sex, religion and physical handicap is a part of the unholy parallel of the ice-cold, deep-freeze mentality.

The most immediate responsibility and obligation of those who truly seek holistic living harmony upon the planet are to implement urgent attitude adjustments and super urgent behavior modifications that reject toxic consumption. The resurrection of a sacred few is an absolute necessity in order for Man, He and She, to go forward and multiply divine change in the offspring. It must be absolutely clear that children learn by example and not by words.

It must be absolutely clear that it is impossible for the sacred spirit presence of Man, He and She, to exist under the guidance and leadership of the sons and daughters of the ice-cold, deep-freeze mentality. It must be forever in the mindset of Man, He and She, that the death consumption culture will forever have its accent on the consumption of dead, devitalized, and depleted food substances. It must be crystal clear that the consumption of dead, devitalized, and depleted food substances is the fuel that breeds lust, lies, illusions, confusion, death and deadly destruction. The simplest mind must come to comprehend that the scavenger mentality and the predator mentality require one to be cunning, conniving and deceptive. Whereas the predator is a cold-blooded opportunist that thrives on the quick kill, the scavenger is a cold-blooded opportunist that thrives on the spoils of the kill.

The Children of the Sun with the golden tan and the Children of the Sun who lost their tan must comprehend that divine oneness requires an emergence forward into a divine social economic family community. However, there will be many who find this as an unacceptable option; therefore, there will be many who will be unwilling to heal from the toxic vibrations of the lost and astray mind.

There are indeed a sacred few who will come to comprehend the toxic and depleted damage that has been done and will seek to heal from the toxicity, be they perpetrator or be they victim. It will require a tremendous amount of trust and divine humility for the Children of the Sun to go beyond the deceptive ways and means of superficial coexistence. Establishing trust and divine humility is impossible within the ice-cold, deep-freeze mentality. The lost and astray Children who lost their tan have maintained a vicious and cold-blooded historical pattern. This historical pattern of rape, murder and theft has been highlighted by deceptive morals and values that are entrenched in lust, lies, illusions, confusion, death and deadly destruction. Who would want to trust such a cold-blooded, cruel, greedy, and deadly vibration ever again?

The suntanned Children would definitely be in a dilemma on this question. In order to establish any level and degree of trust, the suntanned Children would have to close their eyes to the holistic living truth about the facts of history. However to close one's eyes to the holistic living truth about the facts of history would be a greater indulgence in deception. Additionally, closing one's eyes to the historical realities would be to indulge in utter stupidity and ignorance with serious suicidal intent. On the other hand, if one opens one's eyes to the historical phenomena of the lost and astray Children who lost their tan, the entire peace-seeking mission would be quickly aborted to avoid an historical replay. It is indeed a fact of life that the "white man speaks with forked tongue" of the ice-cold, deep-freeze mentality.

EXPOSING THE ICE-COLD, DEEP-FREEZE MENTALITY AND WHOLE LIFE HEALING OF SEXUAL ENERGY WITHIN THE DIVINE PARALLEL

Notwithstanding historical facts, it is indeed necessary for all of Man, He and She, to come to the realization that whole life healing is essential and that all healing must begin from within. Within divine spirit consciousness, toxic energy patterns of the unholy parallel are seen as foreign and comprehended as being outside of the supreme love vibration. Within divine spirit consciousness, the process of self-healing is revealed as the corrective actions that are required to regain one's mental, physical and spiritual integrity and wholeness. The greatest self-healing is experienced when one releases all toxic residues within self by aligning oneself within the supreme love vibration.

The justice of divine order is well-comprehended within divine spirit consciousness. One must reap from what one sows. Therefore, the bitter herbs of being accountable for one's own toxic thoughts, attitudes and behaviors lead one to a greater sense of divine humility and whole life healing. Those who have indulged most deeply in toxic consumption have the most damage to repair.

What the I in I am saying here is that anyone who has consumed of toxic energy must de-tox or purge the last detail of that toxic consumption from the mind of thought, body of flesh and sacred spirit presence. In the de-tox process, there is no room for scapegoats or for finger pointing. There must be a focus on the divine actions required to de-tox the cesspool of toxic waste. It is often assumed that one can state a prayer of forgiveness or can attempt to meditate pains or negative behaviors away. However, the true act of forgiveness is, in fact, the act of de-toxing and purging the toxic and depleting attitudes and behaviors.

There is absolutely no question that de-toxing is not an act of momentary enthusiasm, but rather an intense course of action requiring tenacity, patience and consistent work efforts to purge. One must be most aware that throughout the de-toxing process there will be a tendency to move back into one's comfort zone, i.e. the addictions, habits, attitudes and behaviors that one has known best. Therefore, throughout the de-tox process, one must learn to work tenaciously to focus from a place of divine clarity. One must focus on divine spirit consciousness so as to dismiss the toxic attitudes and behaviors of every unwholesome space and place that once provided comfort.

Indeed, there are many encounters that have a very draining, dreadful, fruitless and unwholesome feel. It is the divine duty, obligation and responsibility of Man, He and She, to reach deeper within their whole life presence to reconcile these indifferences without becoming distracted. Man, He and She, must come to understand their divine presence and the Most Supreme Unseen energy force field that is available for He and She to tap into. The most objective way to reconcile toxic reasoning and toxic attitudes and toxic behaviors is to cease and desist from consuming those toxic energies.

The I in I want to make it clear that all of Man, He and She, must honor their whole life presence. Therefore, regardless of one being blonde or bald or natty, natty dread, one must honor and appreciate one's physical presence. However, any attitude or behavior that rejects the divine and innate characteristics of Man, He and She is a contradiction to the whole life presence. Esteem and self-love are the key and the backbone to divine spirit consciousness. Esteem and self-love can never ever be at the mercy of evaluating one's self-worth by degrading and devaluing the self worth of another.

The I in I have come to set the record straight. There is absolutely no way that any of Man, He and She, can claim any supreme self-love and self-esteem while one continues to reject one's sacred and most glorious origin, i.e. the Divine Children of the Sun with the golden tan. Only one who has maintained and honored the divine principles and practices of the sacred garden culture within divine spirit consciousness is in the position to guide the steps forward into divinity.

It is very clear that the buck must stop somewhere. The toxic emergence of the ice-cold, deep-freeze mentality must be seen as nothing less than a divine lesson regarding the consequences of disobeying the divine laws of the universe. If the divine lesson is not learned and corrective action is not immediately implemented, these toxic and depleting energies will become even more of a threat and danger to the whole life presence of Man, He and She, the glory of mother earth, and every whole life presence upon the planet Earth.

Absolutely and beyond a shadow of a doubt, the first divine act and requirement of Man, He and She, in emerging forward into divine oneness is the emergence into divine consumption. Divine consumption is for the body, i.e. raw and living fruits, vegetables, seeds and nuts. Divine consumption is for the brain, i.e. divine spirit consciousness and the total and absolute rejection of the consciousness of the ice-cold, deep-freeze mentality and all of its parts and parcels thereof.

Eventually, by the grace of the Most Supreme Seen and Unseen, the emergence into divine union once again will be the anointing of Man, He and She, into the fullness and the wholeness of the Divine Children of the Sun, i.e. the divine and sacred spirit presence of Man, He and She. Once again the sacred garden culture will flourish upon this glorious planet where life is for the living. And so now the work intensifies.

### *Divine Spirit Consciousness: the Sacred Energy for Masculine Healing*

The basic principles of life within the sacred garden culture honor the divine nurturing presence of the mother spirit. The mother spirit as a life energy presence nurtures what is brought to her mentally, physically and spiritually. With that understanding, it is an absolute duty, obligation and responsibility for the father presence of Man He to go into serious and intense relationship studies. His studies must establish the basic groundwork of principles, morals and values to enable him to provide divine guidance and divine protection for the sacred and most blessed presence of Man She, the mother spirit. Within the teachings of the sacred garden culture, the mother spirit is recognized as the gateway to life.

It is well understood within the sacred garden culture that the mother spirit, the mother presence, of Man, He and She, is the first and primary teacher from the point of inception of that newborn life. When the mother spirit is within the pride and the glory of the sacred garden culture and her holistic living existence upon the seen of the planet Earth, she goes forward to multiply that sacred and most blessed energy within the offspring. The children are recognized as the ancestral recycling of Man, He and She. Therefore, in order to secure the sacred social order, it becomes an absolute obligation of every Man He to gain the greatest degree of development, knowledge, wisdom and understanding available in order to be able to give divine guidance and divine protection to the mother spirit. For this reason, Man He enters into the unified manifestation of the masculine spirit within the male society of the divine social economic family community setting.

Every male child gains membership and entry into the male society simply by his birth rites as Man He, the masculine spirit of the holistic living presence of Man, He and She. One of the first divine principles that Man He of the male society learns is that Man She, the mother spirit, must be honored, adored, protected, and divinely guided, because any damage done to her as the keeper of the gateway of life damages the entire social order. Moreover, it is reasoned that any damage done to her is damage inflicted upon the ancestral spirits who pass through her in the recycling vibration as the spirit presence of newborn life again. When one begins to comprehend that this whole life reasoning existed millions of years prior to the unwholly intervention of the death consumption culture and the energy that is opposite of Supreme Love, one will begin to understand how disorder has interrupted the wholly existence of Man, He and She. If one pays close attention and begins to understand that divine action speaks louder than words, one will be able to reason with the whole life necessity for corrective action.

Oftentimes, the I in I have been asked, "How did Man He gain his sexual experience in the sacred garden culture?" In other words, the question is: "How is the male to learn to master his sexual arts and enhance his sexual skills if he doesn't get practice?" The point of fact is that Man He has absolutely no right to practice on, misuse, and abuse the feminine spirit, the mother spirit. If he behaves in such a toxic manner, Man He is totally dishonorable to his presence as the giver of divine guidance and protection. Unquestionably, what he is doing is asking for the toxic energy of his practices to become a norm, a way of life that will be passed on through the mother spirit.

Within the sacred garden culture, the male would be considered totally insane and dangerous if he were to follow the old adage, "My mama told me, you'd better shop around." However, within the death consumption culture, it is no wonder that "Papa was a rolling stone, and anywhere he laid his hat was his home." In truth and reality, the greatest practice that Man He could receive would be to begin practicing the attitudes and behaviors of divine spirit consciousness. Every mental, physical and spiritual element of sexual expression is already interwoven in the genetic existence of Man, He and She; it is just a matter of gaining that divine spirit consciousness and sacred insight into one's higher self. Indeed, there is no greater sexual expression beyond that which is experienced when Man, He and She, has entered the most high state of divine oneness of brain, body and spirit...What a magnificent and invigorating experience it is. Therefore, within the society of Man He of the sacred garden culture it is an absolute duty, obligation and responsibility of the masculine presence to hold very dear his innercourse with the mother spirit. Divine innercourse is comprehended to be far more than an ejaculation of fluids and juices, and a few moments of pleasure and satisfaction. Divine innercourse is in fact an ejaculation of the male's whole life presence, his energy, his divine duty, obligation and responsibility to the feminine presence.

### *Divine Spirit Consciousness: the Sacred Energy for Feminine Healing*

It is about time for the sacred resurrection of the sacred mother spirit. The feminine presence has been so twisted and turned by the ice-cold, deep-freeze mentality that she can not even remember her divine self. Indeed, the feminine presence has assumed a completely opposite identity within the energy that is opposite of Supreme Love, and she is acting out the most degraded and corrupted attitudes and behaviors based on the disrespect and disregard that has been brought to her by the masculine presence. The divinity of the mother spirit has only been hinted at throughout modern history in pieces of myth and spiritual teachings of what has remained and what has survived from the vicious invasions against the sacred garden culture. The original context of a holistic living way of life of the sacred garden culture has been long-forgotten in the distortions and ignorance of the ice-cold, deep-freeze mentality. Nevertheless, the existing images of the "black" goddess, the "black" Madonna, and the "black" earth-mother figure are references to the sacred origin of the feminine presence of Man, He and She, within the sacred garden culture.

Within the sacred garden culture, the mother spirit is exalted as the master of the physical as she brings forward the physical presence of Man, He and She. It is well comprehended within divine spirit consciousness that the feminine presence is fertilized by the whole-life energy radiating from the masculine presence as symbolized by the sun radiating upon the earth to bring forward the fruits of the garden. The divine union of Man, He and She, is the harmony and balance of the father spirit and mother spirit functioning within their duties, obligations and responsibilities as the Most Supreme Seen Essence of Life and Supreme Love. The "black" goddess figure represented the physical presence of the collective feminine energy that would be embodied within the divine sisterhood. To honor the mother spirit, is recognized as the expression of honoring the ancestral spirits and securing the future of one's own presence and the presence of the divine social economic family community.

The feminine presence holds the utmost adoration for and devotion to the masculine presence for his strong and comforting position as the giver of divine guidance and divine protection. The divine spirit consciousness of the father spirit provides a harmonizing effect that allows the mother spirit to focus with full allegiance on nurturing the practices and principles established within a holistic living way of life. The divine spirit consciousness of the mother spirit provides her with the intense spirit focus and insight that enables her to organize, coordinate and master the physical. The level and degree of mutual respect and appreciation between Man He and Man She in divine union is a powerful inspiration and stimulation.

Within the sisterhood society, the feminine presence is instructed in her innate worth and beauty as a manifestation of the nurturing vibration. Her naturally soft and gentle tendencies are enhanced with the comprehension that the ability to soothe and nurture is an unparalleled strength, just as the ability of the earth to provide the generation of life and the food to nurture that life is the ultimate glory of the earth. The sacred presence of the mother spirit radiates tenderness and abundant, gracious fertility. In divine order, the mother spirit honors the divine guidance and divine protection given to her by the father spirit. When one begins to gain a sense of what was lost due to the degeneration and mutation of the feminine presence, the present state of Man She within the death consumption culture becomes almost unbearable.

Within divine order, the female, by nature of her nurturing qualities, is a sensitive and sensual being. These characteristics are often seen as reflecting her emotional processes. This emotional process refers to receiving vibrations of thought and sensations, absorbing those signals and translating them into a physical presentation. The feminine presence is sensitive to her surroundings meaning that her senses are attuned to absorb the vibrations of her environment and those around her as a means for directing her relationships. The ability to attune to the vibrations of others is a key factor in securing the mother's relationship with her newborn. This ability to sensitize to others is a key factor that promotes the unity, strength and harmony of the sisterhood relationships in divine order.

The ability to receive and absorb vibrations is a key factor in the feminine presence being a divine nurturer and bringing forward the fruit of the masculine presence, mentally, physically and spiritually. However, because the feminine presence functions as a nurturer of energy, she suffers the adverse effects of toxic consumption to a worse degree than the male. Within the death consumption culture, the feminine presence suffers emotional traumas and mental disorders at an alarming rate. Depression, eating disorders, and a string of addictions are symptoms of the emotional distress of the mother spirit out of alignment with her divine spirit presence.

Either one makes the commitment to stay within the death consumption culture, consuming the same toxic substances again and again while expecting different results, or one must make whole life change into an alignment with the principles, morals and values of the sacred garden culture. It has been a long time for the mother spirit to remain out of alignment with her holistic living presence as Man She. It has been a long time for the mother spirit to continue producing offspring who idolize and worship the vibrations and sensations of the death consumption culture. It has been a long time for the mother spirit to be disconnected from the divine protection and guidance of the father spirit who is totally devoted to the Most Supreme Spirit of Love as the Most High Essence of Life.

The consequences of this longtime disorder and this plague of mental insanity strike a fatal blow against the sacred garden culture. Imagine such a fatal and dilapidated state of mind that would cause Man He to perpetuate religious orders and social economic systems that actually pinpoint Man He as the birthplace of Man, He and She. Such religious orders actually claim that, in fact, the rib of Man He was taken to create a partner as an afterthought. This rib-born partner would be identified as the mother spirit, or Man She. Worst of all, her creation was said to come about as an afterthought after Man He could not get enough satisfaction with the sheep and other animals. The I in I have heard the issue of not getting enough satisfaction with the sheep debated in modern times among those of the ice-cold, deep-freeze mentality. This point is made, because many of Man He choose alternative mating relationships that deviate from the divine order of Man He with Man She. In fact, it seems that many of Man She have decided that what goes around comes around and, therefore, also seek an alternative mating relationship that deviates from the divine order of Man She with Man He.

Imagine how this toxic disorder born and bred of the ice-cold, deep-freeze mentality has affected the mother spirit upon the planet. Imagine this toxicity being the basic principle of all teachings and beliefs that she consumes. Imagine these teachings and beliefs being honored as the foundation of a civilized way of life. Imagine the mental disorder that the mother spirit faces when she begins to think that she is even one degree less important than Man He. Know and understand full well that this disorder has been part and parcel of a plague of deception to degrade and dishonor the mother spirit.

It must be clearly comprehended that the mother spirit is the first teacher. She is either the first teacher of the sacred garden culture of her origin as part and parcel of the divine union of Man, He and She. Or, she is the teacher of the lust, lies, illusions, confusion, death and deadly destruction that are born and bred within the death consumption culture.

And all that the mother spirit teaches is all that will come out of her through the birth and nurturing of the offspring and all that will come back to her through her relationships upon the planet. It is therefore safe to say that the mother spirit is in grave danger and has been reduced to her lowest terms when she finds herself aligned and confined to vibrations and sensations of the death consumption culture. Let it be known that any time that one finds mental or physical disease and social disorder that causes the mother spirit to be placed in grave danger, one has truly reached the last critical stage of total destruction. And the only way to possibly resurrect a people within this last critical stage of total destruction is to rescue and secure as many as possible among the feminine presence. Divine spirit consciousness of a holistic living way of life is the only alternative that will guide Man, He and She, to a sacred path away from a most painful and bloody trail that leads to total destruction.

It has indeed been a long time for the mother spirit to be out of synch, out of focus, and out of time with the Supreme Love spirit of the sacred garden culture. However, if Man She is not receiving divine guidance and divine protection from Man He, then only chaos can manifest. It must be comprehended that it is not possible for Man She to receive divine guidance and divine protection from Man He unless Man He is totally and absolutely devoted to the holistic living way of life of the sacred garden culture. Clearly and beyond a shadow of a doubt, Man He must have an absolute relationship of divine humility to the Most High Essence of Life and Supreme Love in order to provide divine guidance and divine protection to the mother spirit.

Man, He and She, must comprehend that the death consumption culture is simply a malignant cancer and a rampaging plague. Within the death consumption culture, everyone is a victim of prey and a predator at the same time. So the mother spirit became a victim of prey, and she became a cold-blooded, envious, jealous, greedy and vengeful predator at the same time. From this cold-blooded, cruel, and callous mentality came a vibration of I, me, my where one would seek to have advantage over another by any means necessary. With a cold-blooded, cruel, and vicious way of life as the dominating position of thought and reasoning among Man, He and She, how would it be possible for Man He, and most especially Man She, to maintain the vibration of looking out for sisters?

It would be innate and instinctual for the mother spirit to push the vibrations and sensations of integration, assimilation, and association as ways and means of protecting herself and her offspring. Even when these characteristics had the most fatal outcomes, she would continue to grip this vibration in the hopes that it would provide greater returns in the long run. The goal was to feel accepted by those in victory lane no matter how blatant it was that she was not the same. The mother spirit works to discolor herself and actually works to develop characteristics, physical appearances and presentations that show clearly and beyond a shadow of a doubt that she is humble and submissive to the dominant culture of the ice-cold, deep-freeze mentality.

Remember within the death consumption culture, it is not what a thing is but rather what something looks like or appears to be that matters more than anything else. It doesn't matter how unhappy or unwholesome one feels on the inside; the only thing that matters is the glamour and the expressions of integration and assimilation that one displays externally. The dominant culture perpetuates the idea of acceptance of one's natural characteristics based on how closely one resembles the degeneration and mutation of the ice-cold, deep-freeze mentality.

Honoring divine consumption as the consumption of raw and living fruits, vegetables, seeds and nuts is enough to make one an outcast even among family members. It matters not that it is a biological fact that the raw and living energy of these foods divinely nourishes the whole life presence of Man, He and She. In other words, within the death consumption culture, if one honors the vibrations of the sacred garden culture by upholding the principles and practices of divine consumption, then one would have no place and is considered a social deviant, an extremist, or a weirdo cultist. One would be ridiculed and looked upon as one who is outside of the status quo of the death consumption culture, i.e. not normal. To be considered "not normal" seems to be the worst curse that one could experience, yet to be normal within this vicious and esteemless vibration of the ice-cold, deep-freeze mentality is to honor lust, lies, illusions, confusion, death and deadly destruction. Although many have walked the borderline of lifestyle change, as long as one still maintains toxic habits and behaviors of death consumption in some manner or degree, one remains entrenched in the ice-cold, deep-freeze mentality.

So many of Man She walk around with great pride about accomplishments and material gains in a culture of disorder that has used their physical presence to enhance an economic way of life. In fact, the natural and innate characteristics that were born and bred within the sacred garden culture are totally and absolutely rejected and ridiculed as being ugly. Forget about the principles of divine sisterhood, for it is nowhere in the memory as the feminine spirit goes about her day-to-day business being a victim of prey and a predator while losing at every turn. Although it is very clear that when a feminine spirit within the death consumption culture is young and fresh, she is in her best days, or least it appears that way, peddling her wares for sale or trade or to capture a masculine presence for a few moments of "bip, bam, thank you ma'am." However, as she grows older, the competition stiffens with those younger ones coming after her, and her physical attraction begins to take a back seat to the newer models. She finds herself in a state of being where the most precious part of her life is spent in idle relationships with television, movies, games, shopping, pets, or gossip.

The time of life when the feminine spirit should be on a Council of Elders advising younger females and providing wholesome wisdom through the sisterhood of her family structure is spent bitter, angry, hostile and frustrated about the masculine presence and about the condition of her life. So, instead of daughters growing up in a sisterhood vibration with a Council of Elders, each daughter grows up falling into the same traps, playing the same loser games and ending up in the same frustrated and spiteful state of mind. In other words, Man She, as well as Man He, continues to do the same thing over and over again while expecting different results. The game gets watered down, polluted and diluted, and there continues to be a more sophisticated level and degree of mutation and degeneration that is inflicted upon the mind.

What then is the fate of the mother spirit, lost and astray in the vibrations and sensations of the death consumption culture? What else can she produce but lust, lies, illusions, confusion, death and deadly destruction if she is consuming of an energy that is opposite of Supreme Love? Let us keep in mind here that the mother spirit nurtures what is brought to her. Let us also keep in mind that the mother spirit is an emotional being innately.

It has become very clear that emotional sensitivity and compassion have been lost in so many of Man She. Let us also be aware that there is absolutely no way to turn around this toxic and confused state of reasoning except by providing a divine, whole-life energy of consumption for the mother spirit. Let us also be well aware that it requires a tremendous amount of de-toxing of very toxic memories that have been programmed into the feminine presence.

### *Divine Innercourse*

Divine innercourse establishes a contractual agreement that bonds the male to the female and vice versa. After such an encounter, the male is spiritually bound to maintain his divine duty, obligation and responsibility of giving divine guidance and divine protection for that feminine presence. By the same token, the female has a divine duty, obligation, and responsibility not to engage in sexual activities unless she is 100% mentally, physically and spiritually prepared to nurture what that male brings to her. Thus, within the sacred garden culture, the most unifying state of "marriage" was, and remains, the act of divine innercourse or the act of the two parts, Man He and Man She, coming together in divine oneness, i.e. consummation. Thus, the true act of "marriage" is the act of consummation of Man, He and She, into a state of divine oneness to forward and multiply all that they have come together to be. Therefore, every Man He and every Man She must come to understand that sexual intercourse bears far more responsibility than getting a nut, ejaculating, or getting a few moments of pleasure. What is now known as sexual intercourse within the death consumption culture is an unwhole practice of the lost and astray mind that begins with toxic consumption and ends with toxic consumption, breeding disorder and disease.

Within divine union, the male honors his duty, obligation and responsibility to provide divine guidance and protection for that feminine presence. By the same token, the feminine presence honors her duty, obligation and responsibility to nurture the lifestyle structure, values, principles, and morals of that masculine presence. Within divine union, Man, He and She, both have a most sacred and blessed duty, obligation and responsibility to honor the holistic living presence of the sacred garden culture. If He or She is functioning outside of divine order, it should be very clear that He or She is functioning from the ice-cold, deep-freeze mentality. Therefore, it is toxic and a massive contradiction for either Man He or Man She to consummate a union of disorder and expect anything to come out of it other than the vibrations and sensations of the ice-cold, deep-freeze mentality.

In keeping with the holistic living way of life of the sacred garden culture, each individual must emerge into a state of divine spirit consciousness before considering a union. It is imperative that the masculine presence emerge into divine spirit consciousness prior to any attempt to establish a relationship with the feminine presence. Anything other than that is to plot and scheme for failure as well as the destabilization of the feminine presence. It is absolutely unquestionable that emerging into divine spirit consciousness will require divine spiritual guidance from a master or grand master presence. Know for a fact that a master or grand master presence must be represented by Man, He and She in divine union, living a holistic living way of life within the sacred garden culture. Anything other than this represents a perpetrator and a fraud, playing the same game with another name in honor of the ice-cold, deep-freeze mentality.

The overall duty, obligation and responsibility of Man He and Man She is to give absolute humility to the Most Supreme Seen and Unseen. The honor extends to all the senior elders and ancestral keepers of the divine spirit presence of Man, He and She. The basic principles of the sacred garden culture are rooted in the first divine act and requirement of a holistic living way of life, i.e. divine union, divine consumption, and going forward to multiply divinity in the offspring. The basic foundation of the sacred garden culture principles is the honoring of every living thing just as one honors the gift of life that one receives from the Most Supreme Unseen. These sacred principles are established with the understanding that Man, He and She, have forwarded from the Most Supreme Unseen.

Man, He and She, must be clear that the Most Supreme Unseen is the Most High Essence of Life and Supreme Love, and therefore, Man, He and She, must live as the Most Supreme Seen Essence of Life. As the Most High Essence of Life and Supreme Love, the Most Supreme Unseen is unquestionably the most sacred ancestral presence. Every Man, He and She, in divine order must comprehend this holistic living truth about Supreme Love. Within the sacred garden culture, comprehension is the sum total of one's attitudes and behaviors. Therefore, within the sacred garden culture, Man, He and She, must maintain the most supreme mental, physical and spiritual presence as the Most Supreme Seen.

Man came to the planet Earth in divine union as Man, He and She, to honor divine union, divine consumption and going forward to multiply divinity in the offspring. The social order of Man, He and She, within the sacred garden culture, i.e. the Royal Family and the Council of Elders, has a duty, obligation and responsibility to uphold the sacred principles. Therefore, within the social order of the brotherhood society, the masculine presence has a duty, obligation and responsibility to master comprehension of his physical, mental and spirit presence. After mastering the divine comprehension of his whole life self, he then has the duty, obligation and responsibility to master the comprehension of Man She and her mental, physical and spirit presence. This is the primary education source that takes Man He from his early days of learning through puberty and into manhood.

The mother spirit, the sacred feminine presence, of Man She holds a similar line of duty, obligation and responsibility. That is to say, she has a divine duty, obligation and responsibility to master the comprehension of her mental, physical and spirit presence. Only after such self-mastery is she obligated to master the comprehension of Man He and his mental, physical and spirit presence. The collective education process is structured where the brotherhood society studies and comprehends within that grouping, and the sisterhood society studies within that grouping. When coming together, Man, He and She, come together in joy, celebration and honor of life, for harvest, for acknowledgement, and for divine social economic family community gatherings.

Within the sacred social order, there is a sacred and blessed principle of honoring each other and abstaining from sexual interaction before matehood. Celibacy until matehood is simply in divine order as a phase of preparation for divine union. The mating process declares the union of a specific Man He with a specific Man She, a union where the entire divine social economic family community is fully aware of the relationship. The mating process involves those first sacred acts that bond that particular Man He and that particular Man She into a holistic living union geared towards going forward to multiply divinity through the offspring. Therefore, divine union is a consummation that provides the holistic living order for the re-emergence of the ancestral presence of life and the Supreme Love vibration.

Yes, Man He would learn the vigor and vitality of his penis, the power and the glory of the semen, and he would learn how the various acts of stimulation cause great arousal within him. He would learn the various manners and degrees of maintaining holistic living health. He would learn how to control the acts of ejaculation to create greater stimulation for himself and the feminine presence by opening the gateway to life more profoundly. The feminine presence would be inspired to accept the ejaculation of his mental, physical and spirit presence into her through the semen and sperm that is forwarded through his sacred temple.

There would be comprehension of the fullness of bringing her to the point of ecstasy with the understanding that she, the mother spirit, has a connected vibration from her sexual organs to her brain. This means that her thoughts, vibrations and sensations play a vital role in how wide she will open to receive with appreciation the glory of the masculine presence. This will determine how far the feminine presence will reach inside herself to sensitize and respond to her own internal stimulation. Within the values of the sacred garden culture, Man She would learn to comprehend every way and every means of expressing appreciation to Man He, and Man He would learn to graciously accept that appreciation through his response to her call. Man She would comprehend that Man He gives his life force energy to her in order to go forward and multiply divinity in the offspring. Man He would learn to comprehend every way and every means of expressing appreciation to Man She for being the nurturing presence, and Man She would learn to graciously accept that appreciation through her response to his call.

Man, He and She, would learn every manner and every degree of physical expression, from the communication of the eyes, fingers, as well as the oral expressions of the tongue and the lips. Man, He and She, would learn every manner and degree of stimulation, every manner and degree of release within the energy of reciprocation—the flow of giving and receiving that is a pulsating rhythm of life. As a result, divine union, truly and sincerely, is divine. A harmonious and peaceful situation would occur: a heavenly paradise state of being which is formulated upon the vibrations of Man He and Man She in divine union.

Within the sacred garden culture, the utmost care and tenderness is given to the body, starting with the consumption of raw and living fruits, vegetables, seeds and nuts. The sexual organs are kept clean and orderly, well-preserved and protected, and are held in high esteem. Oral expressions are in such sacred order that every inch of the male's body and every inch of the female's body is a point of sensory stimulation and arousal through the kiss, the touch, the smell, the sound, the sight and the taste. Divine innercourse is a cherished act each and every time it occurs.

It must be clearly pointed out that within the sacred garden culture, acts of envy, greed and jealousy have absolutely no place. The primary duties, obligations and responsibilities of

Man He and Man She are to insure that the sacred and blessed vibrations of the sacred garden culture are upheld and maintained by every divine means necessary. Therefore, there would never be a situation where Man She, a feminine presence, would be left without the divine guidance and protection of the masculine presence, even if every available male was already in a divine union and the female happened to be in the extras or surplus of the feminine presence. However, within the death consumption culture, a single female must either charm a man away from another female, wait for a divorce, wait for another female to die, choose a homosexual relationship, become celibate or become part of a promiscuous relationship, an affair, or a down-low syndrome.

Within the sacred garden culture, such things are unheard of, totally unthinkable, totally in disorder, totally a disgusting contradiction to the divine presence of Man, He and She, and a dishonoring of the most sacred and blessed ancestral essence of life. Every Man She is ordained by her life presence to have a mate relationship where she is given divine guidance and protection. Man She has the duty, obligation, and responsibility to nurture divinity. Every Man He is ordained by his life presence to uphold the duties, obligations and responsibilities of providing divine guidance and divine protection for the feminine presence. Therefore, if there are females in excess numbers, the male would simply have to extend his duty, obligation and responsibility. In fact, the feminine presence within the sacred sisterhood society would automatically assist each other through divine sisterhood and make sure that no sister is left stranded.

Within the sacred garden culture, the securing of the feminine spirit is not even a vibration of thought. It is simply a holistic living way of life. Just like it is a known fact with the elephants, the gazelles, just like it is a known fact with the chimpanzees, gorillas and monkeys of all assorted kind. Even with the carnivorous animals, it is a known fact with the lion.

It is a known fact by all keepers of family order that, in fact, the feminine presence must have divine guidance and protection, or she will run astray and perpetuate disorder within the social order or she will become a victim of prey.

A misguided and unprotected feminine presence will cause chaos and will breed the vibrations and sensations of lust, lies, illusions, confusion, death and deadly destruction. She will, in fact, be the instrument of breeding wars and conflict, deception, murder, rape and theft. She will directly or indirectly breed the toxic vibrations into the male offspring who will grow to perpetuate the same vicious cycle. In fact, the very same male who did not fulfill his divine duties, obligations and responsibilities will cause what was inflicted upon the feminine presence by the masculine energy to come back around to the masculine energy through the offspring. In fact, the manner and degree of disorder is well played out within the death consumption culture as the energy that is opposite of Supreme Love runs amok in the lost and astray mind of Man, He and She, who have become disciples and followers of this culture of disorder.

Within the sacred garden culture, Man He looks upon additional responsibilities of giving divine guidance and divine protection as just that, a greater degree of duty, obligation and responsibility in honoring the whole life presence. Within this sacred social order, Man He honors the sisterhood relationship. The sisterhood society is the primary factor in insuring that sisters are not left out, abandoned, rejected or neglected for any reason that may arise.

Within the sacred garden culture, matehood relationships are not determined by mere acts of fashion and style. They are not determined by mere acts of glamour and sex appeal. Nor are they determined by the sensations and vibrations of momentary enthusiasm and great lustful desire to plunge into a cute, sexy, voluptuous, hot body. Matehood relationships are inspired by a greater sense of duty, obligation and responsibility to maintain the divine social order of the sacred garden culture. Additionally, there is a strong sense of honoring the Most Supreme Spirit of Life and Supreme Love and the ancestral presence of life given forward to Man, He and She, by the Most Supreme Unseen.

It is impossible for one to expect to receive divine healing unless one deals with a divine healing process led by a divine healer. It is impossible to receive divine healing without submitting to the holistic living way of life of the sacred garden culture. On many occasions an individual will declare that he or she is going through self-healing while he or she is still maintaining the ways and means of the death consumption cultural patterns of the ice-cold, deep-freeze mentality. Many individuals will claim a holistic position, because they have taken the religious dogma that evolved from the ice-cold, deep-freeze mentality and colored it a different tone. A specific pattern that occurs is that one may change some of the eating patterns by eliminating some items like pork or animal products, some of the dress styles, some of the language patterns, but beneath the surface one will find some level and degree of the death consumption culture still lurking.

Regardless of religious rhetoric, or social economic or political ideologies, the sacred laws of divine healing still apply. Within the death consumption culture, it is amazing how many individuals can walk around in a dazed state of mind without even realizing how much damage is being inflicted on one's whole life presence. Even more profoundly, it seems that individuals have an even harder time realizing that their unwholesome relationships with the mother spirit reflect the energy that is opposite of Supreme Love and will perpetuate the ice-cold, deep-freeze mentality. There are no and's, if's or but's about it, Man He is in a desperate need for divine healing. If the masculine presence responsible for divine guidance and divine protection is in a weak, depleted, dilapidated, incarcerated, and intoxicated state of mental, physical and spiritual disease and disorder, then the primary mission of a genocidal plan against that population has been basically completed.

In order to resurrect from such a toxic and diseased state of being, the sacred masculine presence of Man, He and She, must accelerate the move into a holistic living way of life within the sacred garden culture. Divine spirit consciousness must remain the top priority influencing every act and every behavior of every thought of every way of life. The masculine spirit energy must be focused on the rescue and resurrection of the sacred origin of self so as to be able to divinely focus on the rescue and resurrection of the sacred mother spirit. The rescued spirit of Man He must focus on the holistic living way of life of the sacred garden culture and the forward multiplication of divinity through the offspring. This task, this duty, this responsibility, these goals and these objectives are beyond urgent, and there is absolutely no priority of greater urgency. What we are talking about here is a divine innercourse with the Most Supreme Seen and Unseen Essence of Life and Supreme Love. We are talking about going forward to multiply the holistic living truth about Supreme Love.

The Most Supreme Seen feminine presence of the Earth shall continue to offer the divine fuel of the Most High Essence of Life to the sacred sons and daughters of Man, He and She. The Most Supreme Seen masculine presence of the Sun shall continue to radiate and ejaculate the most sacred semen of life into the Most Supreme Seen feminine presence of the Earth. The most supreme expressions of the earth and the sun, i.e. the supreme presence of the wind and the rain, shall continue to formulate the breath of life. The supreme breath of life shall continue to be anointed by the wetness of Supreme Love. Within this divine union, the Most Supreme Seen masculine and feminine presence go forward and multiply the Essence of Life, i.e. the Divine Children of the Sun, the generation of the sacred fruits of the trees of life for divine consumption, and every living thing within the divine order of earth, wind, rain and sun. Every encounter outside of the divine relationship of earth, wind, rain and sun must serve as a divine lesson to cause Man, He and She, to become most aware of the energy that is opposite of Supreme Love.

The manifestation of divine examples is the only possible saving grace for Man, He and She. Man, He and She, must, therefore, be tenacious and unbending in going forward to multiply divinity through divine union and divine consumption. Thus, Man, He and She, must come to reason with the fact that the whole life presence of Man, He and She, is at stake. The level of high-risk and threat that is posed by the ice-cold, deep-freeze mentality will escalate as long as the ice-cold, deep-freeze mentality is nurtured, honored, worshipped and adored through the acts of consuming toxic attitudes and behaviors.

The I in I urge the sacred few among Man, He and She, to awaken to the glory of the Essence of Life and Supreme Love and to cease and desist from following the lost and astray mind of the ice-cold, deep-freeze mentality that has perpetuated a god in its own image. We are indeed earth children born of the glory of the most supreme seen feminine presence of the Earth in divine union with the most supreme seen masculine presence of the sun. We are energized by the expressions of the divine union of the earth and the sun, i.e. the wind and the rain. Unquestionably, the sacred origin of Man, He and She, emerges from the sacred womb of the earth as the Divine Children of the Sun.

The I in I beckon that all of Man, He and She, come to divine clarity about the fact that the Most Supreme Unseen Essence of Life manifests the magnificence of the Most Supreme Seen of the glorious earth and the glorious sun and a divine relationship of He and She. The Most Supreme Essence of Life is the Supreme Love vibration of that most blessed encounter.

The Divine and Sacred Few must be dedicated to the glory of that most supreme union of the masculine and feminine presence that has come forward to give the Most Supreme Essence of Life to Man, He and She. The I in I am of the Most Supreme Seen and Unseen Essence of Life. The I in I have come forward from the Most Supreme Unseen into the Seen to inspire divine community. A holistic living way of life is all that the I in I can give to you as advice. Now that you know that the I in I have come to do what I do, take my advice and concentrate on you.

It must be clear that divine spirit consciousness is structured on divine union, divine consumption and going forward to multiply divinity in the offspring. Divine consumption is the essence of the fuel that will manifest the Divine Children of the Sun once again upon this glorious planet of ours. Of course, the sacred garden culture is the divine presence of Man, He and She.

***Let Man, He and She, be reminded that life is for the living. As it was, as it is, and as it continues to be.***

# Reference and Research Sources

*The web sites cited below were used to compile statistical and background information. However, this list in no way implies an endorsement of the general information content from any of these sources.*

**AIDS.: UNAIDS -- Joint United Nations Programme on HIV/AIDS**
http://www.unAIDS.org/wad2004/report.html

**Alliance for Lupus Research**
http://www.lupusresearch.org/press_sept4.html

**American Cancer. Society**
http://www.cancer.org/docroot/home/index.asp

**American Medical Student Association**
http://www.amsa.org/hp/RandD.cfm

**The American Slave Code in Theory and Practice. Dinsmore Documentation.**
http://www.dinsdoc.com/goodell-1-1-7.htm

**American Social Health Association (ASHA)**
http://www.ashastd.org/stdfaqs/chancroid.html

**Black Genocide.: The "Negro" Project**
http://blackgenocide.org/"Negro".html

**Black Women's Health: Fibroids**
http://www.blackwomenshealth.com/fibroids.htm

**Congressional Black Caucus Foundation Health.org**
http://www.cbcfhealth.org/

**Descent of Man. Author: Charles Darwin (1871)**
http://www.infidels.org/library/historical/charles_darwin/descent_of_man/index.shtml

**Center for Disease Control, National Center for HIV, STD and TB Prevention**
http://www.cdc.gov/std/Chlamydia/STDFact-Chlamydia.htm

**The Digital Urology Journal, A Peer-Reviewed Online Journal of Adult and Pediatric Urology**
http://www.duj.com/venereal.html

**eMedicine Consumer Health**
http://www.emedicinehealth.com/articles/6668-1.asp

**The Endometriosis Association**
http://www.endometriosisassn.org/endo.html

**Eugenics.: Images Archive on the American Eugenics Movement**
http://www.eugenicsarchive.org/html/eugenics/essay2text.html

**Health Central**
http://www.healthcentral.com/library/library.cfm

**Incidents in the Life of Slave Girl. Author: Harriet Jacobs**
http://xroads.virginia.edu/~HYPER/JACOBS/hj-site-index.htm

**Melanin.: Perspectives in Biology and Melanin Chemistry, Rodolfo Nicklaus**
http://www.tightrope.it/nicolaus/ponta.htm

**National Cancer Institute, National Institutes of Health**
http://www.nci.nih.gov/

**National Foundation for Cancer Research**
http://www2.nfcr.org/site/PageServer?pagename=cancers_uterine

**National Institute of Allergy and Infectious Diseases, National Institutes of Health.**
http://www.niaid.nih.gov/default.htm

**An Introduction to Sexually Transmitted Infections**
http://www.niaid.nih.gov/factsheets/stdinfo.htm

**National Institute of Environmental Health Sciences, National Institutes of Health**
http://www.niehs.nih.gov/oc/crntnws/2001mar/fibroids.htm

**National Institute of Mental Health**
http://www.nimh.nih.gov/studies/2mooddisordersmen.cfm

**The National Women's Health Information Center, A Project of the U.S. Department of Health and Human Services, Office of Women's Health**

**Fibroids**
http://www.4woman.gov/faq/fibroids.htm

**HIV/**
http://www.4woman.gov/HIV/whatis.cfm

**New York City Department of Health and Mental Hygiene**
http://www.nyc.gov/html/doh/html/std/std5.html

**The Office of Minority Health, U.S. Department of Health and Human Services**
http://www.omhrc.gov/OMHRC/

**Small Pox: Amherst and Small Pox Blankets**
http://www.nativeweb.org/pages/legal/amherst/lord_jeff.html

**United Nations: Convention on the Prevention and Punishment of the Crime of Genocide**
http://www.civicwebs.com/cwvlib/constitutions/un/e_un_convention_genocide_1948.htm

**Wikipedia, The Free Encyclopedia**
http://en.wikipedia.org/wiki/Apoptosis#Homeostasis

**Yeast Infection Resource.com**
http://www.yeastinfectionresource.com/yeast/article_basics.asp

# Index

## H



## I



## J



## K



## L



## M



## N



## O



## P



## R

***The High Priest Kwatamani and the Kwatamani Royal Family***

# Holistic Living Resource Materials

## DVD Productions

*Holistic Living DVD Series: Raw & Living Foods Preparation Class Live Sweet Potato Pie with delicious live potato greens* $49.99

## Books

*Fulfilling the Sacred Ancestral Prophecy of the Triple Nine: Unveiling the Prophetic 2012 Meltdown of the Lost and Astray Pale State of Mind* $39.99

*Exposing the Ice-Cold, Deep-Freeze Mentality and Whole Life Healing of Sexual Energy within the Divine Parallel...And the Sacred Resurrection of the Divine Garden Culture* $39.99
*(A classic and historic reading of this text by Royal Priestess Gail Kwatamani available by special order)*

*The Holistic Living Truth About Supreme Love...And the Sacred Resurrection of the Divine Garden Culture: Book 1-Resurrecting the Divine Body of Flesh; Book 2-Resurrecting Divine Thought and Reasoning;*
$35 ea. *Book 3-Resurrecting Divine Spirit Consciousness* $39.99

*Raw and Living Foods: The First Divine Act and Requirement of a Holistic Living Way of Life. Living Fruits, Vegetables, Seeds, Nuts, & Grains. The Natural Foods for Human Consumption* $29.99

*The Divine Gathering of the Sacred Few through a Holistic Living Way of Life* $25

## CD Productions

### Truth Lyrics

*Supernatural Healing Serum* *$14.99*
*Supernatural Healing Serum: Dose Two* *$14.99*
*Supernatural Healing Serum: Dose Three* *$14.99*
*Conjuring Ancestral Spirit Consciousness* *$19.99*
*12th Hour Prophecy: The Pale Curse and the Solarized Energy Shift* *$20.12*

**TO ORDER:** Please visit our website at: **www.livefoodsunchild.com**

www.ingramcontent.com/pod-product-compliance
Lightning Source LLC
LaVergne TN
LVHW020516100826
845148LV00010B/1246

* 9 7 8 0 9 7 9 2 6 2 6 0 9 *